THE INTERNATIONAL LAW OF THE SEA
VOLUME II DOCUMENTS, CASES AND TABLES

The International Law of the Sea
Volume II Documents, Cases and Tables

E.D. BROWN B
Professor of Inte
Director, Centre

Dartm

Aldershot •

Published by
Dartmouth Publishing Company Limited
Gower House
Croft Road
Aldershot
Hants GU11 3HR
England

Dartmouth Publishing Company
Old Post Road
Brookfield
Vermont 05036
USA

British Library Cataloguing in Publication Data
Brown, E. D.
  International Law of the Sea
  I. Title
  341.45

Library of Congress Cataloging-in-Publication Data
Brown, E. D. (Edward Duncan)
    The international law of the sea / E.D. Brown.
      p.   cm.
    Includes indexes.
    Contents: v. 1. Introductory manual – v. 2. Documents, cases and tables.
    ISBN 1-85521-306-0 (HB : set) : $149.95 (approx.). – ISBN
  1-85521-330-3 (PB : set) : $75.00 (approx.)
    1. Maritime law. I. Title.
  JX4411.B725   1994
  341.7'566–dc20   94-21352
                                                                       CIP

ISBN 1 85521 306 0 (Hbk)
ISBN 1 85521 330 3 (Pbk)

Printed and Bound in Great Britain by
Hartnolls Limited, Bodmin, Cornwall.

Contents

Table of cases

Table of statutes and other municipal instruments

Table of treaties

Acknowledgements

The author is indebted to copyright owners for permission to reproduce copyright materials in this volume.   In particular, he wishes to thank the Director of the Publications Division of Her Majesty's Stationery Office for advice on the reproduction of Documents numbers 4.5-4.5.2 and 12.6 which are protected by Crown copyright and the Registrar of the International Court of Justice for advice on the reproduction of the excerpts from the Court's Judgments in Documents numbers 3.3, 3.4 and 5.3.   Every effort has been made to contact the copyright owners of other documents reproduced in this volume.

Introduction

If students are to acquire a sound understanding of the international law of the sea, it is essential that they should be thoroughly familiar with the sources and forms of evidence of rules of international law and should learn to use the raw materials of the subject. It is for this reason that the exposition of the law of the sea in Volume I is complemented by the collection of selected documents included in this second volume and is fully cross-referenced to it.

There now exists a vast and ever-growing body of documentation on the law of the sea and the task of selection has not been easy. To some extent the choice has been dictated by the emphasis in Volume I and by experience in teaching the subject. A conscious effort has been made to include a wide range of treaties and other forms of State practice. Excerpts from decided cases have been included in Section 3 on the Sources of the International Law of the Sea, and in Section 5 on Straits Used for International Navigation. In addition, extensive quotations from judgments in delimitation cases will be found in Chapter 11 of Volume I.

In designing this volume, the first question which had to be considered was whether or not to include the whole of the United Nations Convention on the Law of the Sea, 1982, including its nine annexes and, if so, whether to present it as a single document or to incorporate its various Parts in sections dealing with particular topics. As will be seen, the great bulk of the Convention has been included and has been distributed among the substantive sections into which this volume is divided. There are, however, two exceptions.

The first exception relates to those provisions of the Convention and its annexes which are concerned with the regime of seabed mining in the Area beyond the limits of national jurisdiction. Given the length of Part XI and related Annexes, it ws possible to include in Section 12 of this volume only excerpts from Article 1 and Part XI of the

Convention. As noted in Chapter 17 of Volume I, the regime of seabed mining laid down in Part XI has been substantially amended by the New York Agreement of 28 July 1994. Fortunately, it has been possible to add at the end of Section 12 the texts of the New York Agreement and related resolution adopted by the UN General Assembly.

The second exception relates to the provisions of the Convention on dispute settlement. Part XV of the Convention on Settlement of Disputes will be found in Section 2 but Annexes V-VIII have been excluded. They are concerned with Conciliation (Annex V); the Statute of the International Tribunal for the Law of the Sea (Annex VI); and Arbitration and Special Arbitration (Annexes VII and VIII).

Section 13 on the Status of Conventions offers checklists of the parties to the UN Convention and to the Geneva Conventions on the Law of the Sea of 1958. Given the complexity of the interrelationship among the conventions on civil liability for oil pollution damage, details of the status of these instruments as at 31 December 1993 have also been provided.

Finally, in Section 14, information will be found on the series of excellent bibliographies on the law of the sea published by the United Nations.

In general, full citations have not been given for documents reproduced in this volume. They are, however, given in footnote references in Volume I and can be traced through the *Table of treaties* in Volume I. Similarly, abbreviations used in this volume will be found in the list of *Abbreviations* in Volume I.

2 United Nations Convention on the Law of the Sea, 1982

This Section includes:

2.1 The Preamble and Part I: Introduction;

2.2 Part XV: Settlement of Disputes;

2.3 Part XVI: General Provisions; and

2.4 Part XVII: Final Provisions.

Other Parts of the Convention are reproduced in later Sections dealing with particular aspects of the law of the sea. For example, Part II of the Convention, on the Territorial Sea and Contiguous Zone, is included in Section 4 below on Internal Waters, Territorial Sea and Contiguous Zone.

2.1 UNITED NATIONS CONVENTION ON THE LAW OF THE SEA, 1982: PREAMBLE AND PART I: INTRODUCTION

PREAMBLE

The States Parties to this Convention,

Prompted by the desire to settle, in a spirit of mutual understanding and co-operation, all issues relating to the law of the sea and aware of the historic significance of this Convention as an important contribution to the maintenance of peace, justice and progress for all peoples of the world,

Noting that developments since the United Nations Conferences on the Law of the Sea held at Geneva in 1958 and 1960 have accentuated the need for a new and generally acceptable Convention on the law of the sea,

Conscious that the problems of ocean space are closely interrelated and need to be considered as a whole,

Recognizing the desirability of establishing through this Convention, with due regard for the sovereignty of all States, a legal order for the seas and oceans which will facilitate international communication, and will promote the peaceful uses of the seas and oceans, the equitable and efficient utilization of their resources, the conservation of their living resources, and the study, protection and preservation of the marine environment,

Bearing in mind that the achievement of these goals will contribute to the realization of a just and equitable international economic order which takes into account the interests and needs of mankind as a whole and, in particular, the special interests and needs of developing countries, whether coastal or land-locked,

Desiring by this Convention to develop the principles embodied in resolution 2749 (XXV) of 17 December 1970 in which the General Assembly of the United Nations solemnly declared *inter alia* that the area of the sea-bed and ocean floor and the subsoil thereof, beyond the limits of national jurisdiction, as well as its resources, are the common heritage of mankind, the exploration and exploitation of which shall be carried out for the benefit of mankind as a whole, irrespective of the geographical location of States,

Believing that the codification and progressive development of the law of the sea achieved in this Convention will contribute to the strengthening of peace, security, co-operation and friendly relations among all nations in conformity with the principles of justice and equal rights and will promote the economic and social advancement of all peoples of the world, in accordance with the Purposes and Principles of the United Nations as set forth in the Charter,

Affirming that matters not regulated by this Convention continue to be governed by the rules and principles of general international law,

Have agreed as follows:

PART I
INTRODUCTION

Article 1
Use of terms and scope

1.   For the purposes of this Convention:

(1) "Area" means the sea-bed and ocean floor and subsoil thereof, beyond the limits of national jurisdiction;

(2) "Authority" means the International Sea-Bed Authority;

(3) "activities in the Area" means all activities of exploration for, and exploitation of, the resources of the Area;

(4) "pollution of the marine environment" means the introduction by man, directly or indirectly, of substances or energy into the marine environment, including estuaries, which results or is likely to result in such deleterious effects as harm to living resources and marine life, hazards to human health, hindrance to marine activities, including fishing and other legitimate uses of the sea, impairment of quality for use of sea water and reduction of amenities;

(5) (a) "dumping" means:
  (i) any deliberate disposal of wastes or other matter from vessels, aircraft, platforms or other man-made structures at sea;
  (ii) any deliberate disposal of vessels, aircraft, platforms or other man-made structures at sea;
(b) "dumping" does not include:
  (i) the disposal of wastes or other matter incidental to, or derived from the normal operations of vessels, aircraft, platforms or other man-made structures at sea and their equipment, other than wastes or other matter transported by or to vessels, aircraft, platforms or other man-made structures at sea, operating for the purpose of disposal of such matter or derived from the treatment of such wastes or other matter on such vessels, aircraft, platforms or structures;
  (ii) placement of matter for a purpose other than the mere disposal thereof, provided that such placement is not contrary to the aims of this Convention.

2. (1) "States Parties" means States which have consented to be bound by this Convention and for which this Convention is in force.

(2) This Convention applies *mutatis mutandis* to the entities referred to in article 305, paragraph 1(b), (c), (d), (e) and (f), which become Parties to this Convention in accordance with the conditions relevant to each, and to that extent "States Parties" refers to those entities.

2.2 UNITED NATIONS CONVENTION ON THE LAW OF THE SEA, 1982: PART XV: SETTLEMENT OF DISPUTES

SECTION 1. GENERAL PROVISIONS

Article 279
Obligation to settle disputes by peaceful means

States Parties shall settle any dispute between them concerning the interpretation or application of this Convention by peaceful means in accordance with Article 2, paragraph 3, of the Charter of the United Nations and, to this end, shall seek a solution by the means indicated in Article 33, paragraph 1, of the Charter.

Article 280
Settlement of disputes by any peaceful means chosen by the parties

Nothing in this Part impairs the right of any States Parties to agree at any time to settle a dispute between them concerning the interpretation or application of this Convention by any peaceful means of their own choice.

Article 281
Procedure where no settlement has been reached by the parties

1. If the States Parties which are parties to a dispute concerning the interpretation or application of this Convention have agreed to seek settlement of the dispute by a peaceful means of their own choice, the procedures provided for in this Part apply only

where no settlement has been reached by recourse to such means and the agreement between the parties does not exclude any further procedure.

2. If the parties have also agreed on a time-limit, paragraph 1 applies only upon the expiration of that time-limit.

Article 282
Obligations under general, regional or bilateral agreements

If the States Parties which are parties to a dispute concerning the interpretation or application of this Convention have agreed, through a general, regional or bilateral agreement or otherwise, that such dispute shall, at the request of any party to the dispute, be submitted to a procedure that entails a binding decision, that procedure shall apply in lieu of the procedures provided for in this Part, unless the parties to the dispute otherwise agree.

Article 283
Obligation to exchange views

1. When a dispute arises between States Parties concerning the interpretation or application of this Convention, the parties to the dispute shall proceed expeditiously to an exchange of views regarding its settlement by negotiation or other peaceful means.

2. The parties shall also proceed expeditiously to an exchange of views where a procedure for the settlement of such a dispute has been terminated without a settlement or where a settlement has been reached and the circumstances require consultation regarding the manner of implementing the settlement.

Article 284
Conciliation

1. A State Party which is a party to a dispute concerning the interpretation or application of this Convention may invite the other party or parties to submit the dispute to conciliation in accordance with the procedure under Annex V, section 1, or another conciliation procedure.

2. If the invitation is accepted and if the parties agree upon the conciliation procedure to be applied, any party may submit the dispute to that procedure.

3. If the invitation is not accepted or the parties do not agree upon the procedure, the conciliation proceedings shall be deemed to be terminated.

4. Unless the parties otherwise agree, when a dispute has been submitted to conciliation, the proceedings may be terminated only in accordance with the agreed conciliation procedure.

Article 285
Application of this section to disputes submitted pursuant to Part XI

This section applies to any dispute which pursuant to Part XI, section 5, is to be settled in accordance with procedures provided for in this Part.   If an entity other than a State Party is a party to such a dispute, this section applies *mutatis mutandis*.

SECTION 2. COMPULSORY PROCEDURES ENTAILING BINDING DECISIONS

Article 286
Application of procedures under this section

Subject to section 3, any dispute concerning the interpretation or application of this Convention shall, where no settlement has been reached by recourse to section 1, be submitted at the request of any party to the dispute to the court or tribunal having jurisdiction under this section.

Article 287
Choice of procedure

1. When signing, ratifying or acceding to this Convention or at any time thereafter, a State shall be free to choose, by means of a written declaration, one or more of the following means for the settlement of disputes concerning the interpretation or application of this Convention:
(a) the International Tribunal for the Law of the Sea established in accordance with Annex VI;
(b) the International Court of Justice;
(c) an arbitral tribunal constituted in accordance with Annex VII;
(d) a special arbitral tribunal constituted in accordance with Annex VIII for one or more of the categories of disputes specified therein.

2. A declaration made under paragraph 1 shall not affect or be affected by the obligation of a State Party to accept the jurisdiction of the Sea-Bed Disputes Chamber of the International Tribunal for the Law of the Sea to the extent and in the manner provided for in Part XI, section 5.

3. A State Party, which is a party to a dispute not covered by a declaration in force, shall be deemed to have accepted arbitration in accordance with Annex VII.

4. If the parties to a dispute have accepted the same procedure for the settlement of the dispute, it may be submitted only to that procedure, unless the parties otherwise agree.

5. If the parties to a dispute have not accepted the same procedure for the settlement of the dispute, it may be submitted only to arbitration in accordance with Annex VII, unless the parties otherwise agree.

6. A declaration made under paragraph 1 shall remain in force until three months after notice of revocation has been deposited with the Secretary-General of the United Nations.

7. A new declaration, a notice of revocation or the expiry of a declaration does not in any way affect proceedings pending before a court or tribunal having jurisdiction under this article, unless the parties otherwise agree.

8. Declarations and notices referred to in this article shall be deposited with the Secretary-General of the United Nations, who shall transmit copies thereof to the States Parties.

Article 288
Jurisdiction

1. A court or tribunal referred to in article 287 shall have jurisdiction over any dispute concerning the interpretation or application of this Convention which is submitted to it in accordance with this Part.

2. A court or tribunal referred to in article 287 shall also have jurisdiction over any dispute concerning the interpretation or application of an international agreement related to the purposes of this Convention, which is submitted to it in accordance with the agreement.

3. The Sea-Bed Disputes Chamber of the International Tribunal for the Law of the Sea established in accordance with Annex VI, and any other chamber or arbitral tribunal referred to in Part XI, section 5, shall have jurisdiction in any matter which is submitted to it in accordance therewith.

4. In the event of a dispute as to whether a court or tribunal has jurisdiction, the matter shall be settled by decision of that court or tribunal.

Article 289
Experts

In any dispute involving scientific or technical matters, a court or tribunal exercising jurisdiction under this section may, at the request of a party or *proprio motu*, select in consultation with the parties no fewer than two scientific or technical experts chosen preferably from the relevant list prepared in accordance with Annex VIII, article 2, to sit with the court or tribunal but without the right to vote.

Article 290
Provisional measures

1. If a dispute has been duly submitted to a court or tribunal which considers that *prima facie* it has jurisdiction under this Part or Part XI, section 5, the court or tribunal may prescribe any provisional measures which it considers appropriate under the circumstances to preserve the respective rights of the parties to the dispute or to prevent serious harm to the marine environment, pending the final decision.

2. Provisional measures may be modified or revoked as soon as the circumstances justifying them have changed or ceased to exist.

3. Provisional measures may be prescribed, modified or revoked under this article only at the request of a party to the dispute and after the parties have been given an opportunity to be heard.

4. The court or tribunal shall forthwith give notice to the parties to the dispute, and to such other States Parties as it considers appropriate, of the prescription, modification or revocation of provisional measures.

5. Pending the constitution of an arbitral tribunal to which a dispute is being submitted under this section, any court or tribunal agreed upon by the parties or, failing such agreement within two weeks from the date of the request for provisional measures, the International Tribunal for the Law of the Sea or, with respect to activities in the Area, the Sea-Bed Disputes Chamber, may prescribe, modify or revoke provisional measures in accordance with this article if it considers that *prima facie* the tribunal which is to be constituted would have jurisdiction and that the urgency of the situation so requires. Once constituted, the tribunal to which the dispute has been submitted may modify, revoke or affirm those provisional measures, acting in conformity with paragraphs 1 to 4.

6. The parties to the dispute shall comply promptly with any provisional measures prescribed under this article.

Article 291
Access

1.   All the dispute settlement procedures specified in this Part shall be open to States Parties.
2.   The dispute settlement procedures specified in this Part shall be open to entities other than States Parties only as specifically provided for in this Convention.

Article 292
Prompt release of vessels and crews

1.   Where the authorities of a State Party have detained a vessel flying the flag of another State Party and it is alleged that the detaining State has not complied with the provisions of this Convention for the prompt release of the vessel or its crew upon the posting of a reasonable bond or other financial security, the question of release from detention may be submitted to any court or tribunal agreed upon by the parties or, failing such agreement within 10 days from the time of detention, to a court or tribunal accepted by the detaining State under article 287 or to the International Tribunal for the Law of the Sea, unless the parties otherwise agree.
2.   The application for release may be made only by or on behalf of the flag State of the vessel.
3.   The court or tribunal shall deal without delay with the application for release and shall deal only with the question of release, without prejudice to the merits of any case before the appropriate domestic forum against the vessel, its owner or its crew.   The authorities of the detaining State remain competent to release the vessel or its crew at any time.
4.   Upon the posting of the bond or other financial security determined by the court or tribunal, the authorities of the detaining State shall comply promptly with the decision of the court or tribunal concerning the release of the vessel or its crew.

Article 293
Applicable law

1.   A court or tribunal having jurisdiction under this section shall apply this Convention and other rules of international law not incompatible with this Convention.
2.   Paragraph 1 does not prejudice the power of the court or tribunal having jurisdiction under this section to decide a case *ex aequo et bono*, if the parties so agree.

Article 294
Preliminary proceedings

1.   A court or tribunal provided for in article 287 to which an application is made in respect of a dispute referred to in article 297 shall determine at the request of a party, or may determine *proprio motu*, whether the claim constitutes an abuse of legal process or whether *prima facie* it is well founded.   If the court or tribunal determines that the claim constitutes an abuse of legal process or is *prima facie* unfounded, it shall take no further action in the case.
2.   Upon receipt of the application, the court or tribunal shall immediately notify the other party or parties of the application, and shall fix a reasonable time-limit within which they may request it to make a determination in accordance with paragraph 1.

3. Nothing in this article affects the right of any party to a dispute to make preliminary objections in accordance with the applicable rules of procedure.

Article 295
Exhaustion of local remedies

Any dispute between States Parties concerning the interpretation or application of this Convention may be submitted to the procedures provided for in this section only after local remedies have been exhausted where this is required by international law.

Article 296
Finality and binding force of decisions

1. Any decision rendered by a court or tribunal having jurisdiction under this section shall be final and shall be complied with by all the parties to the dispute.
2. Any such decision shall have no binding force except between the parties and in respect of that particular dispute.

SECTION 3. LIMITATIONS AND EXCEPTIONS TO APPLICABILITY OF SECTION 2

Article 297
Limitations on applicability of section 2

1. Disputes concerning the interpretation or application of this Convention with regard to the exercise by a coastal State of its sovereign rights or jurisdiction provided for in this Convention shall be subject to the procedures provided for in section 2 in the following cases:
(a) when it is alleged that a coastal State has acted in contravention of the provisions of this Convention in regard to the freedoms and rights of navigation, overflight or the laying of submarine cables and pipelines, or in regard to other internationally lawful uses of the sea specified in article 58;
(b) when it is alleged that a State in exercising the aforementioned freedoms, rights or uses has acted in contravention of this Convention or of laws or regulations adopted by the coastal State in conformity with this Convention and other rules of international law not incompatible with this Convention; or
(c) when it is alleged that a coastal State has acted in contravention of specified international rules and standards for the protection and preservation of the marine environment which are applicable to the coastal State and which have been established by this Convention or through a competent international organization or diplomatic conference in accordance with this Convention.
2. (a) Disputes concerning the interpretation or application of the provisions of this Convention with regard to marine scientific research shall be settled in accordance with section 2, except that the coastal State shall not be obliged to accept the submission to such settlement of any dispute arising out of:
    (i)   the exercise by the coastal State of a right or discretion in accordance with article 246; or
    (ii)   a decision by the coastal State to order suspension or cessation of a research project in accordance with article 253.
    (b) A dispute arising from an allegation by the researching State that with respect to a specific project the coastal State is not exercising its rights under articles 246 and 253 in a manner compatible with this Convention shall be submitted, at the

request of either party, to conciliation under Annex V, section 2, provided that the conciliation commission shall not call in question the exercise by the coastal State of its discretion to designate specific areas as referred to in article 246, paragraph 6, or of its discretion to withhold consent in accordance with article 246, paragraph 5.

3.   (a)   Disputes concerning the interpretation or application of the provisions of this Convention with regard to fisheries shall be settled in accordance with section 2, except that the coastal State shall not be obliged to accept the submission to such settlement of any dispute relating to its sovereign rights with respect to the living resources in the exclusive economic zone or their exercise, including its discretionary powers for determining the allowable catch, its harvesting capacity, the allocation of surpluses to other States and the terms and conditions established in its conservation and management laws and regulations.

   (b)   Where no settlement has been reached by recourse to section 1 of this Part, a dispute shall be submitted to conciliation under Annex V, section 2, at the request of any party to the dispute, when it is alleged that:

   (i)   a coastal State has manifestly failed to comply with its obligations to ensure through proper conservation and management measures that the maintenance of the living resources in the exclusive economic zone is not seriously endangered;

   (ii)   a coastal State has arbitrarily refused to determine, at the request of another State, the allowable catch and its capacity to harvest living resources with respect to stocks which that other State is interested in fishing; or

   (iii)   a coastal State has arbitrarily refused to allocate to any State, under articles 62, 69 and 70 and under the terms and conditions established by the coastal State consistent with this Convention, the whole or part of the surplus it has declared to exist.

   (c)   In no case shall the conciliation commission substitute its discretion for that of the coastal State.

   (d)   The report of the conciliation commission shall be communicated to the appropriate international organizations.

   (e)   In negotiating agreements pursuant to articles 69 and 70, States Parties, unless they otherwise agree, shall include a clause on measures which they shall take in order to minimize the possibility of a disagreement concerning the interpretation or application of the agreement, and on how they should proceed if a disagreement nevertheless arises.

Article 298
Optional exceptions to applicability of section 2

1. When signing, ratifying or acceding to this Convention or at any time thereafter, a State may, without prejudice to the obligations arising under section 1, declare in writing that it does not accept any one or more of the procedures provided for in section 2 with respect of one or more of the following categories of disputes:

(a) (i) disputes concerning the interpretation or application of articles 15, 74 and 83 relating to sea boundary delimitations, or those involving historic bays or titles, provided that a State having made such a declaration shall, when such a dispute arises subsequent to the entry into force of this Convention and where no agreement within a reasonable period of time is reached in negotiations between the parties, at the request of any party to the dispute, accept submission of the matter to conciliation under Annex V, section 2; and provided further that any dispute that necessarily involves the concurrent consideration of any unsettled dispute concerning sovereignty or other rights over continental or insular land territory shall be excluded from such submission;

(ii) after the conciliation commission has presented its report, which shall state the reasons on which it is based, the parties shall negotiate an agreement on the basis of that report; if these negotiations do not result in an agreement, the parties shall, by mutual consent, submit the question to one of the procedures provided for in section 2, unless the parties otherwise agree;

(iii) this subparagraph does not apply to any sea boundary dispute finally settled by an arrangement between the parties, or to any such dispute which is to be settled in accordance with a bilateral or multilateral agreement binding upon those parties;

(b) disputes concerning military activities, including military activities by government vessels and aircraft engaged in non-commercial service, and disputes concerning law enforcement activities in regard to the exercise of sovereign rights or jurisdiction excluded from the jurisdiction of a court or tribunal under article 297, paragraph 2 or 3;

(c) disputes in respect of which the Security Council of the United Nations is exercising the functions assigned to it by the Charter of the United Nations, unless the Security Council decides to remove the matter from its agenda or calls upon the parties to settle it by the means provided for in this Convention.

2. A State Party which has made a declaration under paragraph 1 may at any time withdraw it, or agree to submit a dispute excluded by such declaration to any procedure specified in this Convention.

3. A State Party which has made a declaration under paragraph 1 shall not be entitled to submit any dispute falling within the excepted category of disputes to any procedure in this Convention as against another State Party, without the consent of that party.

4. If one of the States Parties has made a declaration under paragraph 1(a), any other State Party may submit any dispute falling within an excepted category against the declarant party to the procedure specified in such declaration.

5. A new declaration, or the withdrawal of a declaration, does not in any way affect proceedings pending before a court or tribunal in accordance with this article, unless the parties otherwise agree.

6. Declarations and notices of withdrawal of declarations under this article shall be deposited with the Secretary-General of the United Nations, who shall transmit copies thereof to the States Parties.

Article 299
Right of the parties to agree upon a procedure

1. A dispute excluded under article 297 or excepted by a declaration made under article 298 from the dispute settlement procedures provided for in section 2 may be submitted to such procedures only by agreement of the parties to the dispute.

2. Nothing in this section impairs the right of the parties to the dispute to agree to some other procedure for the settlement of such dispute or to reach an amicable settlement.

2.3 UNITED NATIONS CONVENTION ON THE LAW OF THE SEA, 1982: PART XVI: GENERAL PROVISIONS

Article 300
Good faith and abuse of rights

States Parties shall fulfil in good faith the obligations assumed under this Convention and shall exercise the rights, jurisdictions and freedoms recognized in this Convention in a manner which would not constitute an abuse of right.

Article 301
Peaceful uses of the seas

In exercising their rights and performing their duties under this Convention, States Parties shall refrain from any threat or use of force against the territorial integrity or political independence of any State, or in any manner inconsistent with the principles of international law embodied in the Charter of the United Nations.

Article 302
Disclosure of information

Without prejudice to the right of a State Party to resort to the procedures for the settlement of disputes provided for in this Convention, nothing in this Convention shall be deemed to require a State Party, in the fulfilment of its obligations under this Convention, to supply information the disclosure of which is contrary to the essential interests of its security.

Article 303
Archaeological and historical objects found at sea

1. States have the duty to protect objects of an archaeological and historical nature found at sea and shall co-operate for this purpose.
2. In order to control traffic in such objects, the coastal State may, in applying article 33, presume that their removal from the sea-bed in the zone referred to in that article without its approval would result in an infringement within its territory or territorial sea of the laws and regulations referred to in that article.
3. Nothing in this article affects the rights of identifiable owners, the law of salvage or other rules of admiralty, or laws and practices with respect to cultural exchanges.
4. This article is without prejudice to other international agreements and rules of international law regarding the protection of objects of an archaeological and historical nature.

Article 304
Responsibility and liability for damage

The provisions of this Convention regarding responsibility and liability for damage are without prejudice to the application of existing rules and the development of further rules regarding responsibility and liability under international law.

2.4 UNITED NATIONS CONVENTION ON THE LAW OF THE SEA, 1982: PART XVII: FINAL PROVISIONS

Article 305
Signature

1. This Convention shall be open for signature by:
(a) all States;
(b) Namibia, represented by the United Nations Council for Namibia;
(c) all self-governing associated States which have chosen that status in an act of self-determination supervised and approved by the United Nations in accordance with General Assembly resolution 1514 (XV) and which have competence over the matters governed by this Convention, including the competence to enter into treaties in respect of those matters;
(d) all self-governing associated States which, in accordance with their respective instruments of association, have competence over the matters governed by this Convention, including the competence to enter into treaties in respect of those matters;
(e) all territories which enjoy full internal self-government, recognized as such by the United Nations, but have not attained full independence in accordance with General Assembly resolution 1514 (XV) and which have competence over the matters governed by this Convention, including the competence to enter into treaties in respect of those matters;
(f) international organizations, in accordance with Annex IX.
2. This Convention shall remain open for signature until 9 December 1984 at the Ministry of Foreign Affairs of Jamaica and also, from 1 July 1983 until 9 December 1984, at United Nations Headquarters in New York.

Article 306
Ratification and formal confirmation

This Convention is subject to ratification by States and the other entities referred to in article 305, paragraph 1(b), (c), (d) and (e), and to formal confirmation, in accordance with Annex IX, by the entities referred to in article 305, paragraph 1(f). The instruments of ratification and of formal confirmation shall be deposited with the Secretary-General of the United Nations.

Article 307
Accession

This Convention shall remain open for accession by States and the other entities referred to in article 305.   Accession by the entities referred to in article 305, paragraph 1(f), shall be in accordance with Annex IX.   The instruments of accession shall be deposited with the Secretary-General of the United Nations.

Article 308
Entry into force

1. This Convention shall enter into force 12 months after the date of deposit of the sixtieth instrument of ratification or accession.

2. For each State ratifying or acceding to this Convention after the deposit of the sixtieth instrument of ratification or accession, the Convention shall enter into force on the thirtieth day following the deposit of its instrument of ratification or accession, subject to paragraph 1.

3. The Assembly of the Authority shall meet on the date of entry into force of this Convention and shall elect the Council of the Authority. The first Council shall be constituted in a manner consistent with the purpose of article 161 if the provisions of that article cannot be strictly applied.

4. The rules, regulations and procedures drafted by the Preparatory Commission shall apply provisionally pending their formal adoption by the Authority in accordance with Part XI.

5. The Authority and its organs shall act in accordance with resolution II of the Third United Nations Conference on the Law of the Sea relating to preparatory investment and with decisions of the Preparatory Commission taken pursuant to that resolution.

Article 309
Reservations and exceptions

No reservations or exceptions may be made to this Convention unless expressly permitted by other articles of this Convention.

Article 310
Declarations and statements

Article 309 does not preclude a State, when signing, ratifying or acceding to this Convention, from making declarations or statements, however phrased or named, with a view, *inter alia*, to the harmonization of its laws and regulations with the provisions of this Convention, provided that such declarations or statements do not purport to exclude or to modify the legal effect of the provisions of this Convention in their application to that State.

Article 311
Relation to other conventions and international agreements

1. This Convention shall prevail, as between States Parties, over the Geneva Conventions on the Law of the Sea of 29 April 1958.

2. This Convention shall not alter the rights and obligations of States Parties which arise from other agreements compatible with this Convention and which do not affect the enjoyment by other States Parties of their rights or the performance of their obligations under this Convention.

3. Two or more States Parties may conclude agreements modifying or suspending the operation of provisions of this Convention, applicable solely to the relations between them, provided that such agreements do not relate to a provision derogation from which is incompatible with the effective execution of the object and purpose of this Convention, and provided further that such agreements shall not affect the application of the basic principles embodied herein, and that the provisions of such agreements do not affect the enjoyment by other States Parties of their rights or the performance of their obligations under this Convention.

4. States Parties intending to conclude an agreement referred to in paragraph 3 shall notify the other States Parties through the depositary of this Convention of their intention to conclude the agreement and of the modification or suspension for which it provides.

5. This article does not affect international agreements expressly permitted or preserved by other articles of this Convention.

6. States Parties agree that there shall be no amendments to the basic principle relating to the common heritage of mankind set forth in article 136 and that they shall not be party to any agreement in derogation thereof.

Article 312
Amendment

1. After the expiry of a period of 10 years from the date of entry into force of this Convention, a State Party may, by written communication addressed to the Secretary-General of the United Nations, propose specific amendments to this Convention, other than those relating to activities in the Area, and request the convening of a conference to consider such proposed amendments. The Secretary-General shall circulate such communication to all States Parties. If, within 12 months from the date of the circulation of the communication, not less than one half of the States Parties reply favourably to the request, the Secretary-General shall convene the conference.

2. The decision-making procedure applicable at the amendment conference shall be the same as that applicable at the Third United Nations Conference on the Law of the Seas unless otherwise decided by the conference. The conference should make every effort to reach agreement on any amendments by way of consensus and there should be no voting on them until all efforts at consensus have been exhausted.

Article 313
Amendment by simplified procedure

1. A State Party may, by written communication addressed to the Secretary-General of the United Nations, propose an amendment to this Convention, other than an amendment relating to activities in the Area, to be adopted by the simplified procedure set forth in this article without convening a conference. The Secretary-General shall circulate the communication to all States Parties.

2. If, within a period of 12 months from the date of the circulation of the communication, a State Party objects to the proposed amendment or to the proposal for its adoption by the simplified procedure, the amendment shall be considered rejected. The Secretary-General shall immediately notify all States Parties accordingly.

3. If, 12 months from the date of the circulation of the communication, no State Party has objected to the proposed amendment or to the proposal for its adoption by the simplified procedure, the proposed amendment shall be considered adopted.

Article 314
Amendments to the provisions of this Convention relating exclusively to activities in the Area

1. A State Party may, by written communication addressed to the Secretary-General of the Authority, propose an amendment to the provisions of this Convention relating exclusively to activities in the Area, including Annex VI, section 4. The Secretary-General shall circulate such communication to all States Parties. The proposed amendment shall be subject to approval by the Assembly following its approval by the Council. Representatives of States Parties in those organs shall have full powers to consider and approve the proposed amendment. The proposed amendment as approved by the Council and the Assembly shall be considered adopted.

2. Before approving any amendment under paragraph 1, the Council and the Assembly shall ensure that it does not prejudice the system of exploration for and exploitation of the resources of the Area, pending the Review Conference in accordance with article 155.

Article 315
Signature, ratification of, accession to and authentic texts of amendments

1. Once adopted, amendments to this Convention shall be open for signature by States Parties for 12 months from the date of adoption, at United Nations Headquarters in New York, unless otherwise provided in the amendment itself.
2. Articles 306, 307 and 320 apply to all amendments to this Convention.

Article 316
Entry into force of amendments

1. Amendments to this Convention, other than those referred to in paragraph 5, shall enter into force for the States Parties ratifying or acceding to them on the thirtieth day following the deposit of instruments of ratification or accession by two thirds of the States parties or by 60 States Parties, whichever is greater. Such amendments shall not affect the enjoyment by other States Parties of their rights or the performance of their obligations under this Convention.
2. An amendment may provide that a larger number of ratifications or accessions shall be required for its entry into force than are required by this article.
3. For each State Party ratifying or acceding to an amendment referred to in paragraph 1 after the deposit of the required number of instruments of ratification or accession, the amendment shall enter into force on the thirtieth day following the deposit of its instrument of ratification or accession.
4. A State which becomes a Party to this Convention after the entry into force of an amendment in accordance with paragraph 1 shall, failing an expression of a different intention by that State:
(a) be considered as a Party to this Convention as so amended; and
(b) be considered as a Party to the unamended Convention in relation to any State Party not bound by the amendment.
5. Any amendment relating exclusively to activities in the Area and any amendment to Annex VI shall enter into force for all States Parties one year following the deposit of instruments of ratification or accession by three fourths of the States Parties.
6. A State which becomes a Party to this Convention after the entry into force of amendments in accordance with paragraph 5 shall be considered as a Party to this Convention as so amended.

Article 317
Denunciation

1. A State Party may, by written notification addressed to the Secretary-General of the United Nations, denounce this Convention and may indicate its reasons. Failure to indicate reasons shall not affect the validity of the denunciation. The denunciation shall take effect one year after the date of receipt of the notification, unless the notification specifies a later date.
2. A State shall not be discharged by reason of the denunciation from the financial and contractual obligations which accrued while it was a Party to this Convention, nor

shall the denunciation affect any right, obligation or legal situation of that State created through the execution of this Convention prior to its termination for that State.

3. The denunciation shall not in any way affect the duty of any State Party to fulfil any obligation embodied in this Convention to which it would be subject under international law independently of this Convention.

Article 318
Status of Annexes

The Annexes form an integral part of this Convention and, unless expressly provided otherwise, a reference to this Convention or to one of its Parts includes a reference to the Annexes relating thereto.

Article 319
Depositary

1. The Secretary-General of the United Nations shall be the depositary of this Convention and amendments thereto.
2. In addition to his functions as depositary, the Secretary-General shall:
(a) report to all States Parties, the Authority and competent international organizations on issues of a general nature that have arisen with respect to this Convention;
(b) notify the Authority of ratifications and formal confirmations of and accessions to this Convention and amendments thereto, as well as of denunciations of this Convention;
(c) notify States Parties of agreements in accordance with article 311, paragraph 4;
(d) circulate amendments adopted in accordance with this Convention to States Parties for ratification or accession;
(e) convene necessary meetings of States Parties in accordance with this Convention.
3. (a) The Secretary-General shall also transmit to the observers referred to in article 156:
(i) reports referred to in paragraph 2(a);
(ii) notifications referred to in paragraph 2(b) and (c); and
(iii) texts of amendments referred to in paragraph 2(d), for their information.
(b) The Secretary-General shall also invite those observers to participate as observers at meetings of States Parties referred to in paragraph 2(e).

Article 320
Authentic texts

The original of this Convention, of which the Arabic, Chinese, English, French, Russian and Spanish texts are equally authentic, shall, subject to article 305, paragraph 2, be deposited with the Secretary-General of the United Nations.

IN WITNESS WHEREOF, the undersigned Plenipotentiaries, being duly authorized thereto, have signed this Convention.

DONE AT MONTEGO BAY, this tenth day of December, one thousand nine hundred and eighty-two.

3 Sources of the International Law of the Sea

3.1 STATUTE OF THE INTERNATIONAL COURT OF JUSTICE, ARTICLE 38

Article 38

1. The Court whose function is to decide in accordance with international law such disputes as are submitted to it, shall apply:
    (a) international conventions, whether general or particular, establishing rules expressly recognized by the contesting States;
    (b) international custom, as evidence of a general practice accepted as law;
    (c) the general principles of law recognized by civilised nations;
    (d) subject to the provisions of Article 59, judicial decisions and the teachings of the most highly qualified publicists of the various nations, as subsidiary means for the determination of rules of law.
2. This provision shall not prejudice the power of the Court to decide a case *ex aequo et bono*, if the parties agree thereto.

3.2 VIENNA CONVENTION ON THE LAW OF TREATIES, 1969, ARTICLES 34-6 AND 38

SECTION 4. TREATIES AND THIRD STATES

Article 34
General rule regarding third States

A treaty does not create either obligations or rights for a third State without its consent.

Article 35
Treaties providing for obligations for third States

An obligation arises for a third State from a provision of a treaty if the parties to the treaty intend the provision to be the means of establishing the obligation and the third State expressly accepts that obligation in writing.

Article 36
Treaties providing for rights for third States

1.   A right arises for a third State from a provision of a treaty if the parties to the treaty intend the provision to accord that right either to the third State, or to a group of States to which it belongs, or to all States, and the third State assents thereto.   Its assent shall be presumed so long as the contrary is not indicated, unless the treaty otherwise provides.
2.   A State exercising a right in accordance with paragraph 1 shall comply with the conditions for its exercise provides for in the treaty or established in conformity with the treaty.

Article 38
Rules in a treaty becoming binding on third States through international custom

Nothing in articles 34 to 37 precludes a rule set forth in a treaty from becoming binding upon a third State as a customary rule of international law, recognized as such.

3.3 NORTH SEA CONTINENTAL SHELF CASES, 1969

North Sea Continental Shelf, Judgment, ICJ Reports 1969, p.3
Excerpt from Judgment at pp.37-45

60. The conclusions so far reached leave open, and still to be considered, the question whether on some basis other than that of an *a priori* logical necessity, i.e., through positive law processes, the equidistance principle has come to be regarded as a rule of customary international law, so that it would be obligatory for the Federal Republic in that way, even though Article 6 of the Geneva Convention is not, as such, opposable to it.   For this purpose it is necessary to examine the status of the principle as it stood when the Convention was drawn up, as it resulted from the effect of the Convention, and in the light of State practice subsequent to the Convention; but it should be clearly understood that in the pronouncements the Court makes on these matters it has in view solely the delimitation provisions (Article 6) of the Convention, not other parts of it, nor the Convention as such.
61. The first of these questions can conveniently be considered in the form suggested on behalf of Denmark and the Netherlands themselves in the course of the oral hearing, when it was stated that they had not in fact contended that the delimitation article (Article 6) of the Convention "embodied already received rules of customary law in the sense that the Convention was merely declaratory of existing rules".   Their contention was, rather, that although prior to the Conference, continental shelf law was only in the formative stage, and State practice lacked uniformity, yet "the process of the definition and consolidation of the emerging customary law took place through the work of the International Law Commission, the reaction of governments to that work and the

proceedings of the Geneva Conference"; and this emerging customary law became "crystallized in the adoption of the Continental Shelf Convention by the Conference".

62. Whatever validity this contention may have in respect of at least certain parts of the Convention, the Court cannot accept it as regards the delimitation provision (Article 6), the relevant parts of which were adopted almost unchanged from the draft of the International Law Commission that formed the basis of discussion at the Conference. The status of the rule in the Convention therefore depends mainly on the processes that led the Commission to propose it. These processes have already been reviewed in connection with the Danish-Netherlands contention of an *a priori* necessity for equidistance, and the Court considers this review sufficient for present purposes also, in order to show that the principle of equidistance, as it now figures in Article 6 of the Convention, was proposed by the Commission with considerable hesitation, somewhat on an experimental basis, at most *de lege ferenda*, and not at all *de lege lata* or as an emerging rule of customary international law. This is clearly not the sort of foundation on which Article 6 of the Convention could be said to have reflected or crystallized such a rule.

63. The foregoing conclusion received significant confirmation from the fact that Article 6 is one of those in respect of which, under the reservations article of the Convention (Article 12) reservations may be made by any State on signing, ratifying or acceding, – for, speaking generally, it is a characteristic of purely conventional rules and obligations that, in regard to them, some faculty of making unilateral reservations may, within certain limits, be admitted; – whereas this cannot be so in the case of general or customary law rules and obligations which, by their very nature, must have equal force for all members of the international community, and cannot therefore be the subject of any right of unilateral exclusion exercisable at will by any one of them in its own favour. Consequently, it is to be expected that when, for whatever reason, rules or obligations of this order are embodied, or are intended to be reflected in certain provisions of a convention, such provisions will figure amongst those in respect of which a right of unilateral reservation is not conferred, or is excluded. This expectation is, in principle, fulfilled by Article 12 of the Geneva Continental Shelf Convention, which permits reservations to be made to all the articles of the Convention "other than to Articles 1 to 3 inclusive" – these three Articles being the ones which, it is clear, were then regarded as reflecting, or as crystallizing, received or at least emergent rules of customary international law relative to the continental shelf, amongst them the question of the seaward extent of the shelf; the juridical character of the coastal State's entitlement; the nature of the rights exercisable; the kind of natural resources to which these relate; and the preservation intact of the legal status as high seas of the waters over the shelf, and the legal status of the superjacent air-space.

64. The normal inference would therefore be that any articles that do not figure among those excluded from the faculty of reservation under Article 12, were not regarded as declaratory of previously existing or emergent rules of law; and this is the inference the Court in fact draws in respect of Article 6 (delimitation), having regard also to the attitude of the International Law Commission to this provision, as already described in general terms. Naturally this would not of itself prevent this provision from eventually passing into the general *corpus* of customary international law by one of the processes considered in paragraphs 70-81 below. But that is not here the issue. What is now under consideration is whether it originally figured in the Convention as such a rule.

65. It has however been suggested that the inference drawn at the beginning of the preceding paragraph is not necessarily warranted, seeing that there are certain other provisions of the Convention, also not excluded from the faculty of reservation, but

which do undoubtedly in principle relate to matters that lie within the field of received customary law, such as the obligation not to impede the laying or maintenance of submarine cables or pipelines on the continental shelf seabed (Article 4), and the general obligation not unjustifiably to interfere with freedom of navigation, fishing, and so on (Article 5, paragraphs 1 and 6). These matters however, all relate to or are consequential upon principles or rules of general maritime law, very considerably ante-dating the Convention, and not directly connected with but only incidental to continental shelf rights as such. They were mentioned in the Convention, not in order to declare or confirm their existence, which was not necessary, but simply to ensure that they were not prejudiced by the exercise of continental shelf rights as provided for in the Convention. Another method of drafting might have clarified the point, but this cannot alter the fact that no reservation could release the reserving party from obligations of general maritime law existing outside and independently of the Convention, and especially obligations formalized in Article 2 of the contemporaneous Convention on the High Seas, expressed by its preamble to be declaratory of established principles of international law.

66. Article 6 (delimitation) appears to the Court to be in a different position. It does directly relate to continental shelf rights as such, rather than to matters incidental to these; and since it was not, as were Articles 1 to 3, excluded from the faculty of reservation, it is a legitimate inference that it was considered to have a different and less fundamental status and not, like those Articles, to reflect pre-existing or emergent customary law. It was however contended on behalf of Denmark and the Netherlands that the right of reservation given in respect of Article 6 was not intended to be an unfettered right, and that in particular it does not extend to effecting a total exclusion of the equidistance principle of delimitation, – for, so it was claimed, delimitation on the basis of that principle is implicit in articles 1 and 2 of the Convention, in respect of which no reservations are permitted. Hence the right of reservation under Article 6 could only be exercised in a manner consistent with the preservation of at least the basic principle of equidistance. In this connection it was pointed out that, of the no more than four reservations so far entered in respect of Article 6, one at least of which was somewhat far-reaching, none has purported to effect such a total exclusion or denial.

67. The Court finds this argument unconvincing for a number of reasons. In the first place, Articles 1 and 2 of the Geneva Convention do not appear to have any direct connection with inter-State delimitation as such. Article 1 is concerned only with the outer, seaward, limit of the shelf generally, not with boundaries between the shelf areas of opposite or adjacent States. Article 2 is equally not concerned with such boundaries. The suggestion seems to be that the notion of equidistance is implicit in the reference in paragraph 2 of Article 2 to the rights of the coastal State over its continental shelf being "exclusive". So far as actual language is concerned this interpretation if clearly incorrect. The true sense of the passage is that in whatever areas of the continental shelf a coastal State has rights, those rights are exclusive rights, not exercisable by any other State. But this says nothing as to what in fact are the precise areas in respect of which each coastal State possesses these exclusive rights. This question, which can arise only as regards the fringes of a coastal State's shelf area is, as explained at the end of paragraph 20 above, exactly what falls to be settled through the process of delimitation, and this is the sphere of Article 6, not Article 2.

68. Secondly, it must be observed that no valid conclusions can be drawn from the fact that the faculty of entering reservations to Article 6 has been exercised only sparingly and within certain limits. This is the affair exclusively of those States which have not

wished to exercise the faculty, or which have been content to do so only to a limited extent.   Their action or inaction cannot affect the right of other States to enter reservations to whatever is the legitimate extent of the right.

69. In the light of these various considerations, the Court reaches the conclusion that the Geneva Convention did not embody or crystallize any pre-existing or emergent rule of customary law, according to which the delimitation of continental shelf areas between adjacent States must, unless the Parties otherwise agree, be carried out on an equidistance-special circumstances basis.   A rule was of course embodied in Article 6 of the Convention, but as a purely conventional rule.   Whether it has since acquired a broader basis remains to be seen: *qua* conventional rule however, as has already been concluded, it is not opposable to the Federal Republic.

70. The Court must now proceed to the last stage in the argument put forward on behalf of Denmark and the Netherlands.   This is to the effect that even if there was at the date of the Geneva Convention no rule of customary international law in favour of the equidistance principle, and no such rule was crystallized in Article 6 of the Convention, nevertheless such a rule has come into being since the Convention, partly because of its own impact, partly on the basis of subsequent State practice, – and that this rule, being now a rule of customary international law binding on all States, including therefore the Federal Republic, should be declared applicable to the delimitation of the boundaries between the Parties' respective continental shelf areas in the North Sea.

71. In so far as this contention is based on the view that Article 6 of the Convention has had the influence, and has produced the effect, described, it clearly involves treating that Article as a norm-creating provision which has constituted the foundation of, or has generated a rule which, while only conventional or contractual in its origin, has since passed into the general *corpus* of international law, and is now accepted as such by the *opinio juris*, so as to have become binding even for countries which have never, and do not, become parties to the Convention.   There is no doubt that this process is a perfectly possible one and does from time to time occur: it constitutes indeed one of the recognized methods by which new rules of customary international law may be formed.   At the same time this result is not lightly to be regarded as having been attained.

72. It would in the first place be necessary that the provision concerned should, at all events potentially, be of a fundamentally norm-creating character such as could be regarded as forming the basis of a general rule of law.   Considered *in abstracto* the equidistance principle might be said to fulfil this requirement.   Yet in the particular form in which it is embodied in Article 6 of the Geneva Convention, and having regard to the relationship of that Article to other provisions of the Convention, this must be open to some doubt.   In the first place, Article 6 is so framed as to put second the obligation to make use of the equidistance method, causing it to come after a primary obligation to effect delimitation by agreement.   Such a primary obligation constitutes an unusual preface to what is claimed to be a potential general rule of law.   Without attempting to enter into, still less pronounce upon any question of *jus cogens*, it is well understood that, in practice, rules of international law can, by agreement, be derogated from in particular cases, or as between particular parties, – but this is not normally the subject of any express provision, as it is in Article 6 of the Geneva Convention. Secondly the part played by the notion of special circumstances, relative to the principle of equidistance as embodied in Article 6, and the very considerable, still unresolved controversies as to the exact meaning and scope of this notion, must raise further doubts as to the potentially norm-creating character of the rule.   Finally, the

faculty of making reservations to Article 6, while it might not of itself prevent the equidistance principle being eventually received as general law, does add considerably to the difficulty of regarding this result as having been brought about (or being potentially possible) on the basis of the Convention: for so long as this faculty continues to exist, and is not the subject of any revision brought about in consequence of a request made under Article 13 of the Convention – of which there is at present no official indication – it is the Convention itself which would, for the reasons already indicated, seem to deny to the provisions of Article 6 the same norm-creating character as, for instance, Articles 1 and 2 possess.

73. With respect to the other elements usually regarded as necessary before a conventional rule can be considered to have become a general rule of international law, it might be that, even without the passage of any considerable period of time, a very widespread and representative participation in the convention might suffice of itself, provided it included that of States whose interests were specially affected. In the present case however, the Court notes that, even if allowance is made for the existence of a number of States to whom participation in the Geneva Convention is not open, or which, by reason for instance of being land-locked States, would have no interest in becoming parties to it, the number of ratifications and accessions so far secured is, though respectable, hardly sufficient. That non-ratification may sometimes be due to factors other than active disapproval of the convention concerned can hardly constitute a basis on which positive acceptance of its principles can be implied: the reasons are speculative, but the facts remain.

74. As regards the time element, the Court notes that it is over ten years since the Convention was signed, but that it is even now less than five since it came into force in June 1964, and that when the present proceedings were brought it was less than three years, while less than one had elapsed at the time when the respective negotiations between the Federal Republic and the other two Parties for a complete delimitation broke down on the question of the application of the equidistance principle. Although the passage of only a short period of time is not necessarily, or of itself, a bar to the formation of a new rule of customary international law on the basis of what was originally a purely conventional rule, an indispensable requirement would be that within the period in question, short though it might be, State practice, including that of States whose interests are specially affected, should have been both extensive and virtually uniform in the sense of the provision invoked; – and should moreover have occurred in such a way as to show a general recognition that a rule of law or legal obligation is involved.

75. The Court must now consider whether State practice in the matter of continental shelf delimitation has, subsequent to the Geneva Convention, been of such a kind as to satisfy this requirement. Leaving aside cases which, for various reasons, the Court does not consider to be reliable guides as precedents, such as delimitations effected between the present Parties themselves, or not relating to international boundaries, some fifteen cases have been cited in the course of the present proceedings, occurring mostly since the signature of the 1958 Geneva Convention, in which continental shelf boundaries have been delimited according to the equidistance principle – in the majority of the cases by agreement, in a few others unilaterally – or else the delimitation was foreshadowed but has not yet been carried out. Amongst these fifteen are the four North Sea delimitations United Kingdom/Norway-Denmark-Netherlands, and Norway/Denmark already mentioned in paragraph 4 of this Judgment. But even if these various cases constituted more than a very small proportion of those potentially calling for delimitation in the world as a whole, the Court would not think it necessary

to enumerate or evaluate them separately, since there are, *a priori*, several grounds which deprive them of weight as precedents in the present context.

76. To begin with, over half the States concerned, whether acting unilaterally or conjointly, were or shortly became parties to the Geneva Convention, and were therefore presumably, so far as they were concerned, acting actually or potentially in the application of the Convention. From their action no inference could legitimately be drawn as to the existence of a rule of customary international law in favour of the equidistance principle. As regards those States, on the other hand, which were not, and have not become parties to the Convention, the basis of their action can only be problematical and must remain entirely speculative. Clearly, they were not applying the Convention. But from that no inference could justifiably be drawn that they believed themselves to be applying a mandatory rule of customary international law. There is not a shred of evidence that they did and, as has been seen (paragraphs 22 and 23), there is no lack of other reasons for using the equidistance method, so that acting, or agreeing to act in a certain way, does not of itself demonstrate anything of a juridical nature.

77. The essential point in this connection - and it seems necessary to stress it – is that even if these instances of action by non-parties to the Convention were much more numerous than they in fact are, they would not, even in the aggregate, suffice in themselves to constitute the *opinio juris*; – for, in order to achieve this result, two conditions must be fulfilled. Not only must the acts concerned amount to a settled practice, but they must also be such, or be carried out in such a way, as to be evidence of a belief that this practice is rendered obligatory by the existence of a rule of law requiring it. The need for such a belief, i.e., the existence of a subjective element, is implicit in the very notion of the *opinio juris sive necessitatis*. The States concerned must therefore feel that they are conforming to what amounts to a legal obligation. The frequency, or even habitual character of the acts is not in itself enough. There are many international acts, e.g., in the field of ceremonial and protocol, which are performed almost invariably, but which are motivated only by considerations of courtesy, convenience or tradition, and not by any sense of legal duty.

78. In this respect the Court follows the view adopted by the Permanent Court of International Justice in the *Lotus* case, as stated in the following passage, the principle of which is, by analogy, applicable almost word for word, *mutatis mutandis*, to the present case (*P.C.I.J., Series A, No.10*, 1927, at p.28):

"Even if the rarity of the judicial decisions to be found ... were sufficient to prove ... the circumstance alleged ..., it would merely show that States had often, in practice, abstained from instituting criminal proceedings, and not that they recognized themselves as being obliged to do so; for only if such abstention were based on their being conscious of having a duty to abstain would it be possible to speak of an international custom. The alleged fact does not allow one to infer that States have been conscious of having such a duty; on the other hand, ... there are other circumstances calculated to show that the contrary is true."

Applying this dictum to the present case, the position is simply that in certain cases – not a great number – the States concerned agreed to draw or did draw the boundaries concerned according to the principle of equidistance. There is no evidence that they so acted because they felt legally compelled to draw them in this way by reason of a rule of customary law obliging them to do so – especially considering that they might have been motivated by other obvious factors.

79. Finally, it appears that in almost all of the cases cited, the delimitations concerned were median-line delimitations between opposite States, not lateral delimitations between adjacent States.   For reasons which have already been given (paragraph 57) the Court regards the case of median-line delimitations between opposite States as different in various respects, and as being sufficiently distinct not to constitute a precedent for the delimitation of lateral boundaries.   In only one situation discussed by the Parties does there appear to have been a geographical configuration which to some extent resembles the present one, in the sense that a number of States on the same coastline are grouped around a sharp curve or bend of it.   No complete delimitation in this area has however yet been carried out.   But the Court is not concerned to deny to this case, or any other of those cited, all evidential value in favour of the thesis of Denmark and the Netherlands.   It simply considers that they are inconclusive, and insufficient to bear the weight sought to be put upon them as evidence of such a settled practice, manifested in such circumstances, as would justify the inference that delimitation according to the principle of equidistance amounts to a mandatory rule of customary international law, – more particularly where lateral delimitations are concerned.

80. There are of course plenty of cases (and a considerable number were cited) of delimitations of waters, as opposed to seabed, being carried out on the basis of equidistance – mostly of internal waters (lakes, rivers, etc.), and mostly median-line cases.   The nearest analogy is that of adjacent territorial waters, but as already explained (paragraph 59) the Court does not consider this case to be analogous to that of the continental shelf.

81. The Court accordingly concludes that if the Geneva Convention was not in its origins or inception declaratory of a mandatory rule of customary international law enjoining the use of the equidistance principle for the delimitation of continental shelf areas between adjacent States, neither has its subsequent effect been constitutive of such a rule;   and that State practice up-to-date has equally been insufficient for the purpose.

3.4 FISHERIES JURISDICTION CASE, 1974

Fisheries Jurisdiction (United Kingdom v. Iceland), Merits, Judgment,
ICJ Reports 1974, p.3
Excerpt from Judgment at pp.23-27

52. The 1960 Conference failed by one vote to adopt a text governing the two questions of the breadth of the territorial sea and the extent of fishery rights. However, after that Conference the law evolved through the practice of States on the basis of the debates and near-agreements at the Conference.   Two concepts have crystallized as customary law in recent years arising out of the general consensus revealed at that Conference.   The first is the concept of the fishery zone, the area in which a State may claim exclusive fishery jurisdiction independently of its territorial sea;   the extension of that fishery zone up to a 12-mile limit from the baselines appears now to be generally accepted.   The second is the concept of preferential rights of fishing in adjacent waters in favour of the coastal State in a situation of special dependence on its coastal fisheries, this preference operating in regard to other States concerned in the exploitation of the same fisheries, and to be implemented in the way indicated in paragraph 57 below.

53. In recent years the question of extending the coastal State's fisheries jurisdiction has come increasingly to the forefront. The Court is aware that a number of States has asserted an extension of fishery limits. The Court is also aware of present endeavours, pursued under the auspices of the United Nations, to achieve in a third Conference on the Law of the Sea the further codification and progressive development of this branch of the law, as it is of various proposals and preparatory documents produced in this framework, which must be regarded as manifestations of the views and opinions of individual States and as vehicles of their aspirations, rather than as expressing principles of existing law. The very fact of convening the third Conference on the Law of the Sea evidences a manifest desire on the part of all States to proceed to the codification of that law on a universal basis, including the question of fisheries and conservation of the living resources of the sea. Such a general desire is understandable since the rules of international maritime law have been the product of mutual accommodation, reasonableness and co-operation. So it was in the past, and so it necessarily is today. In the circumstances, the Court, as a court of law, cannot render judgment *sub specie legis ferendae*, or anticipate the law before the legislator has laid it down.

54. The concept of a 12-mile fishery zone, referred to in paragraph 52 above, as a *tertium genus* between the territorial sea and the high seas, has been accepted with regard to Iceland in the substantive provisions of the 1961 Exchange of Notes, and the United Kingdom has also applied the same fishery limit to its own coastal waters since 1964; therefore this matter is no longer in dispute between the Parties. At the same time, the concept of preferential rights, a notion that necessarily implies the existence of other legal rights in respect of which that preference operates, has been admitted by the Applicant to be relevant to the solution of the present dispute. Moreover, the Applicant has expressly recognized Iceland's preferential rights in the disputed waters and at the same time has invoked its own historic fishing rights in these same waters, on the ground that reasonable regard must be had to such traditional rights by the coastal State, in accordance with the generally recognized principles embodied in Article 2 of the High Seas Convention. If, as the Court pointed out in its dictum in the *Fisheries* case, cited in paragraph 49 above, any national delimitation of sea areas, to be opposable to other States, requires evaluation in terms of the existing rules of international law, then it becomes necessary for the Court, in its examination of Icelandic fisheries Regulations, to take those elements into consideration as well. Equally it has necessarily to take into account the provisions of the Exchange of Notes of 1961 which govern the relations between the Parties with respect to Iceland's fishery limits. The said Exchange of Notes, which was concluded within the framework of the existing provisions of the law of the sea, was held by the Court, in its Judgment of 2 February 1973, to be a treaty which is valid and in force.

55. The concept of preferential rights for the coastal State in a situation of special dependence on coastal fisheries originated in proposals submitted by Iceland at the Geneva Conference of 1958. Its delegation drew attention to the problem which would arise when, in spite of adequate fisheries conservation measures, the yield ceased to be sufficient to satisfy the requirements of all those who were interested in fishing in a given area. Iceland contended that in such a case, when a catch-limitation becomes necessary, special consideration should be given to the coastal State whose population is overwhelmingly dependent on the fishing resources in its adjacent waters.

56. An Icelandic proposal embodying these ideas failed to obtain the majority required, but a resolution was adopted at the 1958 Conference concerning the situation of countries or territories whose people are overwhelmingly dependent upon coastal

fisheries for their livelihood or economic development. This resolution, after "recognizing that such situations call for exceptional measures befitting particular needs" recommended that:

> "... where, for the purpose of conservation, it becomes necessary to limit the total catch of a stock or stocks of fish in an area of the high seas adjacent to the territorial sea of a coastal State, any other States fishing in that area should collaborate with the coastal State to secure just treatment of such situation, by establishing agreed measures which shall recognize any preferential requirements of the coastal State resulting from its dependence upon the fishery concerned while having regard to the interests of the other States."

The resolution further recommended that "appropriate conciliation and arbitral procedures shall be established for the settlement of any disagreement".

57. At the Plenary Meetings of the 1960 Conference the concept of preferential rights was embodied in a joint amendment presented by Brazil, Cuba and Uruguay which was subsequently incorporated by a substantial vote into a joint United States-Canadian proposal concerning a 6-mile territorial sea and an additional 6-mile fishing zone, thus totalling a 12-mile exclusive fishing zone, subject to a phasing-out period. This amendment provided, independently of the exclusive fishing zone, that the coastal State had:

> "... the faculty of claiming preferential fishing rights in any area of the high seas adjacent to its exclusive fishing zone when it is scientifically established that a special situation or condition makes the exploitation of the living resources of the high seas in that area of fundamental importance to the economic development of the coastal State or the feeding of its population".

It also provided that:

> "A special situation or condition may be deemed to exist when:
> (a) The fisheries and the economic development of the coastal State or the feeding of its population are so manifestly interrelated that, in consequence, that State is greatly dependent on the living resources of the high seas in the area in respect of which preferential fishing is being claimed;
> (b) It becomes necessary to limit the total catch of a stock or stocks of fish in such areas ..."

The contemporary practice of States leads to the conclusion that the preferential rights of the coastal State in a special situation are to be implemented by agreement between the States concerned, either bilateral or multilateral, and, in case of disagreement, through the means for the peaceful settlement of disputes provided for in Article 33 of the Charter of the United Nations. It was in fact an express condition of the amendment referred to above that any other State concerned would have the right to request that a claim made by a coastal State should be tested and determined by a special commission on the basis of scientific criteria and of evidence presented by the coastal State and other States concerned. The commission was to be empowered to determine, for the period of time and under the limitations that it found necessary, the preferential rights of the coastal State, "while having regard to the interests of any other State or States in the exploitation of such stock or stocks of fish".

58. State practice on the subject of fisheries reveals an increasing and widespread acceptance of the concept of preferential rights for coastal States, particularly in favour of countries or territories in a situation of special dependence on coastal fisheries. Both the 1958 Resolution and the 1960 joint amendment concerning preferential rights were approved by a large majority of the Conferences, thus showing overwhelming support for the idea that in certain special situations it was fair to recognize that the coastal State had preferential fishing rights.　After these Conferences, the preferential rights of the coastal State were recognized in various bilateral and multilateral international agreements.　The Court's attention has been drawn to the practice in this regard of the North-West and North-East Atlantic Fisheries Commissions, of which 19 maritime States altogether, including both Parties, are members;　its attention has also been drawn to the Arrangement Relating to Fisheries in Waters Surrounding the Faroe Islands, signed at Copenhagen on 18 December 1973 on behalf of the Governments of Belgium, Denmark, France, the Federal Republic of Germany. Norway, Poland and the United Kingdom, and to the Agreement on the Regulation of the Fishing of North-East Arctic (Arcto-Norwegian) Cod, signed on 15 March 1974 on behalf of the Governments of the United Kingdom, Norway and the Union of Soviet Socialist Republics.　Both the aforesaid agreements, in allocating the annual shares on the basis of the past performance of the parties in the area, assign an additional share to the coastal State on the ground of its preferential right in the fisheries in its adjacent waters.　The Faroese agreement takes expressly into account in its preamble "the exceptional dependence of the Faroese economy on fisheries" and recognizes "that the Faroe Islands should enjoy preference in waters surrounding the Faroe Islands".

59. There can be no doubt of the exceptional dependence of Iceland on its fisheries. That exceptional dependence was explicitly recognized by the Applicant in the Exchange of Notes of 11 March 1961, and the Court has also taken judicial notice of such recognition, by declaring that it is "necessary to bear in mind the exceptional dependence of the Icelandic nation upon coastal fisheries for its livelihood and economic development" (*I.C.J. Reports 1972*, p.16, para.23).

60. The preferential rights of the coastal State come into play only at the moment when an intensification in the exploitation of fishery resources makes it imperative to introduce some system of catch-limitation and sharing of those resources, to preserve the fish stocks in the interests of their rational and economic exploitation.　This situation appears to have been reached in the present case.　In regard to the two main demersal species concerned – cod and haddock – the Applicant has shown itself aware of the need for a catch-limitation which has become indispensable in view of the establishment of catch-limitations in other regions of the North Atlantic.　If a system of catch-limitation were not established in the Icelandic area, the fishing effort displaced from those other regions might well be directed towards the unprotected grounds in that area.

4 Internal Waters, Territorial Sea and Contiguous Zone

4.1 UNITED NATIONS CONVENTION ON THE LAW OF THE SEA, 1982: PART II: TERRITORIAL SEA AND CONTIGUOUS ZONE; AND PART VIII: REGIME OF ISLANDS

PART II
TERRITORIAL SEA AND CONTIGUOUS ZONE

SECTION 1. GENERAL PROVISIONS

Article 2
Legal status of the territorial sea, of the air space over the territorial sea and of its bed and subsoil

1. The sovereignty of a coastal State extends, beyond its land territory and internal waters and, in the case of an archipelagic State, its archipelagic waters, to an adjacent belt of sea, described as the territorial sea.
2. This sovereignty extends to the air space over the territorial sea as well as to its bed and subsoil.
3. The sovereignty over the territorial sea is exercised subject to this Convention and to other rules of international law.

SECTION 2. LIMITS OF THE TERRITORIAL SEA

Article 3
Breadth of the territorial sea

Every State has the right to establish the breadth of its territorial sea up to a limit not exceeding 12 nautical miles, measured from baselines determined in accordance with this Convention.

Article 4
Outer limit of the territorial sea

The outer limit of the territorial sea is the line every point of which is at a distance from the nearest point of the baseline equal to the breadth of the territorial sea.

Article 5
Normal baseline

Except where otherwise provided in this Convention, the normal baseline for measuring the breadth of the territorial sea is the low-water line along the coast as marked on large-scale charts officially recognized by the coastal State.

Article 6
Reefs

In the case of islands situated on atolls or of islands having fringing reefs, the baseline for measuring the breadth of the territorial sea is the seaward low-water line of the reef, as shown by the appropriate symbol on charts officially recognized by the coastal State.

Article 7
Straight baselines

1.   In localities where the coastline is deeply indented and cut into, or if there is a fringe of islands along the coast in its immediate vicinity, the method of straight baselines joining appropriate points may be employed in drawing the baseline from which the breadth of the territorial sea is measured.
2.   Where because of the presence of a delta and other natural conditions the coastline is highly unstable, the appropriate points may be selected along the furthest seaward extent of the low-water line and, notwithstanding subsequent regression of the low-water line, the straight baselines shall remain effective until changed by the coastal State in accordance with this Convention.
3.   The drawing of straight baselines must not depart to any appreciable extent from the general direction of the coast, and the sea areas lying within the lines must be sufficiently closely linked to the land domain to be subject to the regime of internal waters.
4.   Straight baselines shall not be drawn to and from low-tide elevations, unless lighthouses or similar installations which are permanently above sea level have been built on them or except in instances where the drawing of baselines to and from such elevations has received general international recognition.
5.   Where the method of straight baselines is applicable under paragraph 1, account may be taken, in determining particular baselines, of economic interests peculiar to the

region concerned, the reality and the importance of which are clearly evidenced by long usage.

6. The system of straight baselines may not be applied by a State in such a manner as to cut off the territorial sea of another State from the high seas or an exclusive economic zone.

Article 8
Internal waters

1. Except as provided in Part IV, waters on the landward side of the baseline of the territorial sea form part of the internal waters of the State.

2. Where the establishment of a straight baseline in accordance with the method set forth in article 7 has the effect of enclosing as internal waters areas which had not previously been considered as such, a right of innocent passage as provided in this Convention shall exist in those waters.

Article 9
Mouths of rivers

If a river flows directly into the sea, the baseline shall be a straight line across the mouth of the river between points on the low-water line of its banks.

Article 10
Bays

1. This article relates only to bays the coasts of which belong to a single State.

2. For the purposes of this Convention, a bay is a well-marked indentation whose penetration is in such proportion to the width of its mouth as to contain land-locked waters and constitute more than a mere curvature of the coast. An indentation shall not, however, be regarded as a bay unless its area is as large as, or larger than, that of the semi-circle whose diameter is a line drawn across the mouth of that indentation.

3. For the purpose of measurement, the area of an indentation is that lying between the low-water mark around the shore of the indentation and a line joining the low-water mark of its natural entrance points. Where, because of the presence of islands, an indentation has more than one mouth, the semi-circle shall be drawn on a line as long as the sum total of the lengths of the lines across the different mouths. Islands within an indentation shall be included as if they were part of the water area of the indentation.

4. If the distance between the low-water marks of the natural entrance points of a bay does not exceed 24 nautical miles, a closing line may be drawn between these two low-water marks, and the waters enclosed thereby shall be considered as internal waters.

5. Where the distance between the low-water marks of the natural entrance points of a bay exceeds 24 nautical miles, a straight baseline of 24 nautical miles shall be drawn within the bay in such a manner as to enclose the maximum area of water that is possible with a line of that length.

6. The foregoing provisions do not apply to so-called "historic" bays, or in any case where the system of straight baselines provided for in article 7 is applied.

Article 11
Ports

For the purpose of delimiting the territorial sea, the outermost permanent harbour works which form an integral part of the harbour system are regarded as forming part of the coast. Off-shore installations and artificial islands shall not be considered as permanent harbour works.

Article 12
Roadsteads

Roadsteads which are normally used for the loading, unloading and anchoring of ships, and which would otherwise be situated wholly or partly outside the outer limit of the territorial sea, are included in the territorial sea.

Article 13
Low-tide elevations

1. A low-tide elevation is a naturally formed area of land which is surrounded by and above water at low tide but submerged at high tide. Where a low-tide elevation is situated wholly or partly at a distance not exceeding the breadth of the territorial sea from the mainland or an island, the low-water line on that elevation may be used as the baseline for measuring the breadth of the territorial sea.
2. Where a low-tide elevation is wholly situated at a distance exceeding the breadth of the territorial sea from the mainland or an island, it has no territorial sea of its own.

Article 14
Combination of methods for determining baselines

The coastal State may determine baselines in turn by any of the methods provided for in the foregoing articles to suit different conditions.

Article 15
Delimitation of the territorial sea between States with opposite or adjacent coasts

Where the coasts of two States are opposite or adjacent to each other, neither of the two States is entitled, failing agreement between them to the contrary, to extend its territorial sea beyond the median line every point of which is equidistant from the nearest points on the baselines from which the breadth of the territorial seas of each of the two States is measured. The above provision does not apply, however, where it is necessary by reason of historic title or other special circumstances to delimit the territorial seas of the two States in a way which is at variance therewith.

Article 16
Charts and lists of geographical co-ordinates

1. The baselines for measuring the breadth of the territorial sea determined in accordance with articles 7, 9 and 10, or the limits derived therefrom, and the lines of delimitation drawn in accordance with articles 12 and 15 shall be shown on charts of a scale or scales adequate for ascertaining their position. Alternatively, a list of geographical co-ordinates of points, specifying the geodetic datum, may be substituted.
2. The coastal State shall give due publicity to such charts or lists of geographical co-ordinates and shall deposit a copy of each such chart or list with the Secretary-General of the United Nations.

SECTION 3. INNOCENT PASSAGE IN THE TERRITORIAL SEA

SUBSECTION A. RULES APPLICABLE TO ALL SHIPS

Article 17
Right of innocent passage

Subject to this Convention, ships of all States, whether coastal or land-locked, enjoy the right of innocent passage through the territorial sea.

Article 18
Meaning of passage

1. Passage means navigation through the territorial sea for the purpose of:
    (a) traversing that sea without entering internal waters or calling at a roadstead or port facility outside internal waters; or
    (b) proceeding to or from internal waters or a call at such roadstead or port facility.
2. Passage shall be continuous and expeditious. However, passage includes stopping and anchoring, but only in so far as the same are incidental to ordinary navigation or are rendered necessary by *force majeure* or distress or for the purpose of rendering assistance to persons, ships or aircraft in danger or distress.

Article 19
Meaning of innocent passage

1. Passage is innocent so long as it is not prejudicial to the peace, good order or security of the coastal State. Such passage shall take place in conformity with this Convention and with other rules of international law.
2. Passage of a foreign ship shall be considered to be prejudicial to the peace, good order or security of the coastal State if in the territorial sea it engages in any of the following activities:
    (a) any threat or use of force against the sovereignty, territorial integrity or political independence of the coastal State, or in any other manner in violation of the principles of international law embodied in the Charter of the United Nations;
    (b) any exercise or practice with weapons of any kind;
    (c) any act aimed at collecting information to the prejudice of the defence or security of the coastal State;
    (d) any act of propaganda aimed at affecting the defence or security of the coastal State;
    (e) the launching, landing or taking on board of any aircraft;
    (f) the launching, landing or taking on board of any military device;
    (g) the loading or unloading of any commodity, currency or person contrary to the customs, fiscal, immigration or sanitary laws and regulations of the coastal State;
    (h) any act of wilful and serious pollution contrary to this Convention;
    (i) any fishing activities;
    (j) the carrying out of research or survey activities;
    (k) any act aimed at interfering with any systems of communication or any other facilities or installations of the coastal State;
    (l) any other activity not having a direct bearing on passage.

Article 20
Submarines and other underwater vehicles

In the territorial sea, submarines and other underwater vehicles are required to navigate on the surface and to show their flag.

Article 21
Laws and regulations of the coastal State relating to innocent passage

1. The coastal State may adopt laws and regulations, in conformity with the provisions of this Convention and other rules of international law, relating to innocent passage through the territorial sea, in respect of all or any of the following:
    (a) the safety of navigation and the regulation of maritime traffic;
    (b) the protection of navigational aids and facilities and other facilities or installations;
    (c) the protection of cables and pipelines;
    (d) the conservation of the living resources of the sea;
    (e) the prevention of infringement of the fisheries laws and regulations of the coastal State;
    (f) the preservation of the environment of the coastal State and the prevention, reduction and control of pollution thereof;
    (g) marine scientific research and hydrographic surveys;
    (h) the prevention of infringement of the customs, fiscal, immigration or sanitary laws and regulations of the coastal State.
2. Such laws and regulations shall not apply to the design, construction, manning or equipment of foreign ships unless they are giving effect to generally accepted international rules or standards.
3. The coastal State shall give due publicity to all such laws and regulations.
4. Foreign ships exercising the right of innocent passage through the territorial sea shall comply with all such laws and regulations and all generally accepted international regulations relating to the prevention of collisions at sea.

Article 22
Sea lanes and traffic separation schemes in the territorial sea

1. The coastal State may, where necessary having regard to the safety of navigation, require foreign ships exercising the right of innocent passage through its territorial sea to use such sea lanes and traffic separation schemes as it may designate or prescribe for the regulation of the passage of ships.
2. In particular, tankers, nuclear-powered ships and ships carrying nuclear or other inherently dangerous or noxious substances or materials may be required to confine their passage to such sea lanes.
3. In the designation of sea lanes and the prescription of traffic separation schemes under this article, the coastal State shall take into account:
    (a) the recommendations of the competent international organization;
    (b) any channels customarily used for international navigation;
    (c) the special characteristics of particular ships and channels; and
    (d) the density of traffic.
4. The coastal State shall clearly indicate such sea lanes and traffic separation schemes on charts to which due publicity shall be given.

Article 23
Foreign nuclear-powered ships and ships carrying nuclear or other inherently dangerous or noxious substances

Foreign nuclear-powered ships and ships carrying nuclear or other inherently dangerous or noxious substances shall, when exercising the right of innocent passage through the territorial sea, carry documents and observe special precautionary measures established for such ships by international agreements.

Article 24
Duties of the coastal State

1. The coastal State shall not hamper the innocent passage of foreign ships through the territorial sea except in accordance with this Convention. In particular, in the application of this Convention or of any laws or regulations adopted in conformity with this Convention, the coastal State shall not:
(a) impose requirements on foreign ships which have the practical effect of denying or impairing the right of innocent passage; or
(b) discriminate in form or in fact against the ships of any State or against ships carrying cargoes to, from or on behalf of any State.
2. The coastal State shall give appropriate publicity to any danger to navigation, of which it has knowledge, within its territorial sea.

Article 25
Rights of protection of the coastal State

1. The coastal State may take the necessary steps in its territorial sea to prevent passage which is not innocent.
2. In the case of ships proceeding to internal waters or a call at a port facility outside internal waters, the coastal State also has the right to take the necessary steps to prevent any breach of the conditions to which admission of those ships to internal waters or such a call is subject.
3. The coastal State may, without discrimination in form or in fact among foreign ships, suspend temporarily in specified areas of its territorial sea the innocent passage of foreign ships if such suspension is essential for the protection of its security, including weapons exercises. Such suspension shall take effect only after having been duly published.

Article 26
Charges which may be levied upon foreign ships

1. No charge may be levied upon foreign ships by reason only of their passage through the territorial sea.
2. Charges may be levied upon a foreign ship passing through the territorial sea as payment only for specific services rendered to the ship. These charges shall be levied without discrimination.

SUBSECTION B. RULES APPLICABLE TO MERCHANT SHIPS AND GOVERNMENT SHIPS OPERATED FOR COMMERCIAL PURPOSES

Article 27
Criminal jurisdiction on board a foreign ship

1. The criminal jurisdiction of the coastal State should not be exercised on board a foreign ship passing through the territorial sea to arrest any person or to conduct any investigation in connection with any crime committed on board the ship during its passage, save only in the following cases:
   (a) if the consequences of the crime extend to the coastal State;
   (b) if the crime is of a kind to disturb the peace of the country or the good order of the territorial sea;
   (c) if the assistance of the local authorities has been requested by the master of the ship or by a diplomatic agent or consular officer of the flag State; or
   (d) if such measures are necessary for the suppression of illicit traffic in narcotic drugs or psychotropic substances.
2. The above provisions do not affect the right of the coastal State to take any steps authorized by its laws for the purpose of an arrest or investigation on board a foreign ship passing through the territorial sea after leaving internal waters.
3. In the cases provided for in paragraphs 1 and 2, the coastal State shall, if the master so requests, notify a diplomatic agent or consular officer of the flag State before taking any steps, and shall facilitate contact between such agent or officer and the ship's crew. In cases of emergency this notification may be communicated while the measures are being taken.
4. In considering whether or in what manner an arrest should be made, the local authorities shall have due regard to the interests of navigation.
5. Except as provided in Part XII or with respect to violations of laws and regulations adopted in accordance with Part V, the coastal State may not take any steps on board a foreign ship passing through the territorial sea to arrest any person or to conduct any investigation in connection with any crime committed before the ship entered the territorial sea, if the ship, proceeding from a foreign port, is only passing through the territorial sea without entering internal waters.

Article 28
Civil jurisdiction in relation to foreign ships

1. The coastal State should not stop or divert a foreign ship passing through the territorial sea for the purpose of exercising civil jurisdiction in relation to a person on board the ship.
2. The coastal State may not levy execution against or arrest the ship for the purpose of any civil proceedings, save only in respect of obligations or liabilities assumed or incurred by the ship itself in the course or for the purpose of its voyage through the waters of the coastal State.
3. Paragraph 2 is without prejudice to the right of the coastal State, in accordance with its laws, to levy execution against or to arrest, for the purpose of any civil proceedings, a foreign ship lying in the territorial sea, or passing through the territorial sea after leaving internal waters.

SUBSECTION C. RULES APPLICABLE TO WARSHIPS AND OTHER GOVERNMENT SHIPS OPERATED FOR NON-COMMERCIAL PURPOSES

Article 29
Definition of warships

For the purposes of this Convention, "warship" means a ship belonging to the armed forces of a State bearing the external marks distinguishing such ships of its nationality, under the command of an officer duly commissioned by the government of the State and whose name appears in the appropriate service list or its equivalent, and manned by a crew which is under regular armed forces discipline.

Article 30
Non-compliance by warships with the laws and regulations of the coastal State

If any warship does not comply with the laws and regulations of the coastal State concerning passage through the territorial sea and disregards any request for compliance therewith which is made to it, the coastal State may require it to leave the territorial sea immediately.

Article 31
Responsibility of the flag State for damage caused by a warship or other government ship operated for non-commercial purposes

The flag State shall bear international responsibility for any loss or damage to the coastal State resulting from the non-compliance by a warship or other government ship operated for non-commercial purposes with the laws and regulations of the coastal State concerning passage through the territorial sea or with the provisions of this Convention or other rules of international law.

Article 32
Immunities of warships and other government ships operated for non-commercial purposes

With such exceptions as are contained in subsection A and in articles 30 and 31, nothing in this Convention affects the immunities of warships and other government ships operated for non-commercial purposes.

SECTION 4. CONTIGUOUS ZONE

Article 33
Contiguous zone

1. In a zone contiguous to its territorial sea, described as the contiguous zone, the coastal State may exercise the control necessary to:
(a) prevent infringement of its customs, fiscal, immigration or sanitary laws and regulations within its territory or territorial sea;
(b) punish infringement of the above laws and regulations committed within its territory or territorial sea.
2. The contiguous zone may not extend beyond 24 nautical miles from the baselines from which the breadth of the territorial sea is measured.

...

PART VIII
REGIME OF ISLANDS

Article 121
Regime of islands

1. An island is a naturally formed area of land, surrounded by water, which is above water at high tide.
2. Except as provided for in paragraph 3, the territorial sea, the contiguous zone, the exclusive economic zone and the continental shelf of an island are determined in accordance with the provisions of this Convention applicable to other land territory.
3. Rocks which cannot sustain human habitation or economic life of their own shall have no exclusive economic zone or continental shelf.

4.2 GENEVA CONVENTION ON THE TERRITORIAL SEA AND THE CONTIGUOUS ZONE, 1958

The States Parties to this Convention
Have *agreed* as follows:

PART I
TERRITORIAL SEA

SECTION I. GENERAL

Article 1

1. The sovereignty of a State extends, beyond its land territory and its internal waters, to a belt of sea adjacent to its coast, described as the territorial sea.
2. This sovereignty is exercised subject to the provisions of these Articles and to other rules of international law.

Article 2

The sovereignty of a coastal State extends to the air space over the territorial sea as well as to its bed and subsoil.

SECTION II. LIMITS OF THE TERRITORIAL SEA

Article 3

Except where otherwise provided in these Articles, the normal baseline for measuring the breadth of the territorial sea is the low-water line along the coast as marked on large-scale charts officially recognized by the coastal State.

Article 4

1.   In localities where the coastline is deeply indented and cut into, or if there is a fringe of islands along the coast in its immediate vicinity, the method of straight baselines joining appropriate points may be employed in drawing the baseline from which the breadth of the territorial sea is measured.

2.   The drawing of such baselines must not depart to any appreciable extent from the general direction of the coast, and the sea areas lying within the lines must be sufficiently closely linked to the land domain to be subject to the regime of internal waters.

3.   Baselines shall not be drawn to and from low-tide elevations, unless lighthouses or similar installations which are permanently above sea level have been built on them.

4.   Where the method of straight baselines is applicable under the provisions of paragraph 1, account may be taken, in determining particular baselines, of economic interests peculiar to the region concerned, the reality and the importance of which are clearly evidenced by a long usage.

5.   The system of straight baselines may not be applied by a State in such a manner as to cut off from the high seas the territorial sea of another State.

6.   The coastal State must clearly indicate straight baselines on charts, to which due publicity must be given.

Article 5

1.   Waters on the landward side of the baseline of the territorial sea form part of the internal waters of the State.

2.   Where the establishment of a straight baseline in accordance with Article 4 has the effect of enclosing as internal waters areas which previously had been considered as part of the territorial sea or of the high seas, a right of innocent passage, as provided in Articles 14 to 23, shall exist in those waters.

Article 6

The outer limit of the territorial sea is the line every point of which is at a distance from the nearest point of the baseline equal to the breadth of the territorial sea.

Article 7

1.   This Article relates only to bays the coasts of which belong to a single State.

2.   For the purposes of these Articles, a bay is a well-marked indentation whose penetration is in such proportion to the width of its mouth as to contain landlocked waters and constitute more than a mere curvature of the coast.   An indentation shall not, however, be regarded as a bay unless its area is as large as, or larger than, that of the semi-circle whose diameter is a line drawn across the mouth of that indentation.

3.   For the purpose of measurement, the area of an indentation is that lying between the low-water mark around the shore of the indentation and a line joining the low-water mark of its natural entrance points.   Where, because of the presence of islands, an indentation has more than one mouth, the semi-circle shall be drawn on a line as long as the sum total of the lengths of the lines across the different mouths.   Islands within an indentation shall be included as if they were part of the water area of the indentation.

4. If the distance between the low-water marks of the natural entrance points of a bay does not exceed twenty-four miles, a closing line may be drawn between these two low-water marks, and the waters enclosed thereby shall be considered as internal waters.
5. Where the distance between the low-water marks of the natural entrance points of a bay exceeds twenty-four miles, a straight baseline of twenty-four miles shall be drawn within the bay in such a manner as to enclose the maximum area of water that is possible with a line of that length.
6. The foregoing provisions shall not apply to so-called 'historic' bays, or in any case where the straight baseline system provided for in Article 4 is applied.

Article 8

For the purpose of delimiting the territorial sea, the outermost permanent harbour works which form an integral part of the harbour system shall be regarded as forming part of the coast.

Article 9

Roadsteads which are normally used for the loading, unloading, and anchoring of ships, and which would otherwise be situated wholly or partly outside the outer limit of the territorial sea, are included in the territorial sea. The coastal State must clearly demarcate such roadsteads and indicate them on charts together with their boundaries, to which due publicity must be given.

Article 10

1. An island is a naturally-formed area of land, surrounded by water, which is above water at high tide.
2. The territorial sea of an island is measured in accordance with the provisions of these Articles.

Article 11

1. A low-tide elevation is a naturally formed area of land which is surrounded by and above water at low-tide but submerged at high tide. Where a low-tide elevation is situated wholly or partly at a distance not exceeding the breadth of the territorial sea from the mainland or an island, the low-water line on that elevation may be used as the baseline for measuring the breadth of the territorial sea.
2. Where a low-tide elevation is wholly situated at a distance exceeding the breadth of the territorial sea from the mainland or an island, it has no territorial sea of its own.

Article 12

1. Where the coasts of two States are opposite or adjacent to each other, neither of the two States is entitled, failing agreement between them to the contrary, to extend its territorial sea beyond the median line every point of which is equidistant from the nearest points on the baselines from which the breadth of the territorial seas of each of the two States is measured. The provisions of this paragraph shall not apply, however, where it is necessary by reason of historic title or other special circumstances to delimit the territorial seas of the two States in a way which is at variance with this provision.
2. The line of delimitation between the territorial seas of two States lying opposite to each other or adjacent to each other shall be marked on large-scale charts officially recognized by the coastal States.

Article 13

If a river flows directly into the sea, the baseline shall be a straight line across the mouth of the river between points on the low-tide line of its banks.

SECTION III. RIGHT OF INNOCENT PASSAGE

Sub-section A. Rules applicable to all ships

Article 14

1.   Subject to the provisions of these Articles, ships of all States, whether coastal or not, shall enjoy the right of innocent passage through the territorial sea.
2.   Passage means navigation through the territorial sea for the purpose either of traversing that sea without entering internal waters, or of proceeding to internal waters, or of making for the high seas from internal waters.
3.   Passage includes stopping and anchoring, but only in so far as the same are incidental to ordinary navigation or are rendered necessary by *force majeure* or by distress.
4.   Passage is innocent so long as it is not prejudicial to the peace, good order or security of the coastal State.   Such passage shall take place in conformity with these Articles and with other rules of international law.
5.   Passage of foreign fishing vessels shall not be considered innocent if they do not observe such laws and regulations as the coastal State may make and publish in order to prevent these vessels from fishing in the territorial sea.
6.   Submarines are required to navigate on the surface and to show their flag.

Article 15

1.   The coastal State must not hamper innocent passage through the territorial sea.
2.   The coastal State is required to give appropriate publicity to any dangers to navigation, of which it has knowledge, within its territorial sea.

Article 16

1.   The coastal State may take the necessary steps in its territorial sea to prevent passage which is not innocent.
2.   In the case of ships proceeding to internal waters, the coastal State shall also have the right to take the necessary steps to prevent any breach of the conditions to which admission of those ships to those waters is subject.
3.   Subject to the provisions of paragraph 4, the coastal State may, without discrimination amongst foreign ships, suspend temporarily in specified areas of its territorial sea the innocent passage of foreign ships if such suspension is essential for the protection of its security.   Such suspension shall take effect only after having been duly published.
4.   There shall be no suspension of the innocent passage of foreign ships through straits which are used for international navigation between one part of the high seas and another part of the high seas or the territorial sea of a foreign State.

Article 17

Foreign ships exercising the right of innocent passage shall comply with the laws and regulations enacted by the coastal State in conformity with these Articles and other rules of international law and, in particular, with such laws and regulations relating to transport and navigation.

Sub-section B. *Rules applicable to merchant ships*

Article 18

1.   No charge may be levied upon foreign ships by reason only of their passage through the territorial sea.
2.   Charges may be levied upon a foreign ship passing through the territorial sea as payment only for specific services rendered to the ship.   These charges shall be levied without discrimination.

Article 19

1.   The criminal jurisdiction of the coastal State should not be exercised on board a foreign ship passing through the territorial sea to arrest any person or to conduct any investigation in connection with any crime committed on board the ship during its passage, save only in the following cases:
(a) If the consequences of the crime extend to the coastal State; or
(b) If the crime is of a kind to disturb the peace of the country or the good order of the territorial sea; or
(c) If the assistance of the local authorities has been requested by the captain of the ship or by the consul of the country whose flag the ship flies; or
(d) If it is necessary for the suppression of illicit traffic in narcotic drugs.
2.   The above provisions do not affect the right of the coastal State to take any steps authorized by its laws for the purpose of an arrest or investigation on board a foreign ship passing through the territorial sea after leaving internal waters.
3.   In the cases provided for in paragraphs 1 and 2 of this Article, the coastal State shall, if the captain so requests, advise the consular authority of the flag State before taking any steps, and shall facilitate contact between such authority and the ship's crew. In cases of emergency this notification may be communicated while the measures are being taken.
4.   In considering whether or how an arrest should be made, the local authorities shall pay due regard to the interests of navigation.
5.   The coastal State may not take any steps on board a foreign ship passing through the territorial sea to arrest any person or to conduct any investigation in connection with any crime committed before the ship entered the territorial sea, if the ship, proceeding from a foreign port, is only passing through the territorial sea without entering internal waters.

Article 20

1.   The coastal State should not stop or divert a foreign ship passing through the territorial sea for the purpose of exercising civil jurisdiction in relation to a person on board the ship.
2.   The coastal State may not levy execution against or arrest the ship for the purpose of any civil proceedings, save only in respect of obligations or liabilities assumed or

incurred by the ship itself in the course or for the purpose of its voyage through the waters of the coastal State.

3.   The provisions of the previous paragraph are without prejudice to the right of the coastal State, in accordance with its laws, to levy execution against or to arrest, for the purpose of any civil proceedings, a foreign ship lying in the territorial sea, or passing through the territorial sea after leaving internal waters.

Sub-section C. Rules applicable to government ships other than warships

Article 21

The rules contained in sub-sections A and B shall also apply to government ships operated for commercial purposes.

Article 22

1.   The rules contained in sub-section A and in Article 18 shall apply to government ships operated for non-commercial purposes.

2.   With such exceptions as are contained in the provisions referred to in the preceding paragraph, nothing in these Articles affects the immunities which such ships enjoy under these Articles or other rules of international law.

Sub-section D. Rule applicable to warships

Article 23

If any warship does not comply with the regulations of the coastal State concerning passage through the territorial sea and disregards any request for compliance which is made to it, the coastal State may require the warship to leave the territorial sea.

PART II
CONTIGUOUS ZONE

Article 24

1.   In a zone of the high seas contiguous to its territorial sea, the coastal State may exercise the control necessary to:
(a) Prevent infringement of its customs, fiscal, immigration or sanitary regulations within its territory or territorial sea;
(b) Punish infringement of the above regulations committed within its territory or territorial sea.

2.   The contiguous zone may not extend beyond twelve miles from the baseline from which the breadth of the territorial sea is measured.

3.   Where the coasts of two States are opposite or adjacent to each other, neither of the two States is entitled, failing agreement between them to the contrary, to extend its contiguous zone beyond the median line every point of which is equidistant from the nearest points on the baselines from which the breadth of the territorial seas of the two States is measured.

PART III
FINAL ARTICLES

Article 25

The provisions of this Convention shall not affect conventions or other international agreements already in force, as between States Parties to them.

Article 26

This Convention shall, until 31 October 1958, be open for signature by all States Members of the United Nations or of any of the specialized agencies, and by any other State invited by the General Assembly of the United Nations to become a party to the Convention.

Article 27

This Convention is subject to ratification.   The instruments of ratification shall be deposited with the Secretary-General of the United Nations.

Article 28

This Convention shall be open for accession by any States belonging to any of the categories mentioned in Article 26.   The instrument of accession shall be deposited with the Secretary-General of the United Nations.

Article 29

1.   This Convention shall come into force on the thirtieth day following the date of deposit of the twenty-second instrument of ratification or accession with the Secretary-General of the United Nations.
2.   For each State ratifying or acceding to the Convention after the deposit of the twenty-second instrument of ratification or accession, the Convention shall enter into force on the thirtieth day after deposit by such State of its instrument of ratification or accession.

Article 30

1.   After the expiration of a period of five years from the date on which this Convention shall enter into force, a request for the revision of this Convention may be made at any time by any Contracting Party by means of a notification in writing addressed to the Secretary-General of the United Nations.
2.   The General Assembly of the United Nations shall decide upon the steps, if any, to be taken in respect of such request.

Article 31

The Secretary-General of the United Nations shall inform all States Members of the United Nations and the other States referred to in Article 26:
(a) Of signatures to this Convention and of the deposit of instruments of ratification or accession, in accordance with Articles 26, 27, and 28;
(b) Of the date on which this Convention will come into force, in accordance with Article 29;
(c) Of requests for revision in accordance with Article 30.

Article 32

The original of this Convention, of which the Chinese, English, French, Russian, and Spanish texts are equally authentic, shall be deposited with the Secretary-General of the United Nations, who shall send certified copies thereof to all States referred to in Article 26.

IN WITNESS WHEREOF the undersigned plenipotentiaries, being duly authorized thereto by their respective governments, have signed this Convention.

DONE AT GENEVA, this twenty-ninth day of April one thousand nine hundred and fifty-eight.

4.3 CONVENTION AND STATUTE ON THE INTERNATIONAL REGIME OF MARITIME PORTS, 1923

Germany, Belgium, Brazil, The British Empire (with New Zealand and India), Bulgaria, Chile, Denmark, Spain, Estonia, Greece, Hungary, Italy, Japan, Lithuania, Norway, The Netherlands, Salvador, Kingdom of the Serbs, Croats and Slovenes, Siam, Sweden, Switzerland, Czechoslovakia and Uruguay,

Desirous of ensuring in the fullest measure possible the freedom of communications mentioned in Article 23(*e*) of the Covenant by guaranteeing in the maritime ports situated under their sovereignty or authority and for purposes of international trade equality of treatment between the ships of all the Contracting States, their cargoes and passengers;

Considering that the best method of achieving their present purpose is by means of a general convention to which the greatest possible number of States can later accede;

And whereas the Conference which met at Genoa on April 10th, 1922, requested, in a resolution which was transmitted to the competent organisations of the League of Nations with the approval of the Council and the Assembly of the League, that the International Conventions relating to the Regime of Communications provided for in the Treaties of Peace should be concluded and put into operation as soon as possible, and whereas, Article 379 of the Treaty of Versailles and the corresponding articles of the other Treaties provide for the preparation of a General Convention on the International Regime of Ports;

Having accepted the invitation of the League of Nations to take part in a Conference which met at Geneva on November 15th, 1923;

Desirous of bringing into force the provisions of the Statute relating to the International Regime of Ports adopted thereat, and of concluding a General Convention for this purpose, the High Contracting Parties have appointed as their plenipotentiaries:

...

Who, after communicating their full powers, found in good and due form, have agreed as follows:

Article 1

The Contracting States declare that they accept the Statute on the International Regime of Maritime Ports, annexed hereto, adopted by the Second General Conference on Communications and Transit which met at Geneva on November 15, 1923.

This Statute shall be deemed to constitute an integral part of the present Convention.

Consequently, they hereby declare that they accept the obligations and undertakings of the said Statute in conformity with the terms and in accordance with the conditions set out therein.

Article 2

The present Convention does not in any way affect the rights and obligations arising out of the provisions of the Treaty of Peace signed at Versailles on June 28, 1919, or out of the provisions of the other corresponding Treaties, in so far as they concern the Powers which have signed, or which benefit by, such Treaties.

Article 3

The present Convention of which the French and English texts are both authentic, shall bear this day's date, and shall be open for signature until October 31, 1924, by any State represented at the Conference of Geneva, by any Member of the League of Nations and by any States to which the Council of the League of Nations shall have communicated a copy of the Convention for this purpose.

Article 4

The present Convention is subject to ratification. The instruments of ratification shall be deposited with the Secretary-General of the League of Nations, who shall notify their receipt to every State signatory of or acceding to the Convention.

Article 5

On and after November 1st, 1924, the present Convention may be acceded to by any State represented at the Conference referred to in Article 1, by any Member of the League of Nations, or by any State to which the Council of the League of Nations shall have communicated a copy of the Convention for this purpose.

Accession shall be effected by an instrument communicated to the Secretary-General of the League of Nations to be deposited in the archives of the Secretariat. The Secretary-General shall at once notify such deposit to every State signatory of or acceding to the Convention.

Article 6

The present Convention will not come into force until it has been ratified in the name of five States. The date of its coming into force shall be the ninetieth day after the receipt by the Secretary-General of the League of Nations of the fifth ratification. Thereafter, the present Convention will take effect in the case of each Party ninety days after the receipt of its ratification or of the notification of its accession.

In compliance with the provisions of Article 18 of the Covenant of the League of Nations, the Secretary-General will register the present Convention upon the day of its coming into force.

Article 7

A special record shall be kept by the Secretary-General of the League of Nations showing, with due regard to the provisions of Article 9, which of the Parties have signed, ratified, acceded to or denounced the present Convention. This record shall be open to the Members of the League at all times; it shall be published as often as possible, in accordance with the directions of the Council.

Article 8

Subject to the provisions of Article 2 above, the present Convention may be denounced by any Party thereto after the expiration of five years from the date when it came into force in respect of that Party. Denunciation shall be effected by notification in writing addressed to the Secretary-General of the League of Nations. Copies of such notification shall be transmitted forthwith by him to all the other Parties, informing them of the date on which it was received.

A denunciation shall take effect one year after the date on which the notification thereof was received by the Secretary-General, and shall operate only in respect of the notifying State.

Article 9

Any State signing or acceding to the present Convention may declare at the moment either of its signature, ratification or accession, that its acceptance of the present Convention does not include any or all of its colonies, overseas possessions, protectorates, or overseas territories, under its sovereignty or authority, and may subsequently accede, in conformity with the provisions of Article 5, on behalf of any such colony, overseas possession, protectorate or territory excluded by such declaration.

Denunciation may also be made separately in respect of any such colony, overseas possession, protectorate or territory, and the provisions of Article 8 shall apply to any such denunciation.

Article 10

The revision of the present Convention may be demanded at any time by one-third of the Contracting States.

In faith whereof the above-named plenipotentiaires have signed the present Convention.

Done at Geneva the ninth day of December, one thousand nine hundred and twenty-three, in a single copy which shall remain deposited in the Archives of the Secretariat of the League of Nations.

STATUTE

Article 1

All ports which are normally frequented by sea-going vessels and used for foreign trade shall be deemed to be maritime ports within the meaning of the present Statute.

Article 2

Subject to the principle of reciprocity and to the reservation set out in the first paragraph of Article 8, every Contracting State undertakes to grant the vessels of every other Contracting State equality of treatment with its own vessels, or those of any other State whatsoever, in the maritime ports situated under its sovereignty or authority, as regards freedom of access to the port, the use of the port, and the full enjoyment of the benefits as regards navigation and commercial operations which it affords to vessels, their cargoes and passengers.

The equality of treatment thus established shall cover facilities of all kinds, such as allocation of berths, loading and unloading facilities, as well as dues and charges of all kinds levied in the name or for the account of the Government, public authorities, concessionaires or undertakings of any kind.

Article 3

The provisions of the preceding article in no way restrict the liberty of the competent Port Authorities to take such measures as they may deem expedient for the proper conduct of the business of the port provided that these measures comply with the principle of equality of treatment as defined in the said article.

Article 4

All dues and charges levied for the use of maritime ports shall be duly published before coming into force.

The same shall apply to the by-laws and regulations of the port.

In each maritime port, the Port Authority shall keep open for inspection by all persons concerned a table of the dues and charges in force, as well as a copy of the by-laws and regulations.

Article 5

In assessing and applying Customs and other analogous duties, local octroi or consumption duties, or incidental charges, levied on the importation or exportation of goods through the maritime ports situated under the sovereignty or authority of the Contracting States, the flag of the vessel must not be taken into account, and accordingly no distinction may be made to the detriment of the flag of any Contracting State whatsoever as between that flag and the flag of the State under whose sovereignty or authority the port is situated, or the flag of any other State whatsoever.

Article 6

In order that the principle of equal treatment in maritime ports laid down in Article 2 may not be rendered ineffective in practice by the adoption of other methods of discrimination against the vessels of a Contracting State using such ports, each contracting State undertakes to apply the provisions of Articles 4, 20, 21 and 22 of the Statute annexed to the Convention on the International Regime of Railways, signed at Geneva on December 9, 1923 , so far as they are applicable to traffic to or from a maritime port, whether or not such Contracting State is a party to the said Convention on the International Regime of Railways. The aforesaid Articles are to be interpreted in conformity with the provisions of the protocol of Signature of the said Convention. (See Annex.)

Article 7

Unless there are special reasons justifying an exception, such as those based upon special geographical, economic, or technical conditions, the Customs duties levied in any maritime port situated under the sovereignty or authority of a Contracting State may not exceed the duties levied on the other Customs frontiers of the said State on goods of the same kind, source or destination.

If, for special reasons as set out above, a Contracting State grants special Customs facilities on other routes for the importation or exportation of goods, it shall not use these facilities as a means of discriminating unfairly against importation or exportation through the maritime ports situated under its sovereignty or authority.

Article 8

Each of the Contracting States reserves the power, after giving notice through diplomatic channels, of suspending the benefit of equality of treatment from any vessel of a State which does not effectively apply, in any maritime port situated under its sovereignty or authority, the provisions of this Statute to the vessels of the said Contracting State, their cargoes and passengers.

In the event of action being taken as provided in the preceding paragraph, the State which has taken action and the State against which action is taken, shall both alike have the right of applying to the Permanent Court of International Justice by an application addressed to the Registrar; and the Court shall settle the matter in accordance with the rules of summary procedure.

Every Contracting State shall, however, have the right at the time of signing or ratifying this Convention, of declaring that it renounces the right of taking action as provided in the first paragraph of this article against any other State which may make a similar declaration.

Article 9

This Statute does not in any way apply to the maritime coasting trade.

Article 10

Each Contracting State reserves the right to make such arrangements for towage in its maritime ports as it thinks fit, provided that the provisions of Articles 2 and 4 are not thereby infringed.

Article 11

Each Contracting State reserves the right to organise and administer pilotage services as it thinks fit. Where pilotage is compulsory, the dues and facilities offered shall be subject to the provisions of Articles 2 and 4, but each Contracting State may exempt from the obligation of compulsory pilotage such of its nationals as possess the necessary technical qualifications.

Article 12

Each Contracting State shall have the power, at the time of signing or ratifying this convention, of declaring that it reserves the right of limiting the transport of emigrants, in accordance with the provisions of its own legislation to vessels which have been granted special authorisation as fulfilling the requirements of the said legislation. In exercising this right, however, the Contracting State shall be guided, as far as possible, by the principles of this Statute.

The vessels so authorised to transport emigrants shall enjoy all the benefits of this Statute in all maritime ports.

Article 13

This Statute applies to all vessels, whether publicly or privately owned or controlled.

It does not, however, apply in any way to warships or vessels performing police or administrative functions, or, in general, exercising any kind of public authority, or any other vessels which for the time being are exclusively employed for the purposes of the Naval, Military or Air Forces of a State.

Article 14

This Statute does not in any way apply to fishing vessels or to their catches.

Article 15

Where in virtue of a treaty, convention or agreement, a Contracting State has granted special rights to another State within a defined area in any of its maritime ports for the purpose of facilitating the transit of goods or passengers to or from the territory of the said State, no other Contracting State can invoke the stipulations of this Statute in support of any claim for similar special rights.

Every Contracting State which enjoys the aforesaid special rights in a maritime port of another State, whether Contracting or not, shall conform to the provisions of this Statute in its treatment of the vessels trading with it, and their cargoes and passengers.

Every Contracting State which grants the aforesaid special rights to a non-Contracting State is bound to impose, as one of the conditions of the grant, an obligation on the State which is to enjoy the aforesaid rights to conform to the provisions of this Statute in its treatment of the vesels trading with it, and their cargoes and passengers.

Article 16

Measures of a general or particular character which a Contracting State is obliged to take in case of an emergency affecting the safety of the State or the vital interests of the country may, in exceptional cases, and for as short a time as possible, involve a deviation from the provisions of Articles 2 to 7 inclusive; it being understood that the principles of the present Statute must be observed to the utmost possible extent.

Article 17

No Contracting State shall be bound by this Statute to permit the transit of passengers whose admission to its territories is forbidden, or of goods of a kind of which the importation is prohibited, either on grounds of public health or security, or as a precaution against diseases of animals or plants.   As regards traffic other than traffic in transit, no Contracting State shall be bound by this Statute to permit the transport of passengers whose admission to its territories is forbidden, or of goods of which the import or export is prohibited, by its national laws.

Each Contracting State shall be entitled to take the necessary precautionary measures in respect of the transport of dangerous goods or goods of a similar character, as well as general police measures, including the control of emigrants entering or leaving its territory, it being understood that such measures must not result in any discrimination contrary to the principles of the present Statute.

Nothing in this Statute shall affect the measures which one of the Contracting States is or may feel called upon to take in pursuance of general international conventions to which it is a party, or which may be concluded hereafter, particularly conventions concluded under the auspices of the League of Nations, relating to the traffic in women and children, the transit, export or import of particular kinds of articles such as opium or other dangerous drugs, arms, or the produce of fisheries, or in pursuance of general conventions intended to prevent any infringement of industrial, literary or artistic property, or relating to false marks, false indications of origin or other methods of unfair competition.

Article 18

This Statute does not prescribe the rights and duties of belligerents and neutrals in time of war. The Statute shall, however, continue in force in time of war so far as such rights and duties permit.

Article 19

The Contracting States undertake to introduce into those Conventions in force on December 9, 1923, which contravene the provisions of this Statute, so soon as circumstances permit and in any case on the expiry of such conventions, the modifications required to bring them into harmony with such provisions, so far as the geographical, economic or technical circumstance of the countries or areas concerned allow.

The same shall apply to concessions granted before December 9, 1923, for the total or partial exploitation of maritime ports.

Article 20

This Statute does not entail in any way the withdrawal of facilities which are greater than those provided for in the Statute and which have been granted in respect of the use of maritime ports under conditions consistent with its principles. This Statute also entails no prohibition of such grant of greater facilities in the future.

Article 21

Without prejudice to the provisions of the second paragraph of Article 8, disputes which may arise between Contracting States as to the interpretation or the application of the present Statute shall be settled in the following manner:

Should it prove impossible to settle such dispute either directly between the Parties or by any other method of amicable settlement, the Parties to the dispute may, before resorting to any procedure of arbitration or to a judicial settlement, submit the dispute for an advisory opinion to the body established by the League of Nations as the advisory and technical organisation of Members of the League for matters of communications and transit. In urgent cases a preliminary opinion may be given recommending temporary measures, including measures to restore the facilities for international traffic which existed before the act or occurrence which gave rise to the dispute.

Should it prove impossible to settle the dispute by any of the methods of procedure enumerated in the preceding paragraph, the Contracting States shall submit their dispute to arbitration, unless they have decided or shall decide, under an agreement between them, to bring it before the Permanent Court of International Justice.

Article 22

If the case is submitted to the Permanent Court of International Justice, it shall be heard and determined under the conditions laid down in Article 27 of the Statute of the Court.

If arbitration is resorted to, and unless the Parties decide otherwise, each Party shall appoint an arbitrator, and a third member of the arbitral tribunal shall be elected by the arbitrators, or, in case the latter are unable to agree, shall be selected by the Council of the League of Nations from the list of assessors for Communications and Transit cases mentioned in Article 27 of the Statute of the Permanent Court of International Justice; in such latter case, the third arbitrator shall be selected in accordance with the provisions of the penultimate paragraph of Article 4 and the first paragraph of Article 5 of the Covenant of the League.

The arbitral tribunal shall judge the case on the basis of the terms of reference mutually agreed upon between the Parties. If the Parties have failed to reach an agreement, the arbitral tribunal, acting unanimously, shall itself draw up terms of reference after considering the claims formulated by the Parties; if unanimity cannot be obtained, the Council of the League of Nations shall decide the terms of reference under the conditions laid down in the preceding paragraph. If the procedure is not determined by the terms of reference, it shall be settled by the arbitral tribunal.

During the course of the arbitration the Parties, in the absence of any contrary provision in the terms of reference, are bound to submit to the Permanent Court of International Justice any question of international law or question as to the legal meaning of this Statute the solution of which the arbitral tribunal, at the request of one of the Parties, pronounces to be a necessary preliminary to the settlement of the dispute.

Article 23

It is understood that this Statute must not be interpreted as regulating in any way rights and obligations *inter se* of territories forming part of or placed under the protection of the same sovereign State, whether or not these territories are individually Contracting States.

Article 24

Nothing in the preceding Articles is to be construed as affecting in any way the rights or duties of a Contracting State as Member of the League of Nations.

[Annex and Protocol of Signature of Convention omitted].

4.4 TREATY OF COMMERCE, ESTABLISHMENT AND NAVIGATION BETWEEN THE UNITED KINGDOM AND JAPAN, 1962 ARTICLES 20-1

Article 20
[Freedom of access to ports on basis of MFN or national standard]

(1) The vessels of one Contracting Party shall be entitled, *inter alia* –
   (a) to have liberty of access to all ports, waters and places open to international commerce and navigation in any territory of the other;
   (b) to compete for and carry passengers and cargoes, alike in any of the territories of the Contracting Parties and elsewhere.

(2) In all matters referred to in the foregoing paragraph of this Article and, in addition, in all other matters relative to commerce, navigation or the treatment of shipping, the vessels of one Contracting Party, their passengers and cargoes shall be accorded in any territory of the other treatment not less favourable than that accorded to the vessels, passengers and cargoes of the latter contracting Party or of any other foreign country; the vessels of one Contracting Party, their passengers and cargoes shall be accorded all the rights, liberties, favours, privileges, immunities and exemptions accorded to the vessels, passengers and cargoes of the other Contracting Party or of any other foreign country and shall not be subjected to any other or more onerous duties, charges, taxes or other impositions of whatsoever kind or denomination than would be levied in similar circumstances in relation to such vessels, passengers and cargoes.

(3) Neither Contracting Party shall apply exchange restrictions in such a manner as to hamper the participation of vessels of the other Contracting Party in the transportation of passengers or cargoes to or from any territory of either Contracting Party or elsewhere.

(4) The Contracting Parties shall ensure that all dues and charges levied for the use of maritime ports within any of their territories and all byelaws and regulations of such ports shall be duly published before coming into force and that in each maritime port the port authority shall keep open for inspection by all persons concerned a table of the said dues and charges and a copy of the said byelaws and regulations.

(5) The provisions of this Article shall not apply to inland navigation or coasting trade. However,
   (a) the vessels of one Contracting Party, if engaged in trade to or from places not within the limits of the coasting trade or inland navigation in any territory of the other, may engage in the carriage between ports within those limits of passengers holding through tickets or cargoes consigned on through bills of lading to or from such places not within those limits, provided that such vessels obtain permits authorising such carriage in accordance with the law of that territory; and
   (b) the vessels of one Contracting Party may proceed from one port to another in any territory of the other for the purpose of landing the whole or part of their passengers or cargoes brought from places not within those limits or taking on board the whole or part of their passengers or cargoes destined for such places not within those limits.

Article 21
[Treatment of vessels entering internal waters in distress]

(1) A vessel of one Contracting Party which is forced by stress of weather or any other cause to take refuge in any territory of the other shall be entitled to refit therein, to procure all necessary stores, and to put to sea again without paying any duty, charge, tax or other imposition of whatsoever kind or denomination exceeding that which would be levied in similar circumstances in relation to a vessel of the latter Contracting Party or of any other foreign country.

(2) If in the territory of one Contracting Party a vessel of the other Contracting Party is wrecked, runs aground, is under any distress, or requires services, it shall be entitled
–
    (a) to receive all such assistance and protection as would be given by the former Contracting Party to one of its own vessels or to a vessel of any other foreign country;

    (b) to call upon any salvage or other vessels of whatever nationality to render such services as it may consider necessary; and

    (c) to discharge or transship its cargo, equipment or other contents in case of need; no payment of any duty, charge, tax or other imposition of whatsoever kind or denomination shall be levied in respect thereof unless such cargo, equipment or other contents is delivered for use or consumption in that territory; the authorities of the territory may, however, if they think fit, require security for the protection of the revenue in relation to such goods.

(3) Nothing in the foregoing provisions of this Article shall exempt any vessel of one Contracting Party from the operation of any law of the other Contracting Party which permits the removal or sale of any such vessel which is, or is likely to become, an obstruction or danger to navigation, or of any part thereof or property recovered therefrom, provided that the vessels of one Contracting Party shall be accorded in the territory of the other under any such law treatment not less favourable than that accorded to the vessels of the latter Contracting Party or of any other foreign country.

(4) Where a vessel of one Contracting Party, or any part thereof or its cargo, equipment or any other contents, is salved, such vessel or part thereof or such cargo, equipment or other contents, or the proceeds thereof, if sold, shall be delivered up to the owner or his agent when claimed, provided that the claim is made within the period fixed by the law of the other Contracting Party. The owner or his agent shall be liable for the payment of any expenses incurred in the preservation of the vessel and its contents and of the salvage fees and other expenses incurred, but such fees and expenses shall not exceed those which would have been payable in similar circumstances in respect of a vessel of the latter Contracting Party or of any other foreign country.

4.5 UNITED KINGDOM: TERRITORIAL SEA ACT 1987

An Act to provide for the extent of the territorial sea adjacent to the British Islands. [15 May 1987]

    Be it enacted by the Queen's Most Excellent Majesty, by and with the advice and consent of the Lords Spiritual and Temporal, and Commons, in this present Parliament assembled, and by the authority of the same, as follows:-

Extension of territorial sea

1. – (1) Subject to the provisions of this Act –
    (a) the breadth of the territorial sea adjacent to the United Kingdom shall for all purposes be 12 nautical miles; and
    (b) the baselines from which the breadth of that territorial sea is to be measured shall for all purposes be those established by Her Majesty by Order in Council.

(2) Her Majesty may, for the purpose of implementing any international agreement or otherwise, by Order in Council provide that any part of the territorial sea adjacent to the United Kingdom shall extend to such line other than that provided for by subsection (1) above as may be specified in the Order.

(3) In any legal proceedings a certificate issued by or under the authority of the Secretary of State stating the location of any baseline established under subsection (1) above shall be conclusive of what is stated in the certificate.

(4) As from the coming into force of this section the Territorial Waters Order in Council 1964 and the Territorial Waters (Amendment) Order in Council 1979 shall have effect for all purposes as if they were Orders in Council made by virtue of subsection (1)(b) above; and subsection (5) below shall apply to those Orders as it applies to any other instrument.

(5) Subject to the provisions of this Act, any enactment or instrument which (whether passed or made before or after the coming into force of this section) contains a reference (however worded) to the territorial sea adjacent to, or to any part of, the United Kingdom shall be construed in accordance with this section and with any provision made or having effect as if made, under this section.

(6) Without prejudice to the operation of subsection (5) above in relation to a reference to the baselines from which the breadth of the territorial sea adjacent to the United Kingdom is measured, nothing in that subsection shall require any reference in any enactment or instrument to a specified distance to be construed as a reference to a distance equal to the breadth of that territorial sea.

(7) In this section "nautical miles" means international nautical miles of 1,852 metres.

Enactments and instruments not affected

2. – (1) Except in so far as Her Majesty may by Order in Council otherwise provide, nothing in section 1 above shall affect the operation of any enactment contained in a local Act passed before the date on which that section comes into force.

(2) Nothing in section 1 above, or in any Order in Council under that section or subsection (1) above, shall affect the operation of so much of any enactment passed or instrument made before the date on which that section comes into force as for the time being settles the limits within which any harbour authority or port health authority has jurisdiction or is able to exercise any power.

(3) Where any area which is not part of the territorial sea adjacent to the United Kingdom becomes part of that sea by virtue of section 1 above or an Order in Council under that section, subsection (2) of section 1 of the 1964 c.29. Continental Shelf Act 1964 (vesting and exercise of rights with respect to coal) shall continue, on and after the date on which section 1 above or that order comes into force, to have effect with respect to coal in that area as if the area were not part of the territorial sea.

(4) Nothing in section 1 above, or in any Order in Council under that section, shall affect –

1934 c.36. (a) any regulations made under section 6 of the Petroleum (Production) Act 1934 before the date on which that section or Order comes into force; or

(b) any licences granted under the said Act of 1934 before that date or granted on or after that date in pursuance of regulations made under that section before that date.

(5) In this section –

1964 c.59. "coal" has the same meaning as in the Coal Industry Nationalisation Act 1946;

1964 c.40. "harbour authority" means a harbour authority within the meaning of the
1970 c.1. Harbours Act 1964 or the Harbours Act (Northern Ireland) 1970; and
(N.I.).

"port health authority" means a port health authority for the purposes of the
1984 c.22. Public Health (Control of Disease) Act 1984

Amendments and repeals

3. – (1) The enactments mentioned in Schedule 1 to this Act shall have effect with the amendments there specified (being minor amendments and amendments consequential on the provisions of this Act).

(2) Her Majesty may by Order in Council –

(a) make, in relation to any enactment passed or instrument made before the date on which section 1 above comes into force, any amendment corresponding to any of those made by Schedule 1 to this Act;

(b) amend subsection (1) of section 36 of the Wildlife and Countryside

1981 c.69. Act 1981 (marine nature reserves) so as to include such other parts of the territorial sea adjacent to Great Britain as may be specified in the Order in the waters and parts of the sea which, by virtue of paragraph 6 of Schedule 1 to this Act, may be designated under that section;

S.I. (c) amend paragraph 1 of article 20 of the Nature Conservation and
1985/170 Amenity Lands (Northern Ireland) Order 1985 (marine nature reserves) so
(N.I.1). as to include such other parts of the territorial sea adjacent to Northern Ireland as may be specified in the Order in the waters and parts of the sea which, by virtue of paragraph 9 of Schedule 1 to this Act, may be designated under that Article.

(3) Her Majesty may by Order in Council make such modifications of the effect of any Order in Council under section 1(7) of the Continental Shelf

1964 c.29. Act 1964 (designated areas) as appear to Her to be necessary or expedient in consequence of any provision made by or under this Act.

(4) The enactments mentioned in Schedule 2 to this Act are hereby repealed to the extent specified in the third column of that Schedule.

Short title, commencement and extent

4. – (1) This Act may be cited as the Territorial Sea Act 1987.

(2) This Act shall come into force on such day as Her Majesty may by order in Council appoint, and different days may be so appointed for different provisions and for different purposes.

(3) This Act extends to Northern Ireland.

(4) Her Majesty may by Order in Council direct that any of the provisions of this Act shall extend, with such exceptions, adaptations and modifications (if any) as may be specified in the Order, to any of the Channel Islands or to the Isle of Man.

SCHEDULES

Section 3.   **SCHEDULE 1**

Minor and Consequential Amendments

The Coast Protection Act 1949

1949 c.74. 1. – (1)   In section 18(3) of the Coast Protection Act 1949 (prohibition of excavation etc. of materials on or under the seashore) for the words "lying to seaward therefrom" there shall be substituted the words "of the sea-shore lying to seaward of their area but within three nautical miles of the baselines from which the breadth of the territorial sea adjacent to Great Britain is measured,".

(2)   In section 49(1) of that Act (interpretation) after the definition of "mortgage" there shall be inserted the following definition –

"'nautical miles' means international nautical miles of 1,852 metres;".

The Mineral Workings (Offshore Installations) Act 1971

2.   For the definition of "foreign sector of the continental shelf" in
1971 c.61. section 1(4) of the Mineral Workings (Offshore Installations) Act 1971 there shall be substituted the following definition –

"'foreign sector of the continental shelf' means an area within which rights are exercisable with respect to the seabed and subsoil and their natural resources by a country or territory outside the United Kingdom;".

The Salmon and Freshwater Fisheries Act 1975

1975 c.51. 3.   In section 6(1) of the Salmon and Freshwater Fisheries Act 1975 (offence of placing unauthorized fixed engine in inland or tidal waters) after the words "inland or tidal waters" there shall be inserted the words "which are within the area of any water authority".

The Customs and Excise Management Act 1979

1979 c.2. 4. – (1)   In section 1(1) of the Customs and Excise Management Act 1979 (interpretation) after the definition of "transit shed" there shall be inserted the following definition –

"'United Kingdom waters' means any waters (including inland waters within the seaward limits of the territorial sea of the United Kingdom;".

(2)   In section 35(7) of that Act (report inwards of ships and aircraft) for the words "within 12 nautical miles of the coast of the United Kingdom" there shall be substituted the words "in or over United Kingdom waters".

(3)   In that Act the words "in United Kingdom waters" shall be substituted:

(a) In section 64(4) (clearance outwards of ships and aircraft) for the words "within the limits of a port or within 3 nautical miles of the coast of the United Kingdom";

(b) In section 88 (forfeiture of ship, aircraft or vehicle constructed etc. for concealing goods) for the words "within the limits of any port or within 3 or, being a British ship, 12 nautical miles of the coast of the United Kingdom";
(c) In section 89(1) and (2) (forfeiture or ship jettisoning cargo etc.) for the words "within 3 nautical miles of the coast of the United Kingdom";
(d) In section 142(2) (special provision as to forfeiture of larger ships) for the words "within 3 nautical miles of the coast of the United Kingdom".

The Alcoholic Liquor Duties Act 1979

1979 c.4. 5. – (1) In the Table in section 4(3) of the Alcoholic Liquor Duties Act 1979 (expressions defined in the Management Act) after the expression "tons register" there shall be inserted the expression "United Kingdom waters".
(2) In section 26(4) of that Act (importation and exportation of spirits) for the words "in the case of a British ship, within 12 or, in any other case, within 3 nautical miles of the coast of the United Kingdom" there shall be substituted the words "in United Kingdom waters".

The Wildlife and Countryside Act 1981

1981 c.69. 6. In section 36 of the Wildlife and Countryside Act 1981 (marine nature reserves) –
(a) in subsection (1) for the words "in or adjacent to Great Britain up to the seaward limits of territorial waters" there shall be substituted the words "which are landward of the baselines from which the breadth of the territorial sea adjacent to Great Britain is measured or are seaward of those baselines up to a distance of three nautical miles"; and
(b) in subsection (7) after the definition of "local authority" there shall be inserted the following definition:

"'nautical miles' means international nautical miles of 1,852 metres;".

The Oil and Gas (Enterprise) Act 1982

1982 c.23. 7. – (1) For the definition of "cross-boundary field" in section 22(6) of the Oil and Gas (Enterprise) Act 1982 there shall be substituted the following definition:

"'cross-boundary field' means a field that extends across the boundary between waters falling within paragraph (a) or (b) of subsection (4) above and a foreign sector of the continental shelf".

(2) For the definition of "foreign sector of the continental shelf" in section 28(1) of that Act there shall be substituted the following definition –

"'foreign sector of the continental shelf' means an area within which rights are exercisable with respect to the seabed and subsoil and their natural resources by a country or territory outside the United Kingdom;".

The Public Health (Control of Disease) Act 1984

1984 c.22. 8. In section 6 of the Public Health (Control of Disease) Act 1984 (under which the Port of London is for the purposes of that Act not to extend outside territorial waters) for the words "are for the time being" there shall be substituted the words "immediately before the coming into force of the Territorial Sea Act 1987 were".

The Nature Conservation and Amenity Lands (Northern Ireland) Order 1985

S.I. 1985/ 9.　　In Article 20 of the Nature Conservation and Amenity Lands 170 (N.I.1).(Northern Ireland) Order 1985 (marine nature reserves) –

(a) in paragraph (1) for the words "in or adjacent to Northern Ireland up to the seaward limits of territorial waters" there shall be substituted the words "which are landward of the baselines from which the breadth of the territorial sea adjacent to Northern Ireland is measured or are seaward of those baselines up to a distance of three nautical miles"; and

(b) In paragraph (6) before the definition of "relevant body" there shall be inserted the following definition –

"'nautical miles' means international nautical miles of 1,852 metres;".

Section 3.　　　　　　　　**SCHEDULE 2**

REPEALS

Chapter	Short title	Extent of repeal
41 & 42 Vict. c. 73.	The Territorial Waters Jurisdiction Act 1878.	In section 7, the definition of "the territorial waters of Her Majesty's dominions", including the words from "and for the purpose of any offence" to "the territorial waters of Her Majesty's dominions".
1967 c.41.	The Marine, &c., Broadcasting Offences Act 1967.	Section 9(2).
1967 c.72.	The Wireless Telegraphy Act 1967.	Section 9(1).
1979 c.2.	The Customs and Excise Management Act 1979.	In section 1(1), the definition of "nautical mile".
1979 c.4.	The Alcoholic Duties Act 1979.	In section 4(3), the words "nautical mile".

4.5.1　UNITED KINGDOM:　THE TERRITORIAL WATERS ORDER IN COUNCIL 1964

...

1.　This Order may be cited as the Territorial Waters Order in Council, 1964, and shall come into operation on 30th September, 1964.

2.–(1) Except as otherwise provided in Articles 3 and 4 of this Order, the baseline from which the breadth of the territorial sea adjacent to the United Kingdom, the Channel Islands and the Isle of Man is measured shall be low-water line along the coast, including the coast of all islands comprised in those territories.

(2) For the purposes of this Article a low-tide elevation which lies wholly or partly within the breadth of sea which would be territorial sea if all low-tide elevations were disregarded for the purpose of the measurement of the breadth thereof and if Article 3 of this Order were omitted shall be treated as an island.

3.–(1) The baseline from which the breadth of the territorial sea is measured between Cape Wrath and the Mull of Kintyre shall consist of the series of straight lines drawn so as to join successively, in the order in which they are there set out, the points identified by the co-ordinates of latitude and longitude in the first column of the Schedule to this Order, each being a point situate on low-water line and on or adjacent to the feature, if any, named in the second column of that Schedule opposite to the co-ordinates of latitude and longitude of the point in the first column.

(2) The provisions of paragraph (1) of this Article shall be without prejudice to the operation of Article 2 of this Order in relation to any island or low-tide elevation which for the purpose of that Article is treated as if it were an island, being an island or low-tide elevation which lies to seaward of the baseline specified in paragraph (1) of this Article.

4. In the case of the sea adjacent to a bay, the baseline from which the breadth of the territorial sea is measured shall, subject to the provisions of Article 3 of this Order –

(a) if the bay has only one mouth and the distance between the low-water lines of the natural entrance points of the bay does not exceed 24 miles, be a straight line joining the said low-water lines;

(b) if, because of the presence of islands, the bay has more than one mouth and the distances between the low-water lines of the natural entrance points of each mouth added together do not exceed 24 miles, be a series of straight lines across each of the mouths drawn so as to join the said low-water lines;

(c) if neither paragraph (a) nor (b) of this Article applies, be a straight line 24 miles in length drawn from low-water line to low-water line within the bay in such a manner as to enclose the maximum area of water that is possible with a line of that length.

5.– (1) In this Order –

the expression "bay" means an indentation of the coast such that its area is not less than that of the semi-circle whose diameter is a line drawn across the mouth of the indentation, and for the purposes of this definition the area of an indentation shall be taken to be the area bounded by low-water line around the shore of the indentation and the straight line joining the low-water lines of its natural entrance points, and where, because of the presence of islands, an indentation has more than one mouth the length of the diameter of the semi-circle referred to shall be the sum of the lengths of the straight lines drawn across each of the mouths, and in calculating the area of an indentation the area of any islands lying within it shall be treated as part of the area of the indentation;

the expression "island" means a naturally formed area of land surrounded by water which is above water at mean high-water spring tides;   and the expression "low-tide elevation" means a naturally formed area of drying land surrounded by water which is below water at mean high-water spring tides.

(2) For the purposes of this Order, permanent harbour works which form an integral part of a harbour system shall be treated as forming part of the coast.

(3) The Interpretation Act, 1889,[1] shall apply to the interpretation of this order as it applies to the interpretation of an Act of Parliament.
6. This Order shall be published in the London Gazette, the Edinburgh Gazette and the Belfast Gazette.

W.G. Agnew

Article 3   SCHEDULE

Points between Cape Wrath and the Mull Of Kintyre Joined to Form Baselines

| | Co-ordinates of latitude and longitude of point | | Name of Feature |
| | Latitude North | Longitude West | |
	° ′ ″	° ′ ″	
1	58 37 33	5 00 00	Cape Wrath
2	58 31 14	6 15 46	Lith Sgeir
3	58 29 08	6 20 27	Dell Rock
4	58 18 16	6 48 18	Tiumpan
5	58 17 40	6 52 54	Mas Sgeir
6	58 17 06	6 55 31	Stac nam Balg
7	58 14 33	7 02 00	Gallan Head
8	58 13 56	7 03 00	-
9	58 10 38	7 06 58	Eilean Molach
10	57 59 03	7 17 50	Gasker
11	57 41 15	7 43 00	Haskeir Eagach
12	57 32 33	7 43 46	Clettan a Fer
13	57 14 25	7 27 24	Rudha Ardvule
14	57 00 46	7 31 36	Greian Head
15	56 57 21	7 33 43	-
16	56 56 56	7 34 19	Ard Caolas
17	56 56 00	7 34 51	Biruastil
18	56 49 16	7 39 32	Guarsay Point
19	56 48 00	7 40 00	Sron an Duin
20	56 47 07	7 39 37	Berneray Island
21	56 19 22	7 06 48	Skerryvore
22	56 08 00	6 38 03	Dubh Artach
23	55 41 36	6 32 03	Frenchman's Rocks
24	55 40 20	6 30 55	Orsay Island
25	55 35 19	6 20 12	Mull of Oa
26	55 17 57	5 47 52	Mull of Kintyre

1. 52 & 53 Vict. c. 63.

Explanatory Note

(This Note is not part of the order, but is intended to indicate its general purport)

This Order establishes the baseline from which the breadth of the territorial sea adjacent to the United Kingdom, the Channel Islands and the Isle of Man is measured. This, generally, is low-water line round the coast, including the coast of all islands, but between Cape Wrath and the Mull of Kintyre a series of straight lines joining specified points lying generally on the seaward side of the islands lying off the coast are used, and where there are well defined bays elsewhere lines not exceeding 24 miles in length drawn across the bays are used.

4.5.2 UNITED KINGDOM: THE TERRITORIAL SEA (LIMITS) ORDER 1989

...

Her Majesty, in exercise of the powers conferred upon her by section 1(2) of The Territorial Sea Act 1987(a), is pleased, by and with the advice of Her Privy Council, to order, and it is hereby ordered as follows:

1. This Order may be cited as The Territorial Sea (Limits) Order 1989 and shall come into force on 6 April 1989.

2. The seaward limit of the territorial sea adjacent to the United Kingdom between Point 1 and Point 6 indicated in the Schedule to this Order shall consist of a series of straight lines joining, in the sequence given, Points 1 to 6 indicated in the Schedule to this Order.

3. The seaward limit of the territorial sea adjacent to the United Kingdom shall be the median line where the baselines from which the breadth of the territorial sea adjacent to the United Kingdom is measured are less than 24 nautical miles from the baselines from which the breadth of the territorial sea adjacent to the Isle of Man is measured.

4. In this Order:
    (a) "straight line" means a loxodromic line;
    (b) all positions given by means of co-ordinates are defined on European Datum (1st Adjustment 1950);
    (c) "median line" is a line every point of which is equidistant from the nearest points of the baselines from which the breadth of the territorial sea adjacent to the United Kingdom and the Isle of Man respectively is measured.

5. The Territorial Sea (Limits) order 1987(b) is hereby revoked.

SCHEDULE

List of points

Point	Position of Points	
1	50° 49' 30" 95 N	01° 15' 53" 43 E
2	50° 53' 47" 00 N	01° 16' 58" 00 E
3	50° 57' 00" 00 N	01° 21' 25" 00 E
4	51° 02' 19" 00 N	01° 32' 53" 00 E
5	51° 05' 58" 00 N	01° 43' 31" 00 E
6	51° 12' 00" 72 N	01° 53' 20" 07 E

(a) 1987 c.49.
(b) S.I. 1987/1269.

Explanatory Note

(This note is not part of the Order)

This Order provides for the seaward limit of the territorial sea adjacent to the United Kingdom in the Straits of Dover and in the vicinity of the Isle of Man. The limit in the Straits of Dover is constituted by straight lines joining the points indicated in the Schedule and follows the line defined in the Agreement of 2nd November 1988 between the Government of the United Kingdom and the Government of the French Republic (Cm. 557) relating to the Delimitation of the Territorial Sea in the Straits of Dover. The limit in the vicinity of the Isle of Man is the median line.

4.5.2.1 UK DEPENDENT TERRITORIES: TERRITORIAL SEA EXTENSION

In 1989 Orders were made extending the territorial sea from 3 to 12 miles around the Falkland Islands (S.I. 1989/1993); South Georgia and South Sandwich Islands (S.I. 1989/1995); St. Helena and Dependencies (S.I. 1989/1994); and Turks and Caicos Islands (S.I. 1989/1996).

4.6 UNITED STATES: PRESIDENTIAL PROCLAMATION ON THE TERRITORIAL SEA OF THE UNITED STATES OF AMERICA, 27 DECEMBER 1988

BY THE PRESIDENT OF THE UNITED STATES OF AMERICA

A PROCLAMATION

International law recognizes that coastal nations may exercise sovereignty and jurisdiction over their territorial seas.

The territorial sea of the United States is a maritime zone extending beyond the land territory and internal waters of the United States over which the United States exercises sovereignty and jurisdiction, a sovereignty and jurisdiction that extend to the airspace over the territorial sea, as well as to its bed and subsoil.

Extension of the territorial sea by the United States to the limits permitted by international law will advance the national security and other significant interests of the United States.

Now, Therefore, I, Ronald Reagan, by the authority vested in me as President by the Constitution of the United States of America, and in accordance with international law, do hereby proclaim the extension of the territorial sea of the United States of America, the Commonwealth of Puerto Rico, Guam, American Samoa, the United States Virgin Islands, the Commonwealth of the Northern Mariana Islands, and any other territory or possession over which the United States exercises sovereignty.

The territorial sea of the United States henceforth extends to 12 nautical miles from the baselines of the United States determined in accordance with international law.

In accordance with international law, as reflected in the applicable provisions of the 1982 Convention on the Law of the Sea, within the territorial sea of the United

States, the ships of all countries enjoy the right of innocent passage and the ships and aircraft of all countries enjoy the right of transit passage through international straits.

Nothing in this Proclamation:

(a) extends or otherwise alters existing federal or State law or any jurisdiction, rights, legal interests, or obligations derived therefrom, or

(b) impairs the determination, in accordance with international law, of any maritime boundary of the United States with a foreign jurisdiction.

In Witness Whereof, I have hereunto set my hand this twenty-seventh day of December, in the year of our Lord nineteen hundred and eighty-eight, and of the Independence of the United States of America the two hundred and thirteenth.

4.7 USA-USSR: JACKSON HOLE JOINT STATEMENT ON INNOCENT PASSAGE, 1989

Since 1986, representatives of the United States of America and the Union of Soviet Socialist Republics have been conducting friendly and constructive discussions of certain international legal aspects of traditional uses of the oceans, in particular navigation.

The Governments are guided by the provisions of the 1982 United Nations Convention on the Law of the Sea, which, with respect to traditional uses of the oceans, generally constitute international law and practice and balance fairly the interests of all States. They recognize the need to encourage all States to harmonize their internal laws, regulations and practices with those provisions.

The Governments consider it useful to issue the attached Uniform Interpretation of the Rules of International Law Governing Innocent Passage. Both Governments have agreed to take the necessary steps to conform their internal laws, regulations and practices with this understanding of the rules.

...

Jackson Hole, Wyoming   September 23, 1989

UNIFORM INTERPRETATION OF RULES OF INTERNATIONAL LAW GOVERNING INNOCENT PASSAGE

1. The relevant rules of international law governing innocent passage of ships in the territorial sea are stated in the 1982 United Nations Convention on the Law of the Sea (Convention of 1982), particularly in Part II, Section 3.

2. All ships, including warships, regardless of cargo, armament or means of propulsion, enjoy the right of innocent passage through the territorial sea in accordance with international law, for which neither prior notification nor authorization is required.

3. Article 19 of the Convention of 1982 sets out in paragraph 2 an exhaustive list of activities that would render passage not innocent. A ship passing through the territorial sea that does not engage in any of those activities is in innocent passage.

4. A coastal State which questions whether the particular passage of a ship through its territorial sea is innocent shall inform the ship of the reason why it questions the

innocence of the passage, and provide the ship an opportunity to clarify its intentions or correct its conduct in a reasonably short period of time.

5. Ships exercising the right of innocent passage shall comply with all laws and regulations of the coastal State adopted in conformity with relevant rules of international law as reflected in Articles 21, 22, 23 and 25 of the Convention of 1982. These include the laws and regulations requiring ships exercising the right of innocent passage through its territorial sea to use such sea lanes and traffic separation schemes as it may prescribe where needed to protect safety of navigation.   In areas where no such sea lanes or traffic separation schemes have been prescribed, ships nevertheless enjoy the right of innocent passage.

6.   Such laws and regulations of the coastal State may not have the practical effect of denying or impairing the exercise of the right of innocent passage as set forth in Article 24 of the Convention of 1982.

7.   If a warship engages in conduct which violates such laws or regulations or renders its passage not innocent and does not take corrective action upon request, the coastal State may require it to leave the territorial sea, as set forth in Article 30 of the Convention of 1982.   In such case the warship shall do so immediately.

8.   Without prejudice to the exercise of rights of coastal and flag States, all differences which may arise regarding a particular case of passage of ships through the territorial sea shall be settled through diplomatic channels or other agreed means.

5 Straits Used for International Navigation

5.1 UNITED NATIONS CONVENTION ON THE LAW OF THE SEA, 1982:
PART III: STRAITS USED FOR INTERNATIONAL NAVIGATION

SECTION 1. GENERAL PROVISIONS

Article 34
Legal status of waters forming straits used for international navigation

1. The regime of passage through straits used for international navigation established in this Part shall not in other respects affect the legal status of the waters forming such straits or the exercise by the States bordering the straits of their sovereignty or jurisdiction over such waters and their air space, bed and subsoil.
2. The sovereignty or jurisdiction of the States bordering the straits is exercised subject to this Part and to other rules of international law.

Article 35
Scope of this Part

Nothing in this Part affects:
(a) any areas of internal waters within a strait, except where the establishment of a straight baseline in accordance with the method set forth in article 7 has the effect of enclosing as internal waters areas which had not previously been considered as such;
(b) the legal status of the waters beyond the territorial seas of States bordering straits as exclusive economic zones or high seas; or

(c) the legal regime in straits in which passage is regulated in whole or in part by long-standing international conventions in force specifically relating to such straits.

Article 36
High seas routes or routes through exclusive economic zones through straits used for international navigation

This Part does not apply to a strait used for international navigation if there exists through the strait a route through the high seas or through an exclusive economic zone of similar convenience with respect to navigational and hydrographical characteristics; in such routes, the other relevant Parts of this Convention, including the provisions regarding the freedoms of navigation and overflight, apply.

SECTION 2. TRANSIT PASSAGE

Article 37
Scope of this section

This section applies to straits which are used for international navigation between one part of the high seas or an exclusive economic zone and another part of the high seas or an exclusive economic zone.

Article 38
Right of transit passage

1. In straits referred to in article 37, all ships and aircraft enjoy the right of transit passage, which shall not be impeded; except that, if the strait is formed by an island of a State bordering the strait and its mainland, transit passage shall not apply if there exists seaward of the island a route through the high seas or through an exclusive economic zone of similar convenience with respect to navigational and hydrographical characteristics.
2. Transit passage means the exercise in accordance with this Part of the freedom of navigation and overflight solely for the purpose of continuous and expeditious transit of the strait between one part of the high seas or an exclusive economic zone and another part of the high seas or an exclusive economic zone. However, the requirement of continuous and expeditious transit does not preclude passage through the strait for the purpose of entering, leaving or returning from a State bordering the strait, subject to the conditions of entry to that State.
3. Any activity which is not an exercise of the right of transit passage through a strait remains subject to the other applicable provisions of this Convention.

Article 39
Duties of ships and aircraft during transit passage

1. Ships and aircraft, while exercising the right of transit passage, shall:
(a) proceed without delay through or over the strait;
(b) refrain from any threat or use of force against the sovereignty, territorial integrity or political independence of States bordering the strait, or in any other manner in violation of the principles of international law embodied in the Charter of the United Nations;

(c) refrain from any activities other than those incident to their normal modes of continuous and expeditious transit unless rendered necessary by *force majeure* or by distress;

(d) comply with other relevant provisions of this part.

2. Ships in transit passage shall:

(a) comply with generally accepted international regulations, procedures and practices for safety at sea, including the International Regulations for Preventing Collisions at Sea;

(b) comply with generally accepted international regulations, procedures and practices for the prevention, reduction and control of pollution from ships.

3. Aircraft in transit passage shall:

(a) observe the Rules of the Air established by the International Civil Aviation Organization as they apply to civil aircraft;   state aircraft will normally comply with such safety measures and will at all times operate with due regard for the safety of navigation;

(b) at all times monitor the radio frequency assigned by the competent internationally designated air traffic control authority or the appropriate international distress radio frequency.

Article 40
Research and survey activities

During transit passage, foreign ships, including marine scientific research and hydrographic survey ships, may not carry out any research or survey activities without the prior authorization of the States bordering straits.

Article 41
Sea lanes and traffic separation schemes in straits used for international navigation

1. In conformity with this Part, States bordering straits may designate sea lanes and prescribe traffic separation schemes for navigation in straits where necessary to promote the safe passage of ships.

2. Such States may, when circumstances require, and after giving due publicity thereto, substitute other sea lanes or traffic separation schemes for any sea lanes or traffic separation schemes previously designated or prescribed by them.

3. Such sea lanes and traffic separation schemes shall conform to generally accepted international regulations.

4. Before designating or substituting sea lanes or prescribing or substituting traffic separation schemes, States bordering straits shall refer proposals to the competent international organization with a view to their adoption.   The organization may adopt only such sea lanes and traffic separation schemes as may be agreed with the States bordering the straits, after which the States may designate, prescribe or substitute them.

5. In respect of a strait where sea lanes or traffic separation schemes through the waters of two or more States bordering the strait are being proposed, the States concerned shall co-operate in formulating proposals in consultation with the competent international organization.

6. States bordering straits shall clearly indicate all sea lanes and traffic separation schemes designated or prescribed by them on charts to which due publicity shall be given.

7. Ships in transit passage shall respect applicable sea lanes and traffic separation schemes established in accordance with this article.

Article 42
Laws and regulation of States bordering straits relating to transit passage

1. Subject to the provisions of this section, States bordering straits may adopt laws and regulations relating to transit passage through straits, in respect of all or any of the following:
(a) the safety of navigation and the regulation of maritime traffic, as provided in article 41;
(b) the prevention, reduction and control of pollution, by giving effect to applicable international regulations regarding the discharge of oil, oily wastes and other noxious substances in the strait;
(c) with respect to fishing vessels, the prevention of fishing, including the stowage of fishing gear;
(d) the loading or unloading of any commodity, currency or person in contravention of the customs, fiscal, immigration or sanitary laws and regulations of States bordering straits.
2. Such laws and regulations shall not discriminate in form or in fact among foreign ships or in their application have the practical effect of denying, hampering or impairing the right of transit passage as defined in this section.
3. States bordering straits shall give due publicity to all such laws and regulations.
4. Foreign ships exercising the right of transit passage shall comply with such laws and regulations.
5. The flag State of a ship or the State of registry of an aircraft entitled to sovereign immunity which acts in a manner contrary to such laws and regulations or other provisions of this Part shall bear international responsibility for any loss or damage which results to States bordering straits.

Article 43
Navigational and safety aids and other improvements and the prevention, reduction and control of pollution

User States and States bordering a strait should by agreement co-operate:
(a) in the establishment and maintenance in a strait of necessary navigational and safety aids or other improvements in aid of international navigation; and
(b) for the prevention, reduction and control of pollution from ships.

Article 44
Duties of States bordering straits

States bordering straits shall not hamper transit passage and shall give appropriate publicity to any danger to navigation or overflight within or over the strait of which they have knowledge. There shall be no suspension of transit passage.

SECTION 3. INNOCENT PASSAGE

Article 45
Innocent passage

1. The regime of innocent passage, in accordance with Part II, section 3, shall apply in straits used for international navigation:

(a) excluded from the application of the regime of transit passage under article 38, paragraph 1; or

(b) between a part of the high seas or an exclusive economic zone and the territorial sea of a foreign State.

2. There shall be no suspension of innocent passage through such straits.

5.2 GENEVA CONVENTION ON THE TERRITORIAL SEA AND THE CONTIGUOUS ZONE, 1958, ARTICLE 16(4)

Article 16(4)

There shall be no suspension of the innocent passage of foreign ships through straits which are used for international navigation between one part of the high seas and another part of the high seas or the territorial sea of a foreign State.

5.3 CORFU CHANNEL CASE (MERITS), 1949

Corfu Channel case, Judgment of 9 April 1949, ICJ Reports 1949, p.4
Excerpt from Judgment at pp. 15, 17-8, 22-3, 27-31 and 33-6

[In May 1946, two British cruisers, while passing southwards through the North Corfu Channel, in the Albanian territorial sea, were fired at by an Albanian coastal battery. In October 1946, two British warships passing through the Channel struck mines which caused damage to the warships and loss of lives. In November 1946, the Royal Navy mine-swept that part of the Channel lying in the Albanian territorial sea. The Court had to consider Albania's responsibility for the explosions and resulting damage, the legality of the passage of the British warships in October 1946 and the legality of the British minesweeping operation in November 1946. The following excerpts from the Court's Judgment reflect the Court's view of the right of warships to pass through a strait used for international navigation and the duty of the coastal State to warn foreign shipping of dangers to navigation in such straits].

The Court ... finds that the following facts are established. The two ships were mined in Albanian territorial waters in a previously swept and check-swept channel just at the place where a newly laid minefield consisting of moored contact Germany GY mines was discovered three weeks later. The damage sustained by the ships was inconsistent with damage which could have been caused by floating mines, magnetic ground mines, magnetic moored mines, or German GR mines, but its nature and extent were such as would be caused by mines of the type found in the minefield. In such circumstances the Court arrives at the conclusion that the explosions were due to mines belonging to that minefield.

***

... [T]he United Kingdom Government put forward the argument that, whoever the authors of the minelaying were, it could not have been done without the Albanian Government's knowledge.

It is clear that knowledge of the minelaying cannot be imputed to the Albanian Government by reason merely of the fact that a minefield discovered in Albanian territorial waters caused the explosions of which the British warships were the victims. It is true, as international practice shows, that a State on whose territory or in whose waters an act contrary to international law has occurred, may be called upon to give an explanation. It is also true that that State cannot evade such a request by limiting itself to a reply that it is ignorant of the circumstances of the act and of its authors. The State may, up to a certain point, be bound to supply particulars of the use made by it of the means of information and inquiry at its disposal. But it cannot be concluded from the mere fact of the control exercised by a State over its territory and waters that that State necessarily knew, or ought to have known, of any unlawful act perpetrated therein, nor yet that it necessarily knew, or should have known, the authors. This fact, by itself and apart from other circumstances, neither involves *prima facie* responsibility nor shifts the burden of proof.

On the other hand, the fact of this exclusive territorial control exercised by a State within its frontiers has a bearing upon the methods of proof available to establish the knowledge of that State as to such events. By reason of this exclusive control, the other State, the victim of a breach of international law, is often unable to furnish direct proof of facts giving rise to responsibility. Such a State should be allowed a more liberal recourse to inferences of fact and circumstantial evidence. This indirect evidence is admitted in all systems of law, and its use is recognized by international decisions. It must be regarded as of special weight when it is based on a series of facts linked together and leading logically to a single conclusion.

The Court must examine therefore whether it has been established by means of indirect evidence that Albania has knowledge of minelaying in her territorial waters independently of any connivance on her part in this operation. The proof may be drawn from inferences of fact, provided that they leave *no room* for reasonable doubt. The elements of fact on which these inferences can be based may differ from those which are relevant to the question of connivance.

In the present case, two series of facts, which corroborate one another, have to be considered: the first relates to Albania's attitude before and after the disaster of October 22nd, 1946; the other concerns the feasibility of observing minelaying from the Albanian coast.

...

From all the facts and observations mentioned above, the Court draws the conclusion that the laying of the minefield which caused the explosions on October 22nd, 1946, could not have been accomplished without the knowledge of the Albanian Government.

The obligations resulting for Albania from this knowledge are not disputed between the Parties. Counsel for the Albanian Government expressly recognized that [*translation*] "if Albania had been informed of the operation before the incidents of October 22nd, and in time to warn the British vessels and shipping in general of the existence of mines in the Corfu Channel, her responsibility would be involved ...".

The obligations incumbent upon the Albanian authorities consisted in notifying, for the benefit of shipping in general, the existence of a minefield in Albanian territorial waters and in warning the approaching British warships of the imminent danger to which the minefield exposed them. Such obligations are based, not on the Hague Convention of 1907, No.VIII, which is applicable in time of war, but on certain general and well-recognized principles, namely: elementary considerations of humanity, even more exacting in peace than in war; the principle of the freedom of maritime communication; and every State's obligation not to allow knowingly its territory to be used for acts contrary to the rights of other States.

In fact, Albania neither notified the existence of the minefield, nor warned the British warships of the danger they were approaching.

But Albania's obligation to notify shipping of the existence of mines in her waters depends on her having obtained knowledge of that fact in sufficient time before October 22nd; and the duty of the Albanian coastal authorities to warn the British ships depends on the time that elapsed between the moment that these ships were reported and the moment of the first explosion.

On this subject, the Court makes the following observations. As has already been stated, the Parties agree that the mines were recently laid. It must be concluded that the minelaying, whatever may have been its exact date, was done at a time when there was a close Albanian surveillance over the Strait. If it be supposed that it took place at the last possible moment, i.e., in the night of October 21st-22nd, the only conclusion to be drawn would be that a general notification to the shipping of all States before the time of the explosions would have been difficult, perhaps even impossible. But this would certainly not have prevented the Albanian authorities from taking, as they should have done, all necessary steps immediately to warn ships near the danger zone, more especially those that were approaching that zone. When on October 22nd about 13.00 hours the British warships were reported by the look-out post at St. George's Monastery to the Commander of the Coastal Defences as approaching Cape Long, it was perfectly possible for the Albanian authorities to use the interval of almost two hours that elapsed before the explosion affecting *Saumarez* (14.53 hours to 14.55 hours) to warn the vessels of the danger into which they were running.

In fact, nothing was attempted by the Albanian authorities to prevent the disaster. These grave omissions involve the international responsibility of Albania.

The Court therefore reaches the conclusion that Albania is responsible under international law for the explosions which occurred on October 22nd, 1946, in Albanian waters, and for the damage and loss of human life which resulted from them, and that there is a duty upon Albania to pay compensation to the United Kingdom.

...

On May 15th, 1946, the British Cruisers *Orion* and *Superb*, while passing southward through the North Corfu Channel, were fired at by an Albanian battery in the vicinity of Saranda. ... An Albanian note of May 21st states that the Coastal Commander ordered a few shots to be fired in the direction of the ships "in accordance with a General Order founded on international law."

The United Kingdom Government at once protested to the Albanian Government, stating that innocent passage through straits is a right recognized by international law. There ensued a diplomatic correspondence in which the Albanian Government asserted that foreign warships and merchant vessels had no right to pass through Albanian territorial waters without prior notification to, and the permission of, the Albanian authorities. This view was put into effect by a communication of the Albanian Chief of Staff, dated May 17th, 1946, which purported to subject the passage of foreign warships and merchant vessels in Albanian territorial waters to previous notification to and authorization by the Albanian Government. The diplomatic correspondence continued, and culminated in a United Kingdom note of August 2nd, 1946, in which the United Kingdom Government maintained its view with regard to the right of innocent passage through straits forming routes for international maritime traffic between two parts of the high seas. The note ended with the warning that if Albanian coastal batteries in the future opened fire on any British warship passing through the Corfu Channel, the fire would be returned.

The contents of this note were, on August 1st, communicated by the British Admiralty to the Commander-in-Chief, Mediterranean, with the instruction that he should refrain from using the channel until the note had been presented to the Albanian Government. On August 10th, he received from the Admiralty the following telegram: "The Albanians have now received the note. North Corfu Strait may now be used by ships of your fleet, but only when essential and with armament in fore and aft position. If coastal guns fire at ships passing through the Strait, ships should fire back." On September 21st, the following telegram was sent by the Admiralty to the Commander-in-Chief, Mediterranean: "Establishment of diplomatic relations with Albania is again under consideration by His Majesty's Government who wish to know whether the Albanian Government have learnt to behave themselves. Information is requested whether any ships under your command have passed through the North Corfu Strait since August and, if not, whether you intend them to do so shortly." The Commander-in-Chief answered the next day that his ships had not done so yet, but that it was his intention that *Mauritius* and *Leander* and two destroyers should do so when they departed from Corfu on October 22nd.

It was in such circumstances that these two cruisers together with the destroyers *Saumarez* and *Volage* were sent through the North Corfu Strait on that date.

The Court will now consider the Albanian contention that the United Kingdom Government violated Albanian sovereignty by sending the warships through this Strait without the previous authorization of the Albanian Government.

It is, in the opinion of the Court, generally recognized and in accordance with international custom that States in time of peace have a right to send their warships through straits used for international navigation between two parts of the high seas without the previous authorization of a coastal State, provided that the passage is *innocent*. Unless otherwise prescribed in an international convention, there is no right for a coastal State to prohibit such passage through straits in time of peace.

The Albanian Government does not dispute that the North Corfu Channel is a strait in the geographical sense; but it denies that this Channel belongs to the class of international highways through which a right of passage exists, on the grounds that it is only of secondary importance and not even a necessary route between two parts of the high seas, and that it is used almost exclusively for local traffic to and from the ports of Corfu and Saranda.

It may be asked whether the test is to be found in the volume of traffic passing through the Strait or in its greater or lesser importance for international navigation. But in the opinion of the Court the decisive criterion is rather its geographical situation as connecting two parts of the high seas and the fact of its being used for international navigation. Nor can it be decisive that this Strait is not a necessary route between two parts of the high seas but only an alternative passage between the Aegean and the Adriatic Seas. It has nevertheless been a useful route for international maritime traffic. In this respect, the Agent of the United Kingdom Government gave the Court the following information relating to the period from April 1st, 1936, to December 31st, 1937: "The following is the total number of ships putting in at the Port of Corfu after passing through or just before passing through the Channel. During the period of one year nine months, the total number of ships was 2,884. The flags of the ships are Greek, Italian, Roumanian, Yugoslav, French, Albanian and British. Clearly, very small vessels are included, as the entries for Albanian vessels are high, and of course one vessel may make several journeys, but 2,884 ships for a period of one year nine months is quite a large figure. These figures relate to vessels visited by the Customs at Corfu and so do not include the large number of vessels which went through the Strait without calling at Corfu at all." There were also regular sailings through the Strait by Greek vessels three times weekly, by a British ship fortnightly, and by two Yugoslav vessels weekly and by two others fortnightly. The Court is further informed that the British navy has regularly used this Channel for eighty years or more, and that it has also been used by the navies of other States.

One fact of particular importance is that the North Corfu Channel constitutes a frontier between Albania and Greece, that a part of it is wholly within the territorial waters of these States, and that the Strait is of special importance to Greece by reason of the traffic to and from the port of Corfu.

Having regard to these various considerations, the Court has arrived at the conclusion that the North Corfu Channel should be considered as belonging to the class of international highways through which passage cannot be prohibited by a coastal State in time of peace.

On the other hand, it is a fact that the two coastal States did not maintain normal relations, that Greece had made territorial claims precisely with regard to a part of Albanian territory bordering on the Channel, that Greece had declared that she considered herself technically in a state of war with Albania, and that Albania, invoking the danger of Greek incursions, had considered it necessary to take certain measures of vigilance in this region. The Court is of opinion that Albania, in view of these exceptional circumstances, would have been justified in issuing regulations in respect of the passage of warships through the Strait, but not in prohibiting such passage or in subjecting it to the requirement of special authorization.

For these reasons the Court is unable to accept the Albanian contention that the Government of the United Kingdom has violated Albanian sovereignty by sending the warships through the Strait without having obtained the previous authorization of the Albanian Government.

In these circumstances, it is unnecessary to consider the more general question, much debated by the Parties, whether States under international law have a right to send warships in time of peace through territorial waters not included in a strait.

The Albanian Government has further contended that the sovereignty of Albania was violated because the passage of the British warships on October 22nd, 1946, was not an *innocent passage*. The reasons advanced in support of this contention may be summed up as follows: The passage was not an ordinary passage, but a political mission; the ships were maneuvring and sailing in diamond combat formation with soldiers on board; the position of the guns was not consistent with innocent passage; the vessels passed with crews at action stations; the number of the ships and their armament surpassed what was necessary in order to attain their object and showed an intention to intimidate and not merely to pass; the ships had received orders to observe and report upon the coastal defences and this order was carried out.

It is shown by the Admiralty telegram of September 21st, cited above, and admitted by the United Kingdom Agent, that the object of sending the warships through the Strait was not only to carry out a passage for purposes of navigation, but also to test Albania's attitude. As mentioned above, the Albanian Government, on May 15th, 1946, tried to impose by means of gunfire its view with regard to the passage. As the exchange of diplomatic notes did not lead to any clarification, the Government of the United Kingdom wanted to ascertain by other means whether the Albanian Government would maintain its illegal attitude and again impose its view by firing at passing ships. The legality of this measure taken by the Government of the United Kingdom cannot be disputed, provided that it was carried out in a manner consistent with the requirements of international law The "mission" was designed to affirm a right which had been unjustly denied. The Government of the United Kingdom was not bound to abstain from exercising its right of passage, which the Albanian Government had illegally denied.

It remains, therefore, to consider whether the *manner* in which the passage was carried out was consistent with the principle of innocent passage and to examine the various contentions of the Albanian Government in so far as they appear to be relevant.

When the Albanian coastguards at St. George's Monastery reported that the British warships were sailing in combat formation and were manoeuvring, they must have been under a misapprehension. It is shown by the evidence that the ships were not proceeding in combat formation, but in line, one after the other, and that they were not maneouvring until after the first explosion. Their movements thereafter were due to the explosions and were made necessary in order to save human life and the mined ships. It is shown by the evidence of witnesses that the contention that soldiers were on board must be due to a misunderstanding probably arising from the fact that the two cruisers carried their usual detachment of marines.

It is known from the above-mentioned order issued by the British Admiralty on August 10th, 1946, that ships, when using the North Corfu Strait, must pass with armament in fore and aft position. That this order was carried out during the passage on October 22nd is stated by the Commander-in-Chief, Mediterranean, in a telegram of October 26th to the Admiralty. The guns were, he reported "trained fore and aft, which is their normal position at sea in peace time, and were not loaded". It is confirmed by the commanders of *Saumarez* and *Volage* that the guns were in this position before the explosions. The navigating officer on board *Mauritius* explained that all the guns on that cruiser were in their normal stowage position. The main guns were in the line of the ship, and the anti-aircraft guns were pointing outwards and up into the air, which is the normal position of these guns on a cruiser both in harbour and at sea. In the light of this evidence, the Court cannot accept the Albanian contention that the position of the guns was inconsistent with the rules of innocent passage.

In the above-mentioned telegram of October 26th, the Commander-in-Chief reported that the passage "was made with ships at action stations in order that they might be able to retaliate quickly if fired upon again". In view of the firing from the Albanian battery on May 15th, this measure of precaution cannot, in itself, be regarded as unreasonable. But four warships – two cruisers and two destroyers – passed in this manner, with crews at action stations, ready to retaliate quickly if fired upon. They passed one after another through this narrow channel, close to the Albanian coast, at a time of political tension in this region. The intention must have been, not only to test Albania's attitude, but at the same time to demonstrate such force that she would abstain from firing again on passing ships. Having regard, however, to all the circumstances of the case, as described above, the Court is unable to characterize these measures taken by the United Kingdom authorities as a violation of Albania's sovereignty.

...

After the explosions of October 22nd, the United Kingdom Government sent a note to the Albanian Government, in which it announced its intention to sweep the Corfu Channel shortly. The Albanian reply ... stated that the Albanian Government would not give its consent to this unless the operation in question took place outside Albanian territorial waters.

...

... "Operation Retail" took place on November 12th and 13th ... The area swept was in Albanian territorial waters, and within the limits of the channel previously swept.

The United Kingdom Government does not dispute that "Operation Retail" was carried out against the clearly expressed wish of the Albanian Government. It recognizes that the operation had not the consent of the international mine clearance organizations, that it could not be justified as the exercise of a right of innocent passage, and lastly that, in principle, international law does not allow a State to assemble a large number of warships in the territorial waters of another State and to carry out minesweeping in those waters. The United Kingdom Government states that the operation was one of extreme urgency, and that it considered itself entitled to carry it out without anybody's consent.

The United Kingdom put forward two reasons in justification ... [The Court did not consider the first reason convincing. As regards the second reason:]

But in fact, the explosions of October 22nd, 1946, in a channel declared safe for navigation, and one which the United Kingdom Government, more than any other government, had reason to consider safe, raised quite a different problem from that of a routine sweep carried out under the orders of the mineclearance organizations. These explosions were suspicious; they raised a question of responsibility.

Accordingly, this was the ground on which the United Kingdom Government chose to establish its main line of defence. According to that Government, the *corpora delicti* must be secured as quickly as possible, for fear they should be taken away, without leaving traces, by the authors of the minelaying or by the Albanian authorities. This justification took two distinct forms in the United Kingdom Government's arguments. It was presented first as a new and special application of the theory of intervention, by means of which the State intervening would secure possession of evidence in the territory of another State, in order to submit it to an international tribunal and thus facilitate its task.

The Court cannot accept such a line of defence. The Court can only regard the alleged right of intervention as the manifestation of a policy of force, such as has, in the past, given rise to most serious abuses and such as cannot, whatever be the present defects in international organization, find a place in international law. Intervention is perhaps still less admissible in the particular form it would take here; for, from the nature of things, it would be reserved for the most powerful States, and might easily lead to perverting the administration of international justice itself.

The United Kingdom Agent, in his speech in reply, has further classified "Operation Retail" among methods of self-protection or self-help. The Court cannot accept this defence either. Between independent States, respect for territorial sovereignty is an essential foundation of international relations. The Court recognizes that the Albanian Government's complete failure to carry out its duties after the explosions, and the dilatory nature of its diplomatic notes, are extenuating circumstances for the action of the United Kingdom Government. But to ensure respect for international law, of which it is the organ, the Court must declare that the action of the British Navy constituted a violation of Albanian sovereignty.

This declaration is in accordance with the request made by Albania through her Counsel, and is in itself appropriate satisfaction.

...

The Court ...

Gives judgment that the People's Republic of Albania is responsible under international law for the explosions which occurred on October 22nd, 1946, in

Albanian waters, and for the damage and loss of human life that resulted therefrom; and ...

Gives judgment that the United Kingdom did not violate the sovereignty of the People's Republic of Albania by reason of the acts of the British Navy in Albanian waters on October 22nd, 1946; and ...

Gives judgment that by reason of the acts of the British Navy in Albanian waters in the course of the Operation of November 12th and 13th, 1946, the United Kingdom violated the sovereignty of the People's Republic of Albania, and that this declaration by the Court constitutes in itself appropriate satisfaction.

5.4 MONTREUX CONVENTION REGARDING THE REGIME OF THE [TURKISH] STRAITS, 1936

[The fundamental principle upon which the legal status of the straits is based is the principle of the freedom of passage through the Straits, already established by Article 23 of the Peace Treaty of Lausanne, 1923.   In Article 1 of the Montreux Convention, the Parties 'recognise and affirm the principle of freedom of transit and navigation by sea in the Straits'.   Moreover, under Article 28, although the Convention is declared to be for an initial period of only 20 years, the Parties provide that the principle of freedom of transit and navigation 'shall however continue without limit of time'.   In other words, the nine Parties (Bulgaria, France, Great Britain, Greece, Japan, Rumania, Turkey, the Soviet Union and Yugoslavia) considered the principle of freedom of passage in the Straits to be a principle of international law independent of the Convention.]

...

Article 1

The High Contracting Parties recognise and affirm the principles of freedom of transit and navigation by sea in the Straits.

The exercise of this freedom shall henceforth be regulated by the provisions of the present Convention.

SECTION I: MERCHANT VESSELS

Article 2

In time of peace, merchant vessels shall enjoy complete freedom of transit and navigation in the Straits, by day and by night, under any flag and with any kind of cargo, without any formalities, except as provided in Article 3 below.   No taxes or charges other than those authorised by Annex 1 to the present Convention shall be levied by the Turkish authorities on these vessels when passing in transit without calling at a port in the Straits.

In order to facilitate the collection of these taxes or charges merchant vessels passing through the Straits shall communicate to the officials at the stations referred to in Article 3 their name, nationality, tonnage, destination, and last port of call (provenance).

Pilotage and towage remain optional.

Article 3

All ships entering the Straits by the Aegean Sea or by the Black Sea shall stop at a sanitary station near the entrance to the Straits for the purposes of the sanity control prescribed by Turkish law within the framework of international sanitary regulations. This control, in the case of ships possessing a clean bill of health or presenting a declaration of health testifying that they do not fall within the scope of the provisions of the second paragraph of the present Article, shall be carried out by day and by night with all possible speed, and the vessels in question shall not be required to make any other stop during their passage through the Straits.

Vessels which have on board cases of plague, cholera, yellow fever, exanthematic typhus, or small pox, or which have had such cases on board during the previous seven days, and vessels which have left an infected port within less than five times twenty-four hours shall stop at the sanitary stations indicated in the preceding paragraph in order to embark such sanitary guards as the Turkish authorities may direct. No tax or charge shall be levied in respect of these sanitary guards and they shall be disembarked at a sanitary station on departure from the Straits.

Article 4

In time of war, Turkey not being belligerent, merchant vessels, under any flag or with any kind of cargo, shall enjoy freedom of transit and navigation in the Straits subject to the provisions of Articles 2 and 3.

Pilotage and towage remain optional.

Article 5

In time of war, Turkey being belligerent, merchant vessels not belonging to a country at war with Turkey shall enjoy freedom of transit and navigation in the Straits on condition that they do not in any way assist the enemy.

Such vessels shall enter the Straits by day and their transit shall be effected by the route which shall in each case be indicated by the Turkish authorities.

Article 6

Should Turkey consider herself to be threatened with imminent danger of war, the provisions of Article 2 shall nevertheless continue to be applied except that vessels must enter the Straits by day and that their transit must be effected by the route which shall, in each case, be indicated by the Turkish authorities.

Pilotage may, in this case, be made obligatory, but no charge shall be levied.

Article 7

The term 'merchant vessels' applies to all vessels which are not covered by Section II of the present Convention.

SECTION II: VESSELS OF WAR

Article 8

For the purposes of the present Convention, the definitions of vessels of war and of their specification together with those relating to the calculation of tonnage shall be as set forth in Annex II to the present Convention.

Article 9

Naval auxiliary vessels specifically designed for the carriage of fuel, liquid or non-liquid, shall not be subject to the provisions of Article 13 regarding notification, nor shall they be counted for the purpose of calculating the tonnage which is subject to limitation under Articles 14 and 18, on condition that they shall pass through the Straits singly. They shall, however, continue to be on the same footing as vessels of war for the purpose of the remaining provisions governing transit.

The auxiliary vessels specified in the preceding paragraph shall only be entitled to benefit by the exceptional status therein contemplated if their armament does not include: for use against floating targets, more than two guns of a maximum calibre of 105 millimeters; for use against aerial targets, more than two guns of a maximum calibre of 15 millimeters.

Article 10

In time of peace, light surface vessels, minor war vessels and auxiliary vessels, whether belonging to Black Sea or non-Black Sea Powers, and whatever their flag, shall enjoy freedom of transit through the Straits without any taxes or charges whatever, provided that such transit is begun during daylight and subject to the conditions laid down in Article 13 and the Articles following thereafter.

Vessels of war other than those which fall within the categories specified in the preceding paragraph shall only enjoy a right of transit under the special conditions provided by Articles 11 and 12.

Article 11

Black Sea Powers may send through the Straits capital ships of a tonnage greater than that laid down in the first paragraph of Article 14, on condition that these vessels pass through the Straits singly, escorted by not more than two destroyers.

Article 12

Black Sea Powers shall have the right to send through the Straits, for the purpose of rejoining their base, submarines constructed or purchased outside the Black Sea, provided that adequate notice of the laying down or purchase of such submarines shall have been given to Turkey.

Submarines belonging to the said Powers shall also be entitled to pass through the Straits to be repaired in dockyards outside the Black Sea on condition that detailed information on the matter is given to Turkey.

In either case, the said submarines must travel by day and on the surface, and must pass through the Straits singly.

Article 13

The transit of vessels of war through the Straits shall be preceded by a notification given to the Turkish Government through the diplomatic channel. The normal period of notice shall be eight days; but it is desirable that in the case of non Black Sea Powers this period should be increased to fifteen days. The notification shall specify the destination, name, type and number of the vessels, as also the date of entry for the outward passage and, if necessary, for the return journey. Any change of date shall be subject to three days' notice.

Entry into the Straits for the outward passage shall take place within a period of five days from the date given in the original notification.   After the expiry of this period, a new notification shall be given under the same conditions as for the original notification.

When effecting transit, the commander of the naval force shall, without being under any obligation to stop, communicate to a signal station at the entrance to the Dardenelles or the Bosphorus the exact composition of the force under his orders.

Article 14

The maximum aggregate tonnage of all foreign naval forces which may be in course of transit through the Straits shall not exceed 15,000 tons, except in the cases provided for in Article 11 and in Annex III to the present Convention.

The forces specified in the preceding paragraph shall not, however, comprise more than nine vessels.

Vessels, whether belonging to the Black Sea or non-Black Sea Powers, paying visits to a port in the Straits, in accordance with the provisions of Article 17, shall not be included in thus tonnage.

Neither shall vessels of war which have suffered damage during their passage through the Straits be included in this tonnage; such vessels, while undergoing repair, shall be subject to any special provisions relating to security laid down by Turkey.

Article 15

Vessels of war in transit through the Straits shall in no circumstances make use of any aircraft which they may be carrying.

Article 16

Vessels of war in transit through the Straits shall not, except in the event of damage or peril of the sea, remain therein longer than is necessary for them to effect the passage.

Article 17

Nothing in the provisions of the preceding Articles shall prevent a naval force of any tonnage or composition from paying a courtesy visit of limited duration to a port in the Straits, at the invitation of the Turkish Government. Any such force must leave the Straits by the same route as that by which it entered, unless it fulfils the conditions required for passage in transit through the Straits as laid down by Articles 10, 14 and 18.

Article 18

(1) The aggregate tonnage which non-Black Sea Powers may have in that sea in time of peace shall be limited as follows:

(a) Except as provided in paragraph (b) below, the aggregate tonnage of the said Powers shall not exceed 30,000 tons;

(b) If at any time the tonnage of the strongest fleet in the Black Sea shall exceed by at least 10,000 tons the tonnage of the strongest fleet in that sea at the date of the signature of the present Convention, the aggregate tonnage of 30,000 tons mentioned in paragraph (a) shall be increased by the same amount, up to a maximum of 45,000 tons. For this purpose, each Black Sea Power shall, in conformity with Annex IV to the present Convention, inform the Turkish Government, on the 1st January and the 1st

July of each year, of the total tonnage of its fleet in the Black Sea; and the Turkish Government shall transmit this information to the other High Contracting Parties and to the Secretary-General of the League of Nations;

(c) The tonnage which any one non-Black Sea Power may have in the Black Sea shall be limited to two-thirds of the aggregate tonnage provided for in paragraphs (a) and (b) above;

(d) In the event, however, of one or more non-Black Sea Powers desiring to send naval forces into the Black Sea, for a humanitarian purpose, the said forces, which shall be allowed to enter the Black Sea without having to give the notification provided for in Article 13 of the present Convention, provided an authorisation is obtained from the Turkish Government in the following circumstances: if the figure of the aggregate tonnage specified in paragraphs (a) and (b) above has not been reached and will not be exceeded by the despatch of the forces which it is desired to send, the Turkish Government shall grant the said authorization within the shortest possible time after receiving the request which has been addressed to it; if the said figure has already been reached or if the despatch of the forces which it is desired to send will cause it to be exceeded, the Turkish Government will immediately inform the other Black Sea Powers of the request for authorization, and if the said Powers make no objection within twenty-four hours of having received this information, the Turkish Government shall, within forty-eight hours at the latest, inform the interested Powers of the reply which it has decided to make to their request.

Any further entry into the Black Sea of naval forces of non-Black Sea Powers shall only be effected within the available limits of the aggregate tonnage provided for in paragraphs (a) and (b) above.

(2) Vessels of war belonging to non-Black Sea Powers shall not remain in the Black Sea more than twenty-one days, whatever be the object of their presence there.

Article 19

In time of war, Turkey not being belligerent, warships shall enjoy complete freedom of transit and navigation through the Straits under the same conditions as those laid down in Articles 10 to 18.

Vessels of war belonging to belligerent Powers shall not, however, pass through the Straits except in cases arising out of the application of Article 25 of the present Convention, and in cases of assistance rendered to a State victim of aggression in virtue of a treaty of mutual assistance binding Turkey, concluded within the framework of the Covenant of the League of Nations, and registered and published in accordance with the provisions of Article 18 of the Covenant.

In the exceptional cases provided for in the preceding paragraph, the limitations laid down in Articles 10 to 18 of the present Convention shall not be applicable.

Notwithstanding the prohibition of passage laid down in paragraph 2 above, vessels of war belonging to belligerent Powers, whether they are Black Sea Powers or not, which have become separated from their bases, may return thereto.

Vessels of war belonging to belligerent Powers shall not make any capture, exercise the right of visit and search, or carry out any hostile act in the Straits.

Article 20

In time of war, Turkey being belligerent, the provisions of Articles 10 to 18 shall not be applicable; the passage of warships shall be left entirely to the discretion of the Turkish Government.

Article 21

Should Turkey consider herself to be threatened with imminent danger of war she shall have the right to apply the provisions of Article 20 of the present Convention.

Vessels which have passed through the Straits before Turkey has made use of the powers conferred upon her by the preceding paragraph, and which thus find themselves separated from their bases, may return thereto. It is, however, understood that Turkey may deny this right to vessels of war belonging to the State whose attitude has given rise to the application of the present Article.

Should the Turkish Government make use of the powers conferred by the first paragraph of the present Article, a notification to that effect shall be addressed to the High Contracting Parties and to the Secretary-General of the League of Nations.

If the Council of the League of Nations decide by a majority of two-thirds that the measures thus taken by Turkey are not justified, and if such should also be the opinion of the majority of the High Contracting Parties signatories to the present Convention, the Turkish Government undertake to discontinue the measures which may have been taken under Article 6 of the present Convention.

Article 22

Vessels of war which have on board cases of plague, cholera, yellow fever, exathematic typhus or small pox or which have had such cases on board within the last seven days, and vessels of war which have left an infected port within less than five times twenty-four hours must pass through the straits in quarantine and apply by the means on board such prophylactic measures as are necessary in order to prevent any possibility of the Straits being infected.

SECTION III: AIRCRAFT

Article 23

In order to assure the passage of civil aircraft between the Mediterranean and the Black Sea, the Turkish Government will indicate the air routes available for this purpose, outside the forbidden zones which may be established in the Straits. Civil aircraft may use these routes provided that they give the Turkish Government, as regards occasional flights, a notification of three days, and as regards flights on regular services, a general notification of the dates of passage.

The Turkish Government moreover undertake, notwithstanding any remilitarisation of the Straits, to furnish the necessary facilities for the safe passage of civil aircraft authorised under the air regulations in force in Turkey to fly across Turkish territory between Europe and Asia. The route which is to be followed in the Straits zone by aircraft which have obtained an authorisation shall be indicated from time to time.

SECTION IV: GENERAL PROVISIONS

Article 24

The functions of the International Commission set up under the Convention relating to the regime of the Straits of the 24th July, 1923, are hereby transferred to the Turkish Government.

The Turkish Government undertake to collect statistics and to furnish information concerning the application of Articles 11, 12, 14 and 18 of the present Convention.

They will supervise the execution of all the provisions of the present Convention relating to the passage of vessels of war through the Straits.

As soon as they have been notified of the intended passage through the Straits of a foreign naval force the Turkish Government shall inform the representatives at Angora of the High Contracting Parties of the composition of that force, its tonnage, the date fixed for its entry into the Straits, and, if necessary, the probable date of its return.

The Turkish Government shall address to the Secretary-General of the League of Nations and to the High Contracting Parties an annual report giving details regarding the movements of foreign vessels of war through the Straits and furnishing all information which may be of service to commerce and navigation, both by sea and by air, for which provision is made in the present Convention.

Article 25

Nothing in the present Convention shall prejudice the rights and obligations of Turkey, or of any other High Contracting Parties members of the League of Nations, arising out of the Covenant of the League of Nations.

SECTION V: FINAL PROVISIONS

Article 26

The present Convention shall be ratified as soon as possible.

The ratifications shall be deposited in the archives of the Government of the French Republic in Paris.

The Japanese Government shall be entitled to inform the Government of the French Republic through their diplomatic representative in Paris that the ratification has been given, and in that case they shall transmit the instrument of ratification as soon as possible.

The *procès-verbal* of the deposit of ratifications shall be drawn up as soon as six instruments of ratification, including that of Turkey, shall have been deposited. For this purpose the notification provided for in the preceding paragraph shall be taken as the equivalent of the deposit of an instrument of ratification.

The present Convection shall come into force on the date of the said *procès-verbal*.

The French Government will transmit to all the High Contracting Parties an authentic copy of the *procès-verbal* provided for in the preceding paragraphs and of the *procès-verbaux* of the deposit of any subsequent ratifications.

Article 27

The present Convention shall, as from the date of its entry into force, be open to accession by any Power signatory to the Treaty of Peace at Lausanne signed on the 24th July, 1923.

Each accession shall be notified, through the diplomatic channel, to the Government of the French Republic, and by the latter to all the High Contracting Parties.

Accessions shall come into force as from the date of notification to the French Government.

Article 28

The present Convention shall remain in force for twenty years from the date of its entry into force.

The principle of freedom of transit and navigation affirmed in Article 1 of the present Convention shall however continue without limit of time.

If, two years prior to the expiry of the said period of twenty years, no High Contracting Party shall have given notice of denunciation to the French Government the present Convention shall continue in force until two years after such notice shall have been given. Any such notice shall be communicated by the French Government to the High Contracting Parties.

In the event of the present Convention being denounced in accordance with the provisions of the present Article, the High Contracting Parties agree to be represented at a conference for the purpose of concluding a new Convention.

Article 29

At the expiry of each period of five years from the date of the entry into force of the present Convention each of the High Contracting Parties shall be entitled to initiate a proposal for amending one or more of the provisions of the present Convention.

To be valid, any request for revision formulated by one of the High Contracting Parties must be supported, in the case of modifications to Articles 14 or 18, by one other High Contracting Party, and, in the case of modifications to any other Article, by two other High Contracting Parties.

Any request for revision thus supported must be notified to all the High Contracting Parties three months prior to the expiry of the current period of five years. This notification shall contain details of the proposed amendments and the reasons which have given rise to them.

Should it be found impossible to reach an agreement on these proposals through the diplomatic channel, the High Contracting Parties agree to be represented at a conference to be summoned for this purpose.

Such a conference may only take decisions by a unanimous vote, except as regards cases of revision involving Articles 14 and 18, for which a majority of three-quarters of the High Contracting Parties shall be sufficient.

The said majority shall include three-quarters of the High Contracting Parties which are Black Sea Powers, including Turkey.

ANNEX I

The taxes and charges which may be levied in accordance with Article 2 of the present Convention shall be those set forth in the following table. Any reductions in these taxes or charges which the Turkish Government may grant shall be applied without any distinction based on the flag of the vessel.

ANNEX II

A. Standard Displacement

(1) The standard displacement of a surface vessel is the displacement of the vessel, complete, fully manned, engined, and equipped ready for sea, including all armament and ammunition, equipment, outfit, provisions and fresh water for crew, miscellaneous

stores and implements of every description that are intended to be carried in war, but without fuel or reserve feed water on board.

(2) The standard displacement of a submarine is the surface displacement of the vessel complete (exclusive of the water in non-watertight structure), fully manned, engined and equipped ready for sea, including all armament and ammunition, equipment, outfit, provisions for crew, miscellaneous stores and implements of every description that are intended to be carried in war, but without fuel, lubricating oil, fresh water or ballast water of any kind on board.

(3) The word 'ton' except in the expression 'metric tons' denotes the ton of 2,240 lb (1,016 kilos).

B. Categories

(1) *Capital Ships* are surface vessels of war belonging to one of the two following sub-ca 4tegories: (a) Surface vessels of war, other than aircraft-carriers, auxiliary vessels, or capital ships of sub-category (b), the standard displacement of which exceeds 10,000 tons (10,160 metric tons) or which carry a gun with a calibre exceeding 8 in. (203 mm.); (b) Surface vessels of war, other than aircraft-carriers, the standard displacement of which does not exceed 8,000 tons (8,128 metric tons) and which carry a gun with a calibre exceeding 8 in. (203 mm.).

(2) *Aircraft-Carriers* are surface vessels of war, whatever their displacement, designed or adapted primarily for the purpose of carrying and operating aircraft at sea. The fitting of a landing-on or flying-off deck on any vessel of war, provided such vessel has not been designed or adapted primarily for the purpose of carrying and operating aircraft at sea, shall not cause any vessel so fitted to be classified in the category of aircraft-carriers.

The category of aircraft-carriers is divided into two sub-categories as follows: (a) Vessels fitted with a flight deck, from which aircraft can take off, or on which aircraft can land from the air;

(b) Vessels not fitted with a flight deck as described in (a) above.

(3) *Light surface vessels* are surface vessels of war other than aircraft-carriers, minor war vessels or auxiliary vessels, the standard displacement of which exceeds 100 tons (102 metric tons) and does not exceed 10,000 tons (10,160 metric tons), and which do not carry a gun with a calibre exceeding 8 in. (203 mm.).

...

(4) *Submarines* are vessels designed to operate below the surface of the sea.

...

PROTOCOL

At the moment of signing the Convention bearing this day's date, the undersigned Plenipotentiaries declare for the respective Governments that they accept the following provisions:

(1) Turkey may immediately remilitarise the zone of the Straits as defined in the Preamble to the said Convention.

(2) As from the 15th August, 1936, the Turkish Government shall provisionally apply the regime specified in the said Convention.

(3) The present Protocol shall enter into force as from this day's date.

5.5 DOCUMENTS ON THE STRAIT OF TIRAN AND THE GULF OF AQABA

5.5.1 SECURITY COUNCIL RESOLUTIONS

Resolution 242 of 22 November, 1967

The Security Council,
Expressing its continuing concern with the grave situation in the Middle East,
...
2. *Affirms further* the necessity
(a) For guaranteeing freedom of navigation through international waterways in the area;

Resolution 338 of 22 October 1973

The Security Council
...
2. *Calls upon* the parties concerned to start immediately after the cease-fire the implementation of Security Council Resolution 242 (1967) in all of its parts;

5.5.2 TREATY OF PEACE BETWEEN EGYPT AND ISRAEL, 1979

The Government of the Arab Republic of Egypt and the Government of the State of Israel;

Preamble

Convinced of the urgent necessity of the establishment of a just, comprehensive and lasting peace in the Middle East in accordance with Security Council Resolutions 242 and 338;
    Reaffirming their adherence to the 'Framework for Peace in the Middle East Agreed at Camp David,' dated September 17, 1978;
...
    Agree to the following provisions in the free exercise of their sovereignty, in order to implement the 'Framework for the Conclusion of a Peace Treaty Between Egypt and Israel':
...

Article V

1. Ships of Israel, and cargoes destined for or coming from Israel, shall enjoy the right of free passage through the Suez Canal and its approaches through the Gulf of Suez and the Mediterranean Sea on the basis of the Constantinople Convention of 1888, applying to all nations. Israeli nationals, vessels and cargoes, as well as persons, vessels and cargoes destined for or coming from Israel, shall be accorded non-discriminatory treatment in all matters connected with usage of the canal.

2. The Parties consider the Strait of Tiran and the Gulf of Aqaba to be international waterways open to all nations for unimpeded and non-suspendable freedom of navigation and overflight. The Parties will respect each other's right to navigation and overflight for access to either country through the Strait of Tiran and the Gulf of Aqaba.

...

Agreed Minute to Article V

Article V

The second sentence of paragraph 2 of Article V shall not be construed as limiting the first sentence of that paragraph. The foregoing is not to be construed as contravening the second sentence of paragraph 2 of Article V, which reads as follows:

"The Parties will respect each other's right to navigation and overflight for access to either country through the Strait of Tiran and the Gulf of Aqaba."

5.5.3 ISRAELI NOTE TO UN SECRETARY-GENERAL ON STRAIT OF TIRAN AND GULF OF AQABA, 9 DECEMBER 1984

The Permanent Mission of Israel to the United Nations sent to the Secretary-General of the United Nations a Note dated 9 December 1984, which reads as follows:

The concerns of the Government of Israel, with regard to the law of the sea, relate principally to ensuring maximum freedom of navigation and overflight everywhere and particularly through straits used for international navigation.

In this regard, the Government of Israel states that the regime of navigation and overflight, confirmed by the 1979 Treaty of Peace between Israel and Egypt, in which the Strait of Tiran and the Gulf of Aqaba are considered by the Parties to be international waterways open to all nations for unimpeded and non-suspendable freedom of navigation and overflight, is applicable to the said areas. Moreover, being fully compatible with the United Nations Convention on the Law of the Sea, the regime of the Peace Treaty will continue to prevail and to be applicable to the said areas.

It is the understanding of the Government of Israel that the declaration of the Arab Republic of Egypt in this regard, upon its ratification of the Convention (C.N.272.1983 Treaties 16 Depositary Notification, 10 November 1983), is consonant with the above declaration.

[Source: *Law of the Sea Bulletin*, No.4, February 1985, p.23.]

5.6 DOCUMENTS ON THE STRAITS OF MALACCA AND SINGAPORE

5.6.1 JOINT STATEMENT OF THE GOVERNMENTS OF INDONESIA, MALAYSIA AND SINGAPORE, 16 NOVEMBER 1971

1. The Governments of the Republic of Indonesia, Malaysia and the Republic of Singapore held consultations with a view to adopting a common position on matters relating to the Straits of Malacca and Singapore.
...
4. The results of the above mentioned consultations were as follows:
(i) The three governments agreed that the safety of navigation in the Straits of Malacca and Singapore is the responsibility of the coastal states concerned;
(ii) the three governments agreed on the need for tripartite co-operation on the safety of navigation in the two straits;
(iii) the three governments agreed that a body for cooperation to co-ordinate efforts for the safety of navigation in the Straits of Malacca and Singapore be established as soon as possible and that such body should be composed of only the three coastal states concerned;
(iv) the three governments also agreed that the problem of the safety of navigation and the question of internationalisation of the straits are two separate issues;
(v) the Governments of the Republic of Indonesia and of Malaysia agreed that the Straits of Malacca and Singapore are not international straits while fully recognizing their use for international shipping in accordance with the principle of innocent passage. The Government of Singapore takes note of the position of the Governments of the Republic of Indonesia and of Malaysia on this point;
(vi) on the basis of this understanding the three governments approved the continuation of the hydrographic survey.

[Source: Department of Foreign Affairs of Republic of Indonesia]

5.6.2 JOINT STATEMENT ON SAFETY OF NAVIGATION IN THE STRAITS OF MALACCA AND SINGAPORE, 24 FEBRUARY 1977

The meeting of the foreign ministers of Indonesia, Malaysia and Singapore was held in Manila on 24 February 1977 to consider measures to enhance safety of navigation and to promote close co-operation and co-ordination on anti-pollution policy and measures in the Straits of Malacca and Singapore.
...
The Foreign Ministers considered and reviewed the report of the senior officials meeting in Jakarta from 20 to 21 December 1976 and signed the agreement on safety of navigation in the Straits of Malacca and Singapore, adopting the following recommendations:
(i) Vessels maintain a single under keel clearance (UKC) of at least 3.5 metres at all times during the entire passage through the Straits of Malacca and Singapore

and that they also take all necessary safety precautions especially when navigating through critical areas.

(ii) The delineation of the traffic separation scheme (TSS) in three specified critical areas of the Straits of Malacca and Singapore, namely in the One Fathom Bank area, the Main Strait and Phillip Channel, and off Horsburgh Lighthouse.

(iii) Deep draught vessels, namely vessels having draughts of 15 metres and above, are required to pass through the designated deep water route (DWR) in the Strait of Singapore up to Buffalo Rock and are recommended to navigate in the specified route from Buffalo Rock up to Batu Berhanti area. Other vessels are recommended not to enter the DWR except in an emergency.

(iv) Navigational aids and facilities be improved for the effective and efficient implementation of the TSS.

(v) The existing voluntary reporting procedure and mechanism for large vessels be maintained.

(vi) The principle of voluntary pilotage through the critical areas in the Strait of Singapore be applied.

(vii) VLCCs and deep draught vessels are advised to navigate at a speed of not more than 12 knots during their passage through critical areas, and that no overtaking be allowed in the DWR.

(viii) Charts and current and tidal data be improved.

(ix) Rule 10 of the International Regulations for Preventing Collisions at Sea, 1972, be applied as far as practicable within the TSS.

(x) The implementation of the TSS should not pose a financial burden on the coastal states and the necessary funds be obtained from the users.

(xi) A joint policy to deal with marine pollution be formulated.

(xii) All tankers and large vessels navigating through the Straits of Malacca and Singapore be adequately covered by insurance and compensation schemes.

...

[Source: Department of Foreign Affairs of Republic of Indonesia]

5.6.3 IMCO ASSEMBLY RESOLUTION A.375(X) ON NAVIGATION THROUGH THE STRAITS OF MALACCA AND SINGAPORE, 14 NOVEMBER 1977

THE ASSEMBLY,

NOTING Article 16(i) of the Convention on the Inter-Governmental Maritime Consultative Organization concerning the functions of the Assembly,

BEING AWARE of the close relationship between safety of navigation and the prevention of pollution from ships,

BEING INFORMED of the decisions and measures taken by the Governments of Indonesia, Malaysia and Singapore concerning the safety of navigation and the protection of the marine environment in the Straits of Malacca and Singapore, given in the Annexes to this Resolution,

CONSIDERING Resolution A.378(X) by which the Assembly adopted general provisions on ships. routing,

HAVING EXAMINED the Recommendation by the Maritime Safety Committee at its thirty-seventh session,

ADOPTS the new routing system for the Straits of Malacca and Singapore including traffic separation schemes, deep-water routes and rules described in Annexes I to V to this Resolution,

ENDORSES the necessity that all oil tankers navigating through the Straits shall be adequately covered by relevant insurance and compensation schemes for oil pollution damage, including clean-up costs,

AGREES that the additional and improved aids to navigation listed in Part II of Annex VI to this Resolution will represent an important contribution to the safety of navigation of ships using the new routing system,

INVITES the Governments concerned to advise ships to comply with this Resolution,

REQUESTS the Secretary-General to advise all concerned of the details of this routing system described in the Annexes to this Resolution and to promulgate the date of entry into force as determined by the Governments concerned.

...

ANNEX V
Rules for vessels navigating through the Straits of Malacca and Singapore

I. *Definitions*
For the purpose of these Rules the following definitions should apply:
1. A vessel having a draught of 15 metres or more shall be deemed to be a deep draught vessel.
2. A tanker of 150,00 dwt and above shall be deemed to be a Very Large Crude Carrier (VLCC).
Note: The above definitions do not prejudice the definition of "vessel constrained by her draught" described in Rule 3(h) of the International Regulations for Preventing Collisions at Sea, 1972.

II. *General Provisions*
1. Deep draught vessels and VLCC's shall allow for an Under Keel Clearance (UKC) of at least 3.5 metres at all times during the entire passage through the Straits of Malacca and Singapore and shall also take all necessary safety precautions especially when navigating through the traffic separation schemes.
2. Masters of deep draught vessels and VLCCs shall have particular regard to navigational constraints when planning their passage through the Straits.
3. All deep draught vessels and VLCCs navigating within the traffic separation schemes are recommended to use the pilotage service of the respective countries when they become available.
4. [All tankers navigating through the Straits shall be adequately covered by insurance and compensation schemes.]

III. *Rules*
Rule 1(a) Deep draught vessels shall use the designated Deep-Water Route (DWR) between positions 01°09'57"N., 103°48'17"E, and 01°02'58"N., 103°39'06"E. Other vessels should as far as practicable, avoid the deep-water route.

(b) Deep draught vessels are advised to use the deep-water route between Buffalo Rock and Batu Berhanti.
Rule 2 – Deep draught vessels navigating in the deep-water route shall, as far as practicable, avoid overtaking.

Rule 3 – All vessels navigating within the traffic separation scheme shall proceed in the appropriate traffic lane in the general direction of traffic flow for that lane and maintain as steady a course as possible consistent with safe navigation.

Rule 4 – In the event of an emergency or breakdown of a vessel in the traffic lane it shall, as far as practicable and safe, leave the lane by pulling out to the starboard side.

Rule 5 – Westbound vessels when approaching Raffles Lighthouse in the Strait of Singapore shall proceed with caution, taking note of locally established signals, and give way to deep draught vessels approaching the Single Buoy Mooring facility (in approximate position Lat. 1°11'25"N., long. 103°47'30"E.) from Phillip Channel.

Rule 6 – VLCCs and deep draught vessels are advised to navigate at a speed of not more than 12 knots over the ground.

Rule 7 – All vessels navigating in the traffic separation scheme shall maintain at all times a safe speed consistent with safe navigation, shall proceed with caution and shall be in a maximum state of manoeuvering readiness.

Rule 8 – VLCCs and deep draught vessels navigating in the Straits of Malacca and Singapore are advised to participate in the existing voluntary ships' reporting system. Under this system, such vessels broadcast eight hours before entering the Straits/traffic separation schemes, navigational warnings giving names, deadweight tonnage, draught, speed and times of passing One Fathom Bank Lighthouse, Raffles Lighthouse and Horsburgh Lighthouse. Difficult and unwieldy tows also broadcast similar warnings giving the type, length, speed of tows and times of passing the three above-mentioned areas.

Rule 9 – All vessels navigating in the Straits of Malacca and Singapore are requested to report by radio to the nearest shore authority any damage or malfunction of the aids to navigation in the Straits, or any aids out of position in the Straits.

Rule 10 – Flag States, owners and operators should ensure that their vessels are adequately equipped in accordance with the appropriate international conventions/ recommendations.

IV. *Warning*

Mariners are warned that local traffic which could be unaware of the internationally agreed regulations and practices of seafarers, may be encountered in or near the traffic separation schemes, and should take any precautions which may be required by the ordinary practice of seamen or by the special circumstances of the case.

5.6.4 STATEMENT RELATING TO ARTICLE 233 OF THE DRAFT CONVENTION ON THE LAW OF THE SEA IN ITS APPLICATION TO THE STRAITS OF MALACCA AND SINGAPORE

[This statement was made in the Annex to a Letter dated 28 April 1982 from Malaysia to the President of UNCLOS III (A/CONF.62/L.145, *UNCLOS III Off. Rec.*, Vol.XVI, p.251).   The Draft Convention on the Law of the Sea (A/CONF.62/L.78, 28 August 1981) to which it refers was the last of a succession of UNCLOS III negotiating texts prior to the adoption of the UN Convention on 30 April 1982.]

Following consultations held among the delegations of States concerned, a common understanding regarding the purpose and meaning of article 233 of the draft convention on the law of the sea in its application to the Straits of Malacca and Singapore has been confirmed. This understanding, which takes cognizance of the peculiar geographic and traffic conditions in the Straits, and which recognizes the need to promote safety of navigation and to protect and preserve the marine environment in the Straits, is as follows:

1. Laws and regulations enacted by States bordering the Straits under article 42, paragraph 1(a) of the convention, refer to laws and regulations relating to traffic separation schemes, including the determination of under keel clearance for the Straits provided in article 41.

2. Accordingly, a violation of the provision of resolution A.375(X),[a] by the Inter-Governmental Maritime Consultative Organization adopted on 14 November 1977, whereby the vessels referred to therein shall allow for an under keel clearance of at least 3.5 metres during passage through the Straits of Malacca and Singapore, shall be deemed, in view of the peculiar geographic and traffic conditions of the Straits, to be a violation within the meaning of article 233. The States bordering the Straits may take appropriate enforcement measures, as provided for in article 233. Such measures may include preventing a vessel violating the required under keel clearance from proceeding. Such action shall not constitute denying, hampering, impairing or suspending the right of transit passage in breach of articles 42, paragraph 2 or 44 of the draft convention.

3. States bordering the Straits may take appropriate enforcement measures in accordance with article 233, against vessels violating the laws and regulations referred to in article 42, paragraph 1(a) and (b) causing or threatening major damage to the marine environment of the Straits.

4. States bordering the Straits shall, in taking the enforcement measures, observe the provisions on safeguards in Section 7, Part XII of the draft convention.

5. Articles 42 and 233 do not affect the rights and obligations of States bordering the Straits regarding appropriate enforcement measures with respect to vessels in the Straits not in transit passage.

6. Nothing in the above understanding is intended to impair:

(a) the sovereign immunity of ships and the provisions of article 236 as well as the international responsibility of the flag State in accordance with paragraph 5 of article 42;

(b) the duty of the flag State to take appropriate measures to ensure that its ships comply with article 39, without prejudice to the rights of States bordering the Straits under Parts III and XII of the draft convention and the provisions of paragraphs 1, 2, 3 and 4 of this statement.

a. Note omitted.

5.7 UNITED KINGDOM AND FRANCE: JOINT DECLARATION ON TRANSIT PASSAGE IN STRAITS OF DOVER, 2 NOVEMBER 1988

On the occasion of the signature of the Agreement relating to the delimitation of the territorial sea in the Straits of Dover, the two Governments agreed on the following declaration:

The existence of a specific regime of navigation in straits is generally accepted in the current state of international law. The need for such a regime is particularly clear in straits, such as the Straits of Dover, used for international navigation and linking two parts of the high seas or economic zones in the absence of any other route of similar convenience with respect to navigation.

In consequence, the two Governments recognize rights of unimpeded transit passage for merchant vessels, State vessels and, in particular, warships following their normal mode of navigation, as well as the right of overflight for aircraft, in the Straits of Dover. It is understood that, in accordance with the principles governing this regime under the rules of international law, such passage will be exercised in a continuous and expeditious manner.

The two Governments will continue to co-operate closely, both bilaterally and through the International Maritime Organization, in the interests of ensuring the safety of navigation in the Straits of Dover, as well as in the southern North Sea and the Channel. In particular, the traffic separation scheme in the Straits of Dover will not be affected by the entry into force of the Agreement.

With due regard to the interests of the coastal States the two Governments will also take, in accordance with international agreements in force and generally accepted rules and regulations, measures necessary in order to prevent, reduce and control pollution of the marine environment by vessels.

5.8 UNITED STATES: PRESIDENTIAL STATEMENT ON UNITED STATES OCEANS POLICY, 10 MARCH 1983: EXCERPT

...

The United States has long been a leader in developing customary and conventional law of the sea. Our objectives have consistently been to provide a legal order that will, among other things, facilitate peaceful, international uses of the oceans and provide for equitable and effective management and conservation of marine resources. The United States also recognizes that all nations have an interest in these issues.

Last July I announced that the United States will not sign the United Nations Law of the Sea Convention that was opened for signature on December 10.

...

However, the convention also contains provisions with respect to traditional uses of the oceans which generally confirm existing maritime law and practice and fairly balance the interests of all states.

Today I am announcing three decisions to promote and protect the oceans interests of the United States in a manner consistent with those fair and balanced results in the Convention and international law.

...

Second, the United States will exercise and assert its navigation and overflight rights and freedoms on a worldwide basis in a manner that is consistent with the balance of interests reflected in the convention. The United States will not, however, acquiesce in unilateral acts of other states designed to restrict the rights and freedoms of the international community in navigation and overflight and other related high seas uses.

[See also Document 8.3 for other parts of the Presidential Statement.]

6 Archipelagos

Article 46
Use of terms

For the purposes of this Convention:
(a) "archipelagic State" means a State constituted wholly by one or more archipelagos and may include other islands;
(b) "archipelago" means a group of islands, including parts of islands, interconnecting waters and other natural features which are so closely interrelated that such islands, waters and other natural features form an intrinsic geographical, economic and political entity, or which historically have been regarded as such.

Article 47
Archipelagic baselines

1. An archipelagic State may draw straight archipelagic baselines joining the outermost points of the outermost islands and drying reefs of the archipelago provided that within such baselines are included the main islands and an area in which the ratio of the area of the water to the area of the land, including atolls, is between 1 to 1 and 9 to 1.
2. The length of such baselines shall not exceed 100 nautical miles, except that up to 3 per cent of the total number of baselines enclosing any archipelago may exceed that length, up to a maximum length of 125 nautical miles.
3. The drawing of such baselines shall not depart to any appreciable extent from the general configuration of the archipelago.

4. Such baselines shall not be drawn to and from low-tide elevations, unless lighthouses or similar installations which are permanently above sea level have been built on them or where a low-tide elevation is situated wholly or partly at a distance not exceeding the breadth of the territorial sea from the nearest island.

5. The system of such baselines shall not be applied by an archipelagic State in such a manner as to cut off from the high seas or the exclusive economic zone the territorial sea of another State.

6. If a part of the archipelagic waters of an archipelagic State lies between two parts of an immediately adjacent neighbouring State, existing rights and all other legitimate interests which the latter State has traditionally exercised in such waters and all rights stipulated by agreement between those States shall continue and be respected.

7. For the purpose of computing the ratio of water to land under paragraph 1, land areas may include waters lying within the fringing reefs of islands and atolls, including that part of a steep-sided oceanic plateau which is enclosed or nearly enclosed by a chain of limestone islands and drying reefs lying on the perimeter of the plateau.

8. The baselines drawn in accordance with this article shall be shown on charts of a scale or scales adequate for ascertaining their position. Alternatively, lists of geographical co-ordinates of points, specifying the geodetic datum, may be substituted.

9. The archipelagic State shall give due publicity to such charts or lists of geographical co-ordinates and shall deposit a copy of each such chart or list with the Secretary-General of the United Nations.

Article 48
Measurement of the breadth of the territorial sea, the contiguous zone, the exclusive economic zone and the continental shelf

The breadth of the territorial sea, the contiguous zone, the exclusive economic zone and the continental shelf shall be measured from archipelagic baselines drawn in accordance with article 47.

Article 49
Legal status of archipelagic waters, of the air space over archipelagic waters and of their bed and subsoil

1. The sovereignty of an archipelagic State extends to the waters enclosed by the archipelagic baselines drawn in accordance with article 47, described as archipelagic waters, regardless of their depth or distance from the coast.

2. This sovereignty extends to the air space over the archipelagic waters, as well as to their bed and subsoil, and the resources contained therein.

3. This sovereignty is exercised subject to this Part.

4. The regime of archipelagic sea lanes passage established in this Part shall not in other respects affect the status of the archipelagic waters, including the sea lanes, or the exercise by the archipelagic State of its sovereignty over such waters and their air space, bed and subsoil, and the resources contained therein.

Article 50
Delimitation of internal waters

Within its archipelagic waters, the archipelagic State may draw closing lines for the delimitation of internal waters, in accordance with articles 9, 10 and 11.

Article 51
Existing agreements, traditional fishing rights and existing submarine cables

1. Without prejudice to article 49, an archipelagic State shall respect existing agreements with other States and shall recognize traditional fishing rights and other legitimate activities of the immediately adjacent neighbouring States in certain areas falling within archipelagic waters. The terms and conditions for the exercise of such rights and activities, including the nature, the extent and the areas to which they apply, shall, at the request of any of the States concerned, be regulated by bilateral agreements between them. Such rights shall not be transferred to or shared with third States or their nationals.
2. An archipelagic State shall respect existing submarine cables laid by other States and passing through its waters without making a landfall. An archipelagic State shall permit the maintenance and replacement of such cables upon receiving due notice of their location and the intention to repair or replace them.

Article 52
Right of innocent passage

1. Subject to article 53 and without prejudice to article 50, ships of all States enjoy the right of innocent passage through archipelagic waters, in accordance with Part II, section 3.
2. The archipelagic State may, without discrimination in form or in fact among foreign ships, suspend temporarily in specified areas of its archipelagic waters the innocent passage of foreign ships if such suspension is essential for the protection of its security. Such suspension shall take effect only after having been duly published.

Article 53
Right of archipelagic sea lanes passage

1. An archipelagic State may designate sea lanes and air routes thereabove, suitable for the continuous and expeditious passage of foreign ships and aircraft through or over its archipelagic waters and the adjacent territorial sea.
2. All ships and aircraft enjoy the right of archipelagic sea lanes passage in such sea lanes and air routes.
3. Archipelagic sea lanes passage means the exercise in accordance with this Convention of the rights of navigation and overflight in the normal mode solely for the purpose of continuous, expeditious and unobstructed transit between one part of the high seas or an exclusive economic zone and another part of the high seas or an exclusive economic zone.
4. Such sea lanes and air routes shall traverse the archipelagic waters and the adjacent territorial sea and shall include all normal passage routes used as routes for international navigation or overflight through or over archipelagic waters and, within such routes, so far as ships are concerned, all normal navigational channels, provided that duplication of routes of similar convenience between the same entry and exit points shall not be necessary.
5. Such sea lanes and air routes shall be defined by a series of continuous axis lines from the entry points of passage routes to the exit points. Ships and aircraft in archipelagic sea lanes passage shall not deviate more than 25 nautical miles to either side of such axis lines during passage, provided that such ships and aircraft shall not navigate closer to the coasts than 10 per cent of the distance between the nearest points on islands bordering the sea lane.

6.   An archipelagic State which designates sea lanes under this article may also prescribe traffic separation schemes for the safe passage of ships through narrow channels in such sea lanes.

7.   An archipelagic State may, when circumstances require, after giving due publicity thereto, substitute other sea lanes or traffic separation schemes for any sea lanes or traffic separation schemes previously designated or prescribed by it.

8.   Such sea lanes and traffic separation schemes shall conform to generally accepted international regulations.

9.   In designating or substituting sea lanes or prescribing or substituting traffic separation schemes, an archipelagic State shall refer proposals to the competent international organization with a view to their adoption.   The organization may adopt only such sea lanes and traffic separation schemes as may be agreed with the archipelagic State, after which the archipelagic State may designate, prescribe or substitute them.

10. The archipelagic State shall clearly indicate the axis of the sea lanes and the traffic separation schemes established in accordance with this article.

11. Ships in archipelagic sea lanes passage shall respect applicable sea lanes and traffic separation schemes established in accordance with this article.

12. If an archipelagic State does not designate sea lanes or air routes, the right of archipelagic sea lanes passage may be exercised through the routes normally used for international navigation.

Article 54
Duties of ships and aircraft during their passage, research and survey activities, duties of the archipelagic State and laws and regulations of the archipelagic State relating to archipelagic sea lanes passage

Articles 39, 40, 42 and 44 apply *mutatis mutandis* to archipelagic sea lanes passage.

6.2 INDONESIA: ACT NO.4 OF 18 FEBRUARY 1960 CONCERNING INDONESIAN WATERS

The President of the Republic of Indonesia

Considering:
1.   that the geographical configuration of Indonesia as an archipelagic State which consists of thousands of islands has its own characteristics and peculiarities,
2.   that since time immemorial the Indonesian archipelago has constituted one entity,
3.   that in the interest of the territorial integrity of the Indonesian State all the islands and the waters lying between those islands should be regarded as a single unit,
4.   that the delimitation of the territorial waters as provided for in article 1, paragraph 1 of the Territorial Sea and Maritime Circles Ordinance of 1939 (Government Gazette 1939 No.442) is not in accordance with the above considerations, as it divided the territory of Indonesia into separate parts having their own territorial sea,
5.   that it is therefore deemed necessary to enact an Act concerning the Indonesian waters in accordance with the above considerations,

Having regard to:
Article 5 paragraph I of the Constitution of the Republic of Indonesia

Having heard:
The deliberations of the Cabinet of Ministers of 20 January 1960,

Decides to enact:

Act Concerning Indonesian Waters:

Article 1

(1) The Indonesian waters consist of the territorial sea and the internal waters of Indonesia.
(2) The Indonesian territorial sea is a maritime belt of a width of 12 nautical miles, the outer limit of which is measured perpendicular to the baselines or points on the baselines which consist of straight lines connecting the outermost points on the low water mark of the outermost islands or part of such islands comprising Indonesian territory with the provision that in case straits of a width of not more than 24 nautical miles and Indonesia is not the only coastal state the outer limit of the Indonesian territorial sea shall be drawn at the middle of the strait.
(3) The Indonesian internal waters are all waters lying within the baselines mentioned in paragraph (2).
(4) One nautical mile is one sixtieth of a meridian.

Article 2

On the map annexed to this Act is indicated the position of the points and baselines mentioned in article 1 paragraph (2).

Article 3

(1) Innocent passage through the internal waters of Indonesia is open to foreign vessels.
(2) The innocent passage which is mentioned in paragraph 1 shall be regulated by Government Ordinance.

Article 4

(1) This Act comes into force on the date of its promulgation.
(2) Article 1 paragraph 1 sub-paragraphs 1 to 4 of the Territorial Sea and Maritime Circles Ordinance of 1939 is no longer valid as from the date mentioned in paragraph 1.

[Annexed map and list of co-ordinates for straight baselines omitted.]

6.3 THE PHILIPPINES: AN ACT TO DEFINE THE BASELINES OF THE TERRITORIAL SEA OF THE PHILIPPINES ACT NO.3046 OF 17 JUNE 1961

Whereas, the Constitution of the Philippines describes the national territory as comprising all the territory ceded to the United States by the Treaty of Paris concluded between the United States and Spain on December 10, 1898, the limits of which are set forth in Article III of said treaty together with all the islands embraced in the treaty concluded at Washington, between the United States and Spain on November 7, 1900, and in the treaty concluded between the United States and Great Britain on January 2, 1930, and all the territory over which the Government of the Philippine Islands exercised jurisdiction at the time of the adoption of the Constitution.

Whereas, all the waters within the limits set forth in the above-mentioned treaties have always been regarded as part of the territory of the Philippine Islands;

Whereas, all the waters around, between and connecting the various islands of the Philippine archipelago, irrespective of their width or dimension, have always been considered as necessary appurtenances of the land territory, forming part of the inland or internal waters of the Philippines;

Whereas, all waters beyond the outermost islands of the archipelago but within the limits of the boundaries set forth in the aforementioned treaties comprise the territorial sea of the Philippines;

Whereas, the baselines from which the territorial sea of the Philippines is determined consist of straight lines joining appropriate points of the outermost islands of the archipelago; and

Whereas, the said baselines should be clarified and specifically defined and described for the information of all concerned; Now, therefore,

Be it enacted by the Senate and House of Representatives of the Philippines in Congress assemblage.

Sec.1. The baselines for the territorial sea of the Philippines are hereby defined and described specifically as follows: [list of co-ordinates for straight baselines omitted.]

Sec.2. All waters within the baselines provided for in Section one hereof are considered inland or internal waters of the Philippines.

Sec.3. This Act shall take effect upon its approval.

6.4 THE PHILIPPINES: DECLARATION MADE UPON SIGNATURE AND CONFIRMED UPON RATIFICATION OF THE UN CONVENTION ON THE LAW OF THE SEA, 1982, 10 DECEMBER 1982 AND 8 MAY 1984

1. The signing of the Convention by the Government of the Republic of the Philippines shall not in any manner impair or prejudice the sovereign rights of the Republic of the Philippines under and arising from the Constitution of the Philippines;

2. Such signing shall not in any manner affect the sovereign rights of the Republic of the Philippines as successor of the United States of America, under and arising out of

the Treaty of Paris between Spain and the United States of America of December 10, 1898, and the Treaty of Washington between the United States of America and Great Britain of January 2, 1930;

3. Such signing shall not diminish or in any manner affect the rights and obligations of the contracting parties under the Mutual Defence Treaty between the Philippines and the United States of America of August 30, 1951, and its related interpretative instruments; nor those under any other pertinent bilateral or multilateral treaty or agreement to which the Philippines is a party.

4. Such signing shall not in any manner impair or prejudice the sovereignty of the Republic of the Philippines over any territory over which it exercises sovereign authority, such as the Kalayaan Islands, and the waters appurtenant thereto;

5. The Convention shall not be construed as amending in any manner any pertinent laws and Presidential Decrees or Proclamations of the Republic of the Philippines; the Government of the Republic of the Philippines maintains and reserves the right and authority to make any amendments to such laws, decrees or proclamations pursuant to the provisions of the Philippine Constitution;

6. The provisions of the Convention on archipelagic passage through sea lanes do not nullify or impair the sovereignty of the Philippines as an archipelagic state over the sea lanes and do not deprive it of authority to enact legislation to protect its sovereignty, independence, and security;

7. The concept of archipelagic waters is similar to the concept of internal waters under the Constitution of the Philippines, and removes straits connecting these waters with the economic zone or high sea from the rights of foreign vessels to transit passage for international navigation;

8. The agreement of the Republic of the Philippines to the submission for peaceful resolution, under any of the procedures provided in the Convention, of disputes under Article 298 shall not be considered as a derogation of Philippine sovereignty.

6.5 RUSSIAN FEDERATION (USSR): OBJECTION TO DECLARATION MADE BY THE PHILIPPINES CONCERNING THE UN CONVENTION ON THE LAW OF THE SEA, 1982, 25 FEBRUARY 1985

The Union of Soviet Socialist Republics considers that the statement made by the Philippines upon signature, and then confirmed upon ratification, of the United Nations Convention on the Law of the Sea in essence contains reservations and exceptions to the Convention, which is prohibited under article 309 of the Convention. At the same time, the statement of the Philippines is incompatible with article 310 of the Convention, under which a State, when signing or ratifying the Convention, may make declarations or statements only "provided that such declarations or statements do not purport to exclude or to modify the legal effect of the provisions of this Convention in their application to that State".

The discrepancy between the Philippine statement and the Convention can be seen, *inter alia*, from the affirmation by the Philippines that "The concept of archipelagic waters is similar to the concept of internal waters under the Constitution of the Philippines, and removes straits connecting these waters with the economic zone or high sea from the rights of foreign vessels to transit passage for international navigation". Moreover, the statement emphasizes more than once that, despite its ratification of the Convention, the Philippines will continue to be guided in matters relating to the sea, not by the Convention and the obligations under it, but by its domestic law and by agreements it has already concluded which are not in line with the Convention.   Thus, the Philippines not only is evading the harmonization of its legislation with the Convention but also is refusing to fulfil one of its most fundamental obligations under the Convention − namely, to respect the regime of archipelagic waters, which provides that foreign ships enjoy the right of archipelagic passage through, and foreign aircraft the right of overflight over, such waters.

In view of the foregoing, the USSR cannot recognize as lawful the statement of the Philippines and considers it to be without legal effect in the light of the provisions of the Convention.

Furthermore, the Soviet Union is gravely concerned by the fact that, upon signing the Convention, a number of other States have also made statements of a similar type conflicting with the Convention.   If such statements are also made later on, at the ratification stage or upon accession to the Convention, the purport and meaning of the Convention, which establishes a universal and uniform regime for the use of the oceans and seas and their resources, could be undermined and this important instrument of international law impaired.

Taking into account the statement of the Philippines and the statements made by a number of other countries upon signing the Convention, together with the statements that might possibly be made subsequently upon ratification of and accession to the Convention, the Permanent Mission of the USSR considers that it would be appropriate for the Secretary-General of the United Nations to conduct, in accordance with article 319, paragraph 2(a), a study of a general nature on the problem of ensuring universal application of the provisions of the Convention, including the question of the harmonization of the national legislation of States with the Convention.   The results of such a study should be included in the report of the Secretary-General to the United Nations General Assembly at its fortieth session under the agenda item entitled "Law of the sea".

6.6 AUSTRALIA: OBJECTION TO DECLARATION MADE BY THE PHILIPPINES CONCERNING THE UN CONVENTION ON THE LAW OF THE SEA, 1982, 3 AUGUST 1988

Australia considers that this declaration made by the Republic of the Philippines is not consistent with article 309 of the Law of the Sea Convention, which prohibits the making of reservations, nor with article 310 which permits declarations to be made 'provided that such declarations or statements do not purport to exclude or to modify the legal effect of the provisions of this Convention in their application to that State'.

The declaration of the Republic of the Philippines asserts that the Convention shall not affect the sovereign rights of the Philippines arising from its Constitution, its domestic legislation and any treaties to which the Philippines is a party.   This indicates, in effect, that the Philippines does not consider that it is obliged to harmonize its laws with the provisions of the Convention.   By making such an assertion, the Philippines is seeking to modify the legal effect of the Convention's provisions.

This view is supported by the specific reference in the declaration to the status of archipelagic waters.   The declaration states that the concept of archipelagic waters in the Convention is similar to the concept of internal waters held under former constitutions of the Philippines and recently reaffirmed in article 1 of the New

Constitution of the Philippines in 1987.   It is clear, however, that the Convention distinguishes the two concepts and that different obligations and rights are applicable to archipelagic waters from those which apply to internal waters.   In particular, the Convention provides for the exercise by foreign ships of the rights of innocent passage and of archipelagic sea lanes passage in archipelagic waters.

Australia cannot, therefore, accept that the statement of the Philippines has any legal effect or will have any effect when the Convention comes into force and considers that the provisions of the Convention should be observed without being made subject to the restrictions asserted in the declaration of the Republic of the Philippines.

6.7 THE PHILIPPINES: DECLARATION CONCERNING AN OBJECTION BY AUSTRALIA, 26 OCTOBER 1988

The Philippines declaration was made in conformity with article 310 of the United Nations Convention on the Law of the Sea.   The declaration consists of interpretative statements concerning certain provisions of the Convention.

The Philippine Government intends to harmonize its domestic legislation with the provisions of the Convention.

The necessary steps are being undertaken to enact legislation dealing with archipelagic sea lanes passage and the exercise of Philippine sovereign rights over archipelagic waters, in accordance with the Convention.

The Philippine Government, therefore, wishes to assure the Australian Government and the States Parties to the Convention that the Philippines will abide by the provisions of the said Convention.

7 The Continental Shelf

7.1 UNITED NATIONS CONVENTION ON THE LAW OF THE SEA, 1982: PART VI: CONTINENTAL SHELF

Article 76
Definition of the continental shelf

1. The continental shelf of a coastal State comprises the sea-bed and subsoil of the submarine areas that extend beyond its territorial sea throughout the natural prolongation of its land territory to the outer edge of the continental margin, or to a distance of 200 nautical miles from the baselines from which the breadth of the territorial sea is measured where the outer edge of the continental margin does not extend up to that distance.

2. The continental shelf of a coastal State shall not extend beyond the limits provided for in paragraphs 4 to 6.

3. The continental margin comprises the submerged prolongation of the land mass of the coastal State, and consists of the sea-bed and subsoil of the shelf, the slope and the rise. It does not include the deep ocean floor with its oceanic ridges or the subsoil thereof.

4. (a) For the purposes of this Convention, the coastal State shall establish the outer edge of the continental margin wherever the margin extends beyond 200 nautical miles from the baselines from which the breadth of the territorial sea is measured, by either:

    (i)   a line delineated in accordance with paragraph 7 by reference to the outermost fixed points at each of which the thickness of sedimentary rocks is at least 1 per cent of the shortest distance from such point to the foot of the continental slope; or

(ii)   a line delineated in accordance with paragraph 7 by reference to fixed points not more than 60 nautical miles from the foot of the continental slope.

(b) In the absence of evidence to the contrary, the foot of the continental slope shall be determined as the point of maximum change in the gradient at its base.

5.   The fixed points comprising the line of the outer limits of the continental shelf on the sea-bed, drawn in accordance with paragraph 4(a)(i) and (ii), either shall not exceed 350 nautical miles from the baselines from which the breadth of the territorial sea is measured or shall not exceed 100 nautical miles from the 2,500 metre isobath, which is a line connecting the depth of 2,500 metres.

6.   Notwithstanding the provisions of paragraph 5, on submarine ridges, the outer limit of the continental shelf shall not exceed 350 nautical miles from the baselines from which the breadth of the territorial sea is measured. This paragraph does not apply to submarine elevations that are natural components of the continental margin, such as its plateaux, rises, caps, banks and spurs.

7.   The coastal State shall delineate the outer limits of its continental shelf, where that shelf extends beyond 200 nautical miles from the baselines from which the breadth of the territorial sea is measured, by straight lines not exceeding 60 nautical miles in length, connecting fixed points, defined by co-ordinates of latitude and longitude.

8.   Information on the limits of the continental shelf beyond 200 nautical miles from the baselines from which the breadth of the territorial sea is measured shall be submitted by the coastal State to the Commission on the Limits of the Continental Shelf set up under Annex II on the basis of equitable geographical representation. The Commission shall make recommendations to coastal States on matters related to the establishment of the outer limits of their continental shelf. The limits of the shelf established by a coastal State on the basis of these recommendations shall be final and binding.

9.   The coastal State shall deposit with the Secretary-General of the United Nations charts and relevant information, including geodetic data, permanently describing the outer limits of its continental shelf. The Secretary-General shall give due publicity thereto.

10. The provisions of this article are without prejudice to the question of delimitation of the continental shelf between States with opposite or adjacent coasts.

Article 77
Rights of the coastal State over the continental shelf

1.   The coastal State exercises over the continental shelf sovereign rights for the purpose of exploring it and exploiting its natural resources.

2.   The rights referred to in paragraph 1 are exclusive in the sense that if the coastal State does not explore the continental shelf or exploit its natural resources, no one may undertake these activities without the express consent of the coastal State.

3.   The rights of the coastal State over the continental shelf do not depend on occupation, effective or notional, or on any express proclamation.

4.   The natural resources referred to in this Part consist of the mineral and other non-living resources of the sea-bed and subsoil together with living organisms belonging to sedentary species, that is to say, organisms which, at the harvestable stage, either are immobile on or under the sea-bed or are unable to move except in constant physical contact with the sea-bed or the subsoil.

Article 78
Legal status of the superjacent waters and air space and the rights and freedoms of other States

1.   The rights of the coastal State over the continental shelf do not affect the legal status of the superjacent waters or of the air space above those waters.

2.   The exercise of the rights of the coastal State over the continental shelf must not infringe or result in any unjustifiable interference with navigation and other rights and freedoms of other States as provided for in this Convention.

Article 79
Submarine cables and pipelines on the continental shelf

1.   All States are entitled to lay submarine cables and pipelines on the continental shelf, in accordance with the provisions of this article.

2.   Subject to its right to take reasonable measures for the exploration of the continental shelf, the exploitation of its natural resources and the prevention, reduction and control of pollution from pipelines, the coastal State may not impede the laying or maintenance of such cables or pipelines.

3.   The delineation of the course for the laying of such pipelines on the continental shelf is subject to the consent of the coastal State.

4.   Nothing in this Part affects the right of the coastal State to establish conditions for cables or pipelines entering its territory or territorial sea, or its jurisdiction over cables and pipelines constructed or used in connection with the exploration of its continental shelf or exploitation of its resources or the operations of artificial islands, installations and structures under its jurisdiction.

5.   When laying submarine cables or pipelines, States shall have due regard to cables or pipelines already in position.   In particular, possibilities of repairing existing cables or pipelines shall not be prejudiced.

Article 80
Artificial islands, installations and structures on the continental shelf

Article 60 applies *mutatis mutandis* to artificial islands, installations and structures on the continental shelf.

Article 81
Drilling on the continental shelf

The coastal State shall have the exclusive right to authorize and regulate drilling on the continental shelf for all purposes.

Article 82
Payments and contributions with respect to the exploitation of the continental shelf beyond 200 nautical miles

1.   The coastal State shall make payments or contributions in kind in respect of the exploitation of the non-living resources of the continental shelf beyond 200 nautical miles from the baselines from which the breadth of the territorial sea is measured.

2.   The payments and contributions shall be made annually with respect to all production at a site after the first five years of production at that site.   For the sixth year, the rate of payment or contribution shall be 1 per cent of the value or volume of production at the site.   The rate shall increase by 1 per cent for each subsequent year

until the twelfth year and shall remain at 7 per cent thereafter. Production does not include resources used in connection with exploitation.

3. A developing State which is a net importer of a mineral resource produced from its continental shelf is exempt from making such payments or contributions in respect of that mineral resource.

4. The payments or contributions shall be made through the Authority, which shall distribute them to States Parties to this Convention, on the basis of equal sharing criteria, taking into account the interests and needs of developing States, particularly the least developed and the land-locked among them.

Article 83
Delimitation of the continental shelf between States with opposite or adjacent coasts

1. The delimitation of the continental shelf between States with opposite or adjacent coasts shall be effected by agreement on the basis of international law, as referred to in Article 38 of the Statute of the International Court of Justice, in order to achieve an equitable solution.

2. If no agreement can be reached within a reasonable period of time, the States concerned shall resort to the procedures provided for in Part XV.

3. Pending agreement as provided for in paragraph 1, the States concerned, in a spirit of understanding and co-operation, shall make every effort to enter into provisional arrangements of a practical nature and, during this transitional period, not to jeopardize or hamper the reaching of the final agreement. Such arrangements shall be without prejudice to the final delimitation.

4. Where there is an agreement in force between the States concerned, questions relating to the delimitation of the continental shelf shall be determined in accordance with the provisions of that agreement.

Article 84
Charts and lists of geographical co-ordinates

1. Subject to this Part, the outer limit lines of the continental shelf and the lines of delimitation drawn in accordance with article 83 shall be shown on charts of a scale or scales adequate for ascertaining their position. Where appropriate, lists of geographical co-ordinates of points, specifying the geodetic datum, may be substituted for such outer limit lines or lines of delimitation.

2. The coastal State shall give due publicity to such charts or lists of geographical co-ordinates and shall deposit a copy of each such chart or list with the Secretary-General of the United Nations and, in the case of those showing the outer limit lines of the continental shelf, with the Secretary-General of the Authority.

Article 85
Tunnelling

This Part does not prejudice the right of the coastal State to exploit the subsoil by means of tunnelling, irrespective of the depth of water above the subsoil.

7.1.1 UNITED NATIONS CONVENTION ON THE LAW OF THE SEA, 1982: ANNEX II: COMMISSION ON THE LIMITS OF THE CONTINENTAL SHELF

Article 1

In accordance with the provisions of article 76, a Commission on the Limits of the Continental Shelf beyond 200 nautical miles shall be established in conformity with the following articles.

Article 2

1. The Commission shall consist of 21 members who shall be experts in the field of geology, geophysics or hydrography, elected by States Parties to this Convention from among their nationals, having due regard to the need to ensure equitable geographical representation, who shall serve in their personal capacities.
2. The initial election shall be held as soon as possible but in any case within 18 months after the date of entry into force of this Convention.   At least three months before the date of each election, the Secretary-General of the United Nations shall address a letter to the States Parties, inviting the submission of nominations, after appropriate regional consultations, within three months.   The Secretary-General shall prepare a list in alphabetical order of all persons thus nominated and shall submit it to all the States Parties.
3. Elections of the members of the Commission shall be held at a meeting of States Parties convened by the Secretary-General at United Nations Headquarters.   At that meeting, for which two-thirds of the States Parties shall constitute a quorum, the persons elected to the Commission shall be those nominees who obtain a two-thirds majority of the votes of the representatives of States Parties present and voting.   Not less than three members shall be elected from each geographical region.
4. The members of the Commission shall be elected for a term of five years.   They shall be eligible for re-election.
5. The State Party which submitted the nomination of a member of the Commission shall defray the expenses of that member while in performance of Commission duties. The coastal State concerned shall defray the expenses incurred in respect of the advice referred to in article 3, paragraph 1(b), of this Annex.   The secretariat of the Commission shall be provided by the Secretary-General of the United Nations.

Article 3

1. The functions of the Commission shall be:
(a) to consider data and other material submitted by coastal States concerning the outer limits of the continental shelf in areas where those limits extend beyond 200 nautical miles, and to make recommendations in accordance with article 76 and the Statement of Understanding adopted on 29 August 1980 by the Third United Nations Conference on the Law of the Sea;
(b) to provide scientific and technical advice, if requested by the coastal State concerned during the preparation of the data referred to in subparagraph (a).
2. The Commission may co-operate, to the extent considered necessary and useful, with the Intergovernmental Oceanographic Commission of UNESCO, the International Hydrographic Organization and other competent international organizations with a view

to exchanging scientific and technical information which might be of assistance in discharging the Commission's responsibilities.

Article 4

Where a coastal State intends to establish, in accordance with article 76, the outer limits of its continental shelf beyond 200 nautical miles, it shall submit particulars of such limits to the Commission along with supporting scientific and technical data as soon as possible but in any case within 10 years of the entry into force of this Convention for that State. The coastal State shall at the same time give the names of any Commission members who have provided it with scientific and technical advice.

Article 5

Unless the Commission decides otherwise, the Commission shall function by way of sub-commissions composed of seven members, appointed in a balanced manner taking into account the specific elements of each submission by a coastal State. Nationals of the coastal State making the submission who are members of the Commission and any Commission member who has assisted a coastal State by providing scientific and technical advice with respect to the delineation shall not be a member of the sub-commission dealing with that submission but has the right to participate as a member in the proceedings of the Commission concerning the said submission. The coastal State which has made a submission to the Commission may send its representatives to participate in the relevant proceedings without the right to vote.

Article 6

1. The sub-commission shall submit its recommendations to the Commission.
2. Approval by the Commission of the recommendations of the sub-commission shall be by a majority of two-thirds of Commission members present and voting.
3. The recommendations of the Commission shall be submitted in writing to the coastal State which made the submission and to the Secretary-General of the United Nations.

Article 7

Coastal States shall establish the outer limits of the continental shelf in conformity with the provisions of article 76, paragraph 8, and in accordance with the appropriate national procedures.

Article 8

In the case of disagreement by the coastal State with the recommendations of the Commission, the coastal State shall, within a reasonable time, make a revised or new submission to the Commission.

Article 9

The actions of the Commission shall not prejudice matters relating to delimitation of boundaries between States with opposite or adjacent coasts.

7.2 GENEVA CONVENTION ON THE CONTINENTAL SHELF, 1958

The States Parties to this Convention
Have agreed as follows:

Article 1

For the purpose of these Articles, the term 'continental shelf' is used as referring (a) to the seabed and subsoil of the submarine areas adjacent to the coast but outside the area of the territorial sea, to a depth of 200 metres or, beyond that limit, to where the depth of the superjacent waters admits of the exploitation of the natural resources of the said areas; (b) to the seabed and subsoil of similar submarine areas adjacent to the coasts of islands.

Article 2

1. The coastal State exercises over the continental shelf sovereign rights for the purpose of exploring it and exploiting its natural resources.
2. The rights referred to in paragraph 1 of this Article are exclusive in the sense that if the coastal State does not explore the continental shelf or exploit its natural resources, no one may undertake these activities, or make a claim to the continental shelf, without the express consent of the coastal State.
3. The rights of the coastal State over the continental shelf do not depend on occupation, effective or notional, or on any express proclamation.
4. The natural resources referred to in these Articles consist of the mineral and other non-living resources of the seabed and subsoil together with living organisms belonging to sedentary species, that is to say, organisms which, at the harvestable stage, either are immobile on or under the seabed or are unable to move except in constant physical contact with the seabed or the subsoil.

Article 3

The rights of the coastal State over the continental shelf do not affect the legal status of the superjacent waters as high seas, or that of the air space above those waters.

Article 4

Subject to its right to take reasonable measures for the exploration of the continental shelf and the exploitation of its natural resources, the coastal State may not impede the laying or maintenance of submarine cables or pipelines on the continental shelf.

Article 5

1. The exploration of the continental shelf and the exploitation of its natural resources must not result in any unjustifiable interference with navigation, fishing or the conservation of the living resources of the sea, nor result in any interference with fundamental oceanographic or other scientific research carried out with the intention of open publication.
2. Subject to the provisions of paragraphs 1 and 6 of this Article, the coastal State is entitled to construct and maintain or operate on the continental shelf installations and other devices necessary for its exploration and the exploitation of its natural resources,

and to establish safety zones around such installations and devices and to take in those zones measures necessary for their protection.

3.   The safety zones referred to in paragraph 2 of this Article may extend to a distance of 500 metres around the installations and other devices which have been erected, measured from each point of their outer edge. Ships of all nationalities must respect these safety zones.

4.   Such installations and devices, though under the jurisdiction of the coastal State, do not possess the status of islands. They have no territorial sea of their own, and their presence does not affect the delimitation of the territorial sea of the coastal State.

5.   Due notice must be given of the construction of any such installations, and permanent means for giving warning of their presence must be maintained. Any installations which are abandoned or disused must be entirely removed.

6.   Neither the installations or devices, nor the safety zones around them, may be established where interference may be caused to the use of recognized sea lanes essential to international navigation.

7.   The coastal State is obliged to undertake, in the safety zones, all appropriate measures for the protection of the living resources of the sea from harmful agents.

8.   The consent of the coastal State shall be obtained in respect of any research concerning the continental shelf and undertaken there. Nevertheless, the coastal State shall not normally withhold its consent if the request is submitted by a qualified institution with a view to purely scientific research into the physical or biological characteristics of the continental shelf, subject to the proviso that the coastal State shall have the right, if it so desires, to participate or to be represented in the research, and that in any event the results shall be published.

Article 6

1.   Where the same continental shelf is adjacent to the territories of two or more States whose coasts are opposite each other, the boundary of the continental shelf appertaining to such States shall be determined by agreement between them.   In the absence of agreement, and unless another boundary line is justified by special circumstances, the boundary is the median line, every point of which is equidistant from the nearest points of the baselines from which the breadth of the territorial sea of each State is measured.

2.   Where the same continental shelf is adjacent to the territories of two adjacent States, the boundary of the continental shelf shall be determined by agreement between them.   In the absence of agreement, and unless another boundary line is justified by special circumstances, the boundary shall be determined by application of the principle of equidistance from the nearest points of the baselines from which the breadth of the territorial sea of each State is measured.

3.   In delimiting the boundaries of the continental shelf, any lines which are drawn in accordance with the principles set out in paragraphs 1 and 2 of this Article should be defined with reference to charts and geographical features as they exist at a particular date, and reference should be made to fixed permanent identifiable points on the land.

Article 7

The provisions of these Articles shall not prejudice the right of the coastal State to exploit the subsoil by means of tunnelling irrespective of the depth of water above the subsoil.

Article 8

This Convention shall, until 30 October 1958, be open for signature by all States Members of the United Nations or of any of the specialized agencies, and by any other State invited by the General Assembly of the United Nations to become a party to the Convention.

Article 9

This Convention is subject to ratification. The instruments of ratification shall be deposited with the Secretary-General of the United Nations.

Article 10

This Convention shall be open for accession by any States belonging to any of the categories mentioned in Article 8. The instruments of accession shall be deposited with the Secretary-General of the United Nations.

Article 11

1.   This Convention shall come into force on the thirtieth day following the date of deposit of the twenty-second instrument of ratification or accession with the Secretary-General of the United Nations.
2.   For each State ratifying or acceding to the Convention after the deposit of the twenty-second instrument of ratification or accession, the Convention shall enter into force on the thirtieth day after deposit by such State of its instrument of ratification or accession.

Article 12

1.   At the time of signature, ratification or accession, any State may make reservations to Articles of the Convention other than to articles 1 to 3 inclusive.
2.   Any contracting State making a reservation in accordance with the preceding paragraph may at any time withdraw the reservation by a communication to that effect addressed to the Secretary-General of the United Nations.

Article 13

1.   After the expiration of a period of five years from the date on which this Convention shall enter into force, a request for the revision of this Convention may be made at any time by any contracting party by means of a notification in writing addressed to the Secretary-General of the United Nations.
2.   The General Assembly of the United Nations shall decide upon the steps, if any, to be taken in respect of such request.

Article 14

The Secretary-General of the United Nations shall inform all States Members of the United Nations and the other States referred to in Article 8:
(a) Of signatures to this Convention and of the deposit of instruments of ratification or accession, in accordance with Articles 8, 9 and 10;
(b) Of the date on which this Convention will come into force, in accordance with Article 11;
(c) Of requests for revision in accordance with Article 13;

(d) Of reservations to this Convention, in accordance with Article 12.

Article 15

The original of this Convention, of which the Chinese, English, French, Russian and Spanish texts are equally authentic, shall be deposited with the Secretary-General of the United Nations, who shall send certified copies thereof to all States referred to in Article 8.

IN WITNESS WHEREOF the undersigned plenipotentiaries, being duly authorized thereto by their respective governments, have signed this Convention.

DONE AT GENEVA, this twenty-ninth day of April one thousand nine hundred and fifty-eight.

7.3 TRUMAN PROCLAMATION ON THE CONTINENTAL SHELF (PRESIDENTIAL PROCLAMATION NO.2667, 28 SEPTEMBER 1945)

Presidential Proclamation No.2667 concerning the policy of the United States with respect to the natural resources of the subsoil and sea bed of the continental shelf, 28 September 1945

Whereas the Government of the United States of America, aware of the long range world-wide need for new sources of petroleum and other minerals, holds the view that efforts to discover and make available new supplies of these resources should be encouraged; and

Whereas its competent experts are of the opinion that such resources underlie many parts of the continental shelf off the coasts of the United States of America, and that with modern technological progress their utilization is already practicable or will become so at an early date; and

Whereas recognized jurisdiction over these resources is required in the interest of their conservation and prudent utilization when and as development is undertaken; and

Whereas it is the view of the Government of the United States that the exercise of jurisdiction over the natural resources of the subsoil and sea bed of the continental shelf by the contiguous nation is reasonable and just, since effectiveness of measures to utilize or conserve these resources would be contingent upon co-operation and protection from the shore, since the continental shelf may be regarded as an extension of the land mass of the coastal nation and thus naturally appurtenant to it, since these resources frequently form a seaward extension of a pool or deposit lying within the territory, and since self-protection compels the coastal nation to keep close watch over activities off its shores which are of the nature necessary for utilization of these resources;

Now, therefore, I, Harry S. Truman, President of the United States of America, do hereby proclaim the following policy of the United States of America with respect to the natural resources of the subsoil and sea bed of the continental shelf.

Having concern for the urgency of conserving and prudently utilizing its natural resources, the Government of the United States regards the natural resources of the subsoil and sea bed of the continental shelf beneath the high seas but contiguous to the coasts of the United States as appertaining to the United States, subject to its jurisdiction and control. In cases where the continental shelf extends to the shores of another State, or is shared with an adjacent State, the boundary shall be determined by the United States in accordance with equitable principles. The character as high seas of the waters above the continental shelf and the right to their free and unimpeded navigation are in no way thus affected.

7.4 PROTOCOL FOR THE SUPPRESSION OF UNLAWFUL ACTS AGAINST THE SAFETY OF FIXED PLATFORMS LOCATED ON THE CONTINENTAL SHELF, 1988

The States Parties to this Protocol,
BEING PARTIES to the Convention for the Suppression of Unlawful Acts against the Safety of Maritime Navigation,
RECOGNIZING that the reasons for which the Convention was elaborated also apply to fixed platforms located on the continental shelf,
TAKING ACCOUNT of the provisions of that Convention,
AFFIRMING that matters not regulated by this Protocol continue to be governed by the rules and principles of general international law,
HAVE AGREED as follows:

Article 1

1. The provisions of articles 5 and 7 and of articles 10 to 16 of the Convention for the Suppression of Unlawful Acts against the Safety of Maritime Navigation (hereinafter referred to as "the Convention") shall also apply *mutatis mutandis* to the offences set forth in article 2 of this Protocol where such offences are committed on board or against fixed platforms located on the continental shelf.
2. In cases where the Protocol does not apply pursuant to paragraph 1, it nevertheless applies when the offender or the alleged offender is found in the territory of a State Party other than the State in whose internal waters or territorial sea the fixed platform is located.
3. For the purposes of this Protocol, "fixed platform" means an artificial island, installation or structure permanently attached to the sea-bed for the purpose of exploration or exploitation of resources or for other economic purposes.

Article 2

1. Any person commits an offence if that person unlawfully and intentionally:
    (a) seizes or exercises control over a fixed platform by force or threat thereof or any other form of intimidation; or
    (b) performs an act of violence against a person on board a fixed platform if that act is likely to endanger its safety; or
    (c) destroys a fixed platform or causes damage to it which is likely to endanger its safety; or
    (d) places or causes to be placed on a fixed platform, by any means whatsoever, a device or substance which is likely to destroy that fixed platform or likely to endanger its safety; or
    (e) injures or kills any person in connection with the commission or the attempted commission of any of the offences set forth in subparagraphs (a) to (d).
2. Any person also commits an offence if that person:
    (a) attempts to commit any of the offences set forth in paragraph 1; or

(b) abets the commission of any such offences perpetrated by any person or is otherwise an accomplice of a person who commits such an offence; or

(c) threatens, with or without a condition, as is provided for under national law, aimed at compelling a physical or juridical person to do or refrain from doing any act, to commit any of the offences set forth in paragraph 1, subparagraphs (b) and (c), if that threat is likely to endanger the safety of the fixed platform.

Article 3

1. Each State Party shall take such measures as may be necessary to establish its jurisdiction over the offences set forth in article 2 when the offence is committed:

(a) against or on board a fixed platform while it is located on the continental shelf of that State; or

(b) by a national of that State.

2. A State Party may also establish its jurisdiction over any such offences when:

(a) it is committed by a stateless person whose habitual residence is in that State;

(b) during its commission a national of that State is seized, threatened, injured or killed; or

(c) it is committed in an attempt to compel that State to do or abstain from doing any act.

3. Any State Party which has established jurisdiction mentioned in paragraph 2 shall notify the Secretary-General of the International Maritime Organization (hereinafter referred to as "the Secretary-General"). If such State Party subsequently rescinds that jurisdiction, it shall notify the Secretary-General.

4. Each State Party shall take such measures as may be necessary to establish its jurisdiction over the offences set forth in article 2 in cases where the alleged offender is present in its territory and it does not extradite him to any of the States Parties which have established their jurisdiction in accordance with paragraphs 1 and 2 of this article.

5. This Protocol does not exclude any criminal jurisdiction exercised in accordance with national law.

Article 4

Nothing in this Protocol shall affect in any way the rules of international law pertaining to fixed platforms located on the continental shelf.

Article 5

1. This Protocol shall be open for signature at Rome on 10 March 1988 and at the Headquarters of the International Maritime Organization (hereinafter referred to as "the Organization") from 14 March 1988 to 9 March 1989 by any State which has signed the Convention. It shall thereafter remain open for accession.

2. States may express their consent to be bound by this Protocol by:

(a) signature without reservation as to ratification, acceptance or approval; or

(b) signature subject to ratification, acceptance or approval, followed by ratification, acceptance or approval; or

(c) accession.

3. Ratification, acceptance, approval or accession shall be effected by the deposit of an instrument to that effect with the Secretary-General.

4. Only a State which has signed the Convention without reservation as to ratification, acceptance or approval, or has ratified, accepted, approved or acceded to the Convention may become a Party to this Protocol.

Article 6

1. This Protocol shall enter into force ninety days following the date on which three States have either signed it without reservation as to ratification, acceptance or approval, or have deposited an instrument of ratification, acceptance, approval or accession in respect thereof. However, this Protocol shall not enter into force before the Convention has entered into force.
2. For a State which deposits an instrument of ratification, acceptance, approval or accession in respect of this Protocol after the conditions for entry into force thereof have been met, the ratification, acceptance, approval or accession shall take effect ninety days after the date of such deposit.

Article 7

1. This Protocol may be denounced by any State Party at any time after the expiry of one year from the date on which this Protocol enters into force for that State.
2. Denunciation shall be effected by the deposit of an instrument of denunciation with the Secretary-General.
3. A denunciation shall take effect one year, or such longer period as may be specified in the instrument of denunciation, after the receipt of the instrument of denunciation by the Secretary-General.
4. A denunciation of the Convention by a State Party shall be deemed to be a denunciation of this Protocol by that Party.

Article 8

1. A conference for the purpose of revising or amending this Protocol may be convened by the Organization.
2. The Secretary-General shall convene a conference of the States Parties to this protocol for revising or amending the Protocol, at the request of one-third of the States Parties, or five States Parties, whichever is the higher figure.
3. Any instrument of ratification, acceptance, approval or accession deposited after the date of entry into force of an amendment to this Protocol shall be deemed to apply to the Protocol as amended.

Article 9

1. This Protocol shall be deposited with the Secretary-General.
2. The Secretary-General shall:
   (a) inform all States which have signed this Protocol or acceded thereto, and all Members of the Organization, of:
       (i) each new signature or deposit of an instrument of ratification, acceptance, approval or accession, together with the date thereof;
       (ii) the date of entry into force of this Protocol;
       (iii) the deposit of any instrument of denunciation of this Protocol together with the date on which it is received and the date on which the denunciation takes effect;
       (iv) the receipt of any declaration or notification made under this Protocol or under the Convention, concerning this Protocol;
   (b) transmit certified true copies of this Protocol to all States which have signed this Protocol or acceded thereto.

3. As soon as this Protocol enters into force, a certified true copy thereof shall be transmitted by the Depositary to the Secretary-General of the United Nations for registration and publication in accordance with Article 102 of the Charter of the United Nations.

Article 10

This Protocol is established in a single original in the Arabic, Chinese, English, French, Russian and Spanish languages, each text being equally authentic.

IN WITNESS WHEREOF the undersigned, being duly authorized by their respective Governments for that purpose, have signed this Protocol.

DONE AT ROME this tenth day of March one thousand nine hundred and eighty-eight.

7.5 IMO GUIDELINES AND STANDARDS FOR THE REMOVAL OF OFFSHORE INSTALLATIONS AND STRUCTURES ON THE CONTINENTAL SHELF AND IN THE EXCLUSIVE ECONOMIC ZONE

IMO Resolution A.672(16), 19 October 1989

THE ASSEMBLY,

RECALLING Article 15(j) of the Convention on the International Maritime Organization concerning the functions of the Assembly in relation to regulations and guidelines concerning maritime safety and the prevention and control of marine pollution,

BEARING IN MIND article 60 of the United Nations Convention on the Law of the Sea, 1982, which prescribes that any installations or structures which are abandoned or disused shall be removed to ensure safety of navigation, taking into account any generally accepted international standards established in this regard by the competent international organization, and that such removal shall also have due regard to fishing, protection of the marine environment and the rights and duties of other States,

BEARING IN MIND ALSO that the International Maritime Organization is the competent Organization to deal with this subject,

HAVING CONSIDERED the draft guidelines and standards approved by the Maritime Safety Committee at its fifty-seventh session which were developed in co-operation with the Marine Environment Protection Committee,

1. ADOPTS the Guidelines and Standards for the Removal of Offshore Installations and Structures on the Continental Shelf and in the Exclusive Economic Zone set out in the Annex to the present resolution;

2. RECOMMENDS that Member Governments take into account the aforesaid Guidelines and Standards when making decisions regarding the removal of abandoned or disused installations or structures.

ANNEX

GUIDELINES AND STANDARDS FOR THE REMOVAL OF OFFSHORE
INSTALLATIONS AND STRUCTURES ON THE CONTINENTAL SHELF AND IN
THE EXCLUSIVE ECONOMIC ZONE

1 *General removal requirement*
1.1 Abandoned or disused offshore installations or structures on any continental shelf
or in any exclusive economic zone are required to be removed, except where non-
removal or partial removal is consistent with the following guidelines and standards.
1.2 The coastal State having jurisdiction over the installation or structure should ensure
that it is removed in whole or in part in conformity with these guidelines and standards
once it is no longer serving the primary purpose for which it was originally designed
and installed, or serving a subsequent new use, or where no other reasonable
justification cited in these guidelines and standards exists for allowing the installation or
structure or parts thereof to remain on the sea-bed. Such removal should be performed
as soon as reasonably practicable after abandonment or permanent disuse of such
installation or structure.
1.3 Notification of such non-removal or partial removal should be forwarded to the
Organization.
1.4 Nothing in these guidelines and standards is intended to preclude a coastal State
from imposing more stringent removal requirements for existing or future installations
or structures on its continental shelf or in its exclusive economic zone.

2 *Guidelines*
2.1 The decision to allow an offshore installation, structure, or parts thereof, to remain
on the sea-bed should be based, in particular, on a case-by-case evaluation, by the
coastal State with jurisdiction over the installation or structure, of the following
matters:

.1	any potential effect on the safety of surface or subsurface navigation, or of other uses of the sea;
.2	the rate of deterioration of the material and its present and possible future effect on the marine environment;
.3	the potential effect on the marine environment, including living resources;
.4	the risk that the material will shift from its position at some future time;
.5	the costs, technical feasibility, and risks of injury to personnel associated with removal of the installation or structure; and
.6	the determination of a new use or other reasonable justification for allowing the installation or structure or parts thereof to remain on the sea-bed.

2.2 The determination of any potential effect on safety of surface or subsurface
navigation or of other uses of the sea should be based on: the number, type and
draught of vessels expected to transit the area in the foreseeable future; the cargoes
being carried in the area; the tide, current, general hydrographic conditions and
potentially extreme climatic conditions; the proximity of designated or customary sea
lanes and port access routes; the aids to navigation in the vicinity; the location of
commercial fishing areas; the width of the available navigable fairway; and whether
the area is an approach to or in straits used for international navigation or routes used
for international navigation through archipelagic waters.

2.3 The determination of any potential effect on the marine environment should be based upon scientific evidence taking into account: the effect on water quality; geological and hydrographic characteristics; the presence of endangered or threatened species; existing habitat types; local fishery resources; and the potential for pollution or contamination of the site by residual products from, or deterioration of, the offshore installation or structure.

2.4 The process for allowing an offshore installation or structure, or parts thereof, to remain on the sea-bed should also include the following actions by the coastal State with jurisdiction over the installation or structure: specific official authorization identifying the conditions under which an installation or structure, or parts thereof, will be allowed to remain on the sea-bed; the drawing up of a specific plan, adopted by the coastal State, to monitor the accumulation and deterioration of material left on the sea-bed to ensure there is no subsequent adverse impact on navigation, other uses of the sea or the marine environment; advance notice to mariners as to the specific position, dimensions, surveyed depth and markings of any installations or structures not entirely removed from the sea-bed; and advance notice to appropriate hydrographic services to allow for timely revision of nautical charts.

3 *Standards*

The following standards should be taken into account when a decision is made regarding the removal of an offshore installation or structure.

3.1 All abandoned or disused installations or structures standing in less than 75m of water and weighing less than 4,000 tonnes in air, excluding the deck and superstructure, should be entirely removed.

3.2 All abandoned or disused installations or structures emplaced on the sea-bed on or after 1 January 1998, standing in less than 100m of water and weighing less than 4,000 tonnes in air, excluding the deck and superstructure, should be entirely removed.

3.3 Removal should be performed in such a way as to cause no significant adverse effects upon navigation or the marine environment. Installations should continue to be marked in accordance with IALA recommendations prior to the completion of any partial or complete removal that may be required. Details of the position and dimensions of any installations remaining after the removal operations should be promptly passed to the relevant national authorities and to one of the world charting hydrographic authorities. The means of removal or partial removal should not cause a significant adverse effect on living resources of the marine environment, especially threatened and endangered species.

3.4 The coastal State may determine that the installation or structure may be left wholly or partially in place where:

.1　an existing installation or structure, including one referred to in paragraphs 3.1 or 3.2, or a part thereof, will serve a new use if permitted to remain wholly or partially in place on the sea-bed (such as enhancement of a living resource); or

.2　an existing installation or structure, other than one referred to in paragraphs 3.1 and 3.2, or part thereof, can be left there without causing unjustifiable interference with other uses of the sea.

3.5 Notwithstanding the requirements of paragraphs 3.1 and 3.2, where entire removal is not technically feasible or would involve extreme cost, or an unacceptable risk to personnel or the marine environment, the coastal State may determine that it need not be entirely removed.

3.6 Any abandoned or disused installation or structure, or part thereof, which projects above the surface of the sea should be adequately maintained to prevent structural failure. In cases of partial removal referred to in paragraphs 3.4.2 or 3.5, an unobstructed water column sufficient to ensure safety of navigation, but not less than 55m, should be provided above any partially removed installation or structure which does not project above the surface of the sea.

3.7 Installations or structures which no longer serve the primary purpose for which they were originally designed or installed and are located in approaches to or in straits used for international navigation or routes used for international navigation through archipelagic waters, in customary deep-draught sea lanes, or in, or immediately adjacent to, routeing systems which have been adopted by the Organization should be entirely removed and should not be subject to any exceptions.

3.8 The coastal State should ensure that the position, surveyed depth and dimensions of material from any installation or structure which has not been entirely removed from the sea-bed are indicated on nautical charts and that any remains are, where necessary, properly marked with aids to navigation. The coastal State should also ensure that advance notice of at least 120 days is issued to advise mariners and appropriate hydrographic services of the change in the status of the installation or structure.

3.9 Prior to giving consent to the partial removal of any installation or structure, the coastal State should satisfy itself that any remaining materials will remain on location on the sea-bed and not move under the influence of waves, tides, currents, storms or other foreseeable natural causes so as to cause a hazard to navigation.

3.10 The coastal State should identify the party responsible* for maintaining the aids to navigation, if they are deemed necessary to mark the position of any obstruction to navigation, and for monitoring the condition of remaining material. The coastal State should also ensure that the responsible party* conducts periodic monitoring, as necessary, to ensure continued compliance with these guidelines and standards.

3.11 The coastal State should ensure that legal title to installations and structures which have not been entirely removed from the sea-bed is unambiguous and that responsibility for maintenance and the financial ability to assume liability for future damages are clearly established.

3.12 Where living resources can be enhanced by the placement on the sea-bed of material from removed installations or structures (e.g. to create an artificial reef), such material should be located well away from customary traffic lanes, taking into account these guidelines and standards and other relevant standards for the maintenance of maritime safety.

3.13 On or after 1 January 1998, no installation or structure should be placed on any continental shelf or in any exclusive economic zone unless the design and construction of the installation or structure is such that entire removal upon abandonment or permanent disuse would be feasible.

3.14 Unless otherwise stated, these standards should be applied to existing as well as future installations or structures.

---

* The phrase "party responsible" refers to any juridical or physical person identified by the coastal State for a purpose mentioned in the above paragraph 3.10.

7.6 OSLO COMMISSION GUIDELINES FOR THE DISPOSAL OF OFFSHORE INSTALLATIONS AT SEA

adopted at Seventeenth Meeting of Oslo Commission, The Hague, 10-12 June 1991

Preface

At its Seventeenth Meeting in June 1991, the Oslo Commission adopted these Guidelines on a trial basis. Contracting Parties intending to dispose of offshore installations at sea should notify the other Contracting Parties by providing the information requested in the Guidelines and the reasons for disposing of the offshore installation at sea. This would make consultation possible.

In drafting these guidelines, the Oslo Commission took note of the 1982 United Nations Convention on the Law of the Sea and also of the 1958 Convention on the Continental Shelf (Geneva Convention).

In principle the following options are available once fixed offshore installations (steel and concrete platforms) are disused:
1. leaving in place;
2. complete or partial removal:
   a) reuse or scrapping on land;
   b) disposal *in situ*;
   c) disposal at sea elsewhere;

The "Guidelines and Standards for the Removal of Offshore Installations and Structures on the Continental Shelf and in the Exclusive Economic Zone" (IMO – Guidelines and Standards) apply in each of the above cases. The Oslo Commission Guidelines for the Disposal of Offshore Installations apply to the disposal *at sea* of fixed installations and structures or parts thereof and are complementary to the IMO – Guidelines and Standards.

The Oslo Commission guidelines should be applied under the assumption that any abandonment plan prepared by the industry and the national authority already includes requirements such as:
1. sealing of the wells;
2. the removal of all hazardous or noxious materials, e.g. PCBs, biocides, toxic chemicals, hydrocarbons, corrosion inhibitors;
3. the provision of satisfactory evidence on the stability of the materials when deposited;
4. a survey of the area surrounding the placed materials to locate and remove debris that could interfere with other legitimate uses of the sea.

Introduction

1. These guidelines are designed to assist Contracting Parties in the management of disposal of offshore installations and structures so as to prevent pollution in Oslo Convention waters.
2. The Guidelines are in two parts. Part A deals with the assessment and management of disposal at sea, while part B provides guidance on the conduct of monitoring of marine disposal sites.
3. The Guidelines commence with a summary of those Articles and Annexes to the Oslo Convention which relate to the control of all disposal operations at sea, followed

by guidance on the conditions under which permits might be issued for the disposal of offshore installations and structures. Sections 3, 4 and 5 address those considerations of Annex III of the Convention relevant to the disposal of offshore installations and structures.

PART A:

1 Assessment and Management of Disposal Operations at Sea

1.1 In accordance with Article 5 of the Oslo Convention, Contracting Parties shall prohibit the disposal at sea of offshore installations or structures containing substances listed in Annex I unless these substances can be exempted under Article 8(2) (trace contaminants) or, in the case of organohalogen compounds, "rapidly converted in the sea into substances which are biologically harmless" (Annex I, para. 1).

1.2 Furthermore, in accordance with Article 6 of the Convention, Contracting Parties shall issue a specific permit for the disposal at sea of substances and materials listed in Annex II to the Convention.

1.3 The relevant provisions of Annex III to the Convention shall be taken into account when a specific permit for disposal of offshore installations or structures at sea is issued.

2 Conditions under which Permits for the Disposal at Sea of Offshore Installations or Structures May be Issued

2.1 Disposal of an offshore installation or structure at sea requires a specific permit.

2.2 In order to define the conditions under which specific permits may be issued, Contracting Parties should develop criteria to be applied on a case by case basis.

2.3 These criteria may involve:
1.   reference data linked to particular methods of disposal or disposal sites, such as data on seabed condition, quantities and position of discharged cuttings and concentrations of oil in the sediments.
2.   the residual quantities of Annex I and II substances (cleaning efficiency) after completion of the cleaning of the installation to be disposed of at sea, and
3.   a comparison of the incremental impact of disposal of a component in or around the stump of an installation against that at a second site.

2.4 In the event that the criteria cannot be met, a Contracting Party should not issue a permit unless a detailed consideration of Annex III, section 3(b) indicates that sea disposal is nonetheless the option of least detriment. If such a conclusion is drawn and a permit is issued, the Contracting Party should take all practical steps to mitigate the impact of the disposal operation on the marine environment. In such a case it is necessary to prepare a detailed Impact Hypothesis and to initiate monitoring designed to assess the consequences of the disposal at sea.

NB: Annex III section 3(b) reads as follows: "In applying these principles the practical availability of alternative means of disposal or elimination will be taken into consideration".

2.5 With a view to evaluation of the possibilities for harmonisation or consolidation of the criteria for disposal at sea of offshore installations and structures, Contracting Parties are requested to address in their notifications the criteria adopted, the scientific basis for the development of these criteria and the reasons for granting the permit.

3 Assessment of the Characteristics and Composition of Materials for Disposal

(a) Amount and composition
(b) Amount of substances and materials to be deposited per day (per week, per month)
(c) Toxicity
(d) Persistence
(e) Accumulation in biological materials or sediments
(f) Chemical and physical changes to the waste after release, including possible formation of new compounds
(g) Probability of production of taints reducing marketability of resources (fish, shellfish, etc.).

3.1 formation on the composition, amount (i.e. weight), dimensions, physical properties and the rate of deterioration of the materials should be obtained.

3.2 oper dump site selection rather than a testing application is recommended. Site selection to minimise a detrimental impact on commercial or recreational fishery areas is a major consideration in resource protection.

4 Characteristics of Dumping Site and Method of Deposit

4.1 Matters related to dump site selection criteria are addressed in greater detail in studies prepared by GESAMP (Reports and Studies no. 16: Scientific Criteria for the Selection of Waste Disposal Sites at Sea, IMO 1982) and by the International Council for the Exploration of the Sea (ICES) (Ninth Annual Report of the Oslo Commission, Annex 6).

NB: GESAMP: IMO/FAO/UNESCO/WMO/WHO/IAEA/UN/UNEP Joint Group of Experts on the Scientific Aspects of Marine Pollution

(a) Geographical position, depth and distance from coast
(b) Location in relation to living resources in adult or juvenile phases
(c) Location in relation to amenity areas
(d) Methods of packing, if any
(e) Initial dilution achieved by proposed method of release
(f) Dispersal, horizontal transport and vertical mixing characteristics
(g) Existence and effects of current and previous disposal operations in the area (including accumulative effects)

4.2 *Assessment of a new disposal site*

Basic site characterisation information to be considered at a very early stage of assessment of a new site should include the co-ordinates (latitude, longitude) of the disposal site, as well as its location with regard to:
−   distance to nearest coastline
−   recreational areas
−   spawning and nursery areas
−   known migration routes of fish or marine mammals
−   sport and commercial fishing areas
−   areas of natural beauty or significant cultural or historical importance
−   areas of special scientific or biological importance (marine sanctuaries, habitats of rare, vulnerable or endangered species)
−   shipping lanes
−   military exclusion zones

- engineering uses of the seabed (e.g. potential or ongoing seabed mining, undersea cables, desalination or energy conversion sites)

Furthermore, hydrological data should be obtained relevant to the disposal area.

4.3 *Assessment of the site in case of disposal in situ*

The basic site characteristics of the location of the offshore installation or structure should be re-assessed as the disposal site. The information to be obtained should include those items given in 4.2, which are relevant for such a re-assessment.

4.4 There should be an examination of the risk that the material will shift from its position at the disposal site at some future time. The risk of a breakdown of the structure should also be addressed.

4.5 At the site in question, the existing stress on biological communities as a result of other human activities should be evaluated before any new or additional disposal operations are established. The possible future uses of the sea area should be kept under consideration.

4.6 Any relevant information from baseline and monitoring studies at already established disposal sites should be taken into account.

5 General Considerations and Conditions

(a) Interference with Shipping, Fishing, Recreation, Mineral Extraction, Desalination, Fish and Shellfish Culture, Areas of Special Scientific Importance and Other Legitimate Uses of the Sea

This section deals only with management considerations to minimise the physical impact of disposal at sea of offshore installations or structures. The need to give due consideration to avoiding unnecessary interference with legitimate uses of the sea has been referred to in Section 4.

Physical impact of the disposal at sea of offshore installations or structures

5.1 All offshore installations or structures disposed of at sea could have a significant physical impact at the disposal site. This impact includes covering of the seabed and local smothering of benthic organisms.

5.2 To avoid excessive use of the seabed, the number of sites should be limited as far as possible and each site should be used to the maximum extent possible without interfering with navigation.

5.3 Interference with fish or crustacean migration or spawning or with seasonal fishery activity may be avoided by timing restrictions on disposal operations.

(b) In Applying These Principles, the Practical Availability of Alternative Means of Disposal or Elimination will be Taken into Consideration

Comparative Assessment

5.4 the special case of disposal at sea of an offshore installation or structure, such activity is to be regarded as an exception taking the Convention area as a whole. Any disposal option should be considered in the light of a comparative assessment of:

- technical feasibility
- environmental costs
- hazards (including accidents) associated with transport and disposal
- economics (including energy costs)
- exclusion of future uses of disposal areas

5.5 If asessment of the foregoing analysis shows a land alternative to be more appropriate, a licence for disposal at sea should not be granted.

PART B:

Monitoring Offshore Installation Disposal Operations

Definition

1. In the context of assessing and regulating environmental impacts of disposal operations monitoring is the repeated measurement of an effect whether direct or indirect on the marine environment and/or of interferences with other legitimate uses of the sea.

Objectives

2. Monitoring of offshore installation disposal operations is generally undertaken for the following reasons:
i)   to establish whether licensing conditions have, as intended, within the framework of the Convention, prevented adverse effects at the disposal site as a consequence of disposal;
ii)   to improve the basis on which licence applications are assessed by improving understanding of field effects of disposal operations which are not readily estimated by laboratory or literature assessment.
3. The ultimate purpose of monitoring is to assess the effects of the disposal activity on the biotic and abiotic environment.

Strategy

4. Monitoring operations are expensive for they require considerable resources both at sea and in subsequent data analysis. In order to approach the monitoring programme in a resource-effective manner, it is essential that the programme should have clearly defined objectives, and be defined so that the measurements made can meet these objectives. A review of monitoring activities will determine whether the programme should be continued, revised or terminated.

Impact Hypothesis

5. The objectives of the monitoring programme depend upon the predicted consquences of the disposal operation. The predicted consequences in terms of potential effects on the marine environment, its living resources and other legitimate uses of the sea, may be described formally as an Impact Hypothesis. This hypothesis will be derived from the characteristics of the structure to be dumped and the nature of the disposal site and will encompass spatial as well as temporal effects.
6. The preliminary evaluation should be as comprehensive as possible, identifying primary areas of potential impact, namely those considered to be most sensitive. Alterations to the physical environment, devaluation of marine resources, and interference with other legitimate uses of the sea should be given priority in these assessments.

7. The predicted consequences of disposal can be described in terms of the effect (e.g. nature of spatial and/or temporal change, response or degree of interference) on a particular target (e.g. habitat, process, biological community use). The prediction for any relevant target/effect combination should be described in sufficient detail such that there is no doubt as to the parameters to be measured during the subsequent monitoring phase.

8. In order to develop an Impact Hypothesis, it may be necessary to conduct a baseline survey or surveys to describe the characteristics of the proposed receiving area and the variability of these characteristics with time. Computer models may also be useful in this respect. Then, before any programme is drawn up and implemented, the following questions must be addressed:

i) what exactly should be measured;
ii) what is the purpose of monitoring a particular variable, or physical, chemical or biological effect;
iii) in what compartment and at which locations can measurements be made most effectively;
iv) for how long should the measurements be carried out to meet the defined aim;
v) what should be the temporal and spatial scale of measurements made to test the Impact Hypothesis?

9. A major requirement is to develop criteria describing the specific environmental effects of disposal that should be prevented (see Part A, para. 2.3).

Monitoring

10. Where it is considered that effects will be largely physical, monitoring may be based on remote methods (e.g. acoustic measurements, sidescan sonar).

11. It may be appropriate in certain cases to demonstrate that the disposed offshore installation or structure or its components do not pose major obstacles to commercial fishing.

12. Where physical effects at the seabed are expected, it may be necessary to examine the benthic community structure in the disposal area.

13. Where it is not possible to remove all potentially contaminating material from an offshore installation or structure before disposal (e.g. in emergencies where the IMO Guidelines and Standards cannot be implemented), and where therefore chemical effects might be expected, it may be necessary to examine the chemical quality of biota and the structure of benthic communities in the vicinity of the disposal site.

14. In order to asess the impact of disposal it may be necessary to compare the physical, and, where appropriate, the chemical or biological quality of the affected area with reference sites located away from the disposal site. Experience with the selection of reference sites for biological and physical monitoring can be drawn from monitoring programmes carried out in the North Sea in the vicinity of offshore installations. Such areas can be identified during the early stages of the impact assessment.

15. The spatial extent of sampling will depend upon the size of the area designated for disposal.

8 The Exclusive Economic Zone

8.1 UNITED NATIONS CONVENTION ON THE LAW OF THE SEA, 1982: PART V: EXCLUSIVE ECONOMIC ZONE

Article 55
Specific legal regime of the exclusive economic zone

The exclusive economic zone is an area beyond and adjacent to the territorial sea, subject to the specific legal regime established in this Part, under which the rights and jurisdiction of the coastal State and the rights and freedoms of other States are governed by the relevant provisions of this Convention.

Article 56
Rights, jurisdiction and duties of the coastal State in the exclusive economic zone

1. In the exclusive economic zone, the coastal State has:
   (a) sovereign rights for the purpose of exploring and exploiting, conserving and managing the natural resources, whether living or non-living, of the waters superjacent to the sea-bed and of the sea-bed and its subsoil, and with regard to other activities for the economic exploitation and exploration of the zone, such as the production of energy from the water, currents and winds;
   (b) jurisdiction as provided for in the relevant provisions of this Convention with regard to:
      (i)   the establishment and use of artificial islands, installations and structures;
      (ii) marine scientific research;
      (iii) the protection and preservation of the marine environment;

(c) other rights and duties provided for in this Convention.

2. In exercising its rights and performing its duties under this Convention in the exclusive economic zone, the coastal State shall have due regard to the rights and duties of other States and shall act in a manner compatible with the provisions of this Convention.
3. The rights set out in this article with respect to the sea-bed and subsoil shall be exercised in accordance with Part VI.

Article 57
Breadth of the exclusive economic zone

The exclusive economic zone shall not extend beyond 200 nautical miles from the baselines from which the breadth of the territorial sea is measured.

Article 58
Rights and duties of other States in the exclusive economic zone

1. In the exclusive economic zone, all States, whether coastal or land-locked, enjoy, subject to the relevant provisions of this Convention, the freedoms referred to in article 87 of navigation and overflight and of the laying of submarine cables and pipelines, and other internationally lawful uses of the sea related to these freedoms, such as those associated with the operation of ships, aircraft and submarine cables and pipelines, and compatible with the other provisions of this Convention.
2. Articles 88 to 115 and other pertinent rules of international law apply to the exclusive economic zone in so far as they are not incompatible with this Part.
3. In exercising their rights and performing their duties under this Convention in the exclusive economic zone, States shall have due regard to the rights and duties of the coastal State and shall comply with the laws and regulations adopted by the coastal State in accordance with the provisions of this Convention and other rules of international law in so far as they are not incompatible with this Part.

Article 59
Basis for the resolution of conflicts regarding the attribution of rights and jurisdiction in the exclusive economic zone

In cases where this Convention does not attribute rights or jurisdiction to the coastal State or to other States within the exclusive economic zone, and a conflict arises between the interests of the coastal State and any other state or States, the conflict should be resolved on the basis of equity and in the light of all the relevant circumstances, taking into account the respective importance of the interests involved to the parties as well as to the international community as a whole.

Article 60
Artificial islands, installations and structures in the exclusive economic zone

1. In the exclusive economic zone, the coastal State shall have the exclusive right to construct and to authorize the construction, operation and use of:
(a) artificial islands;
(b) installations and structures for the purposes provided for in article 56 and other economic purposes;

(c) installations and structures which may interfere with the exercise of the rights of the coastal State in the zone.

2. The coastal State shall have exclusive jurisdiction over such artificial islands, installations and structures, including jurisdiction with regard to customs, fiscal, health, safety and immigration laws and regulations.

3. Due notice must be given of the construction of such artificial islands, installations or structures, and permanent means for giving warning of their presence must be maintained. Any installations or structures which are abandoned or disused shall be removed to ensure safety of navigation, taking into account any generally accepted international standards established in this regard by the competent international organization. Such removal shall also have due regard to fishing, the protection of the marine environment and the rights and duties of other States. Appropriate publicity shall be given to the depth, position and dimensions of any installations or structures not entirely removed.

4. The coastal State may, where necessary, establish reasonable safety zones around such artificial islands, installations and structures in which it may take appropriate measures to ensure the safety both of navigation and of the artificial islands, installations and structures.

5. The breadth of the safety zones shall be determined by the coastal State, taking into account applicable international standards. Such zones shall be designed to ensure that they are reasonably related to the nature and function of the artificial islands, installations or structures, and shall not exceed a distance of 500 metres around them, measured from each point of their outer edge, except as authorized by generally accepted international standards or as recommended by the competent international organization. Due notice shall be given of the extent of safety zones.

6. All ships must respect these safety zones and shall comply with generally accepted international standards regarding navigation in the vicinity of artificial islands, installations, structures and safety zones.

7. Artificial islands, installations and structures and the safety zones around them may not be established where interference may be caused to the use of recognized sea lanes essential to international navigation.

8. Artificial islands, installations and structures do not possess the status of islands. They have no territorial sea of their own, and their presence does not affect the delimitation of the territorial sea, the exclusive economic zone or the continental shelf.

Article 61
Conservation of the living resources

1. The coastal State shall determine the allowable catch of the living resources in its exclusive economic zone.

2. The coastal State, taking into account the best scientific evidence available to it, shall ensure through proper conservation and management measures that the maintenance of the living resources in the exclusive economic zone is not endangered by over-exploitation. As appropriate, the coastal State and competent international organizations, whether subregional, regional or global, shall co-operate to this end.

3. Such measures shall also be designed to maintain or restore populations of harvested species at levels which can produce the maximum sustainable yield, as qualified by relevant environmental and economic factors, including the economic needs of coastal fishing communities and the special requirements of developing States, and taking into account fishing patterns, the interdependence of stocks and any

generally recommended international minimum standards, whether subregional, regional or global.

4.   In taking such measures the coastal State shall take into consideration the effects on species associated with or dependent upon harvested species with a view to maintaining or restoring populations of such associated or dependent species above levels at which their reproduction may become seriously threatened.

5.   Available scientific information, catch and fishing effort statistics, and other data relevant to the conservation of fish stocks shall be contributed and exchanged on a regular basis through competent international organizations, whether subregional, regional or global, where appropriate and with participation by all States concerned, including States whose nationals are allowed to fish in the exclusive economic zone.

Article 62
Utilization of the living resources

1.   The coastal State shall promote the objective of optimum utilization of the living resources in the exclusive economic zone without prejudice to article 61.

2.   The coastal State shall determine its capacity to harvest the living resources of the exclusive economic zone. Where the coastal State does not have the capacity to harvest the entire allowable catch, it shall, through agreements or other arrangements and pursuant to the terms, conditions, laws and regulations referred to in paragraph 4, give other States access to the surplus of the allowable catch, having particular regard to the provisions of articles 69 and 70, especially in relation to the developing States mentioned therein.

3.   In giving access to other States to its exclusive economic zone under this article, the coastal State shall take into account all relevant factors, including, *inter alia*, the significance of the living resources of the area to the economy of the coastal state concerned and its other national interests, the provisions of articles 69 and 70, the requirements of developing States in the subregion or region in harvesting part of the surplus and the need to minimize economic dislocation in States whose nationals have habitually fished in the zone or which have made substantial efforts in research and identification of stocks.

4.   Nationals of other States fishing in the exclusive economic zone shall comply with the conservation measures and with the other terms and conditions established in the laws and regulations of the coastal State. These laws and regulations shall be consistent with this Convention and may relate, *inter alia*, to the following:

(a) licensing of fishermen, fishing vessels and equipment, including payment of fees and other forms of remuneration, which, in the case of developing coastal States, may consist of adequate compensation in the field of financing, equipment and technology relating to the fishing industry;

(b) determining the species which may be caught, and fixing quotas of catch, whether in relation to particular stocks or groups of stocks or catch per vessel over a period of time or to the catch by nationals of any State during a specified period;

(c) regulating seasons and areas of fishing, the types, sizes and amount of gear, and the types, sizes and number of fishing vessels that may be used;

(d) fixing the age and size of fish and other species that may be caught;

(e) specifying information required of fishing vessels, including catch and effort statistics and vessel position reports;

(f) requiring, under the authorization and control of the coastal State, the conduct of specified fisheries research programmes and regulating the conduct of such research, including the sampling of catches, disposition of samples and reporting of associated scientific data;

(g) the placing of observers or trainees on board such vessels by the coastal State;

(h) the landing of all or any part of the catch by such vessels in the ports of the coastal State;

(i) terms and conditions relating to joint ventures or other co-operative arrangements;

(j) requirements for the training of personnel and the transfer of fisheries technology, including enhancement of the coastal State's capability of undertaking fisheries research;

(k) enforcement procedures.

5. Coastal States shall give due notice of conservation and management laws and regulations.

Article 63
Stocks occurring within the exclusive economic zones of two or more coastal States or both within the exclusive economic zone and in an area beyond and adjacent to it

1. Where the same stock or stocks of associated species occur within the exclusive economic zones of two or more coastal States, these States shall seek, either directly or through appropriate subregional or regional organizations, to agree upon the measures necessary to co-ordinate and ensure the conservation and development of such stocks without prejudice to the other provisions of this Part.

2. Where the same stock or stocks of associated species occur both within the exclusive economic zone and in an area beyond and adjacent to the zone, the coastal State and the States fishing for such stocks in the adjacent area shall seek, either directly or through appropriate subregional or regional organizations, to agree upon the measures necessary for the conservation of these stocks in the adjacent area.

Article 64
Highly migratory species

1. The coastal State and other States whose nationals fish in the region for the highly migratory species listed in Annex I shall co-operate directly or through appropriate international organizations with a view to ensuring conservation and promoting the objective of optimum utilization of such species throughout the region, both within and beyond the exclusive economic zone. In regions for which no appropriate international organization exists, the coastal State and other States whose nationals harvest these species in the region shall co-operate to establish such an organization and participate in its work.

2. The provisions of paragraph 1 apply in addition to the other provisions of this Part.

Article 65
Marine mammals

Nothing in this Part restricts the right of a coastal State or the competence of an international organization, as appropriate, to prohibit, limit or regulate the exploitation of marine mammals more strictly than provided for in this Part. States shall co-operate with a view to the conservation of marine mammals and in the case of cetaceans shall in particular work through the appropriate international organizations for their conservation, management and study.

Article 66
Anadromous stocks

1. States in whose rivers anadromous stocks originate shall have the primary interest in and responsibility for such stocks.
2. The State of origin of anadromous stocks shall ensure their conservation by the establishment of appropriate regulatory measures for fishing in all waters landward of the outer limits of its exclusive economic zone and for fishing provided for in paragraph 3(b). The State of origin may, after consultations with the other States referred to in paragraphs 3 and 4 fishing these stocks, establish total allowable catches for stocks originating in its rivers.
3. (a) Fisheries for anadromous stock shall be conducted only in waters landward of the outer limits of exclusive economic zones, except in cases where this provision would result in economic dislocation for a State other than the State of origin. With respect to such fishing beyond the outer limits of the exclusive economic zone, States concerned shall maintain consultations with a view to achieving agreement on terms and conditions of such fishing giving due regard to the conservation requirements and the needs of the State of origin in respect of these stocks.
   (b) The State of origin shall co-operate in minimizing economic dislocation in such other States fishing these stocks, taking into account the normal catch and the mode of operations of such States, and all the areas in which such fishing has occurred.
   (c) States referred to in subparagraph (b), participating by agreement with the State of origin in measures to renew anadromous stocks, particularly by expenditures for that purpose, shall be given special consideration by the State of origin in the harvesting of stocks originating in its rivers.
   (d) enforcement of regulations regarding anadromous stocks beyond the exclusive economic zone shall be by agreement between the State of origin and the other States concerned.
4. In cases where anadromous stocks migrate into or through the waters landward of the outer limits of the exclusive economic zone of a State other than the State of origin, such State shall co-operate with the State of origin with regard to the conservation and management of such stocks.
5. The State of origin of anadromous stocks and other States fishing these stocks shall make arrangements for the implementation of the provisions of this article, where appropriate, through regional organizations.

Article 67
Catadromous species

1. A coastal State in whose waters catadromous species spend the greater part of their life cycle shall have responsibility for the management of these species and shall ensure the ingress and egress of migrating fish.
2. Harvesting of catadromous species shall be conducted only in waters landward of the outer limits of exclusive economic zones. When conducted in exclusive economic zones, harvesting shall be subject to this article and the other provisions of this Convention concerning fishing in these zones.
3. In cases where catadromous fish migrate through the exclusive economic zone of another State, whether as juvenile or maturing fish, the management, including harvesting, of such fish shall be regulated by agreement between the State mentioned in paragraph 1 and the other State concerned. Such agreement shall ensure the rational

management of the species and take into account the responsibilities of the State mentioned in paragraph 1 for the maintenance of these species.

Article 68
Sedentary species

This Part does not apply to sedentary species as defined in article 77, paragraph 4.

Article 69
Right of land-locked States

1. Land-locked States shall have the right to participate, on an equitable basis, in the exploitation of an appropriate part of the surplus of the living resources of the exclusive economic zones of coastal States of the same sub-region or region, taking into account the relevant economic and geographical circumstances of all the States concerned and in conformity with the provisions of this article and of articles 61 and 62.

2. The terms and modalities of such participation shall be established by the States concerned through bilateral, subregional or regional agreements taking into account, *inter alia*:

(a) the need to avoid effects detrimental to fishing communities or fishing industries of the coastal State;

(b) the extent to which the land-locked State, in accordance with the provisions of this article, is participating or is entitled to participate under existing bilateral, subregional or regional agreements in the exploitation of the living resources of the exclusive economic zone of other coastal States;

(c) the extent to which other land-locked States and geographically disadvantaged States are participating in the exploitation of the living resources of the exclusive economic zone of the coastal State and the consequent need to avoid a particular burden for any single coastal State or a part of it;

(d) the nutritional needs of the populations of the respective States.

3. When the harvesting capacity of a coastal State approaches a point which would enable it to harvest the entire allowable catch of the living resources in its exclusive economic zone, the coastal State and other States concerned shall co-operate in the establishment of equitable arrangements on a bilateral, sub-regional or regional basis to allow for participation of developing land-locked States of the same subregion or region in the exploitation of the living resources of the exclusive economic zones of coastal States of the subregion or region, as may be appropriate in the circumstances and on terms satisfactory to all parties. In the implementation of this provision the factors mentioned in paragraph 2 shall also be taken into account.

4. Developed land-locked States shall, under the provisions of this article, be entitled to participate in the exploitation of living resources only in the exclusive economic zones of developed coastal States of the same subregion or region having regard to the extent to which the coastal State, in giving access to other States to the living resources of its exclusive economic zone, has taken into account the need to minimize detrimental effects on fishing communities and economic dislocation in States whose nationals have habitually fished in the zone.

5. The above provisions are without prejudice to arrangements agreed upon in subregions or regions where the coastal States may grant to land-locked States of the same subregion or region equal or preferential rights for the exploitation of the living resources in the exclusive economic zones.

Article 70
Right of geographically disadvantaged States

1. Geographically disadvantaged States shall have the right to participate, on an equitable basis, in the exploitation of an appropriate part of the surplus of the living resources of the exclusive economic zones of coastal States of the same subregion or region, taking into account the relevant economic and geographical circumstances of all the States concerned and in conformity with the provisions of this article and of articles 61 and 62.

2. For the purposes of this Part, "geographically disadvantaged States" means coastal States, including States bordering enclosed or semi-enclosed seas, whose geographical situation makes them dependent upon the exploitation of the living resources of the exclusive economic zones of other States in the subregion or region for adequate supplies of fish for the nutritional purposes of their populations or parts thereof, and coastal States which can claim no exclusive economic zones of their own.

3. The terms and modalities of such participation shall be established by the States concerned through bilateral, subregional or regional agreements taking into account, *inter alia*:

(a) the need to avoid effects detrimental to fishing communities or fishing industries of the coastal State;

(b) the extent to which the geographically disadvantaged State, in accordance with the provisions of this article, is participating or is entitled to participate under existing bilateral, subregional or regional agreements in the exploitation of living resources of the exclusive economic zones of other coastal States;

(c) the extent to which other geographically disadvantaged States and land-locked States are participating in the exploitation of the living resources of the exclusive economic zone of the coastal State and the consequent need to avoid a particular burden for any single coastal State or a part of it;

(d) the nutritional needs of the populations of the respective States.

4. When the harvesting capacity of a coastal State approaches a point which would enable it to harvest the entire allowable catch of the living resources in its exclusive economic zone, the coastal State and other States concerned shall co-operate in the establishment of equitable arrangements on a bilateral, subregional or regional basis to allow for participation of developing geographically disadvantaged States of the same subregion or region in the exploitation of the living resources of the exclusive economic zones of coastal States of the subregion or region, as may be appropriate in the circumstances and on terms satisfactory to all parties. In the implementation of this provision the factors mentioned in paragraph 3 shall also be taken into account.

5. Developed geographically disadvantaged States shall, under the provisions of this article, be entitled to participate in the exploitation of living resources only in the exclusive economic zones of developed coastal States of the same subregion or region having regard to the extent to which the coastal State, in giving access to other States to the living resources of its exclusive economic zone, has taken into account the need to minimize detrimental effects on fishing communities and economic dislocation in States whose nationals have habitually fished in the zone.

6. The above provisions are without prejudice to arrangements agreed upon in subregions or regions where the coastal States may grant to geographically disadvantaged States of the same subregion or region equal or preferential rights for the exploitation of the living resources in the exclusive economic zones.

Article 71
Non-applicability of articles 69 and 70

The provisions of articles 69 and 70 do not apply in the case of a coastal State whose economy is overwhelmingly dependent on the exploitation of the living resources of its exclusive economic zone.

Article 72
Restrictions on transfer of rights

1. Rights provided under articles 69 and 70 to exploit living resources shall not be directly or indirectly transferred to third States or their nationals by lease or licence, by establishing joint ventures or in any other manner which has the effect of such transfer unless otherwise agreed by the States concerned.
2. The foregoing provision does not preclude the States concerned from obtaining technical or financial assistance from third States or international organizations in order to facilitate the exercise of the rights pursuant to articles 69 and 70, provided that it does not have the effect referred to in paragraph 1.

Article 73
Enforcement of laws and regulations of the coastal State

1. The coastal State may, in the exercise of its sovereign rights to explore, exploit, conserve and manage the living resources in the exclusive economic zone, take such measures, including boarding, inspection, arrest and judicial proceedings, as may be necessary to ensure compliance with the laws and regulations adopted by it in conformity with this Convention.
2. Arrested vessels and their crews shall be promptly released upon the posting of reasonable bond or other security.
3. Coastal State penalties for violations of fisheries laws and regulations in the exclusive economic zone may not include imprisonment, in the absence of agreements to the contrary by the States concerned, or any other form of corporal punishment.
4. In cases of arrest or detention of foreign vessels the coastal State shall promptly notify the flag State, through appropriate channels, of the action taken and of any penalties subsequently imposed.

Article 74
Delimitation of the exclusive economic zone between States with opposite or adjacent coasts

1. The delimitation of the exclusive economic zone between States with opposite or adjacent coasts shall be effected by agreement on the basis of international law, as referred to in Article 38 of the Statute of the International Court of Justice, in order to achieve an equitable solution.
2. If no agreement can be reached within a reasonable period of time, the States concerned shall resort to the procedures provided for in Part XV.
3. Pending agreement as provided for in paragraph 1, the States concerned, in a spirit of understanding and co-operation, shall make every effort to enter into provisional arrangements of a practical nature and, during this transitional period, not to jeopardize or hamper the reaching of the final agreement. Such arrangements shall be without prejudice to the final delimitation.

4. Where there is an agreement in force between the States concerned, questions relating to the delimitation of the exclusive economic zone shall be determined in accordance with the provisions of that agreement.

Article 75
Charts and lists of geographical co-ordinates

1. Subject to this Part, the outer limit lines of the exclusive economic zone and the lines of delimitation drawn in accordance with article 74 shall be shown on charts of a scale or scales adequate for ascertaining their position. Where appropriate, lists of geographical co-ordinates of points, specifying the geodetic datum, may be substituted for such outer limit lines or lines of delimitation.
2. The coastal State shall give due publicity to such charts or lists of geographical co-ordinates and shall deposit a copy of each such chart or list with the Secretary-General of the United Nations.

8.1.1 UNITED NATIONS CONVENTION ON THE LAW OF THE SEA, 1982: ANNEX I: HIGHLY MIGRATORY SPECIES

1. Albacore tuna: *Thunnus alalunga.*
2. Bluefin tuna: *Thunnus thynnus.*
3. Bigeye tuna: *Thunnus obesus.*
4. Skipjack tuna: *Katsuwonus pelamis.*
5. Yellowfin tuna: *Thunnus albacares.*
6. Blackfin tuna: *Thunnus atlanticus.*
7. Little tuna: *Euthynnus alletteratus; Euthynnus affinis.*
8. Southern bluefin tuna: *Thunnus maccoyii.*
9. Frigate mackerel: *Auxis thazard; Auxis rochei.*
10. Pomfrets: Family *Bramidae.*
11. Marlins: *Tetrapturus angustirostris; Tetrapturus belone; Tetrapturus pfluegeri; Tetrapturus albidus; Tetrapturus audax; Tetrapturus georgei; Makaira mazara; Makaira indica; Makaira nigricans.*
12. Sail-fishes: *Istiophorus platypterus; Istiophorus albicans.*
13. Swordfish: *Xiphias gladius.*
14. Sauries: *Scomberesox saurus; Cololabis saira; Cololabis adocetus; Scomberesox saurus scombroides.*
15. Dolphin: *Coryphaena hippurus; Coryphaena equiselis.*
16. Oceanic sharks: *Hexanchus griseus; Cetorhinus maximus;* Family *Alopiidae; Rhincodon typus;* Family *Carcharhinidae;* Family *Sphyrnidae;* Family *Isurida.*
17. Cetaceans: Family *Physeteridae;* Family *Balaenopteridae;* Family *Balaenidae;* Family *Eschrichtiidae;* Family *Monodontidae;* Family *Ziphiidae;* Family *Delphinidae.*

8.2 UNITED STATES: PROCLAMATION 5030 ON AN EXCLUSIVE ECONOMIC ZONE, 10 MARCH 1983

By the President of the United States of America
A Proclamation

Whereas the Government of the United States of American desires to facilitate the wise development and use of the oceans consistent with international law;

Whereas international law recognizes that, in a zone beyond its territory and adjacent to its territorial sea, known as the Exclusive Economic Zone, a coastal State may assert certain sovereign rights over natural resources and related jurisdiction; and

Whereas the establishment of an Exclusive Economic Zone by the United States will advance the development of ocean resources and promote the protection of the marine environment, while not affecting other lawful uses of the zone, including the freedoms of navigation and overflight, by other States;

Now, Therefore, I, Ronald Reagan, by the authority vested in me as President by the Constitution and laws of the United States of America, do hereby proclaim the sovereign rights and jurisdiction of the United States of America and confirm also the rights and freedoms of all States within an Exclusive Economic Zone, as described herein.

The Exclusive Economic Zone of the United States is a zone contiguous to the territorial sea, including zones contiguous to the territorial sea of the United States, the Commonwealth of Puerto Rico, the Commonwealth of the North Mariana Islands (to the extent consistent with the Covenant and the United Nations Trusteeship Agreement), and the United States overseas territories and possessions. The Exclusive Economic Zone extends to a distance 200 nautical miles from the baseline from which the breadth of the territorial sea is measured. In cases where the maritime boundary with a neighboring State remains to be determined, the boundary of the Exclusive Economic Zone shall be determined by the United States and other State concerned in accordance with equitable principles.

Within the Exclusive Economic Zone, the United States has, to the extent permitted by international law, (a) sovereign rights for the purpose of exploring, exploiting, conserving and managing natural resources, both living and non-living, of the seabed and subsoil, and the superjacent waters and with regard to other activities for the economic exploitation and exploration of the zone, such as the production of energy from the water, currents and winds; and (b) jurisdiction with regard to the establishment and use of artificial islands, and installations and structures having economic purposes, and the protection and preservation of the marine environment.

This Proclamation does not change existing United States policies concerning the continental shelf, marine mammals and fisheries, including highly migratory species of tuna which are not subject to United States jurisdiction and require international agreements for effective management.

The United States will exercise these sovereign rights and jurisdiction in accordance with the rules of international law.

Without prejudice to the sovereign rights and jurisdiction of the United States, the Exclusive Economic Zone remains an area beyond the territory and territorial sea of the United States in which all States enjoy the high seas freedoms of navigation overflight, the laying of submarine cables and pipelines, and other internationally lawful uses of the sea.

...

8.3 UNITED STATES: PRESIDENTIAL STATEMENT ON UNITED STATES OCEANS POLICY, 10 MARCH 1983: EXCERPT

...

The United States has long been a leader in developing customary and conventional law of the sea. Our objectives have consistently been to provide a legal order that will, among other things, facilitate peaceful, international uses of the oceans and provide for equitable and effective management and conservation of marine resources. The United States also recognizes that all nations have an interest in these issues.

Last July I announced that the United States will not sign the United Nations Law of the Sea Convention that was opened for signature on December 10.

...

However, the convention also contains provisions with respect to traditional uses of the oceans which generally confirm existing maritime law and practice and fairly balance the interests of all states.

Today I am announcing three decisions to promote and protect the oceans interests of the United States in a manner consistent with those fair and balanced results in the Convention and international law.

...

Third, I am proclaiming today an Exclusive Economic Zone in which the United States will exercise sovereign rights in living and nonliving resources within 200 nautical miles of its coast. This will provide United States jurisdiction for mineral resources out to 200 nautical miles that are not on the continental shelf. Recently discovered deposits there could be an important future source of strategic minerals.

Within this Zone all nations will continue to enjoy the high seas rights and freedoms that are not resource related, including the freedoms of navigation and overflight. My proclamation does not change existing United States policies concerning the continental shelf, marine mammals, and fisheries, including highly migratory species of tuna which are not subject to United States jurisdiction. The United States will continue efforts to achieve international agreements for the effective management of these species. The proclamation also reinforces this government's policy of promoting the United States fishing industry.

While international law provides for a right of jurisdiction over marine scientific research within such a zone, the proclamation does not assert this right. I have elected not to do so because of the United States interest in encouraging marine scientific research and avoiding any unnecessary burdens. The United States will nevertheless recognize the right of other coastal states to exercise jurisdiction over marine scientific research within 200 nautical miles of their coasts, if that jurisdiction is exercised reasonably in a manner consistent with international law.

The Exclusive Economic Zone established today will also enable the United States to take limited additional steps to protect the marine environment. In this connection, the United States will continue to work through the International Maritime Organization and other appropriate international organizations to develop uniform international measures while imposing no unreasonable burdens on commercial shipping.

The policy decisions I am announcing today will not affect the application of existing United States law concerning the high seas.

...

8.4 TREATY ON FISHERIES BETWEEN THE GOVERNMENTS OF CERTAIN PACIFIC ISLAND STATES AND THE GOVERNMENT OF THE UNITED STATES OF AMERICA, 1987

The Governments of the Pacific Island States party to this Treaty and the Government of the United States of America:

ACKNOWLEDGING that in accordance with international law, coastal States have sovereign rights for the purposes of exploring and exploiting, conserving and managing the fisheries resources of their exclusive economic zones or fisheries zones;

RECOGNIZING the strong dependence of the Pacific Island parties on fisheries resources and the importance of the continued abundance of those resources;

BEARING IN MIND that some species of fish are found within and beyond the jurisdiction of any of the parties and range throughout a broad region; and

DESIRING to maximize benefits flowing from the development of the fisheries resources within the exclusive economic zones or fisheries zones of the Pacific Island parties;

HAVE AGREED AS FOLLOWS:

Article 1
Definitions and Interpretation

1.1 In this Treaty:

(a) "Administrator" means that person or organization designated by the Pacific Island parties to act as such on their behalf pursuant to this Treaty and notified to the Government of the United States:

(b) "final judgment" means a judgment from which no appeal proceedings have been initiated within sixty days;

(c) "fishing" means:

(i) searching for, catching, taking or harvesting fish;

(ii) attempting to search for, catch, take or harvest fish;

(iii) engaging in any other activity which can reasonably be expected to result in the locating, catching, taking or harvesting of fish;

(iv) placing, searching for or recovering fish aggregating devices or associated electronic equipment such as radio beacons;

(v) any operations at sea directly in support of, or in preparation for any activity described in this paragraph; or

(vi) aircraft use, relating to the activities described in this paragraph except for flights in emergencies involving the health or safety of crew members or the safety of a vessel;

(d) "fishing vessel of the United States" or "vessel" means any boat, ship or other craft which is used for, equipped to be used for, or of a type normally used for commercial fishing, which is documented under the laws of the United States;

(e) "Licensing Area" means all waters in the Treaty Area except for:

(i) waters subject to the jurisdiction of the United States in accordance with international law; and

(ii) waters closed to fishing by fishing vessels of the United States in accordance with Annex I;

(f) "operator" means any person who is in charge of, directs or controls a vessel, including the owner, charterer and master;

(g) "Pacific Island party" means a Pacific Island State party to this Treaty and "Pacific Island parties" means all such States from time to time;

(h) "Pacific Island State" means a party to the South Pacific Forum Fisheries Agency Convention, 1979;

(i) "party" means a State party to this Treaty, and "parties" means all such States, from time to time;

(j) "this Treaty" means this Treaty, its Annexes and Schedules; and

(k) "Treaty Area" means all waters north of 60 degrees south latitude and east of 90 degrees east longitude, subject to the fisheries jurisdiction of Pacific Island parties, and all other waters within rhumb lines connecting the following geographic co-ordinates, designated for the purposes of this Treaty, except for waters subject to the jurisdiction in accordance with international law of a State which is not a party to this Treaty:

2° 35' 39"S	141° 00' 00"E
1° 01' 35"N	140° 48' 35"E
1° 01' 35"N	129° 30' 00"E
10° 00' 00"N	129° 30' 00:E
14° 00' 00"N	140° 00' 00"E
14° 00' 00"N	142° 00' 00"E
12° 30' 00"N	142° 00' 00"E
12° 30' 00"N	158° 00' 00"E
15° 00' 00"N	158° 00' 00"E
15° 00' 00"N	165° 00' 00"E
18° 00' 00"N	165° 00' 00"E
18° 00' 00"N	174° 00' 00"E
12° 00' 00"N	174° 00' 00"E
12° 00' 00"N	176° 00' 00"E
5° 00' 00"N	176° 00' 00"E
1° 00' 00"N	180° 00' 00"
1° 00' 00"N	164° 00' 00"W
8° 00' 00"N	164° 00' 00"W
8° 00' 00"N	158° 00' 00"W
0° 00' 00"	150° 00' 00"W
6° 00' 00"S	150° 00' 00"W
6° 00' 00"S	146° 00' 00"W
12° 00' 00"S	146° 00' 00"W
26° 00' 00"S	157° 00' 00"W
26° 00' 00"S	174° 00' 00"W
40° 00' 00"S	174° 00' 00"W
40° 00' 00"S	171° 00' 00"W
46° 00' 00"S	171° 00' 00"W
55° 00' 00"S	180° 00' 00"
59° 00' 00"S	160° 00' 00"E
59° 00' 00"S	152° 00' 00"E

and north along the 152 degrees of east longitude until intersecting the Australian 200 nautical mile limit.

1.2 Nothing in this Treaty shall be deemed to affect the applicability of any provision of a Pacific Island party's law which is not identified or otherwise described in this Treaty.

Article 2
Broader Co-operation

2.1 The Government of the United States shall, as appropriate, co-operate with the Pacific Island parties through the provision of technical and economic support to assist the Pacific Island parties to achieve the objective of maximizing benefits from the development of their fisheries resources.

2.2 The Government of the United States shall, as appropriate, promote the maximization of benefits generated for the Pacific Island parties from the operations of fishing vessels of the United States licensed pursuant to this Treaty, including:

(a) The use of canning, trans-shipment, slipping and repair facilities located in the Pacific Island parties;

(b) The purchase of equipment and supplies, including fuel supplies, from suppliers located in the Pacific Island parties; and

(c) The employment of nationals of the Pacific Island parties on board licensed fishing vessels of the United States.

Article 3
Access to the Treaty Area

3.1 Fishing vessels of the United States shall be permitted to engage in fishing in the Licensing Area in accordance with the terms and conditions referred to in Annex I and licences issued in accordance with the procedures set out in Annex II.

3.2 It shall be a condition of any licence issued pursuant to this Treaty that the vessel in respect of which the licence is issued is operated in accordance with the requirements of Annex I. No fishing vessel of the United States shall be used for fishing in the Licensing Area without a licence issued in accordance with Annex II or in waters closed to fishing pursuant to Annex I, except in accordance with paragraph 3 of this article, or unless the vessel is used for fishing albacore tuna by the trolling method in high seas areas of the Treaty Area.

3.3 A Pacific Island party may permit fishing vessels of the United States to engage in fishing in waters under the jurisdiction of that party which are:

(a) Within the Treaty Area but outside the Licensing Area; or

(b) Except for purse seine vessels, within the Licensing Area but otherwise than in accordance with the terms and conditions referred to in Annex I,

in accordance with such terms and conditions as may be agreed from time to time with the owners of the said vessels or their representatives. In such a case, if the Pacific Island party gives notice to the Government of the United States of such arrangements, and if the Government of the United States concurs, the procedures of articles 4 and 5.6 shall be applicable to such arrangements.

Article 4
Flag State Responsibility

4.1 The Government of the United States shall enforce the provisions of this Treaty and licences issued thereunder. The Government of the United States shall take the necessary steps to ensure that nationals and fishing vessels of the United States refrain from fishing in the Licensing Area and in waters closed to fishing pursuant to Annex I, except as authorized in accordance with article 3.

4.2 The Government of the United States shall, at the request of the Government of a Pacific Island party, take all reasonable measures to assist that party in the investigation of an alleged breach of this Treaty by a fishing vessel of the United States and promptly communicate all the requested information to that party.

4.3 The Government of the United States shall ensure that:

(a) Each fishing vessel of the United States licensed pursuant to this Treaty is fully insured against all risks and liabilities;

(b) All measures are taken to facilitate:

   (i) Any claim arising out of the activities of a fishing vessel of the United States, including a claim for the total market value of any fish taken from the Licensing Area without authorization pursuant to this Treaty, and the prompt settlement of that claim;

   (ii) The service of legal process by or on behalf of a national or the Government of a Pacific Island party in any action arising out of the activities of a fishing vessel of the United States;

   (iii) The prompt and full adjudication in the United States of any claim made pursuant to this Treaty;

   (iv) The prompt and full satisfaction of any final judgment or other final determination made pursuant to this Treaty; and

   (v) The provision of a reasonable level of financial assurances, if, after consultation with the Government of the United States, all Pacific Island parties agree that the collection of any civil or criminal judgment or judgments or determination or determinations made pursuant to this Treaty has become a serious enforcement problem;

(c) An amount equivalent to the total value of any forfeiture, fine, penalty or other amount collected by the Government of the United States incurred as a result of any actions, judicial or otherwise, taken pursuant to this article is paid to the Administrator as soon as possible following the date that the amount is collected.

4.4 The Government of the United States shall, at the request of the Government of a Pacific Island party, fully investigate any alleged infringement of this Treaty involving a vessel of the United States, and report as soon as practicable and in any case within two months to that Government on that investigation and on any action taken or proposed to be taken by the Government of the United States in relation to the alleged infringement.

4.5 In the event that a report provided pursuant to paragraph 4 of this article shows that a fishing vessel of the United States:

(a) While fishing in the Licensing Area did not have a licence to fish in the Licensing Area, except in accordance with paragraph 2 of article 3; or

(b) Was involved in any incident in which an authorized officer or observer was allegedly assaulted with resultant bodily harm, physically threatened, forcefully resisted, refused boarding or subjected to physical intimidation or physical interference in the performance of his or her duties as authorized pursuant to this Treaty; or

that there was probable cause to believe that a fishing vessel of the United States:

(c) Was used for fishing in waters closed to fishing pursuant to Annex I, except as authorised in accordance with paragraph 3 of article 3;

(d) Was used for fishing in any Limited Area described in Annex I, except as authorized in accordance with that Annex I;

(e) Was used for fishing by any method other than the purse seine method, except in accordance with paragraph 2 of article 3;

(f) Was used for directed fishing for southern bluefin tuna or for fishing for any kinds of fish other than tunas, except that other kinds of fish may be caught as an incidental by-catch;

(g) Used an aircraft for fishing which was not identified on a form provided pursuant to Schedule 1 of Annex II in relation to that vessel; or

(h) Was involved in an incident in which evidence which otherwise could have been used in proceedings concerning the vessel has been intentionally destroyed;

and that such vessel has not submitted to the jurisdiction of the Pacific Island party concerned, the Government of the United States shall, at the request of that party, take all necessary measures to ensure that the vessel concerned leaves the Licensing Area and waters closed to fishing pursuant to Annex I immediately and does not return except for the purpose of submitting to the jurisdiction of the party, or after action has been taken by the Government of the United States to the satisfaction of that party.

4.6 In the event that a report provided pursuant to paragraph 4 of this article shows that a fishing vessel of the United States has been involved in a probable infringement of this Treaty, including an infringement of an applicable national law as identified in Schedule 1 of Annex I, other than an infringement of the kind described in paragraph 5 of this article, and that the vessel has not submitted to the jurisdiction of the Pacific Island party concerned, the Government of the United States shall, at the request of that party, take all necessary measures to ensure that the vessel concerned:

(a) Submits to the jurisdiction of that party; or

(b) Is penalized by the Government of the United States at such level as may be provided for like violations in United States law relating to foreign fishing vessels licensed to fish in the exclusive economic zone of the United States but not to exceed the sum of $US 250,000.

4.7 Financial assurances provided pursuant to this Treaty may be drawn against by any Pacific Island party to satisfy any civil or criminal judgment or other determination in favour of a national or the Government of a Pacific Island party.

4.8 Prior to instituting any legal proceedings pursuant to this article concerning an alleged infringement of this Treaty in waters within the jurisdiction, for any purpose, as recognized by international law, of a Pacific Island party, the Government of the United States shall notify the Government of that Pacific Island party that such proceedings shall be instituted. Such notice shall include a statement of the facts believed to show an infringement of this Treaty and the nature of the proposed proceedings, including the proposed charges and the proposed penalties to be sought. The Government of the United States shall not institute such proceedings if the Government of that Pacific Island party objects within 30 days of the effective date of such notice.

4.9 The Government of the United States shall ensure that an agent is appointed and maintained in accordance with the requirements of subparagraphs (a) and (b) of this paragraph, with authority to receive and respond to any legal process issued by a Pacific Island party in respect of an operator of any fishing vessel of the United States (identified in the form set out in Schedule 1 of Annex II) and shall notify the Administrator of the name and address of such agent, who:

(a) Shall be located in Port Moresby for the purpose of receiving and responding to any legal process issued in accordance with this article; and

(b) Shall, within 21 days of notification that legal process has been issued in accordance with this article, travel to any Pacific Island party, at no expense to that party, for the purpose of receiving and responding to that process.

Article 5
Compliance Powers

5.1 It is recognized that the respective Pacific Island parties may enforce the provisions of this Treaty and licences issued thereunder, including arrangements made pursuant to article 3.3 and licences issued thereunder, in waters under their respective jurisdictions.

5.2 The Governments of the Pacific Island parties shall promptly notify the Government of the United States of any arrest of a fishing vessel of the United States or any of its crew or of any charges filed or proceedings instituted following the arrest, in accordance with this article.

5.3 Fishing vessels of the United States and their crews arrested for breach of this Treaty shall be promptly released upon the posting of a reasonable bond or other security. Penalties applied in accordance with this Treaty for fishing violations shall not be unreasonable in relation to the offence and shall not include imprisonment or corporal punishment.

5.4 The Government of the United States shall not apply sanctions of any kind including deductions, however effected, from any amounts which might otherwise have been paid to any Pacific Island party, and restrictions on trade with any Pacific Island party as a result of any enforcement measures taken by a Pacific Island party in accordance with this article.

5.5 The Governments of the parties shall adopt and inform the other parties of such provisions in their national laws as may be necessary to give effect to this Treaty.

5.6 Where legal proceedings have been instituted by the Government of the United States pursuant to article 4, no Pacific Island party shall proceed with any legal action in respect of the same alleged infringement as long as such proceedings are maintained. Where penalties are levied or proceedings are otherwise concluded by the Government of the United States pursuant to article 4, the Pacific Island party which has received notice of such final determination shall withdraw any legal charges or proceedings in respect of the same alleged infringement.

5.7 During any period in which a party is investigating any infringement of this Treaty involving a fishing vessel of the United States, being an infringement which is alleged to have taken place in waters within the jurisdiction, for any purpose, as recognized by international law, of a Pacific Island party, and if that Pacific Island party so notifies the other parties, any licence issued in respect of that vessel shall, for the purposes of article 3, be deemed not to authorize fishing in the waters of that Pacific Island party.

5.8 If full payment of any amount due as a result of a final judgment or other final determination deriving from an occurrence in waters within the jurisdiction, for any purpose, of a Pacific Island party is not made to that party within sixty (60) days, the licence for the vessel involved shall be suspended at the request of that party and that vessel shall not be authorized to fish in the Licensing Area until that amount is paid to that party.

Article 6
Consultations and Dispute Settlement

6.1 At the request of any party, consultations shall be held with any other party within sixty (60) days of the date of receipt of the request. All other parties shall be notified of the request for consultations and any party shall be permitted to participate in such consultations.

6.2 Any dispute between the Government of the United States and the Government of one or more Pacific Island parties in relation to or arising out of this Treaty may be submitted by any such party to an arbitral tribunal for settlement by arbitration no earlier that one hundred and twenty (120) days following a request for consultations under article 6.1.   Unless the parties to the dispute agree otherwise, the Arbitration Rules of the United Nations Commission on International Trade Law, as at present in force, shall be used.

6.3 The Government or Governments of the Pacific Island party or parties to the dispute shall appoint one arbitrator and the Government of the United States shall appoint one arbitrator.   The third arbitrator, who shall act as presiding arbitrator of the tribunal, shall be appointed by agreement of the parties to the dispute.   In the event of a failure to appoint any arbitrator within the time period provided in the Rules, the arbitrator shall be appointed by the Secretary-General of the Permanent Court of Arbitration at The Hague.

6.4 Unless the parties to the dispute agree otherwise, the place of arbitration shall be Port Moresby.   The tribunal may hold meetings at such other place or places within the territory of a Pacific Island party or elsewhere within the Pacific Islands region as it may determine.   An award or other decision shall be final and binding on the parties to the arbitration, and unless the parties agree otherwise, shall be made public.   The parties shall promptly carry out any award or other decision of the tribunal.

6.5 The fees and expenses of the tribunal shall be paid half by the Government or Governments of the Pacific Island party or parties to the arbitration and half by the Government of the United States, unless the parties to the arbitration agree otherwise.

Article 7
Review of the Treaty

7.   The parties shall meet once each year for the purpose of reviewing the operation of this Treaty.

Article 8
Amendment of the Treaty

8.   The following procedures shall apply to the adoption and entry into force of any amendment to this Treaty:

(a) Any party may propose amendments to this Treaty;

(b) A proposed amendment shall be notified to the depositary not less than forty-five (45) days before the meeting at which the proposed amendment will be considered;

(c) The depositary shall promptly notify all parties of such proposal;

(d) The parties shall consider proposed amendments to this Treaty at the annual meeting described in article 7, or at any other time that may be agreed by all parties;

(e) Any amendment to this Treaty shall be adopted by the approval of all the parties, and shall enter into force upon receipt by the depositary of instruments of ratification, acceptance or approval by the parties;

(f) The depositary shall promptly notify all parties of the entry into force of the amendment.

Article 9
Amendment of Annexes

9. The following procedures may apply to the adoption and entry into force of any amendment to an Annex of this Treaty, at the request of the party proposing the amendment, in lieu of the procedure set out in article 8, unless otherwise provided in the Annex:

(a) Any party may propose an amendment to an Annex of this Treaty at any time by notifying such proposal to the depositary, which shall promptly notify all parties of the proposed amendment;

(b) A party approving a proposed amendment to an Annex shall notify its acceptance to the depositary, which shall promptly notify all the parties of each acceptance. Upon receipt by the depositary of notices of acceptance from all parties, such amendment shall be incorporated in the appropriate Annex and shall have effect from that date, or from such other date as may be specified in such amendment. The depositary shall promptly notify all parties of the adoption of the amendment and its effective date.

Article 10
Notification

10.1 The Administrator and each party shall notify the depositary of their current addresses for the receipt of notices given pursuant to this Treaty, and the depositary shall notify the Administrator and each of the parties of such addresses or any changes thereof. Unless otherwise specified in this Treaty, any notice given in accordance with this Treaty shall be in writing and may be served by hand or sent by telex or, where either method cannot readily be effected, by registered airmail to the address of the party or the Administrator as currently listed with the depositary.

10.2 Delivery by hand shall be effective when made. Delivery by telex shall be deemed to be effective on the business day following the day when the "answer back" appears on the sender's telex machine. Delivery by registered airmail shall be deemed to be effective twenty-one (21) days after posting.

Article 11
Depositary

11. The depositary for this Treaty shall be the Government of Papua New Guinea.

Article 12
Final Clauses

12.1 This Treaty shall be open for signature by the Governments of all the Pacific Island States and the Government of the United States of America.

12.2 This Treaty is subject to ratification by the States referred to in paragraph 1 of this article. The instruments of ratification shall be deposited with the depositary.

12.3 This Treaty shall remain open for accession by States referred to in paragraph 1 of this article. The instruments of accession shall be deposited with the depositary.

12.4 This Treaty shall enter into force upon receipt by the depositary of instruments of ratification by the Government of the United States and by the Governments of ten Pacific Island States which shall include the Federated States of Micronesia, the Republic of Kiribati and Papua New Guinea.

12.5 This Treaty shall enter into force for any State ratifying or acceding after the entry into force of this Treaty on the thirtieth day after the date on which its instrument of ratification or accession is received by the depositary.

12.6 This Treaty shall cease to have effect at the expiry of one year following the receipt by the depositary of an instrument signifying withdrawal or denunciation by the United States, any of the Pacific Island States named in article 12.4, or such number of Pacific Island States as would leave fewer than ten such States as parties.

12.7 This Treaty shall cease to have effect for a party at the expiry of the sixth month following the receipt by the depositary of an instrument signifying withdrawal or denunciation by that party, except that where this Treaty would cease to have effect under the last preceding paragraph as the result of the receipt of the said instrument, it shall cease to have effect for that party in the manner provided in the last preceding paragraph.

12.8 Any licence in force pursuant to this Treaty shall not cease to have effect as a result of this Treaty ceasing to have effect either generally or for any party, and articles 1, 3, 4 and 5 shall be regarded as continuing in force between the United States and the Pacific Island State party in respect of such licence until such licence expires in accordance with its terms.

12.9 No reservations may be made to this Treaty.

12.10 Paragraph 9 of this article does not preclude a State, when signing, ratifying or acceding to this Treaty, from making declarations or statements, provided that such declarations or statements do not purport to exclude or modify the legal effect of the provisions of this Treaty in their application to that State.

DONE at Port Moresby on the second day of April, 1987.

[Annexes I and II omitted]

8.5 BRAZIL: DECLARATION MADE UPON RATIFICATION OF THE UN CONVENTION ON THE LAW OF THE SEA, 1982, 22 DECEMBER 1988

In accordance with article 310 of the United Nations Convention on the Law of the Sea, the Government of the Federal Republic of Brazil makes the following statement:

(I) The Brazilian Government understands that the provisions of article 301 prohibiting 'any threat or use of force against the territorial integrity of any State, or in other manner inconsistent with the principles of international law embodied in the Charter of the United Nations' apply in particular to the maritime areas under the sovereignty or jurisdiction of the coastal State.

(II) The Brazilian Government understands that the provisions of the Convention do not authorize other States to carry out military exercises or manoeuvres, in particular those involving the use of weapons or explosives, in the exclusive economic zone without the consent of the coastal State.

(III) The Brazilian Government understands that in accordance with the provisions of the Convention the coastal State has, in the exclusive economic zone and on the continental shelf, the exclusive right to construct and to authorize and to regulate the construction, operation and use of all kinds of installations and structures, without exception, whatever their nature or purpose.

8.6 ITALY: DECLARATION MADE UPON SIGNATURE OF THE UN CONVENTION ON THE LAW OF THE SEA, 1982, 7 DECEMBER 1984: EXCERPT

Italy wishes also to confirm the following points made in its written statement dated 7 March 1983:

> – according to the Convention, the Coastal State does not enjoy residual rights in the exclusive economic zone.   In particular, the rights and jurisdiction of the Coastal State in such zone do not include the right to obtain notification of military exercises or manoeuvres or to authorize them.

Moreover, the rights of the Coastal State to build and to authorize the construction operation and the use of installations and structures in the exclusive economic zone and on the continental shelf is limited only to the categories of such installations and structures as listed in art.60 of the Convention.

9 The High Seas

9.1 **UNITED NATIONS CONVENTION ON THE LAW OF THE SEA, 1982: PART VII: HIGH SEAS**

SECTION 1. GENERAL PROVISIONS

Article 86
Application of the provisions of this Part

The provisions of this Part apply to all parts of the sea that are not included in the exclusive economic zone, in the territorial sea or in the internal waters of a State, or in the archipelagic waters of an archipelagic State.   This article does not entail any abridgement of the freedoms enjoyed by all States in the exclusive economic zone in accordance with article 58.

Article 87
Freedom of the high seas

1.   The high seas are open to all States, whether coastal or land-locked.   Freedom of the high seas is exercised under the conditions laid down by this Convention and by other rules of international law.   It comprises, *inter alia*, both for coastal and land-locked states:
(a) freedom of navigation;
(b) freedom of overflight;
(c) freedom to lay submarine cables and pipelines, subject to Part VI;

(d) freedom to construct artificial islands and other installations permitted under international law, subject to Part VI;

(e) freedom of fishing, subject to the conditions laid down in section 2;

(f) freedom of scientific research, subject to Parts VI and XIII.

2.   These freedoms shall be exercised by all States with due regard for the interests of other States in their exercise of the freedom of the high seas, and also with due regard for the rights under this Convention with respect to activities in the Area.

Article 88
Reservation of the high seas for peaceful purposes

The high seas shall be reserved for peaceful purposes.

Article 89
Invalidity of claims of sovereignty over the high seas

No State may validly purport to subject any part of the high seas to its sovereignty.

Article 90
Right of navigation

Every State, whether coastal or land-locked, has the right to sail ships flying its flag on the high seas.

Article 91
Nationality of ships

1.   Every State shall fix the conditions for the grant of its nationality to ships, for the registration of ships in its territory, and for the right to fly its flag.   Ships have the nationality of the State whose flag they are entitled to fly.   There must exist a genuine link between the State and the ship.

2.   Every State shall issue to ships to which it has granted the right to fly its flag documents to that effect.

Article 92
Status of ships

1.   Ships shall sail under the flag of one State only and, save in exceptional cases expressly provided for in international treaties or in this Convention, shall be subject to its exclusive jurisdiction on the high seas.   A ship may not change its flag during a voyage or while in a port of call, save in the case of a real transfer of ownership or change of registry.

2.   A ship which sails under the flags of two or more States, using them according to convenience, may not claim any of the nationalities in question with respect to any other State, and may be assimilated to a ship without nationality.

Article 93
Ships flying the flag of the United Nations, its specialized agencies and the International Atomic Energy Agency

The preceding articles do not prejudice the question of ships employed on the official service of the United Nations, its specialized agencies or the International Atomic Energy Agency, flying the flag of the organization.

Article 94
Duties of the flag State

1. Every State shall effectively exercise its jurisdiction and control in administrative, technical and social matters over ships flying its flag.

2. In particular every State shall:

(a) maintain a register of ships containing the names and particulars of ships flying its flag, except those which are excluded from generally accepted international regulations on account of their small size; and

(b) assume jurisdiction under its internal law over each ship flying its flag and its master, officers and crew in respect of administrative, technical and social matters concerning the ship.

3. Every State shall take such measures for ships flying its flag as are necessary to ensure safety at sea with regard, *inter alia*, to:

(a) the construction, equipment and seaworthiness of ships;

(b) the manning of ships, labour conditions and the training of crews, taking into account the applicable international instruments;

(c) the use of signals, the maintenance of communications and the prevention of collisions.

4. Such measures shall include those necessary to ensure:

(a) that each ship, before registration and thereafter at appropriate intervals, is surveyed by a qualified surveyor of ships, and has on board such charts, nautical publications and navigational equipment and instruments as are appropriate for the safe navigation of the ship;

(b) that each ship is in the charge of a master and officers who possess appropriate qualifications, in particular in seamanship, navigation, communications and marine engineering, and that the crew is appropriate in qualification and numbers for the type, size, machinery and equipment of the ship;

(c) that the master, officers and, to the extent appropriate, the crew are fully conversant with and required to observe the applicable international regulations concerning the safety of life at sea, the prevention of collisions, the prevention, reduction and control of marine pollution, and the maintenance of communications by radio.

5. In taking the measures called for in paragraphs 3 and 4 each State is required to conform to generally accepted international regulations, procedures and practices and to take any steps which may be necessary to secure their observance.

6. A State which has clear grounds to believe that proper jurisdiction and control with respect to a ship have not been exercised may report the facts to the flag State. Upon receiving such a report, the flag State shall investigate the matter and, if appropriate, take any action necessary to remedy the situation.

7. Each State shall cause an inquiry to be held by or before a suitably qualified person or persons into every marine casualty or incident of navigation on the high seas involving a ship flying its flag and causing loss of life or serious injury to nationals of another State or to the marine environment. The flag State and the other State shall co-operate in the conduct of any inquiry held by that other State into any such marine casualty or incident of navigation.

Article 95
Immunity of warships on the high seas

Warships on the high seas have complete immunity from the jurisdiction of any State other than the flag State.

Article 96
Immunity of ships used only on government non-commercial service

Ships owned or operated by a State and used only on government non-commercial service shall, on the high seas, have complete immunity from the jurisdiction of any State other than the flag State.

Article 97
Penal jurisdiction in matters of collision or any other incident of navigation

1. In the event of a collision or any other incident of navigation concerning a ship on the high seas, involving the penal or disciplinary responsibility of the master or of any other person in the service of the ship, no penal or disciplinary proceedings may be instituted against such person except before the judicial or administrative authorities either of the flag State or of the State of which such person is a national.

2.   In disciplinary matters, the State which has issued a master's certificate or a certificate of competence or licence shall alone be competent, after due legal process, to pronounce the withdrawal of such certificates, even if the holder is not a national of the State which issued them.

3. No arrest or detention of the ship, even as a measure of investigation, shall be ordered by any authorities other than those of the flag State.

Article 98
Duty to render assistance

1. Every State shall require the master of a ship flying its flag, in so far as he can do so without serious danger to the ship, the crew or the passengers:
(a) to render assistance to any person found at sea in danger of being lost;
(b) to proceed with all possible speed to the rescue of persons in distress, if informed of their need of assistance, in so far as such action may reasonably be expected of him;
(c) after a collision, to render assistance to the other ship, its crew and its passengers and, where possible, to inform the other ship of the name of his own ship, its port of registry and the nearest port at which it will call.

2. Every coastal State shall promote the establishment, operation and maintenance of an adequate and effective search and rescue service regarding safety on and over the sea and, where circumstances so require, by way of mutual regional arrangements co-operate with neighbouring States for this purpose.

Article 99
Prohibition of the transport of slaves

Every State shall take effective measures to prevent and punish the transport of slaves in ships authorized to fly its flag and to prevent the unlawful use of its flag for that purpose. Any slave taking refuge on board any ship, whatever its flag, shall *ipso facto* be free.

Article 100
Duty to co-operate in the repression of piracy

All States shall co-operate to the fullest possible extent in the repression of piracy on the high seas or in any other place outside the jurisdiction of any State.

Article 101
Definition of piracy

Piracy consists of any of the following acts:
(a) any illegal acts of violence or detention, or any act of depredation, committed for private ends by the crew or the passengers of a private ship or a private aircraft, and directed:
    (i)   on the high seas, against another ship or aircraft, or against persons or property on board such ship or aircraft;
    (ii)   against a ship, aircraft, persons or property in a place outside the jurisdiction of any State;
(b) any act of voluntary participation in the operation of a ship or of an aircraft with knowledge of facts making it a pirate ship or aircraft;
(c) any act of inciting or of intentionally facilitating an act described in sub-paragraph (a) or (b).

Article 102
Piracy by a warship, government ship or government aircraft whose crew has mutinied

The acts of piracy, as defined in article 101, committed by a warship, government ship or government aircraft whose crew has mutinied and taken control of the ship or aircraft are assimilated to acts committed by a private ship or aircraft.

Article 103
Definition of a pirate ship or aircraft

A ship or aircraft is considered a pirate ship or aircraft if it is intended by the persons in dominant control to be used for the purpose of committing one of the acts referred to in article 101. The same applies if the ship or aircraft has been used to commit any such act, so long as it remains under the control of the persons guilty of that act.

Article 104
Retention or loss of the nationality of a pirate ship or aircraft

A ship or aircraft may retain its nationality although it has become a pirate ship or aircraft. The retention or loss of nationality is determined by the law of the State from which such nationality was derived.

Article 105
Seizure of a pirate ship or aircraft

On the high seas, or in any other place outside the jurisdiction of any State, every State may seize a pirate ship or aircraft, or a ship or aircraft taken by piracy and under the control of pirates, and arrest the persons and seize the property on board. The courts of the State which carried out the seizure may decide upon the penalties to be imposed, and may also determine the action to be taken with regard to the ships, aircraft or property, subject to the rights of third parties acting in good faith.

Article 106
Liability for seizure without adequate grounds

Where the seizure of a ship or aircraft on suspicion of piracy has been effected without adequate grounds, the State making the seizure shall be liable to the State the nationality of which is possessed by the ship or aircraft for any loss of damage caused by the seizure.

Article 107
Ships and aircraft which are entitled to seize on account of piracy

A seizure on account of piracy may be carried out only by warships or military aircraft, or other ships or aircraft clearly marked and identifiable as being on government service and authorized to that effect.

Article 108
Illicit traffic in narcotic drugs or psychotropic substances

1.   All States shall co-operate in the suppression of illicit traffic in narcotic drugs and psychotropic substances engaged in by ships on the high seas contrary to international conventions.
2.   Any State which has reasonable grounds for believing that a ship flying its flag is engaged in illicit traffic in narcotic drugs or psychotropic substances may request the co-operation of other States to suppress such traffic.

Article 109
Unauthorized broadcasting from the high seas

1.   All States shall co-operate in the suppression of unauthorized broadcasting from the high seas.
2.   For the purposes of this Convention, "unauthorized broadcasting" means the transmission of sound radio or television broadcasts from a ship or installation on the high seas intended for reception by the general public contrary to international regulations, but excluding the transmission of distress calls.
3.   Any person engaged in unauthorized broadcasting may be prosecuted before the court of:
(a) the flag State of the ship;
(b) the State of registry of the installation
(c) the State of which the person is a national;
(d) any State where the transmissions can be received; or
(e) any State where authorized radio communication is suffering interference.
4.   On the high seas, a State having jurisdiction in accordance with paragraph 3 may, in conformity with article 110, arrest any person or ship engaged in unauthorized broadcasting and seize the broadcasting apparatus.

Article 110
Right of visit

1.   Except where acts of interference derive from powers conferred by treaty, a warship which encounters on the high seas a foreign ship, other than a ship entitled to

complete immunity in accordance with articles 95 and 96, is not justified in boarding it unless there is reasonable ground for suspecting that:

(a) the ship is engaged in piracy;

(b) the ship is engaged in the slave trade;

(c) the ship is engaged in unauthorized broadcasting and the flag State of the warship has jurisdiction under article 109;

(d) the ship is without nationality; or

(e) though flying a foreign flag or refusing to show its flag, the ship is, in reality, of the same nationality as the warship.

2. In the cases provided for in paragraph 1, the warship may proceed to verify the ship's right to fly its flag. To this end, it may send a boat under the command of an officer to the suspected ship. If suspicion remains after the documents have been checked, it may proceed to a further examination on board the ship, which must be carried out with all possible consideration.

3. If the suspicions prove to be unfounded, and provided that the ship boarded has not committed any act justifying them, it shall be compensated for any loss or damage that may have been sustained.

4. These provisions apply *mutatis mutandis* to military aircraft.

5. These provisions also apply to any other duly authorized ships or aircraft clearly marked and identifiable as being on government service.

Article 111
Right of hot pursuit

1. The hot pursuit of a foreign ship may be undertaken when the competent authorities of the coastal State have good reason to believe that the ship has violated the laws and regulations of that State. Such pursuit must be commenced when the foreign ship or one of its boats is within the internal waters, the archipelagic waters, the territorial sea or the contiguous zone of the pursuing State, and may only be continued outside the territorial sea or the contiguous zone if the pursuit has not been interrupted. It is not necessary that, at the time when the foreign ship within the territorial sea or the contiguous zone receives the order to stop, the ship giving the order should likewise be within the territorial sea or the contiguous zone. If the foreign ship is within a contiguous zone, as defined in article 33, the pursuit may only be undertaken if there has been a violation of the rights for the protection of which the zone was established.

2. The right of hot pursuit shall apply *mutatis mutandis* to violations in the exclusive economic zone or on the continental shelf, including safety zones around continental shelf installations, of the laws and regulations of the coastal State applicable in accordance with this Convention to the exclusive economic zone or the continental shelf, including such safety zones.

3. The right of hot pursuit ceases as soon as the ship pursued enters the territorial sea of its own State or of a third State.

4. Hot pursuit is not deemed to have begun unless the pursuing ship has satisfied itself by such practicable means as may be available that the ship pursued or one of its boats or other craft working as a team and using the ship pursued as a mother ship is within the limits of the territorial sea, or, as the case may be, within the contiguous zone or the exclusive economic zone or above the continental shelf. The pursuit may only be commenced after a visual or auditory signal to stop has been given at a distance which enables it to be seen or heard by the foreign ship.

5. The right of hot pursuit may be exercised only by warships or military aircraft, or other ships or aircraft clearly marked and identifiable as being on government service and authorized to that effect.

6. Where hot pursuit is effected by an aircraft:

(a) the provisions of paragraphs 1 to 4 shall apply *mutatis mutandis*;

(b) the aircraft giving the order to stop must itself actively pursue the ship until a ship or another aircraft of the coastal State, summoned by the aircraft, arrives to take over the pursuit, unless the aircraft is itself able to arrest the ship. It does not suffice to justify an arrest outside the territorial sea that the ship was merely sighted by the aircraft as an offender or suspected offender, if it was not both ordered to stop and pursued by the aircraft itself or other aircraft or ships which continue the pursuit without interruption.

7. The release of a ship arrested within the jurisdiction of a State and escorted to a port of that State for the purposes of an inquiry before the competent authorities may not be claimed solely on the ground that the ship, in the course of its voyage, was escorted across a portion of the exclusive economic zone or the high seas, if the circumstances rendered this necessary.

8. Where a ship has been stopped or arrested outside the territorial sea in circumstances which do not justify the exercise of the right of hot pursuit, it shall be compensated for any loss or damage that may have been thereby sustained.

Article 112
Right to lay submarine cables and pipelines

1. All States are entitled to lay submarine cables and pipelines on the bed of the high seas beyond the continental shelf.

2. Article 79, paragraph 5, applies to such cables and pipelines.

Article 113
Breaking or injury of a submarine cable or pipeline

Every State shall adopt the laws and regulations necessary to provide that the breaking or injury by a ship flying its flag or by a person subject to its jurisdiction of a submarine cable beneath the high seas done wilfully or through culpable negligence, in such a manner as to be liable to interrupt or obstruct telegraphic or telephonic communications, and similarly the breaking or injury of a submarine pipeline or high-voltage power cable, shall be a punishable offence. This provision shall apply also to conduct calculated or likely to result in such breaking or injury. However, it shall not apply to any break or injury caused by persons who acted merely with the legitimate object of saving their lives or their ships, after having taken all necessary precautions to avoid such break or injury.

Article 114
Breaking or injury by owners of a submarine cable or pipeline of another submarine cable or pipeline

Every State shall adopt the laws and regulations necessary to provide that, if persons subject to its jurisdiction who are the owners of a submarine cable or pipeline beneath the high seas, in laying or repairing that cable or pipeline, cause a break in or injury to another cable or pipeline, they shall bear the cost of the repairs.

Article 115
Indemnity for loss incurred in avoiding injury to a submarine cable or pipeline

Every State shall adopt the laws and regulations necessary to ensure that the owners of ships who can prove that they have sacrificed an anchor, a net or any other fishing gear, in order to avoid injuring a submarine cable or pipeline, shall be indemnified by the owner of the cable or pipeline, provided that the owner of the ship has taken all reasonable precautionary measures beforehand.

SECTION 2. CONSERVATION AND MANAGEMENT OF THE LIVING RESOURCES OF THE HIGH SEAS

Article 116
Right to fish on the high seas

All States have the right for their nationals to engage in fishing on the high seas subject to:
(a) their treaty obligations;
(b) the rights and duties as well as the interests of coastal States provided for, *inter alia*, in article 63, paragraph 2, and articles 64 to 67; and
(c) the provisions of this section.

Article 117
Duty of States to adopt with respect to their nationals measures for the conservation of the living resources of the high seas

All States have the duty to take, or to co-operate with other States in taking, such measures for their respective nationals as may be necessary for the conservation of the living resources of the high seas.

Article 118
Co-operation of States in the conservation and management of living resources

States shall co-operate with each other in the conservation and management of living resources in the areas of the high seas. States whose nationals exploit identical living resources, or different living resources in the same area, shall enter into negotiations with a view to taking the measures necessary for the conservation of the living resources concerned. They shall, as appropriate, co-operate to establish subregional or regional fisheries organizations to this end.

Article 119
Conservation of the living resources of the high seas

1. In determining the allowable catch and establishing other conservation measures for the living resources in the high seas, States shall:
(a) take measures which are designed, on the best scientific evidence available to the States concerned, to maintain or restore populations of harvested species at levels which can produce the maximum sustainable yield, as qualified by relevant environmental and economic factors, including the special requirements of developing States, and taking into account fishing patterns, the interdependence of stocks and any generally recommended international minimum standards, whether subregional, regional or global;

(b) take into consideration the effects on species associated with or dependent upon harvested species with a view to maintaining or restoring populations of such associated or dependent species above levels at which their reproduction may become seriously threatened.

2. Available scientific information, catch and fishing effort statistics, and other data relevant to the conservation of fish stocks shall be contributed and exchanged on a regular basis through competent international organizations, whether subregional, regional or global, where appropriate and with participation by all States concerned.

3. States concerned shall ensure that conservation measures and their implementation do not discriminate in form or in fact against the fishermen of any State.

Article 120
Marine mammals

Article 65 also applies to the conservation and management of marine mammals in the high seas.

9.2 GENEVA CONVENTION ON THE HIGH SEAS, 1958

The States Parties to this Convention,
Desiring to codify the rules of international law relating to the high seas,
Recognizing that the United Nations Conference on the Law of the Sea, held at Geneva from 24 February to 27 April 1958, adopted the following provisions as generally declaratory of established principles of international law,
Have agreed as follows:

Article 1

The term 'high seas' means all parts of the sea that are not included in the territorial sea or in the internal waters of a State.

Article 2

The high seas being open to all nations, no State may validly purport to subject any part of them to its sovereignty. Freedom of the high seas is exercised under the conditions laid down by these articles and by the other rules of international law. It comprises, *inter alia*, both for coastal and non-coastal States:
(1) Freedom of navigation;
(2) Freedom of fishing;
(3) Freedom to lay submarine cables and pipelines;
(4) Freedom to fly over the high seas.
These freedoms, and others which are recognized by the general principles of international law, shall be exercised by all States with reasonable regard to the interests of other States in their exercise of the freedom of the high seas.

Article 3

1. In order to enjoy the freedom of the seas on equal terms with coastal States, States having no sea-coast should have free access to the sea. To this end States situated

between the sea and a State having no sea-coast shall by common agreement with the latter and in conformity with existing international conventions accord:

(a) To the State having no sea-coast, on a basis of reciprocity, free transit through their territory; and

(b) To ships flying the flag of that State treatment equal to that accorded to their own ships, or to the ships of any other States, as regards access to seaports and the use of such ports.

2. States situated between the sea and a State having no sea-coast shall settle, by mutual agreement with the latter, and taking into account the rights of the coastal State or State of transit and the special conditions of the State having no sea-coast, all matters relating to freedom of transit and equal treatment in ports, in case such States are not already parties to existing international conventions.

Article 4

Every State, whether coastal or not, has the right to sail ships under its flag on the high seas.

Article 5

1. Each State shall fix the conditions for the grant of its nationality to ships, for the registration of ships in its territory, and for the right to fly its flag. Ships have the nationality of the State whose flag they are entitled to fly. There must exist a genuine link between the State and the ship; in particular, the State must effectively exercise its jurisdiction and control in administrative, technical and social matters over ships flying its flag.

2. Each State shall issue to ships to which it has granted the right to fly its flag documents to that effect.

Article 6

1. Ships shall sail under the flag of one State only and, save in exceptional cases expressly provided for in international treaties or in these Articles, shall be subject to its exclusive jurisdiction on the high seas. A ship may not change its flag during a voyage or while in a port of call, save in the case of a real transfer of ownership or change of registry.

2. A ship which sails under the flags of two or more States, using them according to convenience, may not claim any of the nationalities in question with respect to any other State, and may be assimilated to a ship without nationality.

Article 7

The provisions of the preceding Articles do not prejudice the question of ships employed on the official service of an intergovernmental organization flying the flag of the organization.

Article 8

1. Warships on the high seas have complete immunity from the jurisdiction of any State other than the flag State.

2. For the purposes of these Articles, the term 'warship' means a ship belonging to the naval forces of a State and bearing the external marks distinguishing warships of its nationality, under the command of an officer duly commissioned by the government

and whose name appears in the Navy List, and manned by a crew who are under regular naval discipline.

Article 9

Ships owned or operated by a State and used only on government non-commercial service shall, on the high seas, have complete immunity from the jurisdiction of any State other than the flag State.

Article 10

1. Every State shall take such measures for ships under its flag as are necessary to ensure safety at sea with regard *inter alia* to:
(a) The use of signals, the maintenance of communications and the prevention of collisions;
(b) The manning of ships and labour conditions for crews taking into account the applicable international labour instruments;
(c) The construction, equipment, and seaworthiness of ships.
2. In taking such measures each State is required to conform to generally accepted international standards and to take any steps which may be necessary to ensure their observance.

Article 11

1. In the event of a collision or of any other incident of navigation concerning a ship on the high seas, involving the penal or disciplinary responsibility of the master or of any other person in the service of the ship, no penal or disciplinary proceedings may be instituted against such persons except before the judicial or administrative authorities either of the flag State or of the State of which such person is a national.
2. In disciplinary matters, the State which has issued a master's certificate or a certificate of competence or licence shall alone be competent, after due legal process, to pronounce the withdrawal of such certificates, even if the holder is not a national of the State which issued them.
3. No arrest or detention of the ship, even as a measure of investigation, shall be ordered by any authorities other than those of the flag State.

Article 12

1. Every State shall require the master of a ship sailing under its flag, in so far as he can do so without serious danger to the ship, the crew, or the passengers:
(a) To render assistance to any person found at sea in danger of being lost;
(b) To proceed with all possible speed to the rescue of persons in distress if informed of their need of assistance, in so far as such action may reasonably be expected of him;
(c) After a collision, to render assistance to the other ship, her crew and her passengers and, where possible, to inform the other ship of the name of his own ship, her port of registry and the nearest port at which she will call.
2. Every coastal State shall promote the establishment and maintenance of an adequate and effective search and rescue service regarding safety on and over the sea and – where circumstances so require – by way of mutual regional arrangements co-operate with neighbouring States for this purpose.

Article 13

Every State shall adopt effective measures to prevent and punish the transport of slaves in ships authorized to fly its flag, and to prevent the unlawful use of its flag for that purpose. Any slave taking refuge on board any ship, whatever its flag, shall, *ipso facto*, be free.

Article 14

All States shall co-operate to the fullest possible extent in the repression of piracy on the high seas or in any other place outside the jurisdiction of any State.

Article 15

Piracy consists of any of the following acts:

(1) Any illegal acts of violence, detention or any act of depredation, committed for private ends by the crew or the passengers of a private ship or a private aircraft, and directed:

(a) On the high seas, against another ship or aircraft, or against persons or property on board such ship or aircraft;

(b) Against a ship, aircraft, persons, or property in a place outside the jurisdiction of any State;

(2) Any act of voluntary participation in the operation of a ship or an aircraft with knowledge of facts making it a pirate ship or aircraft;

(3) Any act of inciting or of intentionally facilitating an act described in sub-paragraph 1 or sub-paragraph 2 of this article.

Article 16

The acts of piracy, as defined in Article 15, committed by a warship, government ship or government aircraft whose crew has mutinied and taken control of the ship or aircraft are assimilated to acts committed by a private ship.

Article 17

A ship or aircraft is considered a pirate ship or aircraft if it is intended by the persons in dominant control to be used for the purpose of committing one of the acts referred to in Article 15. The same applies if the ship or aircraft has been used to commit any such act, so long as it remains under the control of the persons guilty of that act.

Article 18

A ship or aircraft may retain its nationality although it has become a pirate ship or aircraft. The retention or loss of nationality is determined by the law of the State from which such nationality was derived.

Article 19

On the high seas, or in any other place outside the jurisdiction of any State, every State may seize a pirate ship or aircraft, or a ship taken by piracy and under the control of pirates, and arrest the persons and seize the property on board. The courts of the State which carried out the seizure may decide upon the penalties to be imposed, and may also determine the action to be taken with regard to the ships, aircraft or property, subject to the rights of third parties acting in good faith.

Article 20

Where the seizure of a ship or aircraft on suspicion of piracy has been effected without adequate grounds, the State making the seizure shall be liable to the State the nationality of which is possessed by the ship or aircraft, for any loss or damage caused by the seizure.

Article 21

A seizure on account of piracy may only be carried out by warships or military aircraft, or other ships or aircraft on government service authorized to that effect.

Article 22

1.   Except where acts of interference derive from powers conferred by treaty, a warship which encounters a foreign merchant ship on the high seas is not justified in boarding her unless there is reasonable ground for suspecting:
(a) That the ship is engaged in piracy; or
(b) That the ship is engaged in the slave trade; or
(c) That, though flying a foreign flag or refusing to show its flag, the ship is, in reality, of the same nationality as the warship.
2.   In the cases provided for in sub-paragraphs (a), (b) and (c) above, the warship may proceed to verify the ship's right to fly its flag. To this end, it may send a boat under the command of an officer to the suspected ship. If suspicion remains after the documents have been checked, it may proceed to a further examination on board the ship, which must be carried out with all possible consideration.
3.   If the suspicions prove to be unfounded, and provided that the ship boarded has not committed any act justifying them, it shall be compensated for any loss or damage that may have been sustained.

Article 23

1.   The hot pursuit of a foreign ship may be undertaken when the competent authorities of the coastal State have good reason to believe that the ship has violated the laws and regulations of that State. Such pursuit must be commenced when the foreign ship or one of its boats is within the internal waters or the territorial sea or the contiguous zone of the pursuing State, and may only be continued outside the territorial sea or the contiguous zone if the pursuit has not been interrupted. It is not necessary that, at the time when the foreign ship within the territorial sea or the contiguous zone receives the order to stop, the ship giving the order should likewise be within the territorial sea or the contiguous zone.   If the foreign ship is within a contiguous zone, as defined in Article 24 of the Convention on the Territorial Sea and the Contiguous Zone, the pursuit may only be undertaken if there has been a violation of the rights for the protection of which the zone was established.
2.   The right of hot pursuit ceases as soon as the ship pursued enters the territorial sea of its own country or of a third State.
3.   Hot pursuit is not deemed to have begun unless the pursuing ship has satisfied itself by such practicable means as may be available that the ship pursued or one of its boats or other craft working as a team and using the ship pursued as a mother ship are within the limits of the territorial sea, or as the case may be within the contiguous zone.   The

pursuit may only be commenced after a visual or auditory signal to stop has been given at a distance which enables it to be seen or heard by the foreign ship.

4.   The right of hot pursuit may be exercised only by warships or military aircraft, or other ships or aircraft on government service specially authorized to that effect.

5.   Where hot pursuit is effected by an aircraft:

(a) The provisions of paragraphs 1 to 3 of this article shall apply *mutatis mutandis*;

(b) The aircraft giving the order to stop must itself actively pursue the ship until a ship or aircraft of the coastal State, summoned by the aircraft, arrives to take over the pursuit, unless the aircraft is itself able to arrest the ship. It does not suffice to justify an arrest on the high seas that the ship was merely sighted by the aircraft as an offender or suspected offender, if it was not both ordered to stop and pursued by the aircraft itself or other aircraft or ships which continue the pursuit without interruption.

6.   The release of a ship arrested within the jurisdiction of a State and escorted to a port of that State for the purposes of an inquiry before the competent authorities may not be claimed solely on the ground that the ship, in the course of its voyage, was escorted across a portion of the high seas, if the circumstances rendered this necessary.

7.   Where a ship has been stopped or arrested on the high seas in circumstances which do not justify the exercise of the rights of hot pursuit, it shall be compensated for any loss or damage that may have been thereby sustained.

Article 24

Every State shall draw up regulations to prevent pollution of the seas by the discharge of oil from ships or pipelines or resulting from the exploitation and exploration of the seabed and its subsoil, taking account of existing treaty provisions on the subject.

Article 25

1.   Every State shall take measures to prevent pollution of the seas from the dumping of radioactive waste, taking into account any standards and regulations which may be formulated by the competent international organizations.

2.   All States shall co-operate with the competent international organizations in taking measures for the prevention of pollution of the seas or air space above, resulting from any activities with radioactive materials or other harmful agents.

Article 26

1.   All States shall be entitled to lay submarine cables and pipelines on the bed of the high seas.

2.   Subject to its right to take reasonable measures for the exploration of the continental shelf and the exploitation of its natural resources, the coastal State may not impede the laying or maintenance of such cables or pipelines.

3.   When laying such cables or pipelines the State in question shall pay due regard to cables or pipelines already in position on the sea-bed. In particular, possibilities of repairing existing cables or pipelines shall not be prejudiced.

Article 27

Every State shall take the necessary legislative measures to provide that the breaking or injury by a ship flying its flag or by a person subject to its jurisdiction of a submarine cable beneath the high seas done wilfully or through culpable negligence, in such a manner as to be liable to interrupt or obstruct telegraphic or telephonic communications, and similarly the breaking or injury of a submarine pipeline or high-voltage power cable shall be a punishable offence. This provision shall not apply to any break or injury caused by persons who acted merely with the legitimate object of saving their lives or their ships, after having taken all necessary precautions to avoid such break or injury.

Article 28

Every State shall take the necessary legislative measures to provide that, if persons subject to its jurisdiction who are the owners of a cable or pipeline beneath the high seas, in laying or repairing that cable or pipeline, cause a break in or injury to another cable or pipeline, they shall bear the cost of the repairs.

Article 29

Every State shall take the necessary legislative measures to ensure that the owners of ships who can prove that they have sacrificed an anchor, a net or any other fishing gear, in order to avoid injuring a submarine cable or pipeline, shall be indemnified by the owner of the cable or pipeline, provided that the owner of the ship has taken all reasonable precautionary measures beforehand.

Article 30

The provisions of this Convention shall not affect conventions or other international agreements already in force, as between States parties to them.

Article 31

This Convention shall, until 31 October 1958, be open for signature by all States Members of the United Nations or of any of the specialized agencies, and by any other State invited by the General Assembly of the United Nations to become a Party to the Convention.

Article 32

This Convention is subject to ratification. The instruments of ratification shall be deposited with the Secretary-General of the United Nations.

Article 33

This Convention shall be open for accession by any States belonging to any of the categories mentioned in Article 31. The instruments of accession shall be deposited with the Secretary-General of the United Nations.

Article 34

1. This Convention shall come into force on the thirtieth day following the date of deposit of the twenty-second instrument of ratification or accession with the Secretary-General of the United Nations.
2. For each State ratifying or acceding to the Convention after the deposit of the twenty-second instrument of ratification or accession, the Convention shall enter into force on the thirtieth day after deposit by such State of its instrument of ratification or accession.

Article 35

1. After the expiration of a period of five years from the date on which this Convention shall enter into force, a request for the revision of this Convention may be made at any time by any Contracting Party by means of a notification in writing addressed to the Secretary-General of the United Nations.
2. The General Assembly of the United Nations shall decide upon the steps, if any, to be taken in respect of such request.

Article 36

The Secretary-General of the United Nations shall inform all States Members of the United Nations and the other States referred to in Article 31:
(a) Of signatures to this Convention and of the deposit of instruments of ratification or accession, in accordance with Articles 31, 32, and 33;
(b) Of the date on which this Convention will come into force, in accordance with Article 34;
(c) Of requests for revision in accordance with Article 35.

Article 37

The original of this Convention, of which the Chinese, English, French, Russian, and Spanish texts are equally authentic, shall be deposited with the Secretary-General of the United Nations, who shall send certified copies thereof to all States referred to in Article 31.

IN WITNESS THEREOF the undersigned plenipotentiaries, being duly authorized thereto by their respective governments, have signed this Convention.

DONE AT GENEVA, this twenty-ninth day of April one thousand nine hundred and fifty-eight.

9.3 TREATY ON THE PROHIBITION OF THE EMPLACEMENT OF NUCLEAR WEAPONS AND OTHER WEAPONS OF MASS DESTRUCTION ON THE SEABED AND THE OCEAN FLOOR AND IN THE SUBSOIL THEREOF, 1971

The States Parties to this Treaty,

Recognizing the common interest of mankind in the progress of the exploration and use of the seabed and the ocean floor for peaceful purposes,

Considering that the prevention of a nuclear arms race on the seabed and the ocean floor serves the interests of maintaining world peace, reduces international tensions and strengthens friendly relations among States,

Convinced that this Treaty constitutes a step towards the exclusion of the seabed, the ocean floor and the subsoil thereof from the arms race,

Convinced that this Treaty constitutes a step towards a treaty on general and complete disarmament under strict and effective international control, and determined to continue negotiations to this end,

Convinced that this Treaty will further the purposes and principles of the Charter of the United Nations, in a manner consistent with the principles of international law and without infringing the freedoms of the high seas,

Have agreed as follows:

Article I

1. The States Parties to this Treaty undertake not to emplant or emplace on the sea-bed and the ocean floor and in the subsoil thereof beyond the outer limit of a seabed zone, as defined in article II, any nuclear weapons or any other types of weapons of mass destruction as well as structures, launching installations or any other facilities specifically designed for storing, testing or using such weapons.
2. The undertakings of paragraph 1 of this article shall also apply to the seabed zone referred to in the same paragraph, except that within such seabed zone, they shall not apply either to the coastal State or to the seabed beneath its territorial waters.
3. The States Parties to this Treaty undertake not to assist, encourage or induce any State to carry out activities referred to in paragraph 1 of this article and not to participate in any other way in such actions.

Article II

For the purpose of this Treaty, the outer limit of the seabed zone referred to in article I shall be coterminous with the twelve-mile outer limit of the zone referred to in part II of the Convention on the Territorial Sea and the Contiguous Zone, signed at Geneva on 29 April 1958, and shall be measured in accordance with the provisions of part I, section II, of that Convention and in accordance with international law.

Article III

1. In order to promote the objectives of and ensure compliance with the provisions of this Treaty, each State Party to the Treaty shall have the right to verify through observation the activities of other States Parties to the Treaty on the seabed and the ocean floor and in the subsoil thereof beyond the zone referred to in article I, provided that observation does not interfere with such activities.
2. If after such observation reasonable doubts remain concerning the fulfilment of the obligations assumed under the Treaty, the State Party having such doubts and the State Party that is responsible for the activities giving rise to the doubts shall consult with a view to removing the doubts. If the doubts persist, the State Party having such doubts shall notify the other States Parties, and the Parties concerned shall co-operate on such further procedures for verification as may be agreed, including appropriate inspection of objects, structures, installations or other facilities that reasonably may be expected to be of a kind described in article I. The Parties in the region of the activities, including any coastal State, and any other Party so requesting, shall be entitled to participate in such consultation and co-operation. After completion of the further procedures for verification, an appropriate report shall be circulated to other Parties by the Party that initiated such procedures.
3. If the State responsible for the activities giving rise to the reasonable doubts is not identifiable by observation of the object, structure, installation or other facility, the State Party having such doubts shall notify and make appropriate inquiries of States Parties in the region of the activities and of any other State Party. If it is ascertained through these inquiries that a particular State Party is responsible for the activities, that State Party shall consult and co-operate with other Parties as provided in paragraph 2 of this article. If the identity of the State responsible for the activities cannot be ascertained through these inquiries, then further verification procedures, including inspection, may be undertaken by the inquiring State Party, which shall invite the

participation of the Parties in the region of the activities, including any coastal State, and of any other Party desiring to co-operate.

4. If consultation and co-operation pursuant to paragraphs 2 and 3 of this article have not removed the doubts concerning the activities and there remains a serious question concerning fulfilment of the obligations assumed under this Treaty, a State Party may, in accordance with the provisions of the Charter of the United Nations, refer the matter to the Security Council, which may take action in accordance with the Charter.

5. Verification pursuant to this article may be undertaken by any State Party using its own means, or with the full or partial assistance of any other State Party, or through appropriate international procedures within the framework of the United Nations and in accordance with its Charter.

6. Verification activities pursuant to this Treaty shall not interfere with activities of other States Parties and shall be conducted with due regard for rights recognized under international law, including the freedoms of the high seas and the rights of coastal States with respect to the exploration and exploitation of their continental shelves.

Article IV

Nothing in this Treaty shall be interpreted as supporting or prejudicing the position of any State Party with respect to existing international conventions, including the 1958 Convention on the Territorial Sea and the Contiguous Zone, or with respect to rights or claims which such State Party may assert, or with respect to recognition or non-recognition of rights or claims asserted by any other State, related to waters off its coasts, including, *inter alia*, territorial seas and contiguous zones, or to the seabed and the ocean floor, including continental shelves.

Article V

The Parties to this Treaty undertake to continue negotiations in good faith concerning further measures in the field of disarmament for the prevention of an arms race on the seabed, the ocean floor and the subsoil thereof.

Article VI

Any State Party may propose amendments to this Treaty. Amendments shall enter into force for each State Party accepting the amendments upon their acceptance by a majority of the States Parties to the Treaty and, thereafter, for each remaining State Party on the date of acceptance by it.

Article VII

Five years after the entry into force of this Treaty, a conference of Parties to the Treaty shall be held at Geneva, Switzerland, in order to review the operation of this Treaty with a view to assuring that the purposes of the preamble and the provisions of the Treaty are being realized. Such review shall take into account any relevant technological developments. The review conference shall determine, in accordance with the views of a majority of those Parties attending, whether and when an additional review conference shall be convened.

Article VIII

Each State Party to this Treaty shall in exercising its national sovereignty have the right to withdraw from this Treaty if it decides that extraordinary events related to the subject-matter of this Treaty have jeopardized the supreme interests of its country. It shall give notice of such withdrawal to all other States Parties to the Treaty and to the United Nations Security Council three months in advance. Such notice shall include a statement of the extraordinary events it considers to have jeopardized its supreme interests.

Article IX

The provisions of this Treaty shall in no way affect the obligations assumed by States Parties to the Treaty under international instruments establishing zones free from nuclear weapons.

Article X

1. This Treaty shall be open for signature to all States. Any State which does not sign the Treaty before its entry into force in accordance with paragraph 3 of this article may accede to it at any time.
2. This Treaty shall be subject to ratification by signatory States. Instruments of ratification and of accession shall be deposited with the Governments of the Union of Soviet Socialist Republics, the United Kingdom of Great Britain and Northern Ireland and the United States of America, which are hereby designated the Depositary Governments of this Treaty.
3. This Treaty shall enter into force after the deposit of instruments of ratification by twenty-two Governments, including the Governments designated as Depositary Governments of this Treaty.
4. For States whose instruments of ratification or accession are deposited after the entry into force of this Treaty, it shall enter into force on the date of the deposit of their instruments of ratification or accession.
5. The Depositary Governments shall promptly inform the Governments of all signatory and acceding States of the date of each signature, of the date of deposit of each instrument of ratification or of accession, of the date of the entry into force of this Treaty, and of the receipt of other notices.
6. This Treaty shall be registered by the Depositary Governments pursuant to Article 102 of the Charter of the United Nations.

Article XI

This Treaty, the Chinese, English, French, Russian and Spanish texts of which are equally authentic, shall be deposited in the archives of the Depositary Governments. Duly certified copies of this Treaty shall be transmitted by the Depositary Governments to the Governments of the States signatory and acceding thereto.

IN WITNESS WHEREOF the undersigned, being duly authorized thereto, have signed this Treaty.

DONE in triplicate, at the cities of London, Moscow and Washington, this seventh day of February, one thousand nine hundred seventy-one.

9.4 TREATY BANNING NUCLEAR WEAPON TESTS IN THE ATMOSPHERE, IN OUTER SPACE AND UNDER WATER, 1963

The Governments of the United States of America, the United Kingdom of Great Britain and Northern Ireland, and the Union of Soviet Socialist Republics, hereinafter referred to as the "Original Parties",

Proclaiming as their principal aim the speediest possible achievement of an agreement on general and complete disarmament under strict international control in accordance with the objectives of the United Nations which would put an end to the armaments race and eliminate the incentive to the production and testing of all kinds of weapons, including nuclear weapons.

Seeking to achieve the discontinuance of all test explosions of nuclear weapons for all time, determined to continue negotiations to this end, and desiring to put an end to the contamination of man's environment by radioactive substances,

Have agreed as follows:

Article I

1. Each of the Parties to this Treaty undertakes to prohibit, to prevent, and not to carry out any nuclear weapon test explosion, or any other nuclear explosion, at any place under its jurisdiction or control:

(a) in the atmosphere; beyond its limits, including outer space; or under water, including territorial waters or high seas; or

(b) in any other environment if such explosion causes radioactive debris to be present outside the territorial limits of the State under whose jurisdiction or control such an explosion is conducted. It is understood in this connection that the provisions of this subparagraph are without prejudice to the conclusion of a treaty resulting in the permanent banning of all nuclear test explosions, including all such explosions underground, the conclusion of which, as the Parties have stated in the preamble to this Treaty, they seek to achieve.

2. Each of the Parties to this Treaty undertakes furthermore to refrain from causing, encouraging, or in any way participating in, the carrying out of any nuclear weapon test explosion, or any other nuclear explosion, anywhere which would take place in any of the environments described, or have the effect referred to, in paragraph 1 of this Article.

Article II

1. Any Party may propose amendments to this Treaty. The text of any proposed amendment shall be submitted to the Depositary Governments which shall circulate it to all Parties to this Treaty. Thereafter, if requested to do so by one-third or more of the Parties, the Depositary Governments shall convene a conference, to which they shall invite all the Parties, to consider such amendment.

2. Any amendment to this Treaty must be approved by a majority of the votes of all the Parties to this Treaty, including the votes of all of the Original Parties. The amendment shall enter into force for all Parties upon the deposit of instruments of ratification by a majority of all the Parties, including the instruments of ratification of all of the Original Parties.

Article III

1.   This Treaty shall be open to all States for signature.   Any State which does not sign this Treaty before its entry into force in accordance with paragraph 3 of this Article may accede to it at any time.

2.   This Treaty shall be subject to ratification by signatory States.   Instruments of ratification and instruments of accession shall be deposited with the Governments of the Original Parties – the United States of America, the United Kingdom of Great Britain and Northern Ireland, and the Union of Soviet Socialist Republics – which are hereby designated the Depositary Governments.

3.   This Treaty shall enter into force after its ratification by all the Original Parties and the deposit of their instruments of ratification.

4.   For States whose instruments of ratification or accession are deposited subsequent to the entry into force of this Treaty, it shall enter into force on the date of the deposit of their instruments of ratification or accession.

5.   The Depositary Governments shall promptly inform all signatory and acceding States of the date of each signature, the date of deposit of each instrument of ratification of and accession to this Treaty, the date of its entry into force, and the date of receipt of any requests for conferences or other notices.

6.   This Treaty shall be registered by the Depositary Governments pursuant to Article 102 of the Charter of the United Nations.

Article IV

This Treaty shall be of unlimited duration.

Each Party shall in exercising its national sovereignty have the right to withdraw from the Treaty if it decides that extraordinary events, related to the subject matter of this Treaty, have jeopardized the supreme interests of its country.   It shall give notice of such withdrawal to all other Parties to the Treaty three months in advance.

Article V

This Treaty, of which the English and Russian texts are equally authentic, shall be deposited in the archives of the Depositary Governments.   Duly certified copies of this Treaty shall be transmitted by the Depositary Governments to the Governments of the signatory and acceding States.

IN WITNESS WHEREOF the undersigned, duly authorized, have signed this Treaty.

DONE in triplicate at the city of Moscow the fifth day of August, one thousand nine hundred and sixty-three.

9.5   TREATY OF TLATELOLCO FOR THE PROHIBITION OF NUCLEAR WEAPONS IN LATIN AMERICA, 1967

Preamble

In the name of their peoples and faithfully interpreting their desires and aspirations, the Governments of the States which sign the Treaty for the Prohibition of Nuclear Weapons in Latin America,

Desiring to contribute, so far as lies in their power, towards ending the armaments race, especially in the field of nuclear weapons, and towards strengthening a world at peace, based on the sovereign equality of States, mutual respect and good neighbourliness,

Recalling that the United Nations General Assembly, in its Resolution 808 (IX), adopted unanimously as one of the three points of a co-ordinated programme of disarmament "the total prohibition of the use and manufacture of nuclear weapons and weapons of mass destruction of every type",

Recalling that militarily denuclearized zones are not an end in themselves but rather a means for achieving general and complete disarmament at a later stage,

Recalling United Nations General Assembly Resolution 1911 (XVIII), which established that the measures that should be agreed upon for the denuclearization of Latin America should be taken "in the light of the principles of the Charter of the United Nations and of regional agreements",

Recalling United Nations General Assembly Resolution 2028 (XX), which established the principle of an acceptable balance of mutual responsibilities and duties for the nuclear and non-nuclear powers, and

Recalling that the Charter of the Organization of American States proclaims that it is an essential purpose of the Organization to strengthen the peace and security of the hemisphere,

Convinced:

That the incalculable destructive power of nuclear weapons has made it imperative that the legal prohibition of war should be strictly observed in practice if the survival of civilization and of mankind itself is to be assured,

That nuclear weapons, whose terrible effects are suffered, indiscriminately and inexorably, by military forces and civilian population alike, constitute, through the persistence of the radioactivity they release, an attack on the integrity of the human species and ultimately may even render the whole earth uninhabitable,

That general and complete disarmament under effective international control is a vital matter which all the peoples of the world equally demand,

That the proliferation of nuclear weapons, which seems inevitable unless States, in the exercise of their sovereign rights, impose restrictions on themselves in order to prevent it, would make any agreement on disarmament enormously difficult and would increase the danger of the outbreak of a nuclear conflagration,

That the establishment of militarily denuclearized zones is closely linked with the maintenance of peace and security in the respective regions,

That the military denuclearization of vast geographical zones, adopted by the sovereign decision of the States comprised therein, will exercise a beneficial influence on other regions where similar conditions exist,

That the privileged situation of the signatory States, whose territories are wholly free from nuclear weapons, imposes upon them the inescapable duty of preserving that situation both in their own interests and for the good of mankind,

That the existence of nuclear weapons in any country of Latin America would make it a target for possible nuclear attacks and would inevitably set off, throughout the region, a ruinous race in nuclear weapons which would involve the unjustifiable diversion, for warlike purposes, of the limited resources required for economic and social development,

That the foregoing reasons, together with the traditional peace-loving outlook of Latin America, give rise to an inescapable necessity that nuclear energy should be used in that region exclusively for peaceful purposes, and that the Latin American countries should use their right to the greatest and most equitable possible access to this new source of energy in order to expedite the economic and social development of their peoples,

Convinced finally:

That the military denuclearization of Latin America – being understood to mean the undertaking entered into internationally in this Treaty to keep their territories forever free from nuclear weapons – will constitute a measure which will spare their peoples from the squandering of their limited resources on nuclear armaments and will protect them against possible nuclear attacks on their territories, and will also constitute a significant contribution towards preventing the proliferation of nuclear weapons and a powerful factor for general and complete disarmament, and

That Latin America, faithful to its tradition of universality, must not only endeavour to banish from its homelands the scourge of a nuclear war, but must also strive to promote the well-being and advancement if its peoples, at the same time co-operating in the fulfilment of the ideals of mankind, that is to say, in the consolidation of a permanent peace based on equal rights, economic fairness and social justice for all, in accordance with the principles and purposes set forth in the Charter of the United Nations and in the Charter of the Organization of American States,

Have agreed as follows:

Obligations

Article 1

1.   The Contracting Parties hereby undertake to use exclusively for peaceful purposes the nuclear material and facilities which are under their jurisdiction, and to prohibit and prevent in their respective territories:

(a) The testing, use, manufacture, production or acquisition by any means whatsoever of any nuclear weapons, by the Parties themselves, directly or indirectly, on behalf of anyone else or in any other way, and

(b) The receipt, storage, installation, deployment and any form of possession of any nuclear weapons, directly or indirectly, by the Parties themselves, by anyone on their behalf or in any other way.

2.   The Contracting Parties also undertake to refrain from engaging in, encouraging or authorizing, directly or indirectly, or in any way participating in the testing, use, manufacture, production, possession or control of any nuclear weapon.

Definition of the Contracting Parties

Article 2

For the purposes of this Treaty, the Contracting Parties are those for whom the Treaty is in force.

Definition of Territory

Article 3

For the purposes of this Treaty, the term "territory" shall include the territorial sea, air space and any other space over which the State exercises sovereignty in accordance with its own legislation.

Zone of Application

Article 4

1. The zone of application of this Treaty is the whole of the territories for which the Treaty is in force.
2. Upon fulfilment of the requirements of article 28, paragraph 1, the zone of application of this Treaty shall also be that which is situated in the western hemisphere within the following limits (except the continental part of the territory of the United States of America and its territorial waters): starting at a point located at 35° north latitude, 75° west longitude; from this point directly southward to a point at 30° north latitude, 75° west longitude; from there, directly eastward to a point at 30° north latitude, 50° west longitude; from there, along a loxodromic line to a point at 5° north latitude, 20° west longitude; from there, directly southward to a point at 60° south latitude, 20° west longitude; from there, directly westward to a point at 60° south latitude, 115° west longitude; from there, directly northward to a point at 0 latitude, 115° west longitude; from there, along a loxodromic line to a point at 35° north latitude, 150° west longitude; from there, directly eastward to a point at 35° north latitude, 75° west longitude.

Definition of Nuclear Weapons

Article 5

For the purposes of this Treaty, a nuclear weapon is any device which is capable of releasing nuclear energy in an uncontrolled manner and which has a group of characteristics that are appropriate for use for warlike purposes. An instrument that may be used for the transport or propulsion of the device is not included in this definition if it is separable from the device and not an indivisible part thereof.

Meeting of Signatories

Article 6

At the request of any of the signatory States or if the Agency established by article 7 should so decide, a meeting of all the signatories may be convoked to consider in common questions which may affect the very essence of this instrument, including possible amendments to it. In either case, the meeting will be convoked by the General Secretary.

Organization

Article 7

1. In order to ensure compliance with the obligations of this Treaty, the Contracting Parties hereby establish an international organization to be known as the Agency for the Prohibition of Nuclear Weapons in Latin America, hereinafter referred to as "the Agency". Only the Contracting Parties shall be affected by its decisions.
2. The Agency shall be responsible for the holding of periodic or extraordinary consultations among Member States on matters relating to the purposes, measures and procedures set forth in this Treaty and to the supervision of compliance with the obligations arising therefrom.

3. The Contracting Parties agree to extend to the Agency full and prompt co-operation in accordance with the provisions of this Treaty, of any agreements they may conclude with the Agency and of any agreements the Agency may conclude with any other international organization or body.

4. The headquarters of the Agency shall be in Mexico City.

Organs

Article 8

1. There are hereby established as principal organs of the Agency a General Conference, a Council and a Secretariat.

2. Such subsidiary organs as are considered necessary by the General Conference may be established within the purview of this Treaty.

The General Conference

Article 9

1. The General Conference, the supreme organ of the Agency, shall be composed of all the Contracting Parties; it shall hold regular sessions every two years, and may also hold special sessions whenever this Treaty so provides or, in the opinion of the Council, the circumstances so require.

2. The General Conference:

(a) May consider and decide on any matters or questions covered by this Treaty, within the limits thereof, including those referring to powers and functions of any organ provided for in this Treaty;

(b) Shall establish procedures for the control system to ensure observance of this Treaty in accordance with its provisions;

(c) Shall elect the Members of the Council and the General Secretary;

(d) May remove the General Secretary from office if the proper functioning of the Agency so requires;

(e) Shall receive and consider the biennial and special reports submitted by the Council and the General Secretary;

(f) Shall initiate and consider studies designed to facilitate the optimum fulfilment of the aims of this Treaty, without prejudice to the power of the General Secretary independently to carry out similar studies for submission to and consideration by the Conference.

(g) Shall be the organ competent to authorize the conclusion of agreements with Governments and other international organizations and bodies.

3. The General Conference shall adopt the Agency's budget and fix the scale of financial contributions to be paid by Member States, taking into account the systems and criteria used for the same purpose by the United Nations.

4. The General Conference shall elect its officers for each session and may establish such subsidiary organs as it deems necessary for the performance of its functions.

5. Each Member of the Agency shall have one vote. The decisions of the General Conference shall be taken by a two-thirds majority of the Members present and voting in the case of matters relating to the control system and measures referred to in article 20, the admission of new Members, the election or removal of the General Secretary, adoption of the budget and matters related thereto. Decisions on other matters, as well as procedural questions and also determination of which questions must be decided by a

two-thirds majority, shall be taken by a simple majority of the Members present and voting.

6. The General Conference shall adopt its own rules of procedure.

The Council

Article 10

1. The Council shall be composed of five Members of the Agency elected by the General Conference from among the Contracting Parties, due account being taken of equitable geographic distribution.

2. The Members of the Council shall be elected for a term of four years. However, in the first election three will be elected for two years. Outgoing Members may not be re-elected for the following period unless the limited number of States for which the Treaty is in force so requires.

3. Each Member of the Council shall have one representative.

4. The Council shall be so organized as to be able to function continuously.

5. In addition to the functions conferred upon it by this Treaty and to those which may be assigned to it by the General Conference, the Council shall, through the General Secretary, ensure the proper operation of the control system, in accordance with the provisions of this Treaty and with the decisions adopted by the General Conference.

6. The Council shall submit an annual report on its work to the General Conference as well as such special reports as it deems necessary or which the General Conference requests of it.

7. The Council shall elect its officers for each session.

8. The decisions of the Council shall be taken by a simply majority of its Members present and voting.

9. The Council shall adopt its own rules of procedure.

The Secretariat

Article 11

1. The Secretariat shall consist of a General Secretary, who shall be the chief administrative officer of the Agency, and of such staff as the Agency may require. The term of office of the General Secretary shall be four years and he may be re-elected for a single additional term.   The General Secretary may not be a national of the country in which the Agency has its headquarters.   In case the office of General Secretary becomes vacant, a new election shall be held to fill the office for the remainder of the term.

2. The staff of the Secretariat shall be appointed by the General Secretary, in accordance with rules laid down by the General Conference.

3. In addition to the functions conferred upon him by this Treaty and to those which may be assigned to him by the General Conference, the General Secretary shall ensure, as provided by article 10, paragraph 5, the proper operation of the control system established by this Treaty, in accordance with the provisions of the Treaty and the decisions taken by the General Conference.

4. The General Secretary shall act in that capacity in all meetings of the General Conference and of the Council and shall make an annual report to both bodies on the

work of the Agency and any special reports requested by the General Conference or the Council or which the General Secretary may deem desirable.

5. The General Secretary shall establish the procedures for distributing to all Contracting Parties information received by the Agency from governmental sources and such information from non-governmental sources as may be of interest to the Agency.

6. In the performance of their duties the General Secretary and the staff shall not seek or receive instructions from any Government or from any other authority external to the Agency and shall refrain from any action which might reflect on their position as international officials responsible only to the Agency; subject to their responsibility to the Agency, they shall not disclose any industrial secrets or other confidential information coming to their knowledge by reason of their official duties in the Agency.

7. Each of the Contracting Parties undertakes to respect the exclusively international character of the responsibilities of the General Secretary and the staff and not to seek to influence them in the discharge of their responsibilities.

Control System

Article 12

1. For the purpose of verifying compliance with the obligations entered into by the Contracting Parties in accordance with article 1, a control system shall be established which shall be put into effect in accordance with the provisions of articles 13-18 of this Treaty.

2. The control system shall be used in particular for the purpose of verifying:

(a) That devices, services and facilities intended for peaceful uses of nuclear energy are not used in the testing or manufacture of nuclear weapons;

(b) That none of the activities prohibited in article 1 of this Treaty are carried out in the territory of the Contracting Parties with nuclear materials or weapons introduced from abroad; and

(c) That explosions for peaceful purposes are compatible with article 18 of this Treaty.

IAEA Safeguards

Article 13

Each Contracting Party shall negotiate multilateral or bilateral agreements with the International Atomic Energy Agency for the application of its safeguards to its nuclear activities.   Each Contracting Party shall initiate negotiations within a period of 180 days after the date of the deposit of its instrument of ratification of this Treaty.   These agreements shall enter into force, for each Party, not later than eighteen months after the date of the initiation of such negotiations except in case of unforeseen circumstances or *force majeure.*

Reports of the Parties

Article 14

1. The Contracting Parties shall submit to the Agency and to the International Atomic Energy Agency, for their information, semi-annual reports stating that no activity prohibited under this Treaty has occurred in their respective territories.

2. The Contracting Parties shall simultaneously transmit to the Agency a copy of any report they may submit to the International Atomic Energy Agency which relates to matters that are the subject of this Treaty and to the application of safeguards.

3. The Contracting Parties shall also transmit to the Organization of American States, for its information, any reports that may be of interest to it, in accordance with the obligations established by the Inter-American System.

Special Reports Requested by the General Secretary

Article 15

1. With the authorisation of the Council, the General Secretary may request any of the Contracting Parties to provide the Agency with complementary or supplementary information regarding any event or circumstance connected with compliance with this Treaty, explaining his reasons.   The Contracting Parties undertake to co-operate promptly and fully with the General Secretary.

2. The General Secretary shall inform the Council and the Contracting Parties forthwith of such requests and of the respective replies.

Special Inspections

Article 16

1. The International Atomic Energy Agency and the Council established by this Treaty have the power of carrying out special inspections in the following cases:

(a) In the case of the International Atomic Energy Agency, in accordance with the agreements referred to in article 13 of this Treaty;

(b) In the case of the Council:

(i) When so requested, the reasons for the request being stated, by any Party which suspects that some activity prohibited by this Treaty has been carried out or is about to be carried out, either in the territory of any other Party or in any other place on such latter Party's behalf, the Council shall immediately arrange for such an inspection in accordance with article 10, paragraph 5;

(ii) When requested by any Party which has been suspected of or charged with having violated this Treaty, the Council shall immediately arrange for the special inspection requested in accordance with article 10, paragraph 5.

The above requests will be made to the Council through the General Secretary.

2. The costs and expenses of any special inspection carried out under paragraph 1, subparagraph (b), sections (i) and (ii) of this article shall be borne by the requesting Party or Parties, except where the Council concludes on the basis of the report on the special inspection that, in view of the circumstances existing in the case, such costs and expenses should be borne by the Agency.

3. The General Conference shall formulate the procedures for the organization and execution of the special instructions carried out in accordance with paragraph 1, sub-paragraph (b), sections (i) and (ii) of this article.

4. The Contracting Parties undertake to grant the inspectors carrying out such special inspections full and free access to all places and all information which may be necessary for the performance of their duties and which are directly and intimately connected with the suspicion of violation of this Treaty.   If so requested by the authorities of the Contracting Party in whose territory the inspection is carried out, the inspectors designated by the General Conference shall be accompanied by

representatives of said authorities, provided that this does not in any way delay or hinder the work of the inspectors.

5. The Council shall immediately transmit to all the Parties, through the General Secretary, a copy of any report resulting from special inspections.

6. Similarly, the Council shall send through the General Secretary, to the Secretary-General of the United Nations, for transmission to the United Nations Security Council and General Assembly, and to the Council of the Organization of American States, for its information, a copy of any report resulting from any special inspection carried out in accordance with paragraph 1, subparagraph (b), sections (i) and (ii) of this article.

7. The Council may decide, or any Contracting Party may request, the convening of a special session of the General Conference for the purpose of considering the reports resulting from any special inspection. In such a case, the General Secretary shall take immediate steps to convene the special session requested.

8. The General Conference, convened in special session under this article, may make recommendations to the Contracting Parties and submit reports to the Secretary-General of the United Nations to be transmitted to the United Nations Security Council and the General Assembly.

Use of Nuclear Energy for Peaceful Purposes

Article 17

Nothing in the provisions of this Treaty shall prejudice the rights of the Contracting Parties, in conformity with this Treaty, to use nuclear energy for peaceful purposes, in particular for their economic development and social progress.

Explosions for Peaceful Purposes

Article 18

1. The Contracting Parties may carry out explosions of nuclear devices for peaceful purposes – including explosions which involve devices similar to those used in nuclear weapons – or collaborate with third parties for the same purpose, provided that they do so in accordance with the provisions of this article and the other articles of the Treaty, particularly articles 1 and 5.

2. Contracting Parties intending to carry out, or to co-operate in carrying out, such an explosion shall notify the Agency and the International Atomic Energy Agency, as far in advance as the circumstances require, of the date of the explosion and shall at the same time provide the following information:

(a) The nature of the nuclear device and the source from which it was obtained;

(b) The place and purpose of the planned explosion;

(c) The procedures which will be followed in order to comply with paragraph 3 of this article;

(d) The expected force of the device; and

(e) The fullest possible information on any possible radioactive fallout that may result from the explosion or explosions, and measures which will be taken to avoid danger to the population, flora, fauna and territories of any other Party or Parties.

3. The General Secretary and the technical personnel designated by the Council and the International Atomic Energy Agency may observe all the preparations, including the explosion of the device, and shall have unrestricted access to any area in the vicinity of the site of the explosion in order to ascertain whether the device and the

procedures followed during the explosion are in conformity with the information supplied under paragraph 2 of this article and the other provisions of this Treaty.

4.   The Contracting Parties may accept the collaboration of third parties for the purposes set forth in paragraph 1 of the present article, in accordance with paragraphs 2 and 3 thereof.

Relations with Other International Organizations

Article 19

1.   The Agency may conclude such agreements with the International Atomic Energy Agency as are authorized by the General Conference and as it considers likely to facilitate the efficient operation of the control system established by this Treaty.

2.   The Agency may also enter into relations with any international organization or body, especially any which may be established in the future to supervise disarmament or measures for the control of armaments in any part of the world.

3.   The Contracting Parties may, if they see fit, request the advice of the Inter-American Nuclear Energy Commission on all technical matters connected with the application of this Treaty with which the Commission is competent to deal under its Statute.

Measures in the Event of Violation of the Treaty

Article 20

1.   The General Conference shall take note of all cases in which, in its opinion, any Contracting Party is not complying fully with its obligations under this Treaty and shall draw the matter to the attention of the Party concerned, making such recommendations as it deems appropriate.

2.   If, in its opinion, such non-compliance constitutes a violation of this Treaty which might endanger peace and security, the General Conference shall report thereon simultaneously to the United Nations Security Council and the General Assembly through the Secretary-General of the United Nations, and to the Council of the Organization of American States.   The General Conference shall likewise report to the International Atomic Energy Agency for such purposes as are relevant in accordance with its Statute.

United Nations and Organization of American States

Article 21

None of the provisions of this Treaty shall be construed as impairing the rights and obligations of the Parties under the Charter of the United Nations or, in the case of States Members of the Organization of American States, under existing regional treaties.

Privileges and Immunities

Article 22

1. The Agency shall enjoy in the territory of each of the Contracting Parties such legal capacity and such privileges and immunities as may be necessary for the exercise of its functions and the fulfilment of its purposes.
2. Representatives of the Contracting Parties accredited to the Agency and officials of the Agency shall similarly enjoy such privileges and immunities as are necessary for the performance of their functions.
3. The Agency may conclude agreements with the Contracting Parties with a view to determining the details of the application of paragraphs 1 and 2 of this article.

Notification of Other Agreements

Article 23

Once this Treaty has entered into force, the Secretariat shall be notified immediately of any international agreement concluded by any of the Contracting Parties on matters with which this Treaty is concerned; the Secretariat shall register it and notify the other Contracting Parties.

Settlement of Disputes

Article 24

Unless the Parties concerned agree on another mode of peaceful settlement, any question or dispute concerning the interpretation or application of this Treaty which is not settled shall be referred to the International Court of Justice with the prior consent of the Parties to the controversy.

Signature

Article 25

1. This Treaty shall be open indefinitely for signature by:
(a) All the Latin American Republics, and
(b) All other sovereign States situated in their entirety south of latitude 35° north in the western hemisphere; and, except as provided in paragraph 2 of this article, all such States which become sovereign, when they have been admitted by the General Conference.
2. The General Conference shall not take any decision regarding the admission of a political entity part or all of whose territory is the subject, prior to the date when this Treaty is opened for signature, of a dispute or claim between an extra-continental country and one or more Latin American States, so long as the dispute has not been settled by peaceful means.

Ratification and Deposit

Article 26

1. This Treaty shall be subject to ratification by signatory States in accordance with their respective constitutional procedures.
2. This Treaty and the instruments of ratification shall be deposited with the Government of the Mexican United States, which is hereby designated the Depositary Government.
3. The Depositary Government shall send certified copies of this Treaty to the Governments of signatory States and shall notify them of the deposit of each instrument of ratification.

Reservations

Article 27

This Treaty shall not be subject to reservations.

Entry into Force

Article 28

1. Subject to the provisions of paragraph 2 of this article, this Treaty shall enter into force among the States that have ratified it as soon as the following requirements have been met:

   (a) Deposit of the instruments of ratification of this Treaty with the Depositary Government by the Governments of the States mentioned in article 25 which are in existence on the date when this Treaty is opened for signature and which are not affected by the provisions of article 25, paragraph 2;

   (b) Signature and ratification of Additional Protocol I annexed to this Treaty by all extra-continental or continental States having *de jure* or *de facto* international responsibility for territories situated in the zone of application of the Treaty;

   (c) Signature and ratification of the Additional Protocol II annexed to this Treaty by all powers possessing nuclear weapons;

   (d) Conclusion of bilateral or multilateral agreements on the application of the Safeguards System of the International Atomic Energy Agency in accordance with article 13 of this Treaty.

2. All signatory States shall have the imprescriptible right to waive, wholly or in part, the requirements laid down in the preceding paragraph. They may do so by means of a declaration which shall be annexed to their respective instrument of ratification and which may be formulated at the time of deposit of the instrument or subsequently. For those States which exercise this right, this Treaty shall enter into force upon deposit of the declaration, or as soon as those requirements have been met which have not been expressly waived.
3. As soon as this Treaty has entered into force in accordance with the provisions of paragraph 2 for eleven States, the Depositary Government shall convene a preliminary meeting of those States in order that the Agency may be set up and commence its work.
4. After the entry into force of this Treaty for all the countries of the zone, the rise of a new power possessing nuclear weapons shall have the effect of suspending the execution of this Treaty for those countries which have ratified it without waiving requirements of paragraph 1, subparagraph (c) of this article, and which request such

suspension; the Treaty shall remain suspended until the new power, on its own initiative or upon request by the General Conference, ratifies the annexed Additional Protocol II.

Amendments

Article 29

1. Any Contracting Party may propose amendments to this Treaty and shall submit its proposals to the Council through the General Secretary, who shall transmit them to all the other Contracting Parties and, in addition, to all other signatories in accordance with article 6. The Council, through the General Secretary, shall immediately following the meeting of signatories convene a special session of the General Conference to examine the proposals made, for the adoption of which a two-thirds majority of the Contracting Parties present and voting shall be required.

2. Amendments adopted shall enter into force as soon as the requirements set forth in article 28 of this Treaty have been complied with.

Duration and Denunciation

Article 30

1. This Treaty shall be of a permanent nature and shall remain in force indefinitely, but any Party may denounce it by notifying the General Secretary of the Agency if, in the opinion of the denouncing State, there have arisen or may arise circumstances connected with the content of this Treaty or of the annexed Additional Protocols I and II which affect its supreme interests or the peace and security of one or more Contracting Parties.

2. The denunciation shall take effect three months after the delivery to the General Secretary of the Agency of the notification by the Government of the signatory State concerned. The General Secretary shall immediately communicate such notification to the other Contracting Parties and to the Secretary-General of the United Nations for the information of the United Nations Security Council and the General Assembly. He shall also communicate it to the Secretary-General of the Organization of American States.

Authentic Texts and Registration

Article 31

This Treaty, of which the Spanish, Chinese, English, French, Portuguese and Russian texts are equally authentic, shall be registered by the Depositary Government in accordance with article 102 of the United Nations Charter. The Depositary Government shall notify the Secretary-General of the United Nations of the signatures, ratifications and amendments relating to this Treaty and shall communicate them to the Secretary-General of the Organization of American States for its information.

Transitional Article

Denunciation of the declaration referred to in article 28, paragraph 2, shall be subject to the same procedures as the denunciation of this Treaty, except that it will take effect on the date of delivery of the respective notification.

IN WITNESS WHEREOF the undersigned Plenipotentiaries, having deposited their full powers, found in good and due form, sign this Treaty on behalf of their respective Governments.

DONE at Mexico, Distrito Federal, on the Fourteenth day of February, one thousand nine hundred and sixty-seven.

Additional Protocol I

The undersigned Plenipotentiaries, furnished with full powers by their respective Governments,

Convinced that the Treaty for the Prohibition of Nuclear Weapons in Latin America, negotiated and signed in accordance with the recommendations of the General Assembly of the United Nations in Resolution 1911 (XVIII) of 27 November 1963, represents an important step towards ensuring the non-proliferation of nuclear weapons,

Aware that the non-proliferation of nuclear weapons is not an end in itself but, rather, a means of achieving general and complete disarmament at a later stage, and

Desiring to contribute, so far as lies in their power, towards ending the armaments race, especially in the field of nuclear weapons, and towards strengthening a world peace, based on mutual respect and sovereign equality of States,

Have agreed as follows:

Article 1

To undertake to apply the statute of denuclearization in respect of warlike purposes as defined in articles 1, 3, 5 and 13 of the Treaty for the Prohibition of Nuclear Weapons in Latin America in territories for which, *de jure* or *de facto*, they are internationally responsible and which lie within the limits of the geographical zone established in that Treaty.

Article 2

The duration of this Protocol shall be the same as that of the Treaty for the Prohibition of Nuclear Weapons in Latin America of which this Protocol is an annex, and the provisions regarding ratification and denunciation contained in the Treaty shall be applicable to it.

Article 3

This Protocol shall enter into force, for the States which have ratified it, on the date of the deposit of their respective instruments of ratification.

IN WITNESS WHEREOF the undersigned Plenipotentiaries, having deposited their full powers, found in good and due form, sign this Protocol on behalf of their respective Governments.

Additional Protocol II

The undersigned Plenipotentiaries, furnished with full powers by their respective Governments,

Convinced that the Treaty for the Prohibition of Nuclear Weapons in Latin America, negotiated and signed in accordance with the recommendations of the General Assembly of the United Nations in Resolution 1911 (XVIII) of 27 November 1963, represents an important step towards ensuring the non-proliferation of nuclear weapons,

Aware that the non-proliferation of nuclear weapons is not an end in itself but, rather, a means of achieving general and complete disarmament at a later stage, and

Desiring to contribute, so far as lies in their power, towards ending the armaments race, especially in the field of nuclear weapons, and towards promoting and strengthening a world at peace, based on mutual respect and sovereign equality of States,

Have agreed as follows:

Article 1

The statute of denuclearization of Latin America in respect of warlike purposes, as defined, delimited and set forth in the Treaty for the Prohibition of Nuclear Weapons in Latin America of which this instrument is an annex, shall be fully respected by the Parties to this Protocol in all its express aims and provisions.

Article 2

The Governments represented by the undersigned Plenipotentiaries undertake, therefore, not to contribute in any way to the performance of acts involving a violation of the obligations of article 2 of the Treaty in the territories to which the Treaty applies in accordance with article 4 thereof.

Article 3

The Governments represented by the undersigned Plenipotentiaries also undertake not to use or threaten to use nuclear weapons against the Contracting Parties of the Treaty for the prohibition of Nuclear Weapons in Latin America.

Article 4

The duration of this Protocol shall be the same as that of the Treaty for the Prohibition of Nuclear Weapons in Latin America of which this Protocol is an annex, and the definitions of territory and nuclear weapons set forth in articles 3 and 5 of the Treaty shall be applicable to this Protocol, as well as the provisions regarding ratification, reservations, denunciation, authentic texts and registration contained in articles 26, 27, 30 and 31 of the Treaty.

Article 5

This Protocol shall enter into force, for the States which have ratified it, on the date of the deposit of their respective instruments of ratification.

IN WITNESS WHEREOF, the undersigned Plenipotentiaries, having deposited their full powers, found to be in good and due form, hereby sign this Additional Protocol on behalf of their respective Governments.

9.6 TREATY OF RAROTONGA, ESTABLISHING A SOUTH PACIFIC NUCLEAR-FREE ZONE, 1985

Preamble

The Parties to this Treaty,

United in their commitment to a world at peace;

Gravely concerned that the continuing nuclear arms race presents the risk of nuclear war which would have devastating consequences for all people;

Convinced that all countries have an obligation to make every effort to achieve the goal of eliminating nuclear weapons, the terror which they hold for humankind and the threat which they pose to life on earth;

Believing that regional arms control measures can contribute to global efforts to reverse the nuclear arms race and promote the national security of each country in the region and the common security of all;

Determined to ensure, so far as lies within their power, that the bounty and beauty of the land and sea in their region shall remain the heritage of their peoples and their descendants in perpetuity to be enjoyed by all in peace;

Reaffirming the importance of the Treaty on the Non-Proliferation of Nuclear Weapons (NPT) in preventing the proliferation of nuclear weapons and in contributing to world security;

Noting, in particular, that Article VII of the NPT recognizes the right of any group of States to conclude regional treaties in order to assure the total absence of nuclear weapons on their respective territories;

Noting that the prohibitions of emplantation and emplacement of nuclear weapons on the seabed and the ocean floor and in the subsoil thereof contained in the Treaty on the Prohibition of Emplacement of Nuclear Weapons and Other Weapons of Mass Destruction on the Seabed and the Ocean Floor and in the Subsoil Thereof apply in the South Pacific;

Noting also that the prohibition of testing of nuclear weapons in the atmosphere or under water, including territorial waters or high seas, contained in the Treaty Banning Nuclear Weapon Tests in the Atmosphere, in Outer Space and Under Water applies in the South Pacific;

Determined to keep the region free of environmental pollution by radioactive wastes and other radioactive matter;

Guided by the decision of the Fifteenth South Pacific Forum at Tuvalu that a nuclear free zone should be established in the region at the earliest possible opportunity in accordance with the principles set out in the communiqué of that meeting:

Have agreed as follows:

Article 1
Usage of Terms

For the purposes of this Treaty and its Protocols:

(a) "South Pacific Nuclear Free Zone" means the areas described in Annex 1 as illustrated by the map attached to that Annex;

(b) "territory" means internal waters, territorial sea and archipelagic waters, the seabed and subsoil beneath, the land territory and the airspace above them;

(c) "nuclear explosive device" means any nuclear weapon or other explosive device capable of releasing nuclear energy, irrespective of the purpose for which it could be used. The term includes such a weapon or device in unassembled and partly assembled forms, but does not include the means of transport or delivery of such a weapon or device if separable from and not an indivisible part of it;

(d) "stationing" means emplantation, emplacement, transportation on land or inland waters, stockpiling, storage, installation and deployment.

Article 2
Application of the Treaty

1. Except where otherwise specified, this Treaty and its Protocols shall apply to territory within the South Pacific Nuclear Free Zone.
2. Nothing in this Treaty shall prejudice or in any way affect the rights, or the exercise of the rights, of any State under international law with regard to freedom of the seas.

Article 3
Renunciation of Nuclear Explosive Devices

Each Party undertakes:

(a) not to manufacture or otherwise acquire, possess or have control over any nuclear explosive device by any means anywhere inside or outside the South Pacific Nuclear Free Zone;

(b) not to seek or receive any assistance in the manufacture or acquisition of any nuclear explosive device;

(c) not to take any action to assist or encourage the manufacture or acquisition of any nuclear explosive device by any State.

Article 4
Peaceful Nuclear Activities

Each Party undertakes:

(a) not to provide source or special fissionable material, or equipment or material especially designed or prepared for the processing, use or production of special fissionable material for peaceful purposes to:

(i) any non-nuclear-weapon State unless subject to the safeguards required by Article III.1 of the NPT, or

(ii) any nuclear-weapon State unless subject to applicable safeguards agreements with the International Atomic Energy Agency (IAEA).

Any such provisions shall be in accordance with strict non-proliferation measures to provide assurance of exclusively peaceful non-explosive use;

(b) to support the continued effectiveness of the international non-proliferation system based on the NPT and the IAEA safeguards system.

Article 5
Prevention of Stationing of Nuclear Explosive Devices

1. Each Party undertakes to prevent in its territory the stationing of any nuclear explosive device.
2. Each Party in the exercise of its sovereign rights remains free to decide for itself whether to allow visits by foreign ships and aircraft to its ports and airfields, transit of its airspace by foreign aircraft, and navigation by foreign ships in its territorial sea or archipelagic waters in a manner not covered by the rights of innocent passage, archipelagic sea lane passage or transit passage of straits.

Article 6
Prevention of Testing of Nuclear Explosive Devices

Each party undertakes:

(a) to prevent in its territory the testing of any nuclear explosive device;

(b) not to take any action to assist or encourage the testing of any nuclear explosive device by any State.

Article 7
Prevention of Dumping

1. Each party undertakes:
    (a) not to dump radioactive wastes and other radioactive matter at sea anywhere within the South Pacific Nuclear Free Zone;
    (b) to prevent the dumping of radioactive wastes and other radioactive matter by anyone in its territorial sea;
    (c) not to take any action to assist or encourage the dumping by anyone of radioactive wastes and other radioactive matter at sea anywhere within the South Pacific Nuclear Free Zone;
    (d) to support the conclusion as soon as possible of the proposed Convention relating to the protection of the natural resources and environment of the South Pacific region and its Protocol for the prevention of pollution of the South Pacific region by dumping, with the aim of precluding dumping at sea of radioactive wastes and other radioactive matter by anyone anywhere in the region.
2. Paragraphs 1(a) and 1(b) of this Article shall not apply to areas of the South Pacific Nuclear Free Zone in respect of which such a Convention and Protocol have entered into force.

Article 8
Control System

1. The Parties hereby establish a control system for the purpose of verifying compliance with their obligations under this Treaty.
2. The control system shall comprise:
    (a) reports and exchange if information as provided for in Article 9;
    (b) consultations as provided for in Article 10 and Annex 4(1);
    (c) the application to peaceful nuclear activities of safeguards by the IAEA as provided for in Annex 2;
    (d) a complaints procedure as provided for in Annex 4.

Article 9
Reports and Exchanges of Information

1. Each Party shall report to the Director of the South Pacific Bureau for Economic Co-operation (the Director) as soon as possible any significant event within its jurisdiction affecting the implementation of this Treaty. The Director shall circulate such reports promptly to all Parties.
2. The Parties shall endeavour to keep each other informed on matters arising under or in relation to this Treaty. They may exchange information by communicating it to the Director, who shall circulate it to all Parties.
3. The Director shall report annually to the South Pacific Forum on the status of this Treaty and matters arising under or in relation to it, incorporating reports and communications made under paragraphs 1 and 2 of this Article and matters arising under Articles 8(2)(d) and 10 and Annex 2(4).

Article 10
Consultations and Review

Without prejudice to the conduct of consultations among Parties by other means, the Director, at the request of any Party, shall convene a meeting of the Consultative Committee established by Annex 3 for consultation and co-operation on any matter arising in relation to this Treaty or for reviewing its operation.

Article 11
Amendment

The Consultative Committee shall consider proposals for amendment of the provisions of this Treaty proposed by any Party and circulated by the Director to all Parties not less than three months prior to the convening of the Consultative Committee for this purpose. Any proposal agreed upon by consensus by the Consultative Committee shall be communicated to the Director who shall circulate it for acceptance to all Parties. An amendment shall enter into force thirty days after receipt by the depositary of acceptances from all Parties.

Article 12
Signature and Ratification

1. This Treaty shall be open for signature by any member of the South Pacific Forum.
2. This Treaty shall be subject to ratification. Instruments of ratification shall be deposited with the Director who is hereby designated depositary of this Treaty and its Protocols.
3. If a member of the South Pacific Forum whose territory is outside the South Pacific Nuclear Free Zone becomes a Party to this Treaty, Annex 1 shall be deemed to be amended so far as is required to enclose at least the territory of that Party within the boundaries of the South Pacific Nuclear Free Zone. The delineation of any area added pursuant to this paragraph shall be approved by the South Pacific Forum.

Article 13
Withdrawal

1. This treaty is of a permanent nature and shall remain in force indefinitely, provided that in the event of a violation by any Party of a provision of this Treaty essential to the achievement of the objectives of the Treaty or of the spirit of the Treaty, every other Party shall have the right to withdraw from the Treaty.
2. Withdrawal shall be effected by giving notice twelve months in advance to the Director who shall circulate such notice to all other Parties.

Article 14
Reservations

This Treaty shall not be subject to reservations.

Article 15
Entry into Force

1. This Treaty shall enter into force on the date of deposit of the eighth instrument of ratification.

2. For a signatory which ratifies this Treaty after the date of deposit of the eighth instrument of notification, the Treaty shall enter into force on the date of deposit of its instrument of ratification.

Article 16
Depositary Functions

The depositary shall register this Treaty and its Protocols pursuant to Article 102 of the Charter of the United Nations and shall transmit certified copies of the Treaty and its Protocols to all Members of the South Pacific Forum and all States eligible to become Party to the Protocols to the Treaty and shall notify them of signatures and ratifications of the Treaty and its Protocols.

IN WITNESS WHEREOF the undersigned, being duly authorized by their Governments, have signed this Treaty.

DONE at Rarotonga, this sixth day of August, One thousand nine hundred and eight-five, in a single original in the English language.

[The following Annexes are omitted:
Annex 1: South Pacific Nuclear Free Zone with south Pacific Nuclear Free Zone Map
Annex 2: IAEA Safeguards
Annex 3: Consultative Committee
Annex 4: Complaints Procedure]

Protocol I

The Parties to this Protocol
Noting the South Pacific Nuclear Free Zone Treaty (the Treaty)
Have agreed as follows:

Article 1

Each Party undertakes to apply, in respect of the territories for which it is internationally responsible situated within the South Pacific Nuclear Free Zone, the prohibitions contained in Articles 3, 5 and 6, in so far as they relate to the manufacture, stationing and testing of any nuclear explosive device within those territories, and the safeguards specified in Article 8(2)(c) and Annex 2 of the Treaty.

Article 2

Each Party may, by written notification to the depositary, indicate its acceptance from the date of such notification of any alteration to its obligation under this Protocol brought about by the entry into force of an amendment to the Treaty pursuant to Article 11 of the Treaty.

Article 3

This Protocol shall be open for signature by the French Republic, the United Kingdom of Great Britain and Northern Ireland and the United States of America.

Article 4

This Protocol shall be subject to ratification.

Article 5

This Protocol is of a permanent nature and shall remain in force indefinitely, provided that each Party shall, in exercising its national sovereignty, have the right to withdraw from this Protocol if it decides that extraordinary events, related to the subject matter of this Protocol, have jeopardized its supreme interests. It shall give notice of such withdrawal to the depositary three months in advance. Such notice shall include a statement of the extraordinary events it regards as having jeopardized its supreme interests.

Article 6

This Protocol shall enter into force for each State on the date of its deposit with the depositary of its instrument of ratification.

IN WITNESS WHEREOF the undersigned, being duly authorized by their Governments, have signed this Protocol.

DONE at Suva, this Eighth day of August, One thousand nine hundred and eighty-six, in a single original in the English language.

Protocol 2

The Parties to this Protocol
Noting the South Pacific Nuclear Free Zone Treaty (the Treaty)
Have agreed as follows:

Article 1

Each Party undertakes not to use or threaten to use any nuclear explosive device against:
(a) Parties to the Treaty; or
(b) any territory within the South Pacific Nuclear Free Zone for which a State that has become a Party to Protocol 1 is internationally responsible.

Article 2

Each Party undertakes not to contribute to any act of a Party to the Treaty which constitutes a violation of the Treaty, or to any act of another Party to a Protocol which constitutes a violation of a Protocol.

Article 3

Each Party may, by written notification to the depositary, indicate its acceptance from the date of such notification of any alteration to its obligation under this Protocol brought about by the entry into force of an amendment to the Treaty pursuant to Article 11 of the Treaty or by the extension of the South Pacific Nuclear Free Zone pursuant to Article 12(3) of the Treaty.

Article 4

This Protocol shall be open for signature by the French Republic, the People's Republic of China, the Union of Soviet Socialist Republics, the United Kingdom of Great Britain and Northern Ireland and the United States of America.

Article 5

This Protocol shall be subject to ratification.

Article 6

This Protocol is of a permanent nature and shall remain in force indefinitely, provided that each Party shall, in exercising its national sovereignty, have the right to withdraw from this Protocol if it decides that extraordinary events, related to the subject matter of this Protocol, have jeopardized its supreme interests.   It shall give notice of such withdrawal to the depositary three months in advance.   Such notice shall include a statement of the extraordinary events it regards as having jeopardized its supreme interests.

Article 7

This Protocol shall enter into force for each State on the date of its deposit with the depositary of its instrument of ratification.

IN WITNESS WHEREOF the undersigned, being duly authorized by their Governments, have signed this Protocol.

DONE at Suva, this Eighth day of August, One thousand nine hundred and eighty-six, in a single original in the English language.

Protocol 3

The Parties to this Protocol
Noting the South Pacific Nuclear Free Zone Treaty (the Treaty)
Have agreed as follows:

Article 1

Each Party undertakes not to test any nuclear explosive device anywhere within the South Pacific Nuclear Free Zone.

Article 2

Each Party may, by written notification to the depositary, indicate its acceptance from the date of such notification of any alteration to its obligation under this Protocol brought about by the entry into force of an amendment to the Treaty pursuant to Article 11 of the Treaty or by the extension of the South Pacific Nuclear Free Zone pursuant to Article 12(3) of the Treaty.

Article 3

This Protocol shall be open for signature by the French Republic, the People's Republic of China, the Union of Soviet Socialist Republics, the United Kingdom of Great Britain and Northern Ireland and the United States of America.

Article 4

This Protocol shall be subject to ratification.

Article 5

This Protocol is of a permanent nature and shall remain in force indefinitely, provided that each Party shall, in exercising its national sovereignty, have the right to withdraw from this Protocol if it decides that extraordinary events, related to the subject matter of this Protocol, have jeopardized its supreme interests.   It shall give notice of such withdrawal to the depositary three months in advance.   Such notice shall include a statement of the extraordinary events it regards as having jeopardized its supreme interests.

Article 6

This Protocol shall enter into force for each State on the date of its deposit with the depositary of its instrument of ratification.

IN WITNESS WHEREOF the undersigned, being duly authorized by their Governments, have signed this Protocol.

DONE at Suva, this Eighth day of August, One thousand nine hundred and eighty-six, in a single original in the English language.

9.7 AGREEMENT BETWEEN THE UNITED KINGDOM AND THE USSR CONCERNING THE PREVENTION OF INCIDENTS AT SEA BEYOND THE TERRITORIAL SEA, 1986

The Government of the United Kingdom of Great Britain and Northern Ireland and the Government of the Union of Soviet Socialist Republics;

Desiring to ensure the safety of navigation of the ships of their respective armed forces, and of the flight of their military aircraft beyond the territorial sea;

Acknowledging that actions prohibited by this Agreement should also not be taken against non-military ships of the Parties;

Guided by the principles and rules of international law;

Have agreed as follows:

Article I

For the purposes of this Agreement the following definitions shall apply:

1.   "Ship" means:

(a) A warship belonging to the armed forces of the Parties bearing the external marks distinguishing warships of its nationality, under the command of an officer duly commissioned by the Government and whose name appears in the appropriate service list or its equivalent, and manned by a crew who are under regular armed forces discipline; and

(b) Auxiliary ships belonging to the armed forces of the Parties, which include all ships authorized to fly the auxiliary ship flag where such a flag has been established by either Party;

2.   "Aircraft" means all military manned heavier-than-air and lighter-than-air craft, excluding space craft;

3.   "Formation" means an ordered arrangement of two or more ships proceeding in company and normally manoeuvring together.

This Agreement shall apply to ships and aircraft operating beyond the territorial sea.

Article II

The Parties shall take measures to instruct the Commanding Officers of their respective ships to observe strictly the letter and spirit of the 1972 International Regulations for Preventing Collisions at Sea, hereinafter referred to as "the 1972 Collision Regulations". The Parties recognize that their freedom to conduct operations beyond the territorial sea is based on the principles established under recognized international law and codified in the 1958 Geneva Convention on the High Seas.

Article III

1. In all cases ships of the Parties operating in proximity to each other, except when required to maintain course and speed under the 1972 Collision Regulations, shall remain well clear to avoid risk of collision.
2. Ships meeting or operating in the vicinity of a formation of the other Party shall, while conforming to the 1972 Collision Regulations, avoid manoeuvring in a manner which would hinder the evolutions of the formation.
3. Formations shall not conduct manoeuvres through areas of heavy traffic where internationally recognized traffic separation schemes are in effect.
4. Ships engaged in surveillance of ships of the other Party shall stay at a distance which avoids the risk of collision and shall also avoid executing manoeuvres embarrassing or endangering the ships under surveillance. Except when required to maintain course and speed under the 1972 Collision Regulations, a surveillant shall take positive early action so as, in the exercise of good seamanship, not to embarrass or endanger ships under surveillance.
5. When ships of both Parties manoeuvre in sight of one another, such signals (flag, sound and light) as are prescribed by the 1972 Collision Regulations, the International Code of Signals and the Table of Special Signals set forth in the Annex to this Agreement shall be adhered to for signalling operations and intentions. At night or in conditions of reduced visibility, or under conditions of lighting and at such distances when signal flags are not distinct, flashing light or Very High Frequency Radio Channel 16 (156.8 MHz) should be used.
6. Ships of the Parties shall not simulate attacks by aiming guns, missile launchers, torpedo tubes and other weapons in the direction of passing ships of the other Party, nor launch any object in the direction of passing ships of the other Party in such a manner as to be hazardous to those ships or to constitute a hazard to navigation; nor use searchlights or other powerful illumination devices for the purpose of illuminating the navigation bridges of passing ships of the other Party.

   Such actions shall also not be taken by ships of each Party against non-military ships of the other Party.
7. When conducting exercises with submerged submarines, supporting ships shall show the appropriate signals prescribed by the International Code of Signals, or in the Table of Special Signals set forth in the Annex to this Agreement, to warn ships of the presence of submarines in the area.
8. Ships of one Party, when approaching ships of the other Party conducting operations which in accordance with Rule 3(g) of the 1972 Collision Regulations are restricted in their ability to manoeuvre, and particularly ships engaged in launching or landing aircraft as well as ships engaged in replenishment underway, shall take appropriate measures not to hinder manoeuvres of such ships and shall remain well clear.

Article IV

1.   Commanders of aircraft of the Parties shall use the greatest caution and prudence in approaching aircraft and ships of the other Party, in particular ships engaged in launching or landing aircraft, and, in the interest of mutual safety, shall not permit simulated attacks by the simulated use of weapons against aircraft and ships of the other Party, or the performance of aerobatics over ships of the other Party, or dropping objects near them in such a manner as to be hazardous to ships or to constitute a hazard to navigation.

Such actions shall also not be taken by aircraft of each Party against non-military ships of the other Party.

2.   Aircraft of the Parties flying in darkness or under instrument conditions shall, whenever feasible, display navigation lights.

Article V

The Parties shall take measures to notify the non-military ships of each Party about the provisions of this Agreement directed at securing mutual safety.

Article VI

The Parties shall   provide through the established system of radio broadcasts of information and warning to mariners, normally not less than three to five days in advance, notification of actions beyond the territorial seas which represent a danger to navigation or to aircraft in flight.

Article VII

The Parties shall exchange in a timely manner appropriate information concerning instances of collisions, incidents which result in damage, and other incidents at sea between ships and aircraft of the Parties.   The Royal Navy shall provide such information through the Soviet Naval or other Military Attaché in London and the Soviet Navy shall provide such information through the British Naval or other Military Attaché in Moscow.

Article VIII

This Agreement shall enter into force on the date of its signature. It may be terminated by either Party giving six months' written notice of termination to the other Party.

Article IX

Representatives of the Parties shall meet within one year after the date of the signing of this Agreement to review the implementation of its terms, as well as possible ways of promoting a higher level of safety of navigation of their ships and flight of their aircraft beyond the territorial sea.   Similar consultations shall be held thereafter annually, or more frequently as the Parties may decide.

IN WITNESS WHEREOF the undersigned, duly authorized thereto by their respective Governments, have signed this Agreement.

DONE in duplicate at London this 15th day of July, 1986, in the English and Russian languages, both texts being equally authoritative.

[Annex on 'Table of Special Signals' omitted.]

9.8 UNITED NATIONS CONVENTION ON CONDITIONS FOR REGISTRATION OF SHIPS, 1986

The States Parties to this Convention,
Recognizing the need to promote the orderly expansion of world shipping as a whole,
Recalling General Assembly resolution 35/56 of 5 December 1980, the annex to which contains the International Development Strategy for the Third United Nations Development Decade, which called, *inter alia*, in paragraph 128, for an increase in the participation by developing countries in world transport of international trade,
Recalling also that according to the 1958 Geneva Convention on the High Seas and the 1982 United Nations Convention on the Law of the Sea there must exist a genuine link between a ship and a flag State and conscious of the duties of the flag State to exercise effectively its jurisdiction and control over ships flying its flag in accordance with the principle of the genuine link,
Believing that to this end a flag State should have a competent and adequate national maritime administration,
Believing also that in order to exercise its control function effectively a flag State should ensure that those who are responsible for the management and operation of a ship on its register are readily identifiable and accountable,
Believing further that measures to make persons responsible for ships more readily identifiable and accountable could assist in the task of combating maritime fraud,
Reaffirming, without prejudice to this Convention, that each State shall fix the conditions for the grant of its nationality to ships, for the registration of ships in its territory and for the right to fly its flag,
Prompted by the desire among sovereign States to resolve in a spirit of mutual understanding and co-operation all issues relating to the conditions for the grant of nationality to, and for the registration of, ships,
Considering that nothing in this Convention shall be deemed to prejudice any provisions in the national laws and regulations of the Contracting Parties to this Convention, which exceed the provisions container herein,
Recognizing the competences of the specialized agencies and other institutions of the United Nations system, as contained in their respective constitutional instruments, taking into account arrangements which may have been concluded between the United Nations and the agencies, and between individual agencies and institutions in specific fields,
Have agreed as follows,

Article 1
Objectives

For the purpose of ensuring or, as the case may be, strengthening the genuine link between a State and ships flying its flag, and in order to exercise effectively its jurisdiction and control over such ships with regard to identification and accountability of shipowners and operators as well as with regard to administrative, technical, economic and social matters, a flag State shall apply the provisions contained in this Convention.

Article 2
Definitions

For the purposes of this Convention:

"Ship" means any self-propelled sea-going vessel used in international seaborne trade for the transport of goods, passengers, or both with the exception of vessels of less than 500 gross registered tons;

"Flag State" means a State whose flag a ship flies and is entitled to fly,

"Owner" or "shipowner" means, unless clearly indicated otherwise, any natural or juridical person recorded in the register of ships of the State of registration as an owner of a ship;

"Operator" means the owner or bareboat charterer, or any other natural or juridical person to whom the responsibilities of the owner or bareboat charterer have been formally assigned;

"State of registration" means the State in whose register of ships a ship has been entered;

"Register of ships" means the official register or registers in which particulars referred to in article 11 of this Convention are recorded;

"National maritime administration" means any State authority or agency which is established by the State of registration in accordance with its legislation and which, pursuant to that legislation, is responsible, *inter alia*, for the implementation of international agreements concerning maritime transport and for the application of rules and standards concernng ships under its jurisdiction and control;

"Bareboat charter" means a contract for the lease of a ship, for a stipulated period of time, by virtue of which the lessee has complete possession and control of the ship, including the right to appoint the master and crew of the ship, for the duration of the lease;

"Labour-supplying country" means a country which provides seafarers for service on a ship flying the flag of another country.

Article 3
Scope of application

This Convention shall apply to all ships as defined in article 2.

Article 4
General provisions

1. Every State, whether coastal or land-locked, has the right to sail ships flying its flag on the high seas.
2. Ships have the nationality of the State whose flag they are entitled to fly.
3. Ships shall sail under the flag of one State only.
4. No ships shall be entered in the registers of ships of two or more States at a time, subject to the provisions of paragraphs 4 and 5 of article 11 and to article 12.
5. A ship may not change its flag during a voyage or while in a port of call, save in the case of a real transfer of ownership or change of registry.

Article 5
National Maritime Administration

1. The flag State shall have a competent and adequate national maritime administration, which shall be subject to its jurisdiction and control.

2. The flag State shall implement applicable international rules and standards concerning, in particular, the safety of ships and persons on board and the prevention of pollution of the marine environment.

3. The maritime administration of the flag State shall ensure:

(a) That ships flying the flag of such State comply with its laws and regulations concerning registration of ships and with applicable international rules and standards concerning, in particular, the safety of ships and persons on board and the prevention of pollution of the marine environment;

(b) That ships flying the flag of such State are periodically surveyed by its authorized surveyors in order to ensure compliance with applicable international rules and standards;

(c) That ships flying the flag of such State carry on board documents, in particular those evidencing the right to fly its flag and other valid relevant documents, including those required by international conventions to which the State of registration is a Party;

(d) That the owners of ships flying the flag of such State comply with the principles of registration of ships in accordance with the laws and regulations of such State and the provisions of this Convention.

4. The State of registration shall require all the appropriate information necessary for full identification and accountability concerning ships flying its flag.

Article 6
Identification and accountability

1. The State of registration shall enter in its register of ships, *inter alia*, information concerning the ship and its owner or owners. Information concerning the operator, when the operator is not the owner, should be included in the register of ships or in the official record of operators to be maintained in the office of the Registrar or be readily accessible to him, in accordance with the laws and regulations of the State of registration. The State of registration shall issue documentation as evidence of the registration of the ship.

2. The State of registration shall take such measures as are necessary to ensure that the owner or owners, the operator or operators, or any other person or persons who can be held accountable for the management and operation of ships flying its flag can be easily identified by persons having a legitimate interest in obtaining such information.

3. Registers of ships should be available to those with a legitimate interest in obtaining information contained therein, in accordance with the laws and regulations of the flag State.

4. A State should ensure that ships flying its flag carry documentation including information about the identity of the owner or owners, the operator or operators or the person or persons accountable for the operation of such ships, and make available such information to port State authorities.

5. Log-books should be kept on all ships and retained for a reasonable period after the date of the last entry, notwithstanding any change in a ship's name, and should be available for inspection and copying by persons having a legitimate interest in obtaining such information, in accordance with the laws and regulations of the flag State. In the

event of a ship being sold and its registration being changed to another State, log-books relating to the period before such sale should be retained and should be available for inspection and copying by persons having a legitimate interest in obtaining such information, in accordance with the laws and regulations of the former flag State.

6.   A State shall take necessary measures to ensure that ships it enters in its register of ships have owners or operators who are adequately identifiable for the purpose of ensuring their full accountability.

7.   A State should ensure that direct contact between owners of ships flying its flag and its government authorities is not restricted.

Article 7
Participation by nationals in the ownership and/or manning of ships

With respect to the provisions concerning manning and ownerhsip of ships as contained in paragraphs 1 and 2 of article 8 and paragraphs 1 to 3 of article 9, respectively, and without prejudice to the application of any other provisions of this Convention, a State of registration has to comply either with the provisions of paragraphs 1 and 2 of article 8 or with the provisions of paragraphs 1 to 3 of article 9, but may comply with both.

Article 8
Ownership of ships

1.   Subject to the provisions of article 7, the flag State shall provide in its laws and regulations for the ownership of ships flying its flag.

2.   Subject to the provisions of article 7, in such laws and regulations the flag State shall include appropriate provisions for participation by that State or its nationals as owners of ships flying its flag or in the ownership of such ships and for the level of such participation.   These laws and regulations should be sufficient to permit the flag State to exercise effectively its jurisdiction and control over ships flying its flag.

Article 9
Manning of ships

1.   Subject to the provisions of article 7, a State of registration, when implementing this Convention, shall observe the principle that a satisfactory part of the complement consisting of officers and crew of ships flying its flag be nationals or persons domiciled or lawfully in permanent residence in that State.

2.   Subject to the provisions of article 7 and in pursuance of the goal set out in paragraph 1 of this article, and in taking necessary measures to this end, the State of registration shall have regard to the following:

    (a) the availability of qualified seafarers within the State of registration;

    (b) multilateral or bilateral agreements or other types of arrangements valid and enforceable pursuant to the legislation of the State of registration;

    (c) the sound and economically viable operation of its ships.

3.   The State of registration should implement the provision of paragraph 1 of this article on a ship, company or fleet basis.

4.   The State of registration, in accordance with its laws and regulations, may allow persons of other nationalities to serve on board ships flying its flag in accordance with the relevant provisions of this Convention.

5.   In pursuance of the goal set out in paragraph 1 of this article, the State of registration should, in co-operation with shipowners, promote the education and

training of its nationals or persons domiciled or lawfully in permanent residence within its territory.

6.   The State of registration shall ensure:

(a)   that the manning of ships flying its flag is of such a level and competence as to ensure compliance with applicable international rules and standards, in particular those regarding safety at sea;

(b)   that the terms and conditions of employment on board ships flying its flag are in conformity with applicable international rules and standards;

(c)   that adequate legal procedures exist for the settlement of civil disputes between seafarers employed on ships flying its flag and their employers;

(d)   that nationals and foreign seafarers have equal access to appropriate legal processes to secure their contractual rights in their relations with their employers.

Article 10
Role of flag States in respect of the management of shipowning companies and ships

1.   The State of registration, before entering a ship in its register of ships, shall ensure that the shipowning company or a subsidiary shipowning company is established and/or has its principal place of business within its territory in accordance with its laws and regulations.

2.   Where the shipowning company or a subsidiary shipowning company or the principal place of business of the shipowning company is not established in the flag State, the latter shall ensure, before entering a ship in its register of ships, that there is a representative or management person who shall be a national of the flag State, or be domiciled therein.   Such a representative or management person may be a natural or juridical person who is duly established or incorporated in the flag State, as the case may be, in accordance with its laws and regulations, and duly empowered to act on the shipowner's behalf and account.   In particular, this representative or management person should be available for any legal process and to meet the shipowner's responsibilities in accordance with the laws and regulations of the State of registration.

3.   The State of registration should ensure that the person or persons accountable for the management and operation of a ship flying its flag are in a position to meet the financial obligations that may arise from the operation of such a ship to cover risks which are normally insured in international maritime transportation in respect of damage to third parties.   To this end the State of registration should ensure that ships flying its flag are in a position to provide at all times documents evidencing that an adequate guarantee, such as appropriate insurance or any other equivalent means, has been arranged.   Furthermore, the State of registration should ensure that an appropriate mechanism, such as a maritime lien, mutual fund, wage insurance, social security scheme, or any governmental guarantee provided by an appropriate agency of the State of the accountable person, whether that person is an owner or operator, exists to cover wages and related monies owed to seafarers employed on ships flying its flag in the event of default of payment by their employers.   The State of registration may also provide for any other appropriate mechanism to that effect in its laws and regulations.

Article 11
Register of ships

1.   A State of registration shall establish a register of ships flying its flag, which register shall be maintained in a manner determined by that State and in conformity

with the relevant provisions of this Convention.   Ships entitled by the laws and regulations of a State to fly its flag shall be entered in this register in the name of the owner or owners or, where national laws and regulations so provide, the bareboat charterer.

2.   Such register shall, *inter alia*, record the following:

(a) the name of the ship and the previous name and registry if any;

(b) the place or port of registration or home port and the official number or mark of identification of the ship;

(c) the international call sign of the ship, if assigned;

(d) the name of the builders, place of build and year of building of the ship;

(e) the description of the main technical characteristics of the ship;

(f) the name, address and, as appropriate, the nationality of the owner or of each of the owners;

and, unless recorded in another public document readily accessible to the Registrar in the flag State:

(g) the date of deletion or suspension of the previous registration of the ship;

the name, address and, as appropriate, the nationality of the bareboat charterer, where national laws and regulations provide for the registration of ships bareboat chartered-in;

(i) the particulars of any mortgages or other similar charges upon the ship as stipulated by national laws and regulations;

3.   Furthermore, such register should also record:

(a) if there is more than one owner, the proportion of the ship owned by each;

(b) the name, address and, as appropriate, the nationality of the operator, when the operator is not the owner or the bareboat charterer.

4.   Before entering a ship in its register of ships a State should assure itself that the previous registration, if any, is deleted.

5.   In the case of a ship bareboat chartered-in a State should assure itself that right to fly the flag of the former flag State is suspended. Such registration shall be effected on production of evidence, indicating suspension of previous registration as regards the nationality of the ship under the former flag State and indicating particulars of any registered encumbrances.

Article 12
Bareboat charter

1.   Subject to the provisions of article 11 and in accordance with its laws and regulations a State may grant registration and the right to fly its flag to a ship bareboat chartered-in by a charterer in that State, for the period of that charter.

2.   When shipowners or charterers in States Parties to this Convention enter into such bareboat charter activities, the conditions of registration contained in this convention should be fully complied with.

3.   To achieve the goal of compliance and for the purpose of applying the requirements of this Convention in the case of a ship so bareboat chartered-in the charterer will be considered to be the owner.   This Convention, however, does not have the effect of providing for any ownership rights in the chartered ship other than those stipulated in the particular bareboat charter contract.

4.   A State should ensure that a ship bareboat chartered-in and flying its flag, pursuant to paragraphs 1 to 3 of this article, will be subject to its full jurisdiction and control.

5. The State where the bareboat chartered-in ship is registered shall ensure that the former flag State is notified of the deletion of the registration of the bareboat chartered ship.
6. All terms and conditions, other than those specified in this article, relating to the relationship of the parties to a bareboat charter are left to the contractual disposal of those parties.

Article 13
Joint ventures

1. Contracting Parties to this Convention, in conformity with their national policies, legislation and the conditions for registration of ships contained in this Convention, should promote joint ventures between shipowners of different countries, and should, to this end, adopt appropriate arrangements, *inter alia,* by safeguarding the contractual rights of the parties to joint ventures, to further the establishment of such joint ventures in order to develop the national shipping industry.
2. Regional and international financial institutions and aid agencies should be invited to contribute, as appropriate, to the establishment and/or strengthening of joint ventures in the shipping industry of developing countries, particularly in the least developed among them.

Article 14
Measures to protect the interests of labour-supplying countries

1. For the purposes of safeguarding the interests of labour-supplying countries and of minimizing labour displacement and consequent economic dislocation, if any, within these countries, particularly developing countries, as a result of the adoption of this Convention, urgency should be given to the implementation, *inter alia,* of the measures as contained in Resolution 1 annexed to this Convention.
2. In order to create favourable conditions for any contract or arrangement that may be entered into by shipowners or operators and the trade unions of seamen or other representative seamen bodies, bilateral agreements may be concluded between flag States and labour-supplying countries concerning the employment of seafarers of those labour-supplying countries.

Article 15
Measures to minimize adverse economic effects

For the purpose of minimizing adverse economic effects that might occur within developing countries in the process of adapting and implementing conditions to meet the requirements established by this Convention, urgency should be given to the implementation, *inter alia,* of the measures as contained in Resolution 2 annexed to this Convention.

Article 16
Depositary

The Secretary-General of the United Nations shall be the depositary of this Convention.

Article 17
Implementation

1. Contracting Parties shall take any legislative or other measures necessary to implement this Convention.
2. Each Contracting Party shall, at appropriate times, communicate to the depositary the texts of any legislative or other measures which it has taken in order to implement this Convention.
3. The depositary shall transmit upon request to Contracting Parties the texts of the legislative or other measures which have been communicated to him pursuant to paragraph 2 of this article.

Article 18
Signature, ratification, acceptance, approval and accession

1. All States are entitled to become Contracting Parties to this Convention by:
(a) signature not subject to ratification, acceptance or approval; or
(b) signature subject to and followed by ratification, acceptance or approval; or
(c) accession.
2. This Convention shall be open for signature from 1 May 1986 to and including 30 April, 1987, at the Headquarters of the United Nations in New York and shall thereafter remain open for accession.
3. Instruments of ratification, acceptance, approval or accession shall be deposited with the depositary.

Article 19
Entry into force

1. This Convention shall enter into force 12 months after the date on which not less than 40 States, the combined tonnage of which amounts to at least 25 per cent of world tonnage, have become Contracting Parties to it in accordance with article 18. For the purpose of this article the tonnage shall be deemed to be that contained in annex III to this Convention.
2. For each State which becomes a Contracting Party to this Convention after the conditions for entry into force under paragraph 1 of this article have been met, the Convention shall enter into force for that State 12 months after that State has become a Contracting Party.

Article 20
Review and amendments

1. After the expiry of a period of eight years from the date of entry into force of this Convention, a Contracting Party may, by written communication addressed to the Secretary-General of the United Nations, propose specific amendments to this Convention and request the convening of a review conference to consider such proposed amendments. The Secretary-General shall circulate such communication to all Contracting Parties. If, within 12 months from the date of the circulation of the communication, not less than two-fifths of the Contracting Parties reply favourably to the request, the Secretary-General shall convene the Review Conference.
2. The Secretary-General of the United Nations shall circulate to all Contracting Parties the texts of any proposals for, or views regarding, amendments, at least six months before the opening date of the Review Conference.

Article 21
Effect of amendments

1. The decisions of a review conference regarding amendments shall be taken by consensus or, upon request, by a vote of a two-thirds majority of the Contracting Parties present and voting. Amendments adopted by such a conference shall be communicated by the Secretary-General of the United Nations to all the Contracting Parties for ratification, acceptance, or approval and to all the States signatories of the Convention for information.
2. Ratification, acceptance or approval of amendments adopted by a review conference shall be effected by the deposit of a formal instrument to that effect with the depositary.
3. Any amendment adopted by a review conference shall enter into force only for those Contracting Parties which have ratified, accepted or approved it, on the first day of the month following one year after its ratification, acceptance or approval by two-thirds of the Contracting Parties. For any State ratifying, accepting or approving an amendment after it has been ratified, accepted or approved by two-thirds of the Contracting Parties, the amendment shall enter into force one year after its ratification, acceptance or approval by that State.
4. Any State which becomes a Contracting Party to this Convention after the entry into force of an amendment shall, failing an expression of a different intention by that State;
(a) Be considered as a Party to this Convention as amended; and
(b) Be considered as a Party to the unamended Convention in relation to any Contracting Party not bound by the amendment.

Article 22
Denunciation

1. Any Contracting Party may denounce this Convention at any time by means of a notification in writing to this effect addressed to the depositary.
2. Such denunciation shall take effect on the expiration of one year after the notification is received by the depositary, unless a longer period has been specified in the notification.

IN WITNESS WHEREOF the undersigned, being duly authorized thereto, have affixed their signatures hereunder on the dates indicated.

DONE at Geneva on 7 February 1986 in one original in the Arabic, Chinese, English, French, Russian and Spanish languages, all texts being equally authentic.
[Annexes I-III omitted]

9.9 INTERNATIONAL CONVENTION FOR THE SUPPRESSION OF UNLAWFUL ACTS AGAINST THE SAFETY OF MARITIME NAVIGATION, 1988

The States Parties to this Convention,
HAVING IN MIND the purposes and principles of the charter of the United Nations concerning the maintenance of international peace and security and the promotion of friendly relations and co-operation among States,

RECOGNIZING in particular that everyone has the right to life, liberty and security of person, as set out in the Universal Declaration of Human Rights and the International Covenant on Civil and Political Rights,

DEEPLY CONCERNED about the world-wide escalation of acts of terrorism in all its forms, which endanger or take innocent human lives, jeopardize fundamental freedoms and seriously impair the dignity of human beings,

CONSIDERING that unlawful acts against the safety of maritime navigation jeopardize the safety of persons and property, seriously affect the operation of maritime services, and undermine the confidence of the peoples of the world in the safety of maritime navigation,

CONSIDERING that the occurrence of such acts is a matter of grave concern to the international community as a whole,

BEING CONVINCED of the urgent need to develop international co-operation between States in devising and adopting effective and practical measures for the prevention of all unlawful acts against the safety of maritime navigation, and the prosecution and punishment of their perpetrators,

RECALLING resolution 40/61 of the General Assembly of the United Nations of 9 December 1985, which, *inter alia*, "urges all States, unilaterally and in co-operation with other States, as well as relevant United Nations organs, to contribute to the progressive elimination of causes underlying international terrorism and to pay special attention to all situations, including colonialism, racism and situations involving mass and flagrant violations of human rights and fundamental freedoms and those involving alien occupation, that may give rise to international terrorism and may endanger international peace and security",

RECALLING FURTHER that resolution 40/61 "unequivocally condemns, as criminal, all acts, methods and practices of terrorism wherever and by whomever committed, including those which jeopardize friendly relations among States and their security",

RECALLING ALSO that by resolution 40/61, the International Maritime Organization was invited to "study the problem of terrorism aboard or against ships with a view to making recommendations on appropriate measures",

HAVING IN MIND resolution A.584(14) of 20 November 1985, of the Assembly of the International Maritime Organization, which called for development of Measures to Prevent Unlawful Acts which Threaten the Safety of Ships and the Security of their Passengers and Crews,

NOTING that acts of the crew which are subject to normal shipboard discipline are outside the purview of this Convention,

AFFIRMING the desirability of monitoring rules and standards relating to the prevention and control of unlawful acts against ships and persons on board ships, with a view to updating them as necessary, and, to this effect, taking note with satisfaction, of the Measures to Prevent Unlawful Acts against Passengers and Crews on Board Ships, recommended by the Maritime Safety Committee of the International Maritime Organization,

AFFIRMING FURTHER that matters not regulated by this Convention continue to be governed by the rules and principles of general international law,

RECOGNIZING the need for all States, in combating unlawful acts against the safety of maritime navigation, strictly to comply with rules and principles of general international law,

HAVE AGREED as follows:

Article 1

For the purposes of this Convention, "ship" means a vessel of any type whatsoever not permanently attached to the sea-bed, including dynamically supported craft, submersibles, or any other floating craft.

Article 2

1. This Convention does not apply to:
   (a) a warship; or
   (b) a ship owned or operated by a State when being used as a naval auxiliary or for customs or police purposes; or
   (c) a ship which has been withdrawn from navigation or laid up.
2. Nothing in this Convention affects the immunities of warships and other Government ships operated for non-commercial purposes.

Article 3

1. Any person commits an offence if that person unlawfully and intentionally:
   (a) seizes or exercises control over a ship by force or threat thereof or any other form of intimidation; or
   (b) performs an act of violence against a person on board a ship if that act is likely to endanger the safe navigation of that ship; or
   (c) destroys a ship or causes damage to a ship or to its cargo which is likely to endanger the safe navigation of that ship; or
   (d) places or causes to be placed on a ship, by any means whatsoever, a device or substance which is likely to destroy that ship, or cause damage to that ship or its cargo which endangers or is likely to endanger the safe navigation of that ship; or
   (e) destroys or seriously damages maritime navigational facilities or seriously interferes with their operation, if any such act is likely to endanger the safe navigation of a ship; or
   (f) communicates information which he knows to be false, thereby endangering the safe navigation of a ship; or
   (g) injures or kills any person, in connection with the commission or the attempted commission of any of the offences set forth in subparagraphs (a) to (f).
2. Any person also commits an offence if that person:
   (a) attempts to commit any of the offences set forth in paragraph 1; or
   (b) abets the commission of any of the offences set forth in paragraph 1 perpetrated by any person or is otherwise an accomplice of a person who commits such an offence; or
   (c) threatens, with or without a condition, as is provided for under national law, aimed at compelling a physical or juridical person to do or refrain from doing any act, to commit any of the offences set forth in paragraph 1, subparagraphs (b), (c) and (e), if that threat is likely to endanger the safe navigation of the ship in question.

Article 4

1. This Convention applies if the ship is navigating or is scheduled to navigate into, through or from waters beyond the outer limit of the territorial sea of a single State, or the lateral limits of its territorial sea with adjacent States.

2. In cases where the Convention does not apply pursuant to paragraph 1, it nevertheless applies when the offender or the alleged offender is found in the territory of a State Party other than the State referred to in paragraph 1.

Article 5

Each State Party shall make the offences set forth in article 3 punishable by appropriate penalties which take into account the grave nature of those offences.

Article 6

1. Each State Party shall take such measures as may be necessary to establish its jurisdiction over the offences set forth in article 3 when the offence is committed:
   (a) against or on board a ship flying the flag of the State at the time the offence is committed; or
   (b) in the territory of that State, including its territorial sea; or
   (c) by a national of that State.
2. A State Party may also establish its jurisdiction over any such offence when:
   (a) it is committed by a stateless person whose habitual residence is in that State; or
   (b) during its commission a national of that State is seized, threatened, injured or killed; or
   (c) it is committed in an attempt to compel that State to do or abstain from doing any act.
3. Any State Party which has established jurisdiction mentioned in paragraph 2 shall notify the Secretary-General of the International Maritime Organization (hereinafter referred to as "the Secretary-General"). If such State Party subsequently rescinds that jurisdiction, it shall notify the Secretary-General.
4. Each State Party shall take such measures as may be necessary to establish its jurisdiction over the offences set forth in article 3 in cases where the alleged offender is present in its territory and it does not extradite him to any of the State Parties which have established their jurisdiction in accordance with paragraphs 1 and 2 of this article.
5. This Convention does not exclude any criminal jurisdiction exercised in accordance with national law.

Article 7

1. Upon being satisfied that the circumstances so warrant, any State Party in the territory of which the offender or the alleged offender is present shall, in accordance with its law, take him into custody or take other measures to ensure his presence for such time as is necessary to enable any criminal or extradition proceeding to be instituted.
2. Such State shall immediately make a preliminary enquiry into the facts, in accordance with its own legislation.
3. Any person regarding whom the measures referred to in paragraph 1 are being taken shall be entitled to:
   (a) communicate without delay with the nearest appropriate representative of the State of which he is a national or which is otherwise entitled to establish such communication or, if he is a stateless person, the State in the territory of which he has his habitual residence;
   (b) be visited by a representative of that State.

4.   The rights referred to in paragraph 3 shall be exercised in conformity with the laws and regulations of the State in the territory of which the offender or the alleged offender is present, subject to the proviso that the said laws and regulations must enable full effect to be given to the purposes for which the rights accorded under paragraph 3 are intended.

5.   When a State Party, pursuant to this article, has taken a person into custody, it shall immediately notify the States which have established jurisdiction in accordance with article 6, paragraph 1 and, if it considers it advisable, any other interested States, of the fact that such person is in custody and of the circumstances which warrant his detention.   The State which makes the preliminary enquiry contemplated in paragraph 2 of this article shall promptly report its findings to the said States and shall indicate whether it intends to exercise jurisdiction.

Article 8

1.   The master of a ship of a State Party (the "flag State") may deliver to the authorities of any other State Party (the "receiving State") any person who he has reasonable grounds to believe has committed one of the offences set forth in article 3.

2.   The flag State shall ensure that the master of its ship is obliged whenever practicable, and if possible before entering the territorial sea of the receiving State carrying on board any person whom the master intends to deliver in accordance with paragraph 1, to give notification to the authorities of the receiving State of his intention to deliver such person and the reasons therefor.

3.   The receiving State shall accept the delivery, except where it has grounds to consider that the Convention is not applicable to the acts giving rise to the delivery, and shall proceed in accordance with the provisions of article 7.   Any refusal to accept a delivery shall be accompanied by a statement of the reasons for refusal.

4.   The flag State shall ensure that the master of its ship is obliged to furnish the authorities of the receiving State with the evidence in the master's possession which pertains to the alleged offence.

5.   A receiving State which has accepted the delivery of a person in accordance with paragraph 3 may in turn request the flag State to accept delivery of that person.   The flag State shall consider any such request, and if it accedes to the request it shall proceed in accordance with article 7.   If the flag State declines a request, it shall furnish the receiving State with a statement of the reasons therefor.

Article 9

Nothing in this Convention shall affect in any way the rules of international law pertaining to the competence of States to exercise investigative or enforcement jurisdiction on board ships not flying their flag.

Article 10

1.   The State Party in the territory of which the offender or the alleged offender is found shall, in cases to which article 6 applies, if it does not extradite him be obliged, without exception whatsoever and whether or not the offence was committed in its territory, to submit the case without delay to its competent authorities for the purpose of prosecution, through proceedings in accordance with the laws of that State.   Those authorities shall take their decision in the same manner as in the case of any other offence of a grave nature under the law of that State.

2. Any person regarding whom proceedings are being carried out in connection with any of the offences set forth in article 3 shall be guaranteed fair treatment at all stages of the proceedings, including enjoyment of all the rights and guarantees provided for such proceedings by the law of the State in the territory of which he is present.

Article 11

1. The offences set forth in article 3 shall be deemed to be included as extraditable offences in any extradition treaty existing between any of the States Parties. States Parties undertake to include such offences as extraditable offences in every extradition treaty to be concluded between them.
2. If a State Party which makes extradition conditional on the existence of a treaty receives a request for extradition from another State Party with which it has no extradition treaty, the requested State Party may, at its option, consider this Convention as a legal basis for extradition in respect of the offences set forth in article 3. Extradition shall be subject to the other conditions provided by the law of the requested State Party.
3. States Parties which do not make extradition conditional on the existence of a treaty shall recognize the offences set forth in article 3 as extraditable offences between themselves, subject to the conditions provided by the law of the requested State.
4. If necessary, the offences set forth in article 3 shall be treated, for the purposes of extradition between States Parties, as if they had been committed not only in the place in which they occurred but also in a place within the jurisdiction of the State Party requesting extradition.
5. A State Party which received more than one request for extradition from States which have established jurisdiction in accordance with article 7 and which decides not to prosecute shall, in selecting the State to which the offender or alleged offender is to be extradited, pay due regard to the interests and responsibilities of the State Party whose flag the ship was flying at the time of the commission of the offence.
6. In considering a request for the extradition of an alleged offender pursuant to this Convention, the requested State shall pay due regard to whether his rights as set forth in article 7, paragraph 3, can be effected in the requesting State.
7. With respect to the offences as defined in this Convention, the provisions of all extradition treaties and arrangements applicable between States Parties are modified as between States Parties to the extent that they are incompatible with this Convention.

Article 12

1. States Parties shall afford one another the greatest measure of assistance in connection with criminal proceedings brought in respect of the offences set forth in article 3, including assistance in obtaining evidence at their disposal necessary for the proceedings.
2. States Parties shall carry out their obligations under paragraph 1 in conformity with any treaties on mutual assistance that may exist between them. In the absence of such treaties, States Parties shall afford each other assistance in accordance with their national law.

Article 13

1. States Parties shall co-operate in the prevention of the offences set forth in article 3, particularly by:

   (a) taking all practicable measures to prevent preparations in their respective territories for the commission of those offences within or outside their territories;

   (b) exchanging information in accordance with their national law, and co-ordinating administrative and other measures taken as appropriate to prevent the commission of offences set forth in article 3.

2.   When, due to the commission of an offence set forth in article 3, the passage of a ship has been delayed or interrupted, any State Party in whose territory the ship or passengers or crew are present shall be bound to exercise all possible efforts to avoid a ship, its passengers, crew or cargo being unduly detained or delayed.

Article 14

Any State Party having reason to believe that an offence set forth in article 3 will be committed shall, in accordance with its national law, furnish as promptly as possible any relevant information in its possession to those States which it believes would be the States having established jurisdiction in accordance with article 6.

Article 15

1.   Each State Party shall, in accordance with its national law, provide to the Secretary-General as promptly as possible, any relevant information in its possession concerning:

   (a) the circumstances of the offence;

   (b) the action taken pursuant to article 13, paragraph 2;

   (c) the measures taken in relation to the offender or the alleged offender, and, in particular, the results of any extradition proceedings or other legal proceedings.

2.   The State Party where the alleged offender is prosecuted shall, in accordance with its national law, communicate the final outcome of the proceedings to the Secretary-General.

3.   The information transmitted in accordance with paragraphs 1 and 2 shall be communicated by the Secretary-General to all States Parties, to members of the International Maritime Organization (hereinafter referred to as "the Organization"), to the other States concerned, and to the appropriate international inter-governmental organizations.

Article 16

1.   Any dispute between two or more States Parties concerning the interpretation or application of this Convention which cannot be settled through negotiation within a reasonable time shall, at the request of one of them, be submitted to arbitration. If within six months from the date of the request for arbitration, the parties are unable to agree on the organization of the arbitration any one of those parties may refer the dispute to the International Court of Justice by request in conformity with the Statute of the Court.

2.   Each State may at the time of signature or ratification, acceptance or approval of this Convention or accession thereto, declare that it does not consider itself bound by any or all of the provisions of paragraph 1. The other States Parties shall not be bound by those provisions with respect to any State Party which has made such a reservation.

3.   Any State which has made a reservation in accordance with paragraph 2 may at any time withdraw that reservation by notification to the Secretary-General.

Article 17

1.   This Convention shall be open for signature at Rome on 10 March 1988 by States participating in the International Conference on the Suppression of Unlawful Acts against the Safety of Maritime Navigation and at the Headquarters of the Organization by all States from 14 March 1988 to 9 March 1989.   It shall thereafter remain open for accession.

2.   States may express their consent to be bound by this Convention by:
     (a) signature without reservation as to ratification, acceptance or approval; or
     (b) signature subject to ratification, acceptance or approval, followed by ratification, acceptance or approval; or
     (c) accession.

3.   Ratification, acceptance, approval or accession shall be effected by the deposit of an instrument to that effect with the Secretary-General.

Article 18

1.   This Convention shall enter into force ninety days following the date on which fifteen States have either signed it without reservation as to ratification, acceptance or approval, or have deposited an instrument of ratification, acceptance, approval or accession in respect thereof.

2.   For a State which deposits an instrument of ratification, acceptance, approval or accession in respect of this Convention after the conditions for entry into force thereof have been met, the ratification, acceptance, approval or accession shall take effect ninety days after the date of such deposit.

Article 19

1.   This Convention may be denounced by any State Party at any time after the expiry of one year from the date on which this Convention enters into force for that State.

2.   Denunciation shall be effected by the deposit of an instrument of denunciation with the Secretary-General.

3.   A denunciation shall take effect one year, or such longer period as may be specified in the instrument of denunciation, after the receipt of the instrument of denunciation by the Secretary-General.

Article 20

1.   A conference for the purpose of revising or amending this Convention may be convened by the Organization.

2.   The Secretary-General shall convene a conference of the States Parties to this Convention for revising or amending the Convention, at the request of one-third of the States Parties, or ten States Parties, whichever is the higher figure.

3.   Any instrument of ratification, acceptance, approval or accession deposited after the date of entry into force of an amendment to this Convention shall be deemed to apply to the Convention as amended.

Article 21

1. This Convention shall be deposited with the Secretary-General.
2. The Secretary-General shall:
   (a) inform all States which have signed this Convention or acceded thereto, and all Members of the Organization, of:
       (i) each new signature or deposit of an instrument of ratification, acceptance, approval or accession together with the date thereof;
       (ii) the date of the entry into force of this Convention;
       (iii) the deposit of any instrument of denunciation of this Convention together with the date on which it is received and the date on which the denunciation takes effect;
       (iv) the receipt of any declaration or notification made under this Convention;
   (b) transmit certified true copies of this Convention to all States which have signed this Convention or acceded thereto.
3. As soon as this Convention enters into force, a certified true copy thereof shall be transmitted by the Depositary to the Secretary-General of the United Nations for registration and publication in accordance with article 102 of the Charter of the United Nations.

Article 22

This Convention is established in a single original in the Arabic, Chinese, English, French, Russian and Spanish languages, each text being equally authentic.

IN WITNESS WHEREOF the undersigned being duly authorized by their respective Governments for that purpose have signed this Convention.

DONE AT Rome this tenth day of March one thousand nine hundred and eighty-eight.

9.10 VIENNA CONVENTION AGAINST ILLICIT TRAFFIC IN NARCOTIC DRUGS AND PSYCHOTROPIC SUBSTANCES, 1988: EXCERPTS

The Parties to this Convention,
   Deeply concerned by the magnitude of and rising trend in the illicit production of, demand for and traffic in narcotic drugs and psychotropic substances, which pose a serious threat to the health and welfare of human beings and adversely affect the economic, cultural and political foundations of society,
   ...
   Determined to improve international co-operation in the suppression of illicit traffic by sea,
   Recognizing that eradication of illicit traffic is a collective responsibility of all States and that, to that end, co-ordinated action within the framework of international co-operation is necessary,
   Acknowledging the competence of the United Nations in the field of control of narcotic drugs and psychotropic substances and desirous that the international organs concerned with such control should be within the framework of that Organization,
   Reaffirming the guiding principles of existing treaties in the field of narcotic drugs and psychotropic substances and the system of control which they embody.

Recognizing the need to reinforce and supplement the measures provided in the Single Convention on Narcotic Drugs, 1961, that Convention as amended by the 1972 Protocol Amending the Single Convention on Narcotic Drugs, 1961, and the 1971 Convention on Psychotropic Substances, in order to counter the magnitude and extent of illicit traffic and its grave consequences,

Recognizing also the importance of strengthening and enhancing effective legal means for international co-operation in criminal matters for suppressing the international criminal activities of illicit traffic,

Desiring to conclude a comprehensive, effective and operative international convention that is directed specifically against illicit traffic and that considers the various aspects of the problem as a whole, in particular those aspects not envisaged in the existing treaties in the field of narcotic drugs and psychotropic substances,

Hereby agree as follows:

Article 1
Definitions

...

(g) "Controlled delivery" means the technique of allowing illicit or suspect consignments of narcotic drugs, psychotropic substances, substances in Table I and Table II annexed to this Convention, or substances substituted for them, to pass out of, through or into the territory of one or more countries, with the knowledge and under the supervision of their competent authorities, with a view to identifying persons involved in the commission of offences established in accordance with article 3, paragraph 1 of the Convention;

...

Article 2
Scope of the Convention

1. The purpose of this Convention is to promote co-operation among the Parties so that they may address more effectively the various aspects of illicit traffic in narcotic drugs and psychotropic substances having an international dimension. In carrying out their obligations under the Convention, the Parties shall take necessary measures, including legislative and administrative measures, in conformity with the fundamental provisions of their respective domestic legislative systems.

2. The Parties shall carry out their obligations under this Convention in a manner consistent with the principles of sovereign equality and territorial integrity of States and that of non-intervention in the domestic affairs of other States.

3. A Party shall not undertake in the territory of another Party the exercise of jurisdiction and performance of functions which are exclusively reserved for the authorities of that other Party by its domestic law.

Article 3
Offences and Sanctions

1. Each Party shall adopt such measures as may be necessary to establish as criminal offences under its domestic law, when committed intentionally:

(a)　(i)　The production, manufacture, extraction, preparation, offering, offering for sale, distribution, sale, delivery on any terms whatsoever, brokerage, dispatch, dispatch in transit, transport, importation or exportation of any narcotic drug or any psychotropic substance contrary to the provisions of the 1961 Convention, the 1961 Convention as amended or the 1971 Convention.

...

Article 4
Jurisdiction

1. Each Party:
(a) Shall take such measures as may be necessary to establish its jurisdiction over the offences it has established in accordance with article 3, paragraph 1, when:
  (i) The offence is committed in its territory;
  (ii) The offence is committed on board a vessel flying its flag or an aircraft which is registered under its laws at the time the offence is committed;
(b) May take such measures as may be necessary to establish its jurisdiction over the offences it has established in accordance with article 3, paragraph 1, when:
  (i) The offence is committed by one of its nationals or by a person who has his habitual residence in its territory;
  (ii) The offence is committed on board a vessel concerning which that Party has been authorized to take appropriate action pursuant to article 17, provided that such jurisdiction shall be exercised only on the basis of agreements or arrangements referred to in paragraphs 4 and 9 of that article;
  (iii) The offence is one of those established in accordance with article 3, paragraph 1, subparagraph (c)(iv), and is committed outside its territory with a view to the commission, within its territory, of an offence established in accordance with article 3, paragraph 1.
2. Each Party:
(a) Shall also take such measures as may be necessary to establish its jurisdiction over the offences it has established in accordance with article 3, paragraph 1, when the alleged offender is present in its territory and it does not extradite him to another Party on the ground:
  (i) That the offence has been committed in its territory or on board a vessel flying its flag or an aircraft which was registered under its law at the time the offence was committed; or
  (ii) That the offence has been committed by one of its nationals;
(b) May also take such measures as may be necessary to establish its jurisdiction over the offences it has established in accordance with article 3, paragraph 1, when the alleged offender is present in its territory and it does not extradite him to another Party.
3. This Convention does not exclude the exercise of any criminal jurisdiction established by a Party in accordance with its domestic law.
...

Article 6
Extradition

1. This article shall apply to the offences established by the Parties in accordance with article 3, paragraph 1.
2. Each of the offences to which this article applies shall be deemed to be included as an extraditable offence in any extradition treaty existing between Parties. The Parties undertake to include such offences as extraditable offences in every extradition treaty to be concluded between them.
3. If a Party which makes extradition conditional on the existence of a treaty receives a request for extradition from another Party with which it has no extradition treaty, it may consider this Convention as the legal basis for extradition in respect of any offence

to which this article applies.   The Parties which require detailed legislation in order to use this Convention as a legal basis for extradition shall consider enacting such legislation as may be necessary.

4.   The Parties which do not make extradition conditional on the existence of a treaty shall recognize offences to which this article applies as extraditable offences between themselves.

5.   Extradition shall be subject to the conditions provided for by the law of the requested Party or by applicable extradition treaties, including the grounds upon which the requested Party may refuse extradition.

6.   In considering requests received pursuant to this article, the requested State may refuse to comply with such requests where there are substantial grounds leading its judicial or other competent authorities to believe that compliance would facilitate the prosecution or punishment of any person on account of his race, religion, nationality or political opinions, or would cause prejudice for any of these reasons to any person affected by the request.

7.   The Parties shall endeavour to expedite extradition procedures and to simplify evidentiary requirements relating thereto in respect of any offence to which this article applies.

8.   Subject to the provisions of its domestic law and its extradition treaties, the requested Party may, upon being satisfied that the circumstances so warrant and are urgent, and at the request of the requesting Party, take a person whose extradition is sought and who is present in its territory into custody or take other appropriate measures to ensure his presence at extradition proceedings.

9.   Without prejudice to the exercise of any criminal jurisdiction established in accordance with its domestic law, a Party in whose territory an alleged offender is found shall:

(a) If it does not extradite him in respect of an offence established in accordance with article 3, paragraph 1, on the grounds set forth in article 4, paragraph 2, subparagraph (a), submit the case to its competent authorities for the purpose of prosecution, unless otherwise agreed with the requesting Party.

(b) If it does not extradite him in respect of such an offence and has established its jurisdiction in relation to that offence in accordance with article 4, paragraph 2, subparagraph (b), submit the case to its competent authorities for the purpose of prosecution, unless otherwise requested by the requesting Party for the purposes of preserving its legitimate jurisdiction.

10. If extradition, sought for purposes of enforcing a sentence, is refused because the person sought is a national of the requested Party, the requested Party shall, if its law so permits and in conformity with the requirements of such law, upon application of the requesting Party, consider the enforcement of the sentence which has been imposed under the law of the requesting Party, or the remainder thereof.

11. The Parties shall seek to conclude bilateral and multilateral agreements to carry out or to enhance the effectiveness of extradition.

12. The Parties may consider entering into bilateral or multilateral agreements, whether *ad hoc* or general, on the transfer to their country of persons sentenced to imprisonment and other forms of deprivation of liberty for offences to which this article applies, in order that they may complete their sentences there.

...

Article 11
Controlled Delivery

1. If permitted by the basic principles of their respective domestic legal systems, the Parties shall take the necessary measures, within their possibilities, to allow for the appropriate use of controlled delivery at the international level, on the basis of agreements or arrangements mutually consented to, with a view to identifying persons involved in offences established in accordance with article 3, paragraph 1, and to taking legal action against them.

2. Decisions to use controlled delivery shall be made on a case-by-case basis and may, when necessary, take into consideration financial arrangements and understandings with respect to the exercise of jurisdiction by the Parties concerned.

3. Illicit consignments whose controlled delivery is agreed to may, with the consent of the Parties concerned, be intercepted and allowed to continue with the narcotic drugs or psychotropic substances intact or removed or replaced in whole or in part.

...

Article 17
Illicit Traffic by Sea

1. The Parties shall co-operate to the fullest extent possible to suppress illicit traffic by sea, in conformity with the international law of the sea.

2. A Party which has reasonable grounds to suspect that a vessel flying its flag or not displaying a flag or marks of registry is engaged in illicit traffic may request the assistance of other Parties in suppressing its use for that purpose. The Parties so requested shall render such assistance within the means available to them.

3. A party which has reasonable grounds to suspect that a vessel exercising freedom of navigation in accordance with international law and flying the flag or displaying marks of registry of another Party is engaged in illicit traffic may so notify the flag State, request confirmation of registry and, if confirmed, request authorization from the flag State to take appropriate measures in regard to that vessel.

4. In accordance with paragraph 3 or in accordance with treaties in force between them or in accordance with any agreement or arrangement otherwise reached between those Parties, the flag State may authorize the requesting State to, *inter alia*:

(a) Board the vessel;

(b) Search the vessel;

(c) If evidence of involvement in illicit traffic is found, take appropriate action with respect to the vessel, persons and cargo on board.

5. Where action is taken pursuant to this article, the Parties concerned shall take due account of the need not to endanger the safety of life at sea, the security of the vessel and the cargo or to prejudice the commercial and legal interests of the flag State or any other interested State.

6. The flag State may, consistent with its obligations in paragraph 1 of this article, subject its authorization to conditions to be mutually agreed between it and the requesting Party, including conditions relating to responsibility.

7. For the purposes of paragraphs 3 and 4 of this article, a Party shall respond expeditiously to a request from another Party to determine whether a vessel that is flying its flag is entitled to do so, and to requests for authorization made pursuant to paragraph 3. At the time of becoming a Party to this Convention, each Party shall designate an authority or, when necessary, authorities to receive and respond to such

requests. Such designation shall be notified through the Secretary-General to all other Parties within one month of the designation.

8. A Party which has taken any action in accordance with this article shall promptly inform the flag State concerned of the results of that action.

9. The Parties shall consider entering into bilateral or regional agreements or arrangements to carry out, or to enhance the effectiveness of, the provisions of this article.

10. Action pursuant to paragraph 4 of this article shall be carried out only by warships or military aircraft, or other ships or aircraft clearly marked and identifiable as being on government service and authorized to that effect.

11. Any action taken in accordance with this article shall take due account of the need not to interfere with or affect the rights and obligations and the exercise of jurisdiction of coastal States in accordance with the international law of the sea.

Article 18
Free Trade Zones and Free Ports

1. The Parties shall apply measures to suppress illicit traffic in narcotic drugs, psychotropic substances and substances in Table I and Table II in free trade zones and in free ports that are no less stringent than those applied in other parts of their territories.

2. The Parties shall endeavour:

(a) To monitor the movement of goods and persons in free trade zones and free ports, and, to that end, shall empower the competent authorities to search cargoes and incoming and outgoing vessels, including pleasure craft and fishing vessels, as well as aircraft and vehicles and, when appropriate, to search crew members, passengers and their baggage;

(b) To establish and maintain a system to detect consignments suspected of containing narcotic drugs, psychotropic substances and substances in Table I and Table II passing into or out of free trade zones and free ports;

(c) To establish and maintain surveillance systems in harbour and dock areas and at airports and border control points in free trade zones and free ports.

...

Declarations and Objections
[The declarations and objections made by Parties to the Convention include the following:]

BRAZIL

On signing the Convention the Government of Brazil made the following declaration:

...

(b) It is the understanding of the Brazilian Government that paragraph 11 of Article 17 does not prevent a coastal State from requiring prior authorization for any action under this Article by other states in its Exclusive Economic Zone.

UNITED KINGDOM OF GREAT BRITAIN AND NORTHERN IRELAND

On 27 December 1989, the Secretary-General received from the Government of the United Kingdom the following objection with regard to the declaration made by Brazil:

The United Kingdom of Great Britain and Northern Ireland, Member State of the European community, attached to the principle of freedom of navigation, notably in the exclusive economic zone, considers that the declaration of Brazil concerning paragraph 11 of Article 17, of the United Nations Convention against Illicit Traffic in Narcotic Drugs and Psychotropic Substances, adopted in Vienna on 20 December 1988, goes further than the rights accorded to coastal states by international law.

[Similar objections were made by other Member States of the European Community]

9.11 EUROPEAN AGREEMENT FOR THE PREVENTION OF BROADCASTS TRANSMITTED FROM STATIONS OUTSIDE NATIONAL TERRITORIES, 1965

The member States of the Council of Europe signatory hereto,

Considering that the aim of the Council of Europe is to achieve a greater unity between its Members;

Considering that the Radio Regulations annexed to the International Telecommunication Convention prohibit the establishment and use of broadcasting stations on board ships, aircraft or any other floating or airborne objects outside national territories;

Considering also the desirability of providing for the possibility of preventing the establishment and use of broadcasting stations on objects affixed to or supported by the bed of the sea outside national territories;

Considering the desirability of European collaboration in this matter,

Have agreed as follows:

Article 1

This Agreement is concerned with broadcasting stations which are installed or maintained on board ships, aircraft, or any other floating or airborne objects and which, outside national territories, transmit broadcasts intended for reception or capable of being received, wholly or in part, within the territory of any Contracting Party, or which cause harmful interference to any radio-communication service operating under the authority of a Contracting Party in accordance with the Radio Regulations.

Article 2

1. Each Contracting Party undertakes to take appropriate steps to make punishable as offences, in accordance with its domestic law, the establishment or operation of broadcasting stations referred to in Article 1, as well as acts of collaboration knowingly performed.

2. The following shall, in relation to broadcasting stations referred to in Article 1, be acts of collaboration:

(a) the provision, maintenance or repairing of equipment;

(b) the provision of supplies;

(c) the provision of transport for, or the transporting of, persons, equipment or supplies;

(d) the ordering or production of material of any kind, including advertisements, to be broadcast;

(e) the provision of services concerning advertising for the benefit of the stations.

Article 3

Each Contracting Party shall, in accordance with its domestic law, apply the provisions of this Agreement in regard to:
(a) its nationals who have committed any act referred to in Article 2 on its territory, ships or aircraft, or outside national territories on any ships, aircraft or any other floating or airborne object;
(b) non-nationals who, on its territory, ships or aircraft, or on board any floating or airborne object under its jurisdiction have committed any act referred to in Article 2.

Article 4

Nothing in this Agreement shall be deemed to prevent a Contracting Party:
(a) from also treating as punishable offences acts other than those referred to in Article 2 and also applying the provisions concerned to persons other than those referred to in Article 3;
(b) from also applying the provisions of this Agreement to broadcasting stations installed or maintained on objects affixed to or supported by the bed of the sea.

Article 5

The Contracting Parties may elect not to apply the provisions of this Agreement in respect of the services of performers which have been provided elsewhere than on the stations referred to in Article 1.

Article 6

The provisions of Article 2 shall not apply to any acts performed for the purpose of giving assistance to a ship or aircraft or any other floating or airborne object in distress or of protecting human life.

Article 7

No reservation may be made to the provisions of this Agreement.

Article 8

1. This Agreement shall be open to signature by the member States of the Council of Europe, which may become Parties to it either by:
(a) signature without reservation in respect of ratification or acceptance, or
(b) signature with reservation in respect of ratification or acceptance followed by ratification or acceptance.
2. Instruments of ratification or acceptance shall be deposited with the Secretary-General of the Council of Europe.

Article 9

1. This Agreement shall enter into force one month after the date on which three member States of the Council shall, in accordance with the provisions of Article 8, have signed the Agreement without reservation in respect of ratification or acceptance, or shall have deposited their instrument of ratification or acceptance.

2.   As regards any member State which shall subsequently sign the Agreement without reservation in respect of ratification or acceptance or which shall ratify or accept it, the Agreement shall enter into force one month after the date of such signature or the date of deposit of the instrument of ratification or acceptance.

Article 10

1.   After this Agreement has entered into force, any Member or Associate Member of the International Telecommunication Union which is not a Member of the Council of Europe may accede to it subject to the prior agreement of the Committee of Ministers.
2.   Such accession shall be effected by depositing with the Secretary-General of the Council of Europe an instrument of accession which shall take effect one month after the date of its deposit.

Article 11

1.   Any Contracting Party may, at the time of signature or when depositing its instrument of ratification, acceptance or accession, specify the territory or territories to which this Agreement shall apply.
2.   Any Contracting Party may, when depositing its instrument of ratification, acceptance or accession or at any later date, by declaration addressed to the Secretary-General of the Council of Europe, extend this Agreement to any other territory or territories specified in the declaration and for whose international relations it is responsible or on whose behalf it is authorised to give undertakings.
3.   Any declaration made in pursuance of the preceding paragraph may, in respect of any territory mentioned in such declaration, be withdrawn according to the procedure laid down in Article 12 of this Agreement.

Article 12

1.   This Agreement shall remain in force indefinitely.
2.   Any Contracting Party may, in so far as it is concerned, denounce this Agreement by means of a notification addressed to the Secretary-General of the Council of Europe.
3.   Such denunciation shall take effect six months after the date of receipt by the Secretary-General of such notification.

Article 13

The Secretary-General of the Council of Europe shall notify the member States of the Council and the Government of any State which has acceded to this Agreement of:
(a)   any signature without reservation in respect of ratification or acceptance;
(b)   any signature with reservation in respect of ratification or acceptance;
(c)   any deposit of an instrument of ratification, acceptance or accession;
(d)   any date of entry into force of this Agreement in accordance with Articles 9 and 10 thereof;
(e)   any declaration received in pursuance of paragraphs 2 and 3 of Article 11;
(f)   any notification received in pursuance of the provisions of Article 12 and the date on which denunciation takes effect.

IN WITNESS WHEREOF the undersigned, being duly authorised thereto, have signed this Agreement.

DONE at Strasbourg, this 22nd day of January 1965 in English and French, both texts being equally authoritative, in a single copy which shall remain deposited in the archives of the Council of Europe. The Secretary-General of the Council of Europe shall transmit certified copies to each of the signatory and acceding States.

9.12 GENEVA CONVENTION ON FISHING AND CONSERVATION OF THE LIVING RESOURCES OF THE HIGH SEAS, 1958

The States Parties to this Convention,

Considering that the development of modern techniques for the exploitation of the living resources of the sea, increasing man's ability to meet the need of the world's expanding population for food, has exposed some of these resources to the danger of being over-exploited.

Considering also that the nature of the problems involved in the conservation of the living resources of the high seas is such that there is a clear necessity that they be solved, whenever possible, on the basis of international co-operation through the concerted action of all the States concerned,

Have agreed as follows:

Article 1

1. All States have the right for their nationals to engage in fishing on the high seas, subject (a) to their treaty obligations, (b) to the interests and rights of coastal States as provided for in this Convention, (c) to the provisions contained in the following Articles concerning conservation of the living resources of the high seas.

2. All States have the duty to adopt, or to co-operate with other States in adopting, such measures for their respective nationals as may be necessary for the conservation of the living resources of the high seas.

Article 2

As employed in this Convention, the expression 'conservation of the living resources of the high seas' means the aggregate of the measures rendering possible the optimum sustainable yield from those resources so as to secure a maximum supply of food and other marine products. Conservation programmes should be formulated with a view to securing in the first place a supply of food for human consumption.

Article 3

A State whose nationals are engaged in fishing any stock or stocks of fish or other living marine resources in any area of the high seas where the nationals of other States are not thus engaged shall adopt, for its own nationals, measures in that area when necessary for the purpose of the conservation of the living resources affected.

Article 4

1. If the nationals of two or more States are engaged in fishing the same stock or stocks of fish or other living marine resources in any area or areas of the high seas, these States shall, at the request of any of them, enter into negotiations with a view to prescribing by agreement for their nationals the necessary measures for the conservation of the living resources affected.

2. If the States concerned do not reach agreement within twelve months, any of the parties may initiate the procedure contemplated by Article 9.

Article 5

1. If, subsequent to the adoption of the measures referred to in Articles 3 and 4, nationals of other States engage in fishing the same stock or stocks of fish or other living marine resources in any area or areas of the high seas, the other States shall apply the measures, which shall not be discriminatory in form or in fact, to their own nationals not later than seven months after the date on which the measures shall have been notified to the Director-General of the Food and Agriculture Organization of the United Nations. The Director-General shall notify such measures to any State which so requests and, in any case, to any State specified by the State initiating the measure.
2. If these other States do not accept the measures so adopted and if no agreement can be reached within twelve months, any of the interested parties may initiate the procedure contemplated by Article 9. Subject to paragraph 2 of Article 10, the measures adopted shall remain obligatory pending the decision of the special commission.

Article 6

1. A coastal State has a special interest in the maintenance of the productivity of the living resources in any area of the high seas adjacent to its territorial sea.
2. A coastal State is entitled to take part on an equal footing in any system of research and regulation for purposes of conservation of the living resources of the high seas in that area, even though its nationals do not carry on fishing there.
3. A State whose nationals are engaged in fishing in any area of the high seas adjacent to the territorial sea of a State shall, at the request of that coastal State, enter into negotiations with a view to prescribing by agreement the measures necessary for the conservation of the living resources of the high seas in that area.
4. A State whose nationals are engaged in fishing in any area of the high seas adjacent to the territorial sea of a coastal State shall not enforce conservation measures in that area which are opposed to those which have been adopted by the coastal State, but may enter into negotiations with the coastal State with a view to prescribing by agreement the measures necessary for the conservation of the living resources of the high seas in that area.
5. If the States concerned do not reach agreement with respect to conservation measures within twelve months, any of the parties may initiate the procedure contemplated by Article 9.

Article 7

1. Having regard to the provisions of paragraph 1 of Article 6, any coastal State may, with a view to the maintenance of the productivity of the living resources of the sea, adopt unilateral measures of conservation appropriate to any stock of fish or other marine resources in any area of the high seas adjacent to its territorial sea, provided that negotiations to that effect with the other States concerned have not led to an agreement within six months.
2. The measures which the coastal State adopts under the previous paragraphs shall be valid as to other States only if the following requirements are fulfilled:
(a) That there is a need for urgent application of conservation measures in the light of the existing knowledge of the fishery;

(b) That the measures adopted are based on appropriate scientific findings;
(c) That such measures do not discriminate in form or in fact against foreign fishermen.
3. These measures shall remain in force pending the settlement, in accordance with the relevant provisions of this Convention, of any disagreement as to their validity.
4. If the measures are not accepted by the other States concerned, any of the parties may initiate the procedure contemplated by Article 9. Subject to paragraph 2 of Article 10, the measures adopted shall remain obligatory pending the decision of the special commission.
5. The principles of geographical demarcation as defined in Article 12 of the Convention on the Territorial Sea and the Contiguous Zone shall be adopted when coasts of different States are involved.

Article 8

1. Any State which, even if its nationals are not engaged in fishing in an area of the high seas not adjacent to its coast, has a special interest in the conservation of the living resources of the high seas in that area, may request the State or States whose nationals are engaged in fishing there to take the necessary measures of conservation under Articles 3 and 4 respectively, at the same time mentioning the scientific reasons which in its opinion make such measures necessary, and indicating its special interest.
2. If no agreement is reached within twelve months, such State may initiate the procedure contemplated by Article 9.

Article 9

1. Any dispute which may arise between States under Articles 4, 5, 6, 7 and 8 shall, at the request of any of the parties, be submitted for settlement to a special commission of five members, unless the parties agree to seek a solution by another method of peaceful settlement, as provided for in Article 33 of the Charter of the United Nations.
2. The members of the commission, one of whom shall be designated as chairman, shall be named by agreement between the States in dispute within three months of the request for settlement in accordance with the provisions of this Article. Failing agreement they shall, upon the request of any State party, be named by the Secretary-General of the United Nations, within a further three-month period, in consultation with the States in dispute and with the President of the International Court of Justice and the Director-General of the Food and Agriculture Organization of the United Nations, from amongst well-qualified persons being nationals of States not involved in the dispute and specializing in legal, administrative or scientific questions relating to fisheries, depending upon the nature of the dispute to be settled. Any vacancy arising after the original appointment shall be filled in the same manner as provided for the initial selection.
3. Any State party to proceedings under these Articles shall have the right to name one of its nationals to the special commission, with the right to participate fully in the proceedings on the same footing as a member of the commission, but without the right to vote or take part in the writing of the commission's decision.
4. The commission shall determine its own procedure, assuring each party to the proceedings a full opportunity to be heard and to present its case. It shall also determine how the costs and expenses shall be divided between the parties to the dispute, failing agreement by the parties on this matter.

5. The special commission shall render its decision within a period of five months from the time it is appointed unless it decides, in case of necessity, to extend the time limit for a period not exceeding three months.

6. The special commission shall, in reaching its decisions, adhere to these Articles and to any special agreements between the disputing parties regarding settlement of the dispute.

7. Decisions of the commission shall be by majority vote.

Article 10

1. The special commission shall, in disputes arising under Article 7, apply the criteria listed in paragraph 2 of that Article. In disputes under Articles 4, 5, 6 and 8, the commission shall apply the following criteria, according to the issues involved in the dispute:

(a) Common to the determination of disputes arising under Articles 4, 5 and 6, are the requirements:
  (i) That scientific findings demonstrate the necessity of conservation measures;
  (ii) That the specific measures are based on scientific findings and are practicable; and
  (iii) That the measures do not discriminate, in form or in fact, against fishermen of other States;
(b) Applicable to the determination of disputes arising under Article 8 is the requirement that scientific findings demonstrate the necessity for conservation measures, or that the conservation programme is adequate, as the case may be.

2. The special commission may decide that pending its award the measures in dispute shall not be applied, provided that, in the case of disputes under Article 7, the measures shall only be suspended when it is apparent to the commission on the basis of *prima facie* evidence that the need for the urgent application of such measures does not exist.

Article 11

The decisions of the special commission shall be binding on the States concerned and the provisions of paragraph 2 of Article 94 of the Charter of the United Nations shall be applicable to those decisions. If the decisions are accompanied by any recommendations, they shall receive the greatest possible consideration.

Article 12

1. If the factual basis of the award of the special commission is altered by substantial changes in the conditions of the stock or stocks of fish or other living marine resources or in methods of fishing, any of the States concerned may request the other States to enter into negotiations with a view to prescribing by agreement the necessary modifications in the measures of conservation.

2. If no agreement is reached within a reasonable period of time, any of the States concerned may again resort to the procedure contemplated by Article 9 provided that at least two years have elapsed from the original award.

Article 13

1. The regulation of fisheries conducted by means of equipment embedded in the floor of the sea in areas of the high seas adjacent to the territorial sea of a State may be undertaken by that State where such fisheries have long been maintained and conducted

by its nationals, provided that non-nationals are permitted to participate in such activities on an equal footing with nationals except in areas where such fisheries have by long usage been exclusively enjoyed by such nationals. Such regulations will not, however, affect the general status of the areas as high seas.

2. In this Article, the expression 'fisheries conducted by means of equipment embedded in the floor of the sea' means those fisheries using gear with supporting members embedded in the sea floor, constructed on a site and left there to operate permanently or, if removed, restored each season on the same site.

Article 14

In Articles 1, 3, 4, 5, 6 and 8, the terms 'nationals' means fishing boats or craft of any size having the nationality of the State concerned, according to the law of that State, irrespective of the nationality of the members of their crews.

Article 15

This Convention shall, until 31 October 1958, be open for signature by all States Members of the United Nations or of any of the specialized agencies, and by any other State invited by the General Assembly of the United Nations to become a Party to the Convention.

Article 16

This Convention is subject to ratification. The instruments of ratification shall be deposited with the Secretary-General of the United Nations.

Article 17

This Convention shall be open for accession by any States belonging to any of the categories mentioned in Article 15. The instruments of accession shall be deposited with the Secretary-General of the United Nations.

Article 18

1. This Convention shall come into force on the thirtieth day following the date of deposit of the twenty-second instrument of ratification or accession with the Secretary-General of the United Nations.

2. For each State ratifying or acceding to the Convention after the deposit of the twenty-second instrument of ratification or accession, the Convention shall enter into force on the thirtieth day after deposit by such State of its instrument of ratification or accession.

Article 19

1. At the time of signature, ratification or accession, any State may make reservations to articles of the Convention other than to Articles 6, 7, 9, 10, 11 and 12.

2. Any contracting State making a reservation in accordance with the preceding paragraph may at any time withdraw the reservation by a communication to that effect addressed to the Secretary-General of the United Nations.

Article 20

1. After the expiration of a period of five years from the date on which this Convention shall enter into force, a request for the revision of this Convention may be made at any time by any contracting party by means of a notification in writing addressed to the Secretary-General of the United Nations.

2. The General Assembly of the United Nations shall decide upon the steps, if any, to be taken in respect of such request.

Article 21

The Secretary-General of the United Nations shall inform all States Members of the United Nations and the other States referred to in Article 15:

(a) Of signatures to this Convention and of the deposit of instruments of ratification or accession, in accordance with Articles 15, 16 and 17;

(b) Of the date on which this Convention will come into force, in accordance with Article 18;

(c) Of requests for revision in accordance with Article 20;

(d) Of reservations to this Convention, in accordance with Article 19.

Article 22

The original of this Convention, of which the Chinese, English, French, Russian, and Spanish texts are equally authentic, shall be deposited with the Secretary-General of the United Nations, who shall send certified copies thereof to all States referred to in Article 15.

IN WITNESS WHEREOF the undersigned plenipotentiaries, being duly authorized thereto by their respective governments, have signed this Convention.

DONE AT GENEVA, this twenty-ninth day of April one thousand nine hundred and fifty-eight.

9.13 CONVENTION ON FUTURE MULTILATERAL CO-OPERATION IN THE NORTHWEST ATLANTIC FISHERIES, 1978

The Contracting Parties,

Noting that the coastal States of the Northwest Atlantic have, in accordance with relevant principles of international law, extended their jurisdiction over the living resources of their adjacent waters to limits of up to two hundred nautical miles from the baselines from which the breadth of the territorial sea is measured, and exercise within these areas sovereign rights for the purpose of exploring and exploiting, conserving and managing these resources;

Taking into account the work of the Third United Nations Conference on the Law of the Sea in the field of fisheries;

Desiring to promote the conservation and optimum utilization of the fishery resources of the Northwest Atlantic area within a framework appropriate to the regime of extended coastal State jurisdiction over fisheries, and accordingly to encourage international co-operation and consultation with respect to these resources;

Have agreed as follows:

Article I

1.   The area to which this Convention applies, hereinafter referred top as "the Convention Area", shall be the waters of the Northwest Atlantic Ocean north of 35°00' north latitude and west of a line extending due north from 35°00' north latitude and 42°00' west longitude to 59°00' north latitude, thence due west to 44°00' west longitude, and thence due north to the coast of Greenland, and the waters of the Gulf of St. Lawrence, Davis Strait and Baffin Bay south of 78°10' north latitude.

2.   The area referred to in this Convention as "the Regulatory Area" is that part of the Convention Area which lies beyond the areas in which coastal States exercise fisheries jurisdiction.

3.   For the purposes of this Convention, "coastal State" shall hereinafter mean a Contracting Party exercising fisheries jurisdiction in waters forming part of the Convention Area.

4.   This Convention applies to all fishery resources of the Convention Area, with the following exceptions: salmon, tunas and marlins, cetacean stocks managed by the International Whaling Commission or any successor organization, and sedentary species of the Continental Shelf, i.e., organisms which, at the harvestable stage, either are immobile on or under the seabed or are unable to move except in constant physical contact with the seabed or the subsoil.

5.   Nothing in this Convention shall be deemed to affect or prejudice the positions or claims of any Contracting Party in regard to internal waters, the territorial sea or the limits or extent of the jurisdiction of any Party over fisheries;   or to affect or prejudice the views or positions of any Contracting Party with respect to the law of the sea.

Article II

1.   The Contracting Parties agree to establish and maintain an international organization whose object shall be to contribute through consultation and co-operation to the optimum utilization, rational management and conservation of the fishery resources of the Convention Area.   This organization shall be known as the Northwest Atlantic Fisheries Organization, hereinafter referred to as "the Organization", and shall carry out the functions set forth in this Convention.

2.   The Organization shall consist of:

(a)   a General Council;

(b)   a Scientific Council;

(c)   a Fisheries Commission;   and

(d)   a Secretariat.

3.   The Organization shall have legal personality and shall enjoy in its relations with other international organizations and in the territories of the Contracting Parties such legal capacity as may be necessary to perform its functions and achieve its ends.   The immunities and privileges which the Organization and its officers shall enjoy in the territory of a Contracting Party shall be subject to agreement between the Organisation and the Contracting Party concerned.

4.   The headquarters of the Organization shall be at Dartmouth, Nova Scotia, Canada, or at such other place as may be decided by the General Council.

Article III

The functions of the General Council shall be:

(a) to supervise and co-ordinate the organizational, administrative, financial and other internal affairs of the Organization, including the relations among its constituent bodies;

(b) to co-ordinate the external relations of the Organization;

(c) to review and determine the membership of the Fisheries Commission pursuant to Article XIII; and

(d) to exercise such other authority as is conferred upon it by this Convention.

Article IV

1. Each Contracting Party shall be a member of the General Council and shall appoint to the Council not more than three representatives who may be accompanied at any of its meetings by alternates, experts and advisers.

2. The General Council shall elect a Chairman and a Vice-Chairman, each of whom shall serve for a term of two years and shall be eligible for re-election but shall not serve for more than four years in succession. The Chairman shall be a representative of a Contracting Party that is a member of the Fisheries Commission and the Chairman and Vice-Chairman shall be representatives of different Contracting Parties.

3. The Chairman shall be the President of the Organization and shall be its principal representative.

4. The Chairman of the General Council shall convene a regular annual meeting of the Organization at a place decided upon by the General Council and which shall normally be in North America.

5. Any meeting of the General Council, other than the annual meeting, may be called by the Chairman at such time and place as the Chairman may determine, upon the request of a Contracting Party with the concurrence of another Contracting Party.

6. The General Council may establish such Committees and Sub-committees as it considers desirable for the exercise of its duties and functions.

Article V

1. Each Contracting Party shall have one vote in proceedings of the General Council.

2. Except where otherwise provided, decisions of the General Council shall be taken by a majority of the votes of all Contracting Parties present and casting affirmative or negative votes, provided that no vote shall be taken unless there is a quorum of at least two-thirds of the Contracting Parties.

3. The General Council shall adopt, and amend as occasion may require, rules for the conduct of its meetings and for the exercise of its functions.

4. The General Council shall submit to the Contracting Parties an annual report of the activities of the Organization.

Article VI

1. The functions of the Scientific Council shall be:

(a) to provide a forum for consultation and co-operation among the Contracting Parties with respect to the study, appraisal and exchange of scientific information and views relating to the fisheries of the Convention Area, including environmental and ecological factors affecting these fisheries, and to encourage and promote co-operation among the Contracting Parties in scientific research designed to fill gaps in knowledge pertaining to these matters;

(b) to compile and maintain statistics and records and to publish or disseminate reports, information and materials pertaining to the fisheries of the Convention Area, including environmental and ecological factors affecting these fisheries;

(c) to provide scientific advice to coastal States, where requested to do so pursuant to Article VII; and

(d) to provide scientific advice to the Fisheries Commission, pursuant to Article VIII or on its own initiative as required for the purposes of the Commission.

2.　The functions of the Scientific Council may, where appropriate, be carried out in co-operation with other public or private organizations having related objectives.

3.　The Contracting Parties shall furnish to the Scientific Council any available statistical and scientific information requested by the Council for the purpose of this Article.

Article VII

1.　The Scientific Council shall, at the request of a coastal State, consider and report on any question pertaining to the scientific basis for the management and conservation of fishery resources in waters under the fisheries jurisdiction of that coastal State within the Convention Area.

2.　The coastal State shall, in consultation with the Scientific Council, specify terms of reference for the consideration of any question referred to the Council pursuant to paragraph 1.　These terms of reference shall include, along with any other matters deemed appropriate, such of the following as are applicable:

(a) a statement of the question referred, including a description of the fisheries and area to be considered;

(b) where scientific estimates or predictions are sought, a description of any relevant factors or assumptions to be taken into account; and

(c) where applicable, a description of any objectives the coastal State is seeking to attain and an indication of whether specific advice or a range of options should be provided.

Article VIII

The Scientific Council shall consider and report on any question referred to it by the Fisheries Commission pertaining to the scientific basis for the management and conservation of fishery resources within the Regulatory Area and shall take into account the terms of reference specified by the Fisheries Commission in respect of that question.

Article IX

1.　Each Contracting Party shall be a member of the Scientific Council and shall appoint to the Council its own representatives who may be accompanied at any of its meetings by alternates, experts and advisers.

2.　The Scientific Council shall elect a Chairman and a Vice-Chairman, each of whom shall serve a term of two years and shall be eligible for re-election but shall not serve for more than four years in succession.　The Chairman and Vice-Chairman shall be representatives of different Contracting Parties.

3.　Any meeting of the Scientific Council, other than the annual meeting convened pursuant to Article IV, may be called by the Chairman at such time and place as the Chairman may determine, upon the request of a coastal State or upon the request of a Contracting Party with the concurrence of another Contracting Party.

4. The Scientific Council may establish such Committees and Sub-committees as it considers desirable for the exercise of its duties and functions.

Article X

1. Scientific advice to be provided by the Scientific Council pursuant to this Convention shall be determined by consensus. Where consensus cannot be achieved, the Council shall set out in its report all views advanced on the matter under consideration.
2. Decisions of the Scientific Council with respect to the election of officers, the adoption and the amendment of rules and other matters pertaining to the organization of its work shall be taken by a majority of votes of all Contracting Parties present and casting affirmative or negative votes, and for these purposes each Contracting Party shall have one vote. No vote shall be taken unless there is a quorum of at least two-thirds of the Contracting Parties.
3. The Scientific Council shall adopt, and amend as occasion may require, rules for the conduct of its meetings and for the exercise of its functions.

Article XI

1. The Fisheries Commission, hereinafter referred to as "the Commission", shall be responsible for the management and conservation of the fishery resources of the Regulatory Area in accordance with the provisions of this Article.
2. The Commission may adopt proposals for joint action by the Contracting Parties designed to achieve the optimum utilization of the fishery resources of the Regulatory Area. In considering such proposals, the Commission shall take into account any relevant information or advice provided to it by the Scientific Council.
3. In the exercise of its functions under paragraph 2, the Commission shall seek to ensure consistency between:
(a) any proposal that applies to a stock or group of stocks occurring both within the Regulatory Area and within an area under the fisheries jurisdiction of a coastal State, or any proposal that would have an effect through species interrelationships on a stock or group of stocks occurring in whole or in part within an area under the fisheries jurisdiction of a coastal State, and
(b) any measures or decisions taken by the coastal State for the management and conservation of that stock or group of stocks with respect to fishing activities conducted within the area under its fisheries jurisdiction.
The appropriate coastal State and the Commission shall accordingly promote the co-ordination of such proposals, measures and decisions. Each coastal State shall keep the Commission informed of its measures and decisions for the purpose of this Article.
4. Proposals adopted by the Commission for the allocation of catches in the Regulatory Area shall take into account the interests of Commission members whose vessels have traditionally fished within that Area, and, in the allocation of catches from the Grand Banks and Flemish Cap, Commission members shall give special consideration to the Contracting Party whose coastal communities are primarily dependent on fishing for stocks related to these fishing banks and which has undertaken extensive efforts to ensure the conservation of such stocks through international action, in particular, by providing surveillance and inspection of international fisheries on these banks under an international scheme of joint enforcement.

5.   The Commission may also adopt proposals for international measures of control and enforcement within the Regulatory Area for the purpose of ensuring within that Area the application of this Convention and the measures in force thereunder.

6.   Each proposal adopted by the Commission shall be transmitted by the Executive Secretary to all Contracting Parties, specifying the date of transmittal for the purposes of paragraph 1 of Article XII.

7.   Subject to the provisions of Article XII, each proposal adopted by the Commission under this Article shall become a measure binding on all Contracting Parties to enter into force on a date determined by the Commission.

8.   The Commission may refer to the Scientific Council any question pertaining to the scientific basis for the management and conservation of fishery resources within the Regulatory Area and shall specify terms of reference for the consideration of that question.

9.   The Commission may invite the attention of any or all Commission members to any matters which relate to the objectives and purposes of this Convention within the Regulatory Area.

Article XII

1.   If any Commission member presents to the Executive Secretary an objection to a proposal within sixty days of the date of transmittal specified in the notification of the proposal by the Executive Secretary, the proposal shall not become a binding measure until the expiry of forty days following the date of transmittal specified in the notification of that objection to the Contracting Parties.   Thereupon any other Commission member may similarly object prior to the expiration of the additional forty-day period, or within thirty days after the date of transmittal specified in the notification to the Contracting Parties of any objection presented within that additional forty-day period, whichever shall be the later.   The proposal shall then become a measure binding on all Contracting Parties, except those which have presented objections, at the end of the extended period or periods for objecting.   If, however, at the end of such extended period or periods, objections have been presented and maintained by a majority of Commission members, the proposal shall not become a binding measure, unless any or all of the Commission members nevertheless agree as among themselves to be bound by it on an agreed date.

2.   Any Commission member which has objected to a proposal may at any time withdraw that objection and the proposal immediately shall become a measure binding on such a member, subject to the objection procedure provided for in this Article.

3.   At any time after the expiration of one year from the date on which a measure enters into force, any Commission member may give to the Executive Secretary notice of its intention not to be bound by the measure, and, if that notice is not withdrawn, the measure shall cease to be binding on that member at the end of one year from the date of receipt of the notice by the Executive Secretary.   At any time after a measure has ceased to be binding on a Commission member under this paragraph, the measure shall cease to be binding on any other Commission member upon the date a notice of its intention not to be bound is received by the Executive Secretary.

4.   The Executive Secretary shall immediately notify each Contracting Party of:

(a)   the receipt of each objection and withdrawal of objection under paragraphs 1 and 2;

(b)   the date on which any proposal becomes a binding measure under the provisions of paragraph 1; and

(c)   the receipt of each notice under paragraph 3.

Article XIII

1. The membership of the Commission shall be reviewed and determined by the General Council at its annual meeting and shall consist of:
(a) Each Contracting Party which participates in the fisheries of the Regulatory Area; and
(b) any Contracting Party which has provided evidence satisfactory to the General Council that it expects to participate in the fisheries of the Regulatory Area during the year of that annual meeting or during the following calendar year.
2. Each Commission member shall appoint to the Commission not more than three representatives who may be accompanied at any of its meetings by alternates, experts and advisers.
3. Any Contracting Party that is not a Commission member may attend meetings of the Commission as an observer.
4. The Commission shall elect a Chairman and a Vice-Chairman, each of whom shall serve for a term of two years and shall be eligible for re-election but shall not serve for more than four years in succession. The Chairman and Vice-Chairman shall be representatives of different Commission members.
5. Any meeting of the Commission, other than the annual meeting convened pursuant to Article IV, may be called by the Chairman at such time and place as the Chairman may determine, upon the request of any Commission member.
6. The Commission may establish such Committees and Sub-committees as it considers desirable for the exercise of its duties and functions.

Article XIV

1. Each Commission member shall have one vote in proceedings of the Commission.
2. Decisions of the Commission shall be taken by a majority of the votes of all Commission members present and casting affirmative or negative votes, provided that no vote shall be taken unless there is a quorum of at least two-thirds of the Commission members.

Article XV

1. The Secretariat shall provide services to the Organization in the exercise of its duties and functions.
2. The chief administrative officer of the Secretariat shall be the Executive Secretary, who shall be appointed by the General Council according to such procedures and on such terms as it may determine.
3. The staff of the Secretariat shall be appointed by the Executive Secretary in accordance with such rules and procedures as may be determined by the General Council.
4. The Executive Secretary shall, subject to the general supervision of the General Council, have full power and authority over staff of the Secretariat and shall perform such other functions as the General Council shall prescribe.

Article XVI

1. Each Contracting Party shall pay the expenses of its own delegation to all meetings held pursuant to this Convention.
2. The General Council shall adopt an annual budget for the Organization.

3.   The General Council shall establish the contributions due from each Contracting Party under the annual budget on the following basis:
(a) 10 per cent of the budget shall be divided among coastal States in proportion to their nominal catches in the Convention Area in the year ending two years before the beginning of the budget year.
(b) 30 per cent of the budget shall be divided equally among all the Contracting Parties; and
(c) 60 per cent of the budget shall be divided among all Contracting Parties in proportion to their nominal catches in the Convention Area in the year ending two years before the beginning of the budget year.
The nominal catches referred to above shall be the reported catches of the species listed in Annex I, which forms an integral part of this Convention.
4.   The Executive Secretary shall notify each Contracting Party of the contribution due from that party as calculated under paragraph 3, and as soon as possible thereafter each Contracting Party shall pay to the Organization its contribution.
5.   Contributions shall be payable in the currency of the country in which the headquarters of the Organization is located, except if otherwise authorized by the General Council.
6.   Subject to paragraph 11, the General Council shall, at its first meeting, approve a budget for the balance of the first financial year in which the Organization functions and the Executive Secretary shall transmit to the Contracting Parties copies of that budget together with notice of their respective contributions.
7.   For subsequent financial years, drafts of the annual budget shall be submitted by the Executive Secretary to each Contracting Party together with a schedule of contributions, not less than sixty days before the annual meeting of the Organization at which the budgets are to be considered.
8.   A Contracting Party acceding to this Convention during the course of a financial year shall contribute in respect of that year a part of the contribution calculated in accordance with the provisions of this Article that is proportional to the number of complete months remaining in the year.
9.   A Contracting Party which has not paid its contributions for two consecutive years shall not enjoy any right of casting votes and presenting objections under this Convention until it has fulfilled its obligations, unless the General Council decides otherwise.
10. The financial affairs of the Organization shall be audited annually by external auditors to be selected by the General Council.
11. If the Convention enters into force on 1 January 1979, the provisions of Annex II, which forms an integral part of this Convention, shall apply in place of the provisions of paragraph 6.

Article XVII

The Contracting Parties agree to take such action, including the imposition of adequate sanctions for violations, as may be necessary to make effective the provisions of the Convention and to implement any measures which become binding under paragraph 7 of Article XI and any measures which are in force under Article XXIII.   Each Contracting Party shall transmit to the Commission an annual statement of the actions taken by it for these purposes.

Article XVIII

The Contracting Parties agree to maintain in force and to implement within the Regulatory Area a scheme of joint international enforcement as applicable pursuant to Article XXIII or as modified by measures referred to in paragraph 5 of Article XI. This scheme shall include provision for reciprocal rights of boarding and inspection by the Contracting Parties and for flag State prosecution and sanctions on the basis of evidence resulting from such boardings and inspections. A report of such prosecutions and sanctions imposed shall be included in the annual statement referred to in Article XVII.

Article XIX

The Contracting Parties agree to invite the attention of any State not a Party to this Convention to any matter relating to the fishing activities in the Regulatory Area of the nationals or vessels of that State which appear to affect adversely the attainment of the objectives of this Convention. The Contracting Parties further agree to confer when appropriate upon the steps to be taken towards obviating such adverse effects.

Article XX

1. The Convention Area shall be divided into scientific and statistical sub-areas, divisions and subdivisions, the boundaries of which shall be those defined in Annex III to this Convention.
2. On the request of the Scientific Council, the General Council may by a two-thirds majority vote of all Contracting Parties, if deemed necessary for scientific or statistical purposes, modify the boundaries of the scientific and statistical sub-areas, divisions and subdivisions set out in Annex III, provided that each coastal State exercising fisheries jurisdiction in any part of the area affected concurs in such action.
3. On the request of the Fisheries Commission and after having consulted the Scientific Council, the General Council may by a two-thirds majority vote of all Contracting Parties, if deemed necessary for management purposes, divide the Regulatory Area into appropriate regulatory divisions and subdivisions. These may subsequently be modified in accordance with the same procedure. The boundaries of any such divisions and subdivisions shall be defined in Annex III.
4. Annex III to this Convention, either in its present terms or as modified from time to time pursuant to this Article, forms an integral part of this Convention.

Annex XXI

1. Any Contracting Party may propose amendments to this Convention to be considered and acted upon by the General Council at an annual or a special meeting. Any such proposed amendment shall be sent to the Executive Secretary at least ninety days prior to the meeting at which it is proposed to be acted upon, and the Executive Secretary shall immediately transmit the proposal to all Contracting Parties.
2. The adoption of a proposed amendment to the Convention by the General Council shall require a three-fourths majority of the votes of all Contracting Parties. The text of any proposed amendments so adopted shall be transmitted by the Depositary to all Contracting Parties.
3. An amendment shall take effect for all Contracting Parties one hundred and twenty days following the date of transmittal specified in the notification by the Depositary of receipt of written notification of approval by three-fourths of all Contracting Parties

unless any other Contracting Party notifies the Depositary that it objects to the amendment within ninety days of the date of transmittal specified in the notification by the Depositary of such receipt, in which case the amendment shall not take effect for any Contracting Party. Any Contracting Party which has objected to an amendment may at any time withdraw that objection. If all objections to an amendment are withdrawn, the amendment shall take effect for all Contracting Parties one hundred and twenty days following the date of transmittal specified in the notification by the Depositary of receipt of the last withdrawal.

4. Any Party which becomes a Contracting Party to the Convention after an amendment has been adopted in accordance with paragraph 2 shall be deemed to have approved the said amendment.

5. The Depositary shall promptly notify all Contracting Parties of the receipt of notifications of approval of amendments, the receipt of notifications of objection or withdrawal of objections, and the entry into force of amendments.

Article XXII

1. This Convention shall be open for signature at Ottawa until 31 December 1978, by the Parties represented at the Diplomatic Conference on the Future of Multilateral Cooperation in the Northwest Atlantic Fisheries, held at Ottawa from 11 to 21 October 1977. It shall thereafter be open for accession.

2. This Convention shall be subject to ratification, acceptance or approval by the Signatories and the instruments of ratification, acceptance or approval shall be deposited with the Government of Canada, referred to in this Convention as "the Depositary".

3. This Convention shall enter into force upon the first day of January following the deposit of instruments of ratification, acceptance or approval by not less than six Signatories, at least one of which exercises fisheries jurisdiction in waters forming part of the Convention Area.

4. Any party which has not signed this Convention may accede thereto by a notification in writing to the Depositary. Accession received by the Depositary prior to the date of entry into force of this Convention shall become effective on the date this Convention enters into force. Accessions received by the Depositary after the date of entry into force of this Convention shall become effective on the date of receipt by the Depositary.

5. The Depositary shall inform all Signatories and all Contracting Parties of all ratifications, acceptances or approvals deposited and accessions received.

6. The Depositary shall convene the initial meeting of the Organization to be held not more than six months after the coming into force of the Convention, and shall communicate the provisional agenda to each Contracting Party not less than one month before the date of the meeting.

Article XXIII

Upon the entry into force of this Convention, each proposal that has been transmitted or is effective at that time under Article VIII of the International Convention for the Northwest Atlantic Fisheries, 1949, ("the ICNAF Convention") shall, subject to the provisions of the ICNAF Convention, become a measure binding on each Contracting Party with respect to the Regulatory Area immediately, if the proposal has become effective under the ICNAF Convention, or at such time as it becomes effective thereunder. Subject to paragraph 3 of Article XII of this Convention, each such measure shall remain binding on each Contracting Party, until such time as it expires or is replaced by a measure which has become binding pursuant to Article XI of this Convention; provided that no such replacement shall take effect before this Convention has been in force for one year.

Article XXIV

1. Any Contracting Party may withdraw from the Convention on 31 December of any year by giving notice on or before the preceding 30 June to the Depositary, which shall communicate copies of such notice to other Contracting Parties.
2. Any other Contracting Party may thereupon withdraw from the Convention on the same 31 December by giving notice to the Depositary within one month of the receipt of a copy of a notice of withdrawal given pursuant to paragraph 1.

Article XXV

1. The original of the present Convention shall be deposited with the Government of Canada, which shall communicate certified copies thereof to all the Signatories and to all the Contracting Parties.
2. The Depositary shall register the present Convention with the Secretariat of the United Nations.

In witness whereof the undersigned, being duly authorized thereto, have signed this Convention.

Done at Ottawa, this 24th day of October, 1978, in a single original, in the English and French languages, each text being equally authentic.

[The following annexes are omitted:
Annex I: List of Species for the Determination of the Nominal Catches to be Used in Calculating the Annual Budget Pursuant to Article XVI
Annex II: Transitional Financial Arrangements
Annex III: Scientific and Statistical Sub-areas, Divisions and Subdivisions, as amended by Amendment adopted by NAFO's General Council on 7 June 1979 (Misc. No.9 (1980), Cmnd. 7865).]

9.14 TARAWA DECLARATION ON DRIFTNET FISHING, 1989

The South Pacific Forum meeting at Tarawa on 10 and 11 July 1989
Recognizing the crucial dependence of the Pacific Island peoples on marine resources,
Profoundly concerned at the damage now being done by pelagic driftnet fishing to the economy and environment of the South Pacific region,
Convinced that this indiscriminate, irresponsible and destructive fishing technique threatens the survival of the albacore tuna resource, and so the economic well-being of Forum Island Countries,
Deeply regretting that Japan and Taiwan have failed to respond to the concerns of regional countries about this most serious issue,
Noting that it is in the mutual interest of the major fishing nations active in the region, and the Forum, to conserve fisheries stocks,

Noting also that all countries inside and outside the region are affected by the mismanagement of the resources of the world's oceans, by the environmental dangers of driftnet fishing and by the threat to safe navigation,

Recalling the relevant provisions of the 1982 United Nations Convention on the Law of the Sea, and in particular articles 63, 64, 87, 116, 117, 118 and 119,

Recognizing that the use of driftnets as presently employed in the Southern Pacific Albacore Tuna Fishery is not consistent with international legal requirements in relation to rights and obligations of high seas fisheries conservation and management and environmental principles,

Resolves, for the sake of this and succeeding generations of Pacific peoples, to seek the establishment of a régime for the management of albacore tuna in the South Pacific that would ban driftnet fishing from the region; such a ban might then be a first step to a comprehensive ban on such fishing;

Determines, to this end, to convene an urgent meeting of regional diplomatic, legal and fisheries experts to develop a Convention to give effect to its common resolve to create a zone free of driftnet fishing;

Calls upon the international community to support, and co-operate in, the urgent conclusion of a Convention establishing the zone;

Resolves that individual member States of the South Pacific Forum will take all possible measures in the interim to prevent driftnet fishing within their waters, and otherwise actively to discourage the operations of driftnet fishers;

Further resolves that member States, acting individually and collectively, will take what action they can within relevant international organizations to contribute to the cessation of this harmful form of fishing;

Commends the Republic of Korea for its decision to cease driftnet fishing in the region,

Calls upon Japan and Taiwan to follow this example, and abandon immediately their damaging driftnet operations.

Signed at Tarawa, Kiribati, on the eleventh day of July 1989.

9.15 THE CASTRIES DECLARATION ON DRIFTNET FISHING, 1989

The Authority at Castries, St. Lucia, 20-24 November 1989,

We the Prime Ministers, Deputy Prime Minister, Chief Ministers and other ministers plenipotentiaries constituted as the Authority of the Organization of Eastern Caribbean States (OECS):

Recognizing the increasing importance of marine fisheries to the peoples of the OECS region,

Deeply concerned at the damage being caused to the marine environment by driftnets and other unselective fishing gear in the oceans,

Conscious of the increasing fishing activities of foreign fishing vessels using the drift-net technique in the waters of the OECS region at a time when their use is restricted in certain other regions,

Convinced that any proliferation in the use of these indiscreet, irresponsible and disruptive fishing techniques in the waters of the OECS region can permanently change the nature and abundance of the region's living marine resources,

Considering the provisions of the 1982 United Nations Convention on the Law of the Sea, particularly articles 61, 63, 64, 73, 116, 117, 118 and 119,

Mindful that the indiscriminate use of fishing gear, whether on the high seas or in a coastal State's exclusive economic zone, is inconsistent with legal provisions as enunciated in the United Nations Convention on the Law of the Sea,

Acknowledging the rights and duties of States to ensure the proper management and conservation of the living marine resources in their exclusive economic zones and the mutual interest of all OECS States to collaborate in order to conserve and protect fisheries stocks,

Resolve to seek to establish a regional régime for the regulation and management of the pelagic resources in the Lesser Antilles region that would outlaw the use of driftnets and other disruptive fishing methods by commercial fishing vessels, and call upon other States in the region to co-operate in this regard;

Resolve that all member States of OECS will take all possible measures in the interim to prevent the use of indiscriminate fishing methods in their exclusive economic zones;

Further resolve that member States, acting individually and collectively, will take whatever action possible within relevant regional and international organizations that would contribute towards the global restriction of harmful fishing practices.

Castries, Saint Lucia, 24 November 1989

9.16 WELLINGTON CONVENTION FOR THE PROHIBITION OF FISHING WITH LONG DRIFTNETS IN THE SOUTH PACIFIC, 1989

The Parties to this Convention,

RECOGNIZING the importance of marine living resources to the people of the South Pacific region;

PROFOUNDLY CONCERNED at the damage now being done by pelagic driftnet fishing to the albacore tuna resource and to the environment and economy of the South Pacific region;

CONCERNED ALSO for the navigational threat posed by driftnet fishing;

NOTING that the increasing fishing capacity induced by large scale driftnet fishing threatens the fish stocks in the South Pacific;

MINDFUL of the relevant rules of international law, including the provisions of the United Nations Convention on the Law of the Sea, done at Montego Bay on 20 December 1982, in particular Parts V, VII and XVI;

RECALLING the Declaration of the South Pacific Forum at Tarawa, 11 July 1989, that a Convention should be adopted to ban the use of driftnets in the South Pacific region;

RECALLING ALSO the Resolution of the 29th South Pacific Conference at Guam, which called for an immediate ban on the practice of driftnet fishing in the South Pacific Commission region;

HAVE AGREED as follows:

Article 1
Definitions

For the purpose of this Convention and its Protocols:
   (a) The "Convention Area",
   (i) Subject to subparagraph (ii) of this paragraph, shall be the area lying within 10 degrees North latitude and 50 degrees South latitude and 130 degrees East

longitude and 120 degrees West longitude, and shall also include all waters under the fisheries jurisdiction of any Party to this Convention;

   (ii) In the case of a State or Territory which is Party to the Convention by virtue of paragraph 1(b) or 1(c) of article 210, it shall include only waters under the fisheries jurisdiction of that Party, adjacent to the Territory referred to in paragraph 1(b) or 1(c) of article 10.

(b) "driftnet" means a gillnet or other net or a combination of nets which is more than 2.5 kilometres in length the purpose of which is to enmesh, entrap or entangle fish by drifting on the surface of or in the water;

(c) "driftnet fishing activities" means:

   (i) catching, taking or harvesting fish with the use of a driftnet;

   (ii) attempting to catch, take or harvest fish with the use of a driftnet;

   (iii) engaging in any other activity which can reasonably be expected to result in the catching, taking or harvesting of fish with the use of a driftnet, including searching for and locating fish to be taken by that method;

   (iv) any operations at sea in support of, or in preparation for, any activity described in this paragraph, including operations of placing, searching for or recovering fish aggregating devices or associated electronic equipment such as radio beacons;

   (v) aircraft use, relating to the activities described in this paragraph, except for flights in emergencies involving the health or safety of crew members or the safety of a vessel; or

   (vi) transporting, transshipping and processing any driftnet catch, and co-operation in the provision of food, fuel and other supplies for vessels equipped for or engaged in driftnet fishing.

(d) the "FFA" means the South Pacific Forum Fisheries Agency; and

(e) "fishing vessel" means any vessel or boat equipped for or engaged in searching for, catching, processing or transporting fish or other marine organisms.

Article 2
Measures regarding nationals and vessels

Each Party undertakes to prohibit its nationals and vessels documented under its laws from engaging in driftnet fishing activities within the Convention Area.

Article 3
Measures against driftnet fishing activities

1. Each Party undertakes:

   (a) not to assist or encourage the use of driftnets within the Convention Area; and

   (b) to take measures consistent with international law to restrict driftnet fishing activities within the Convention Area, including but not limited to:

   (i) prohibiting the use of driftnets within areas under its fisheries jurisdiction; and

   (ii) prohibiting the transshipment of driftnet catches within areas under its jurisdiction.

2. Each Party may also take measures consistent with international law to:

   (a) prohibit the landing of driftnet catches within its territory;

   (b) prohibit the processing of driftnet catches in facilities under its jurisdiction;

(c) prohibit the importation of any fish or fish product, whether processed or not, which was caught using a driftnet;

(d) restrict port access and port servicing facilities for driftnet fishing vessels; and

(e) prohibit the possession of driftnets on board any fishing vessel within areas under its fisheries jurisdiction.

3. Nothing in this Convention shall prevent a Party from taking measures against driftnet fishing activities which are stricter than those required by the Convention.

Article 4
Enforcement

1. Each Party shall take appropriate measures to ensure the application of the provisions of this Convention.

2. The Parties undertake to collaborate to facilitate surveillance and enforcement of measures taken by Parties pursuant to this Convention.

3. The Parties undertake to take measures leading to the withdrawal of good standing on the Regional Register of Foreign Fishing Vessels maintained by the FFA against any vessel engaging in driftnet fishing activities.

Article 5
Consultation with non-parties

1. The Parties shall seek to consult with any State which is eligible to become a Party to this Convention on any matter relating to driftnet fishing activities which appear to affect adversely the conservation of marine living resources within the Convention Area or the implementation of the Convention and its protocols.

2. The Parties shall seek to reach agreement with any State referred to in paragraph 1 of this article, concerning the prohibitions established pursuant to articles 2 and 3.

Article 6
Institutional arrangements

1. The FFA shall be responsible for carrying out the following functions:

(a) the collection, preparation and dissemination of information on driftnet fishing activities within the Convention area;

(b) the facilitation of scientific analyses on the effects of driftnet fishing activities within the Convention Area, including consultations with appropriate regional and international organisations; and

(c) the preparation and transmission to the Parties of an annual report on any driftnet fishing activities within the Convention Area and the measures taken to implement this Convention or its Protocols.

2. Each Party shall expeditiously convey to the FFA:

(a) information on the measures adopted by it pursuant to the implementation of the Convention; and

(b) information on, and scientific analyses on the effects of, driftnet fishing activities relevant to the Convention Area.

3. All Parties, including States or Territories not members of the FFA, and the FFA shall co-operate to promote the effective implementation of this article.

Article 7
Review and consultation among parties

1. Without prejudice to the conduct of consultations among Parties by other means, the FFA, at the request of three Parties, shall convene meetings of the Parties to review the implementation of this Convention and its Protocols.
2. Parties to the Protocols shall be invited to any such meeting and to participate in a manner to be determined by the Parties to the Convention.

Article 8
Conservation and management measures

Parties to this Convention shall co-operate with each other and with appropriate distant water fishing nations and other entities or organisations in the development of conservation and management measures for South Pacific albacore tuna within the Convention Area.

Article 9
Protocols

This Convention may be supplemented by Protocols or associated instruments to further its objectives.

Article 10
Signature, ratification and accession

1. This Convention shall be open for signature by:
    (a) any member of the FFA; and
    (b) any State in respect of any Territory situated within the Convention Area for which it is internationally responsible; or
    (c) any Territory situated within the Convention Area which has been authorized to sign the Convention and to assume rights and obligations under it by the Government of the State which is internationally responsible for it.
2. This Convention is subject to ratification by members of the FFA and the other States and Territories referred to in paragraph 1 of this article.   The instruments of ratification shall be deposited with the Government of New Zealand which shall be the Depositary.
3. This Convention shall remain open for accession by the members of the FFA and the other States and Territories referred to in paragraph 1 of this article.   The instruments of accession shall be deposited with the Depositary.

Article 11
Reservations

This Convention shall not be subject to reservations.

Article 12
Amendments

1. Any Party may propose amendments to this Convention.
2. Amendments shall be adopted by consensus among the Parties.
3. Any amendments adopted shall be submitted by the Depositary to all Parties for ratification, approval or acceptance.

4. An amendment shall enter into force thirty days after receipt by the Depositary of instruments of ratification, approval or acceptance from all Parties.

Article 13
Entry into force

1. This Convention shall enter into force on the date of deposit of the fourth instrument of ratification or accession.
2. For any member of the FFA or a State or Territory which ratifies or accedes to this Convention after the date of deposit of the fourth instrument of ratification or accession, the Convention shall enter into force on the date of deposit of its instrument of ratification or accession.

Article 14
Certification and registration

1. The original of this Convention and its Protocols shall be deposited with the Depositary, which shall transmit certified copies to all States and Territories eligible to become Party to the Convention and to all States eligible to become Party to a Protocol to the Convention.
2. The Depositary shall register this Convention and its Protocols in accordance with article 102 of the Charter of the United Nations.

DONE at Wellington this twenty-third day of November 1989 in the English and French languages, each text being equally authentic.

IN WITNESS WHEREOF the undersigned, being duly authorized by their Governments, have signed this Convention.

9.17 GENERAL ASSEMBLY RESOLUTION 44/225 OF 22 DECEMBER 1989 ON LARGE-SCALE PELAGIC DRIFTNET FISHING AND ITS IMPACT ON THE LIVING MARINE RESOURCES OF THE WORLD'S OCEANS AND SEAS

The General Assembly,
Noting that many countries are disturbed by the increase in the use of large-scale pelagic driftnets, which can reach or exceed 30 miles (48 kilometres) in total length, to catch living marine resources on the high seas of the world's oceans and seas,
Mindful that large-scale pelagic driftnet fishing, a method of fishing with a net or a combination of nets intended to be held in a more or less vertical position by floats and weights, the purpose of which is to enmesh fish by drifting on the surface of or in the water, can be a highly indiscriminate and wasteful fishing method that is widely considered to threaten the effective conservation of living marine resources, such as highly migratory and anadromous species of fish, birds and marine mammals,
Drawing attention to the fact that the present resolution does not address the question of small-scale driftnet fishing traditionally conducted in coastal waters, especially by developing countries, which provides an important contribution to their subsistence and economic development,
Expressing concern that, in addition to targeted species of fish, non-targeted fish, marine mammals, seabirds and other living marine resources of the world's oceans and

seas can become entangled in large-scale pelagic driftnets, either in those in active use or in those that are lost or discarded, and as a result of such entanglement are often either injured or killed.

Recognizing that more than one thousand fishing vessels use large-scale pelagic driftnets in the Pacific, Atlantic and Indian Oceans, and in other areas of the high seas,

Recognizing also that any regulatory measures to be taken for the conservation and management of living marine resources should take account of the best available scientific data and analysis,

Recalling the relevant principles elaborated in the United Nations Convention on the Law of the Sea,

Affirming that, in accordance with the relevant articles of the Convention, all members of the international community have a duty to co-operate globally and regionally in the conservation and management of living resources on the high seas, and a duty to take, or to co-operate with others in taking, such measures for their nationals as may be necessary for the conservation of those resources,

Recalling that, in accordance with the relevant articles of the Convention, it is the responsibility of all members of the international community to ensure the conservation and management of living marine resources and the protection and preservation of the living marine environment within their exclusive economic zones,

Noting the serious concern, particularly of coastal States and States with fishing interests, that the overexploitation of living marine resources of the high seas adjacent to the exclusive economic zones of coastal States is likely to have an adverse impact on the same resources within such zones, and noting also, in this regard, the responsibility for co-operation in accordance with the relevant articles of the Convention,

Noting further that the countries of the South Pacific Forum and the South Pacific Commission, in recognition of the importance of living marine resources to the people of the South Pacific region, have called for a cessation of such fishing in the South Pacific and the implementation of effective management programmes,

Taking note of the adoption of the Tarawa Declaration on this subject by the Twentieth South Pacific Forum at Tarawa, Kiribati, on 11 July 1989 and the adoption by South Pacific States and territories of the Convention on the Prohibition of Driftnet Fishing in the South Pacific, at Wellington on 24 November 1989,

Noting that some members of the international community have entered into co-operative enforcement and monitoring programmes for the immediate evaluation of the impact of large-scale pelagic driftnet fishing,

Recognizing that some members of the international community have taken steps to reduce their driftnet operations in some regions in response to regional concerns,

1.   *Calls upon* all members of the international community, particularly those with fishing interests, to strengthen their co-operation in the conservation and management of living marine resources;

2.   *Calls upon* all those involved in large-scale pelagic driftnet fishing to co-operate fully with the international community, and especially with coastal States and the relevant international and regional organisations, in the enhanced collection and sharing of statistically sound scientific data in order to continue to assess the impact of such fishing methods and to secure conservation of the world's living marine resources;

3.   *Recommends* that all interested members of the international community, particularly within regional organizations, continue to consider and, by 30 June 1991, review the best available scientific data on the impact of large-scale pelagic driftnet fishing and agree upon further co-operative regulation and monitoring measures, as needed;

4. *Also recommends* that all members of the international community, bearing in mind the special role of regional organizations and regional and bilateral co-operation in the conservation and management of living marine resources as reflected in the relevant articles of the United Nations Convention on the Law of the Sea, agree to the following measures:

(a) Moratoria should be imposed on all large-scale pelagic driftnet fishing by 30 June 1992, with the understanding that such a measure will not be imposed in a region or, if implemented, can be lifted, should effective conservation and management measures be taken based upon statistically sound analysis to be jointly made by concerned parties of the itnernational community with an interest in the fishery resources of the region, to prevent unacceptable impact of such fishing practices on that region, and to ensure the conservation of the living marine resources of that region;

(b) Immediate action should be taken to reduce progressively large-scale pelagic driftnet fishing activities in the South Pacific region with a view to the cessation of such activities by 1 July 1991, as an interim measure, until appropriate conservation and management arrangements for South Pacific albacore tuna resources are entered into by the parties concerned;

(c) Further expansion of large-scale pelagic driftnet fishing on the high seas of the North Pacific and all the other high seas outside the Pacific Ocean should cease immediately, with the understanding that this measure will be reviewed subject to the conditions in paragraph 4(a) of the present resolution;

5. *Encourages* those coastal countries which have exclusive economic zones adjacent to the high seas to take appropriate measures and to co-operate in the collection and submission of scientific information on driftnet fishing in their own exclusive economic zones, taking into account the measures taken for the conservation of living marine resources of the high seas;

6. *Requests* specialized agencies, particularly the Food and Agriculture Organisation of the United Nations, and other appropriate organs, organizations and programmes of the United Nations system, as well as the various regional and subregional fisheries organizations, urgently to study large-scale pelagic driftnet fishing and its impact on living marine resources and to report their views to the Secretary-General.

7. *Requests* the Secretary-General to bring the present resolution to the attention of all members of the international community, intergovernmental organisations, non-governmental organisations in consultative status with the Economic and Social Council, and well-established scientific institutions with expertise in relation to living marine resources;

8. *Requests* the Secretary-General to submit to the General Assembly at its forty-fifth session a report on the implementation of the present resolution.

10 The Protection and Preservation of the Marine Environment

10.1 UNITED NATIONS CONVENTION ON THE LAW OF THE SEA, 1982:
PART XII: PROTECTION AND PRESERVATION OF THE MARINE
ENVIRONMENT

SECTION 1. GENERAL PROVISIONS

Article 192
General obligation

States have the obligation to protect and preserve the marine environment.

Article 193
Sovereign right of States to exploit their natural resources

States have the sovereign right to exploit their natural resources pursuant to their environmental policies and in accordance with their duty to protect and preserve the marine environment.

Article 194
Measures to prevent, reduce and control pollution of the marine environment

1. States shall take, individually or jointly as appropriate, all measures consistent with this Convention that are necessary to prevent, reduce and control pollution of the marine environment from any source, using for this purpose the best practicable means

at their disposal and in accordance with their capabilities, and they shall endeavour to harmonize their policies in this connection.

2. States shall take all measures necessary to ensure that activities under their jurisdiction or control are so conducted as not to cause damage by pollution to other States and their environment, and that pollution arising from incidents or activities under their jurisdiction or control does not spread beyond the areas where they exercise sovereign rights in accordance with this Convention.

3. The measures taken pursuant to this Part shall deal with all sources of pollution of the marine environment. These measures shall include, *inter alia*, those designed to minimize to the fullest extent:

(a) the release of toxic, harmful or noxious substances, especially those which are persistent, from land-based sources, from or through the atmosphere or by dumping;

(b) pollution from vessels, in particular measures for preventing accidents and dealing with emergencies, ensuring the safety of operations at sea, preventing intentional and unintentional discharges, and regulating the design, construction, equipment, operation and manning of vessels;

(c) pollution from installations and devices used in exploration or exploitation of the natural resources of the seabed and subsoil, in particular measures for preventing accidents and dealing with emergencies, ensuring the safety of operations at sea, and regulating the design, construction, equipment, operation and manning of such installations or devices;

(d) pollution from other installations and devices operating in the marine environment, in particular measures for preventing accidents and dealing with emergencies, ensuring the safety of operations at sea, and regulating the design, construction, equipment, operation and manning of such installations or devices.

4. In taking measures to prevent, reduce or control pollution of the marine environment, States shall refrain from unjustifiable interference with activities carried out by other States in the exercise of their rights and in pursuance of their duties in conformity with this Convention.

5. The measures taken in accordance with this Part shall include those necessary to protect and preserve rare or fragile ecosystems as well as the habitat of depleted, threatened or endangered species and other forms of marine life.

Article 195
Duty not to transfer damage or hazards or transform one type of pollution into another

In taking measures to prevent, reduce and control pollution of the marine environment, States shall act so as not to transfer, directly or indirectly, damage or hazards from one area to another or transform one type of pollution into another.

Article 196
Use of technologies or introduction of alien or new species

1. States shall take all measures necessary to prevent, reduce and control pollution of the marine environment resulting from the use of technologies under their jurisdiction or control, or the intentional or accidental introduction of species, alien or new, to a particular part of the marine environment, which may cause significant and harmful changes thereto.

2. This article does not affect the application of this Convention regarding the prevention, reduction and control of pollution of the marine environment.

SECTION 2. GLOBAL AND REGIONAL CO-OPERATION

Article 197
Co-operation on a global or regional basis

States shall co-operate on a global basis and, as appropriate, on a regional basis, directly or through competent international organizations, in formulating and elaborating international rules, standards and recommended practices and procedures consistent with this Convention, for the protection and preservation of the marine environment, taking into account characteristic regional features.

Article 198
Notification of imminent or actual damage

When a State becomes aware of cases in which the marine environment is in imminent danger of being damaged or has been damaged by pollution, it shall immediately notify other States it deems likely to be affected by such damage, as well as the competent international organizations.

Article 199
Contingency plans against pollution

In the cases referred to in article 198, States in the area affected, in accordance with their capabilities, and the competent international organizations shall co-operate, to the extent possible, in eliminating the effects of pollution and preventing or minimizing the damage.   To this end, States shall jointly develop and promote contingency plans for responding to pollution incidents in the marine environment.

Article 200
Studies, research programmes and exchange of information and data

States shall co-operate, directly or through competent international organizations, for the purpose of promoting studies, undertaking programmes of scientific research and encouraging the exchange of information and data acquired about pollution of the marine environment.   They shall endeavour to participate actively in regional and global programmes to acquire knowledge for the assessment of the nature and extent of pollution, exposure to it, and its pathways, risks and remedies.

Article 201
Scientific criteria for regulations

In the light of the information and data acquired pursuant to article 200, States shall co-operate, directly or through competent international organizations, in establishing appropriate scientific criteria for the formulation and elaboration of rules, standards and recommended practices and procedures for the prevention, reduction and control of pollution of the marine environment.

SECTION 3. TECHNICAL ASSISTANCE

Article 202
Scientific and technical assistance to developing States

States shall, directly or through competent international organizations:

(a) promote programmes of scientific, international, technical and other assistance to developing States for the protection and preservation of the marine environment and the prevention, reduction and control of marine pollution. Such assistance shall include, *inter alia*:

    (i) training of their scientific and technical personnel;

    (ii) facilitating their participation in relevant international programmes;

    (iii) supplying them with necessary equipment and facilities;

    (iv) enhancing their capacity to manufacture such equipment;

    (v) advice on and developing facilities for research, monitoring, educational and other programmes;

(b) provide appropriate assistance, especially to developing States, for the minimization of the effects of major incidents which may cause serious pollution of the marine environment;

(c) provide appropriate assistance, especially to developing States, concerning the preparation of environmental assessments.

Article 203
Preferential treatment for developing States

Developing States shall, for the purposes of prevention, reduction and control of pollution of the marine environment or minimization of its effects, be granted preference by international organizations in:

(a) the allocation of appropriate funds and technical assistance; and

(b) the utilization of their specialized services.

SECTION 4. MONITORING AND ENVIRONMENTAL ASSESSMENT

Article 204
Monitoring of the risks or effects of pollution

1. States shall, consistent with the rights of other States, endeavour, as far as practicable, directly or through the competent international organizations, to observe, measure, evaluate and analyse, by recognized scientific methods, the risks or effects of pollution of the marine environment.

2. In particular, States shall keep under surveillance the effects of any activities which they permit or in which they engage in order to determine whether these activities are likely to pollute the marine environment.

Article 205
Publication of reports

States shall publish reports of the results obtained pursuant to article 204 or provide such reports at appropriate intervals to the competent international organizations, which should make them available to all States

Article 206
Assessment of potential effects of activities

When States have reasonable grounds for believing that planned activities under their jurisdiction or control may cause substantial pollution of or significant and harmful changes to the marine environment, they shall, as far as practicable, assess the potential effects of such activities on the marine environment and shall communicate reports of the results of such assessments in the manner provided in article 205.

SECTION 5. INTERNATIONAL RULES AND NATIONAL LEGISLATION TO PREVENT, REDUCE AND CONTROL POLLUTION OF THE MARINE ENVIRONMENT

Article 207
Pollution from land-based sources

1. States shall adopt laws and regulations to prevent, reduce and control pollution of the marine environment from land-based sources, including rivers, estuaries, pipelines and outfall structures, taking into account internationally agreed rules, standards and recommended practices and procedures.
2. States shall take other measures as may be necessary to prevent, reduce and control such pollution.
3. States shall endeavour to harmonize their policies in this connection at the appropriate regional level.
4. States, acting especially through competent international organizations or diplomatic conference, shall endeavour to establish global and regional rules, standards and recommended practices and procedures to prevent, reduce and control pollution of the marine environment from land-based sources, taking into account characteristic regional features, the economic capacity of developing States and their need for economic development.   Such rules, standards and recommended practices and procedures shall be re-examined from time to time as necessary.
5. Laws, regulations, measures, rules, standards and recommended practices and procedures referred to in paragraphs 1, 2 and 4 shall include those designed to minimize, to the fullest extent possible, the release of toxic, harmful or noxious substances, especially those which are persistent, into the marine environment.

Article 208
Pollution from sea-bed activities subject to national jurisdiction

1. Coastal States shall adopt laws and regulations to prevent, reduce and control pollution of the marine environment arising from or in connection with sea-bed activities subject to their jurisdiction and from artificial islands, installations and structures under their jurisdiction, pursuant to articles 60 and 80.
2. States shall take other measures as may be necessary to prevent, reduce and control such pollution.
3. Such laws, regulations and measures shall be no less effective than international rules, standards and recommended practices and procedures.
4. States shall endeavour to harmonize their policies in this connection at the appropriate regional level.
5. States, acting especially through competent international organisations or diplomatic conference, shall establish global and regional rules, standards and recommended practices and procedures to prevent, reduce and control pollution of the

marine environment referred to in paragraph 1. Such rules, standards and recommended practices and procedures shall be re-examined from time to time as necessary.

Article 209
Pollution from activities in the Area

1. International rules, regulations and procedures shall be established in accordance with Part XI to prevent, reduce and control pollution of the marine environment from activities in the Area. Such rules, regulations and procedures shall be re-examined from time to time as necessary.
2. Subject to the relevant provisions of this section, States shall adopt laws and regulations to prevent, reduce and control pollution of the marine environment from activities in the Area undertaken by vessels, installations, structures and other devices flying their flag or of their registry or operating under their authority, as the case may be. The requirements of such laws and regulations shall be no less effective than the international rules, regulations and procedures referred to in paragraph 1.

Article 210
Pollution by dumping

1. States shall adopt laws and regulations to prevent, reduce and control pollution of the marine environment by dumping.
2. States shall take other measures as may be necessary to prevent, reduce and control such pollution.
3. Such laws, regulations and measures shall ensure that dumping is not carried out without the permission of the competent authorities of States.
4. States, acting especially through competent international organizations or diplomatic conference, shall endeavour to establish global and regional rules, standards and recommended practices and procedures to prevent, reduce and control such pollution. Such rules, standards and recommended practices and procedures shall be re-examined from time to time as necessary.
5. Dumping within the territorial sea and the exclusive economic zone or onto the continental shelf shall not be carried out without the express prior approval of the coastal State, which has the right to permit, regulate and control such dumping after due consideration of the matter with other States which by reason of their geographical situation may be adversely affected thereby.
6. National laws, regulations and measures shall be no less effective in preventing, reducing and controlling such pollution than the global rules and standards.

Article 211
Pollution from vessels

1. States, acting through the competent international organization or general diplomatic conference, shall establish international rules and standards to prevent, reduce and control pollution of the marine environment from vessels and promote the adoption, in the same manner, wherever appropriate, of routeing systems designed to minimize the threat of accidents which might cause pollution of the marine environment, including the coastline, and pollution damage to the related interests of coastal States. Such rules and standards shall, in the same manner, be re-examined from time to time as necessary.
2. States shall adopt laws and regulations for the prevention, reduction and control of pollution of the marine environment from vessels flying their flag or of their registry.

Such laws and regulations shall at least have the same effect as that of generally accepted international rules and standards established through the competent international organization or general diplomatic conference.

3. States which establish particular requirements for the prevention, reduction and control of pollution of the marine environment as a condition for the entry of foreign vessels into their ports or internal waters or for a call at their off-shore terminals shall give due publicity to such requirements and shall communicate them to the competent international organization. Whenever such requirements are established in identical form by two or more coastal States in an endeavour to harmonize policy, the communication shall indicate which States are participating in such co-operative arrangements. Every State shall require the master of a vessel flying its flag or of its registry, when navigating within the territorial sea of a State participating in such co-operative arrangements, to furnish, upon the request of that State, information as to whether it is proceeding to a State of the same region participating in such co-operative arrangements and, if so, to indicate whether it complies with the port entry requirements of that State. This article is without prejudice to the continued exercise by a vessel of its right of innocent passage or to the application of article 25, paragraph 2.

4. Coastal States may, in the exercise of their sovereignty within their territorial sea, adopt laws and regulations for the prevention, reduction and control of marine pollution from foreign vessels, including vessels exercising the right of innocent passage. Such laws and regulations shall, in accordance with Part II, section 3, not hamper innocent passage of foreign vessels.

5. Coastal States, for the purpose of enforcement as provided for in section 6, may in respect of their exclusive economic zones adopt laws and regulations for the prevention, reduction and control of pollution from vessels conforming to and giving effect to generally accepted international rules and standards established through the competent international organization or general diplomatic conference.

6.(a) Where the international rules and standards referred to in paragraph 1 are inadequate to meet special circumstances and coastal States have reasonable grounds for believing that a particular, clearly defined area of their respective exclusive economic zones is an area where the adoption of special mandatory measures for the prevention of pollution from vessels is required for recognized technical reasons in relation to its oceanographical and ecological conditions, as well as its utilization or the protection of its resources and the particular character of its traffic, the coastal States, after appropriate consultations through the competent international organization concerned, may, for that area, direct a communication to that organization, submitting scientific and technical evidence in support and information on necessary reception facilities. Within 12 months after receiving such a communication, the organization shall determine whether the conditions in that area correspond to the requirements set out above. If the organization so determines, the coastal States may, for that area, adopt laws and regulations for the prevention, reduction and control of pollution from vessels implementing such international rules and standards or navigational practices as are made applicable, through the organization, for special areas. These laws and regulations shall not become applicable to foreign vessels until 15 months after the submission of the communication to the organization.

(b) The coastal States shall publish the limits of any such particular, clearly defined area.

(c)   If the coastal States intend to adopt additional laws and regulations for the same area for the prevention, reduction and control of pollution from vessels, they shall, when submitting the aforesaid communication, at the same time notify the organization thereof.   Such additional laws and regulations may relate to discharges or navigational practices but shall not require foreign vessels to observe design, construction, manning or equipment standards other than generally accepted international rules and standards;   they shall become applicable to foreign vessels 15 months after the submission of the communication to the organization, provided that the organization agrees within 12 months after the submission of the communication.

7.   The international rules and standards referred to in this article should include *inter alia* those relating to prompt notification to coastal States, whose coastline or related interests may be affected by incidents, including maritime casualties, which involve discharges or probability of discharges.

Article 212
Pollution from or through the atmosphere

1.   States shall adopt laws and regulations to prevent, reduce and control pollution of the marine environment from or through the atmosphere, applicable to the air space under their sovereignty and to vessels flying their flag or vessels or aircraft of their registry, taking into account internationally agreed rules, standards and recommended practices and procedures and the safety of air navigation.

2.   States shall take other measures as may be necessary to prevent, reduce and control such pollution.

3.   States, acting especially through competent international organizations or diplomatic conference, shall endeavour to establish global and regional rules, standards and recommended practices and procedures to prevent, reduce and control such pollution.

SECTION 6. ENFORCEMENT

Article 213
Enforcement with respect to pollution from land-based sources

States shall enforce their laws and regulations adopted in accordance with article 207 and shall adopt laws and regulations and take other measures necessary to implement applicable international rules and standards established through competent international organizations or diplomatic conference to prevent, reduce and control pollution of the marine environment from land-based sources.

Article 214
Enforcement with respect to pollution from sea-bed activities

States shall enforce their laws and regulations adopted in accordance with article 208 and shall adopt laws and regulations and take other measures necessary to implement applicable international rules and standards established through competent international organizations or diplomatic conference to prevent, reduce and control pollution of the marine environment arising from or in connection with sea-bed activities subject to their jurisdiction and from artificial islands, installations and structures under their jurisdiction, pursuant to articles 60 and 80.

Article 215
Enforcement with respect to pollution from activities in the Area

Enforcement of international rules, regulations and procedures established in accordance with Part XI to prevent, reduce and control pollution of the marine environment from activities in the Area shall be governed by that Part.

Article 216
Enforcement with respect to pollution by dumping

1. Laws and regulations adopted in accordance with this Convention and applicable international rules and standards established through competent international organizations or diplomatic conference for the prevention, reduction and control of pollution of the marine environment by dumping shall be enforced:
(a) by the coastal State with regard to dumping within its territorial sea or its exclusive economic zone or onto its continental shelf;
(b) by the flag State with regard to vessels flying its flag or vessels or aircraft of its registry;
(c) by any State with regard to acts of loading of wastes or other matter occurring within its territory or at its off-shore terminals.
2. No State shall be obliged by virtue of this article to institute proceedings when another State has already instituted proceedings in accordance with this article.

Article 217
Enforcement by flag States

1. States shall ensure compliance by vessels flying their flag or of their registry with applicable international rules and standards, established through the competent international organization or general diplomatic conference, and with their laws and regulations adopted in accordance with this Convention for the prevention, reduction and control of pollution of the marine environment from vessels and shall accordingly adopt laws and regulations and take other measures necessary for their implementation. Flag States shall provide for the effective enforcement of such rules, standards, laws and regulations, irrespective of where a violation occurs.
2. States shall, in particular, take appropriate measures in order to ensure that vessels flying their flag or of their registry are prohibited from sailing, until they can proceed to sea in compliance with the requirements of the international rules and standards referred to in paragraph 1, including requirements in respect of design, construction, equipment and manning of vessels.
3. States shall ensure that vessels flying their flag or of their registry carry on board certificates required by and issued pursuant to international rules and standards referred to in paragraph 1. States shall ensure that vessels flying their flag are periodically inspected in order to verify that such certificates are in conformity with the actual condition of the vessels. These certificates shall be accepted by other States as evidence of the condition of the vessels and shall be regarded as having the same force as certificates issued by them, unless there are clear grounds for believing that the condition of the vessel does not correspond substantially with the particulars of the certificates.
4. If a vessel commits a violation of rules and standards established through the competent international organization or general diplomatic conference, the flag State, without prejudice to articles 218, 220 and 228, shall provide for immediate

investigation and where appropriate institute proceedings in respect of the alleged violation irrespective of where the violation occurred or where the pollution caused by such violation has occurred or has been spotted.

5. Flag States conducting an investigation of the violation may request the assistance of any other State whose co-operation could be useful in clarifying the circumstances of the case. States shall endeavour to meet appropriate requests of flag States.

6. States shall, at the written request of any State, investigate any violation alleged to have been committed by vessels flying their flag. If satisfied that sufficient evidence is available to enable proceedings to be brought in respect of the alleged violation, flag States shall without delay institute such proceedings in respect of the alleged violation, flag States shall without delay institute such proceedings in accordance with their laws.

7. Flag States shall promptly inform the requesting State and the competent international organization of the action taken and its outcome. Such information shall be available to all States.

8. Penalties provided for by the laws and regulations of States for vessels flying their flag shall be adequate in severity to discourage violations wherever they occur.

Article 218
Enforcement by port States

1. When a vessel is voluntarily within a port or at an off-shore terminal of a State, that State may undertake investigations and, where the evidence so warrants, institute proceedings in respect of any discharge from that vessel outside the internal waters, territorial sea or exclusive economic zone of that State in violation of applicable international rules and standards established through the competent international organization or general diplomatic conference.

2. No proceedings pursuant to paragraph 1 shall be instituted in respect of a discharge violation in the internal waters, territorial sea or exclusive economic zone of another State unless requested by that State, the flag State, or a State damaged or threatened by the discharge violation, or unless the violation has caused or is likely to cause pollution in the internal waters, territorial sea or exclusive economic zone of the State instituting the proceedings.

3. When a vessel is voluntarily within a port or at an off-shore terminal of a State, that State shall, as far as practicable, comply with requests from any State for investigation of a discharge violation referred to in paragraph 1, believed to have occurred in, caused, or threatened damage to the internal waters, territorial sea or exclusive economic zone of the requesting State. It shall likewise, as far as practicable, comply with requests from the flag State for investigation of such a violation, irrespective of where the violation occurred

4. The records of the investigation carried out by a port State pursuant to this article shall be transmitted upon request to the flag State or to the coastal State. Any proceedings instituted by the port State on the basis of such an investigation may, subject to section 7, be suspended at the request of the coastal State when the violation has occurred within its internal waters, territorial sea or exclusive economic zone. The evidence and records of the case, together with any bond or other financial security posted with the authorities of the port State, shall in that event be transmitted to the coastal State. Such transmittal shall preclude the continuation of proceedings in the port State.

Article 219
Measures relating to seaworthiness of vessels to avoid pollution

Subject to section 7, States which, upon request or on their own initiative, have ascertained that a vessel within one of their ports or at one of their offshore terminals is in violation of applicable international rules and standards relating to seaworthiness of vessels and thereby threatens damage to the marine environment shall, as far as practicable, take administrative measures to prevent the vessel from sailing. Such States may permit the vessel to proceed only to the nearest appropriate repair yard and, upon removal of the causes of the violation, shall permit the vessel to continue immediately.

Article 220
Enforcement by coastal States

1. When a vessel is voluntarily within a port or at an off-shore terminal of a State, that State may, subject to section 7, institute proceedings in respect of any violation of its laws and regulations adopted in accordance with this Convention or applicable international rules and standards for the prevention, reduction and control of pollution from vessels when the violation has occurred within the territorial sea or the exclusive economic zone of that State.

2. Where there are clear grounds for believing that a vessel navigating in the territorial sea of a State has, during its passage therein, violated laws and regulations of that State adopted in accordance with this Convention or applicable international rules and standards for the prevention, reduction and control of pollution from vessels, that State, without prejudice to the application of the relevant provisions of Part II, section 3, may undertake physical inspection of the vessel relating to the violation and may, where the evidence so warrants, institute proceedings, including detention of the vessel, in accordance with its laws, subject to the provisions of section 7.

3. Where there are clear grounds for believing that a vessel navigating in the exclusive economic zone or the territorial sea of a State has, in the exclusive economic zone, committed a violation of applicable international rules and standards for the prevention, reduction and control of pollution from vessels or laws and regulations of that State conforming and giving effect to such rules and standards, that State may require the vessel to give information regarding its identity and port of registry, its last and its next port of call and other relevant information required to establish whether a violation has occurred.

4. States shall adopt laws and regulations and take other measures so that vessels flying their flag comply with requests for information pursuant to paragraph 3.

5. Where there are clear grounds for believing that a vessel navigating in the exclusive economic zone or the territorial sea of a State has, in the exclusive economic zone, committed a violation referred to in paragraph 3 resulting in a substantial discharge causing or threatening significant pollution of the marine environment, that State may undertake physical inspection of the vessel for matters relating to the violation if the vessel has refused to give information or if the information supplied by the vessel is manifestly at variance with the evident factual situation and if the circumstances of the case justify such inspection.

6. Where there is clear objective evidence that a vessel navigating in the exclusive economic zone or the territorial sea of a State has, in the exclusive economic zone, committed a violation referred to in paragraph 3 resulting in a discharge causing major damage or threat of major damage to the coastline or related interests of the coastal

State, or to any resources of its territorial sea or exclusive economic zone, that State may, subject to section 7, provided that the evidence so warrants, institute proceedings, including detention of the vessel, in accordance with its laws.

7. Notwithstanding the provisions of paragraph 6, whenever appropriate procedures have been established, either through the competent international organization or as otherwise agreed, whereby compliance with requirements for bonding or other appropriate financial security has been assured, the coastal State if bound by such procedures shall allow the vessel to proceed.

8. The provisions of paragraphs 3, 4, 5, 6 and 7 also apply in respect of national laws and regulations adopted pursuant to article 211, paragraph 6.

Article 221
Measures to avoid pollution arising from maritime casualties

1. Nothing in this Part shall prejudice the right of States, pursuant to international law, both customary and conventional, to take and enforce measures beyond the territorial sea proportionate to the actual or threatened damage to protect their coastline or related interests, including fishing, from pollution or threat of pollution following upon a maritime casualty or acts relating to such a casualty, which may reasonably be expected to result in major harmful consequences.

2. For the purposes of this article, "maritime casualty" means a collision of vessels, stranding or other incident of navigation, or other occurrence on board a vessel or external to it resulting in material damage or imminent threat of material damage to a vessel or cargo.

Article 222
Enforcement with respect to pollution from or through the atmosphere

States shall enforce, within the air space under their sovereignty or with regard to vessels flying their flag or vessels or aircraft of their registry, their laws and regulations adopted in accordance with article 212, paragraph 1, and with other provisions of this Convention and shall adopt laws and regulations and take other measures necessary to implement applicable international rules and standards established through competent international organizations or diplomatic conference to prevent, reduce and control pollution of the marine environment from or through the atmosphere, in conformity with all relevant international rules and standards concerning the safety of air navigation.

SECTION 7. SAFEGUARDS

Article 223
Measures to facilitate proceedings

In proceedings instituted pursuant to this part, States shall take measures to facilitate the hearing of witnesses and the admission of evidence submitted by authorities of another State, or by the competent international organization, and shall facilitate the attendance at such proceedings of official representatives of the competent international organization, the flag State and any State affected by such pollution arising out of any violation. The official representatives attending such proceedings shall have such rights and duties as may be provided under national laws and regulations or international law.

Article 224
Exercise of powers of enforcement

The powers of enforcement against foreign vessels under this Part may only be exercised by officials or by warships, military aircraft, or other ships or aircraft clearly marked and identifiable as being on government service and authorized to that effect.

Article 225
Duty to avoid adverse consequences in the exercise of the powers of enforcement

In the exercise under this Convention of their powers of enforcement against foreign vessels, States shall not endanger the safety of navigation or otherwise create any hazard to a vessel, or bring it to an unsafe port or anchorage, or expose the marine environment to an unreasonable risk.

Article 226
Investigation of foreign vessels

1. (a) States shall not delay a foreign vessel longer than is essential for purposes of the investigations provided for in articles 216, 218 and 220. Any physical inspection of a foreign vessel shall be limited to an examination of such certificates, records or other documents as the vessel is required to carry by generally accepted international rules and standards or of any similar documents which it is carrying; further physical inspection of the vessel may be undertaken only after such an examination and only when:
     (i) there are clear grounds for believing that the condition of the vessel or its equipment does not correspond substantially with the particulars of those documents;
     (ii) the contents of such documents are not sufficient to confirm or verify a suspected violation; or
     (iii) the vessel is not carrying valid certificates and records.
   (b) If the investigation indicates a violation of applicable laws and regulations or international rules and standards for the protection and preservation of the marine environment, release shall be made promptly subject to reasonable procedures such as bonding or other appropriate financial security.
   (c) Without prejudice to applicable international rules and standards relating to the seaworthiness of vessels, the release of a vessel may, whenever it would present an unreasonable threat of damage to the marine environment, be refused or made conditional upon proceeding to the nearest appropriate repair yard. Where release has been refused or made conditional, the flag State of the vessel must be promptly notified, and may seek release of the vessel in accordance with Part XV.
2. States shall co-operate to develop procedures for the avoidance of unnecessary physical inspection of vessels at sea.

Article 227
Non-discrimination with respect to foreign vessels

In exercising their rights and performing their duties under this Part, States shall not discriminate in form or in fact against vessels of any other State.

Article 228
Suspension and restrictions on institution of proceedings

1. Proceedings to impose penalties in respect of any violation of applicable laws and regulations or international rules and standards relating to the prevention, reduction and control of pollution from vessels committed by a foreign vessel beyond the territorial sea of the State instituting proceedings shall be suspended upon the taking of proceedings to impose penalties in respect of corresponding charges by the flag State within six months of the date on which proceedings were first instituted, unless those proceedings relate to a case of major damage to the coastal State or the flag State in question has repeatedly disregarded its obligation to enforce effectively the applicable international rules and standards in respect of violations committed by its vessels. The flag State shall in due course make available to the State previously instituting proceedings a full dossier of the case and the records of the proceedings, whenever the flag State has requested the suspension of proceedings in accordance with this article. When proceedings instituted by the flag State have been brought to a conclusion, the suspended proceedings shall be terminated. Upon payment of costs incurred in respect of such proceedings, any bond posted or other financial security provided in connection with the suspended proceedings shall be released by the coastal State.
2. Proceedings to impose penalties on foreign vessels shall not be instituted after the expiry of three years from the date on which the violation was committed, and shall not be taken by any State in the event of proceedings having been instituted by another State subject to the provisions set out in paragraph 1.
3. The provisions of this article are without prejudice to the right of the flag State to take any measures, including proceedings to impose penalties, according to its laws irrespective of prior proceedings by another State.

Article 229
Institution of civil proceedings

Nothing in this Convention affects the institution of civil proceedings in respect of any claim for loss or damage resulting from pollution of the marine environment.

Article 230
Monetary penalties and the observance of recognized rights of the accused

1. Monetary penalties only may be imposed with respect to violations of national laws and regulations or applicable international rules and standards for the prevention, reduction and control of pollution of the marine environment, committed by foreign vessels beyond the territorial sea.
2. Monetary penalties only may be imposed with respect to violations of national laws and regulations or applicable international rules and standards for the prevention, reduction and control of pollution of the marine environment, committed by foreign vessels in the territorial sea, except in the case of a wilful and serious act of pollution in the territorial sea.
3. In the conduct of proceedings in respect of such violations committed by a foreign vessel which may result in the imposition of penalties, recognized rights of the accused shall be observed.

Article 231
Notification to the flag State and other States concerned

States shall promptly notify the flag State and any other State concerned of any measures taken pursuant to section 6 against foreign vessels, and shall submit to the flag State all official reports concerning such measures. However, with respect to violations committed in the territorial sea, the foregoing obligations of the coastal State apply only to such measures as are taken in proceedings. The diplomatic agents or consular officers and where possible the maritime authority of the flag State, shall be immediately informed of any such measures taken pursuant to section 6 against foreign vessels.

Article 232
Liability of States arising from enforcement measures

States shall be liable for damage or loss attributable to them arising from measures taken pursuant to section 6 when such measures are unlawful or exceed those reasonably required in the light of available information. States shall provide for recourse in their courts for actions in respect of such damage or loss.

Article 233
Safeguards with respect to straits used for international navigation

Nothing in sections 5, 6 and 7 affects the legal regime of straits used for international navigation. However, if a foreign ship other than those referred to in section 10 has committed a violation of the laws and regulations referred to in article 42, paragraph 1(a) and (b), causing or threatening major damage to the rine environment of the straits, the States bordering the straits may take appropriate enforcement measures and if so shall respect *mutatis mutandis* the provisions of this section.

SECTION 8. ICE-COVERED AREAS

Article 234
Ice-covered areas

Coastal States have the right to adopt and enforce non-discriminatory laws and regulations for the prevention, reduction and control of marine pollution from vessels in ice-covered areas within the limits of the exclusive economic zone, where particularly severe climatic conditions and the presence of ice covering such areas for most of the year create obstructions or exceptional hazards to navigation, and pollution of the marine environment could cause major harm to or irreversible disturbance of the ecological balance. Such laws and regulations shall have due regard to navigation and the protection and preservation of the marine environment based on the best available scientific evidence.

SECTION 9. RESPONSIBILITY AND LIABILITY

Article 235
Responsibility and liability

1.   States are responsible for the fulfilment of their international obligations concerning the protection and preservation of the marine environment.   They shall be liable in accordance with international law.

2.   States shall ensure that recourse is available in accordance with their legal systems for prompt and adequate compensation or other relief in respect of damage caused by pollution of the marine environment by natural or juridical persons under their jurisdiction.

3.   With the objective of assuring prompt and adequate compensation in respect of all damage caused by pollution of the marine environment, States shall co-operate in the implementation of existing international law and the further development of international law relating to responsibility and liability for the assessment of and compensation for damage and the settlement of related disputes, as well as, where appropriate, development of criteria and procedures for payment of adequate compensation, such as compulsory insurance or compensation funds.

SECTION 10. SOVEREIGN IMMUNITY

Article 236
Sovereign immunity

The provisions of this Convention regarding the protection and preservation of the marine environment do not apply to any warship, naval auxiliary, other vessels or aircraft owned or operated by a State and used, for the time being, only on government non-commercial service.   However, each State shall ensure, by the adoption of appropriate measures not impairing operations or operational capabilities of such vessels or aircraft owned or operated by it, that such vessels or aircraft act in a manner consistent, so far as is reasonable and practicable, with this Convention.

SECTION 11. OBLIGATIONS UNDER OTHER CONVENTIONS ON THE PROTECTION AND PRESERVATION OF THE MARINE ENVIRONMENT

Article 237
Obligations under other conventions on the protection and preservation of the marine environment

1.   The provisions of this Part are without prejudice to the specific obligations assumed by States under special conventions and agreements concluded previously which relate to the protection and preservation of the marine environment and to agreements which may be concluded in furtherance of the general principles set forth in this Convention.

2.   Specific obligations assumed by States under special conventions, with respect to the protection and preservation of the marine environment, should be carried out in a manner consistent with the general principles and objectives of this Convention.

10.2 INTERNATIONAL CONVENTION ON CIVIL LIABILITY FOR OIL POLLUTION DAMAGE, 1992

Introduction

The International Convention on Civil Liability for Oil Pollution Damage, 1969[1] (CLC 1969) was amended by a Protocol[2] in 1976 (CLC PROT 1976) in order to change the unit of account prescribed in Article V from the gold franc to the Special Drawing Right (SDR) of the International Monetary Fund. CLC PROT 1976 entered into force on 8 April 1981.

Important substantive amendments to CLC 1969 were introduced by a second Protocol adopted in 1984[3] (CLC PROT 1984). Under Article 11, CLC 1969 and CLC PROT 1984 were, as between the parties to CLC PROT 1984, to be read and interpreted as one instrument and CLC 1969, as amended by CLC PROT 1984, was to be known as the 'International Convention on Civil Liability for Oil Pollution Damage, 1984'. Unfortunately, CLC PROT 1984 failed to attract sufficient support to satisfy the conditions for entry into force prescribed in Article 13. To find a way out of the impasse, an IMO Conference met in 1992 and, 'Aware of the need to ensure the entry into force of *the content* of the 1984 Protocol as soon as possible',[4] drafted the Protocol of 1992 to Amend CLC 1969[5] (CLC PROT 1992). As is evident from Conference Resolution 4,[6] CLC PROT 1992 was intended to replace CLC PROT 1984 and, following the 1984 model, provides in Article 11 that CLC 1969 and CLC PROT 1992 shall, as between the parties to this Protocol, be read and interpreted together as one single instrument and Articles I to XII ter of CLC 1969 as amended by CLC PROT 1992 are to be known as the 'International Convention on Civil Liability for Oil Pollution Damage, 1992' (CLC 1992).

Since no authentic composite text has so far been produced, the writer has prepared such a text below.

CLC PROT 1992 was open for signature from 15 January 1993 to 14 January 1994[7]. According to Conference Resolution 4, '... it is unlikely that the conditions for ... entry into force [of CLC PROT 1984] will be met following the adoption of the 1992 Protocol ...'[8]

COMPOSITE TEXT OF CLC 1992 AND ADDITIONAL PROVISIONS OF CLC PROT 1992

[Preamble and Article 1 of CLC PROT 1992]

THE PARTIES TO THE PRESENT PROTOCOL,

HAVING CONSIDERED the International Convention on Civil Liability for Oil Pollution Damage, 1969, and the 1984 Protocol thereto,

HAVING NOTED that the 1984 Protocol to that Convention, which provides for improved scope and enhanced compensation, has not entered into force,

AFFIRMING the importance of maintaining the viability of the international oil pollution liability and compensation system,

AWARE OF the need to ensure the entry into force of the content of the 1984 Protocol as soon as possible,

RECOGNIZING that special provisions are necessary in connection with the introduction of corresponding amendments to the International Convention on the Establishment of an International Fund for Compensation for Oil Pollution Damage, 1971,

HAVE AGREED as follows:

Article 1

The Convention which the provisions of this Protocol amend is the International Convention on Civil Liability for Oil Pollution Damage, 1969, hereinafter referred to as the '1969 Liability Convention'. For States Parties to the Protocol of 1976 to the 1969 Liability Convention, such reference shall be deemed to include the 1969 Liability Convention as amended by that Protocol.

[Preamble of original CLC 1969]

The States Parties to the present Convention,

CONSCIOUS of the dangers of pollution posed by the worldwide maritime carriage of oil in bulk,

CONVINCED of the need to ensure that adequate compensation is available to persons who suffer damage caused by pollution resulting from the escape or discharge of oil from ships,

DESIRING to adopt uniform international rules and procedures for determining questions of liability and providing adequate compensation in such cases,

HAVE AGREED as follows:

Article I

For the purposes of this Convention:

1. 'Ship' means any sea-going vessel and seaborne craft of any type whatsoever constructed or adapted for the carriage of oil in bulk as cargo, provided that a ship capable of carrying oil and other cargoes shall be regarded as a ship only when it is actually carrying oil in bulk as cargo and during any voyage following such carriage unless it is proved that it has no residues of such carriage of oil in bulk aboard.

2. 'Person' means any individual or partnership or any public or private body, whether corporate or not, including a State or any of its constituent subdivisions.

3. 'Owner' means the person or persons registered as the owner of the ship or, in the absence of registration, the person or persons owning the ship. However in the case of a ship owned by a State and operated by a company which in that State is registered as the ship's owner, 'owner' shall mean such company.

4. 'State of the ship's registry' means in relation to registered ships the State of registration of the ship, and in relation to unregistered ships the State whose flag the ship is flying.

5. 'Oil' means any persistent hydrocarbon mineral oil such as crude oil, fuel oil, heavy diesel oil and lubricating oil, whether carried on board a ship as cargo or in the bunkers of such a ship.

6. 'Pollution damage' means:

(a) loss or damage caused outside the ship by contamination resulting from the escape or discharge of oil from the ship, wherever such escape or discharge may occur, provided that compensation for impairment of the environment other than loss of profit from such impairment shall be limited to costs of reasonable measures of reinstatement actually undertaken or to be undertaken;

(b) the costs of preventive measures and further loss or damage caused by preventive measures.

7. 'Preventive measures' means any reasonable measures taken by any person after an incident has occurred to prevent or minimize pollution damage.

8. 'Incident' means any occurrence, or series of occurrences having the same origin, which causes pollution damage or creates a grave and imminent threat of causing such damage.

9. 'Organization' means the International Maritime Organization.

10. '1969 Liability Convention' means the International Convention on Civil Liability for Oil Pollution Damage, 1969. For States Parties to the Protocol of 1976 to that Convention, the term shall be deemed to include the 1969 Liability Convention as amended by that Protocol.

Article II

This Convention shall apply exclusively:

(a) to pollution damage caused:
  (i) in the territory, including the territorial sea, of a Contracting State, and
  (ii) in the exclusive economic zone of a Contracting State, established in accordance with international law, or, if a Contracting State has not established such a zone, in an area beyond and adjacent to the territorial sea of that State determined by that State in accordance with international law and extending not more than 200 nautical miles from the baselines from which the breadth of its territorial sea is measured;
(b) to preventive measures, wherever taken, to prevent or minimize such damage.

Article III

1. Except as provided in paragraphs 2 and 3 of this Article, the owner of a ship at the time of an incident, or where the incident consists of a series of occurrences, at the time of the first such occurrence, shall be liable for any pollution damage caused by the ship as a result of the incident.

2. No liability for pollution damage shall attach to the owner if he proves that the damage:
  (a) resulted from an act of war, hostilities, civil war, insurrection or a natural phenomenon of an exceptional, inevitable and irresistible character, or
  (b) was wholly caused by an act or omission done with intent to cause damage by a third party, or
  (c) was wholly caused by the negligence or other wrongful act of any Government or other authority responsible for the maintenance of lights or other navigational aids in the exercise of that function.

3. If the owner proves that the pollution damage resulted wholly or partially either from an act or omission done with intent to cause damage by the person who suffered the damage or from the negligence of that person, the owner may be exonerated wholly or partially from his liability to such person.

4. No claim for compensation for pollution damage may be made against the owner otherwise than in accordance with this Convention. Subject to paragraph 5 of this Article, no claim for compensation for pollution damage under this Convention or otherwise may be made against:

(a) the servants or agents of the owner or the members of the crew;
(b) the pilot or any other person who, without being a member of the crew, performs services for the ship;
(c) any charterer (howsoever described, including a bareboat charterer), manager or operator of the ship;
(d) any person performing salvage operations with the consent of the owner or on the instructions of a competent public authority;
(e) any person taking preventive measures;
(f) all servants or agents of persons mentioned in subparagraphs (c), (d) and (e);
unless the damage resulted from their personal act or omission, committed with the intent to cause such damage, or recklessly and with knowledge that such damage would probably result.

Article IV

When an incident involving two or more ships occurs and pollution damage results therefrom, the owners of all the ships concerned, unless exonerated under Article III, shall be jointly and severally liable for all such damage which is not reasonably separable.

Article V

1. The owner of a ship shall be entitled to limit his liability under this Convention in respect of any one incident to an aggregate amount calculated as follows:
(a) 3 million units of account for a ship not exceeding 5,000 units of tonnage;
(b) for a ship with a tonnage in excess thereof, for each additional unit of tonnage, 420 units of account in addition to the amount mentioned in subparagraph (a);
provided, however, that this aggregate amount shall not in any event exceed 59.7 million units of account.
2. The owner shall not be entitled to limit his liability under this Convention if it is proved that the pollution damage resulted from his personal act or omission, committed with the intent to cause such damage, or recklessly and with knowledge that such damage would probably result.
3. For the purpose of availing himself of the benefit of limitation provided for in paragraph 1 of this Article the owner shall constitute a fund for the total sum representing the limit of his liability with the Court or other competent authority of any one of the Contracting States in which action is brought under Article IX or, if no action is brought, with any Court or other competent authority in any one of the Contracting States in which an action can be brought under Article IX. The fund can be constituted either by depositing the sum or by producing a bank guarantee or other guarantee, acceptable under the legislation of the Contracting State where the fund is constituted, and considered to be adequate by the Court or other competent authority.
4. The fund shall be distributed among the claimants in proportion to the amounts of their established claims.
5. If before the fund is distributed the owner or any of his servants or agents or any person providing him insurance or other financial security has as a result of the incident in question, paid compensation for pollution damage, such person shall, up to the amount he has paid, acquire by subrogation the rights which the person so compensated would have enjoyed under this Convention.
6. The right of subrogation provided for in paragraph 5 of this Article may also be exercised by a person other than those mentioned therein in respect of any amount of

compensation for pollution damage which he may have paid but only to the extent that such subrogation is permitted under the applicable national law.

7.   Where the owner or any other person establishes that he may be compelled to pay at a later date in whole or in part any such amount of compensation, with regard to which such person would have enjoyed a right of subrogation under paragraphs 5 or 6 of this Article, had the compensation been paid before the fund was distributed, the Court or other competent authority of the State where the fund has been constituted may order that a sufficient sum shall be provisionally set aside to enable such person at such later date to enforce his claim against the fund.

8.   Claims in respect of expenses reasonably incurred or sacrifices reasonably made by the owner voluntarily to prevent or minimize pollution damage shall rank equally with other claims against the fund.

9(a).   The 'unit of account' referred to in paragraph 1 of this Article is the Special Drawing Right as defined by the International Monetary Fund. The amounts mentioned in paragraph 1 shall be converted into national currency on the basis of the value of that currency by reference to the Special Drawing Right on the date of the constitution of the fund referred to in paragraph 3. The value of the national currency, in terms of the Special Drawing Right, of a Contracting State which is a member of the International Monetary Fund, shall be calculated in accordance with the method of valuation applied by the International Monetary Fund in effect on the date in question for its operations and transactions. The value of the national currency, in terms of the Special Drawing Right, of a Contracting State which is not a member of the International Monetary Fund, shall be calculated in a manner determined by that State.

9(b).   Nevertheless, a Contracting State which is not a member of the International Monetary Fund and whose law does not permit the application of the provisions of paragraph 9(a) may, at the time of ratification, acceptance, approval of or accession to this Convention or at any time thereafter, declare that the unit of account referred to in paragraph 9(a) shall be equal to 15 gold francs. The gold franc referred to in this paragraph corresponds to sixty-five and a half milligrammes of gold of millesimal fineness nine hundred. The conversion of the gold france into the national currency shall be made according to the law of the State concerned.

9(c).   The calculation mentioned in the last sentence of paragraph 9(a) and the conversion mentioned in paragraph 9(b) shall be made in such manner as to express in the national currency of the Contracting State as far as possible the same real value for the amounts in paragraph 1 as would result from the application of the first three sentences of paragraph 9(a). Contracting States shall communicate to the depositary the manner of calculation pursuant to paragraph 9(a), or the result of the conversion in paragraph 9(b) as the case may be, when depositing an instrument of ratification, acceptance, approval of or accession to this Convention and whenever there is a change in either.

10.   For the purpose of this Article the ship's tonnage shall be the gross tonnage calculated in accordance with the tonnage measurement regulations contained in Annex I of the International Convention on Tonnage Measurement of Ships, 1969.

11.   The insurer or other person providing financial security shall be entitled to constitute a fund in accordance with this Article on the same conditions and having the same effect as if it were constituted by the owner. Such a fund may be constituted even if, under the provisions of paragraph 2, the owner is not entitled to limit his liability, but its constitution shall in that case not prejudice the rights of any claimant against the owner.

Article VI

1. Where the owner, after an incident, has constituted a fund in accordance with Article V, and is entitled to limit his liability,

(a) no person having a claim for pollution damage arising out of that incident shall be entitled to exercise any right against any other assets of the owner in respect of such claim;

(b) the Court or other competent authority of any Contracting State shall order the release of any ship or other property belonging to the owner which has been arrested in respect of a claim for pollution damage arising out of that incident, and shall similarly release any bail or other security furnished to avoid such arrest.

2. The foregoing shall, however, only apply if the claimant has access to the Court administering the fund and the fund is actually available in respect of his claim.

Article VII

1. The owner of a ship registered in a Contracting State and carrying more than 2,000 tons of oil in bulk as cargo shall be required to maintain insurance or other financial security, such as the guarantee of a bank or a certificate delivered by an international compensation fund, in the sums fixed by applying the limits of liability prescribed in Article V, paragraph 1 to cover his liability for pollution damage under this Convention.

2. A certificate attesting that insurance or other financial security is in force in accordance with the provisions of this Convention shall be issued to each ship after the appropriate authority of a Contracting State has determined that the requirements of paragraph 1 have been complied with. With respect to a ship registered in a Contracting State such certificate shall be issued or certified by the appropriate authority of the State of the ship's registry; with respect to a ship not registered in a Contracting State it may be issued or certified by the appropriate authority of any Contracting State. This certificate will be in the form of the annexed model and shall contain the following particulars:

(a) name of ship and port of registration;

(b) name and principal place of business of owner;

(c) type of security;

(d) name and principal place of business of insurer or other person giving security and, where appropriate, place of business where the insurance or security is established;

(e) period of validity of certificate which shall not be longer than the period of validity of the insurance or other security.

3. The certificate shall be in the official language or languages of the issuing State. If the language used is neither English nor French, the text shall include a translation into one of these languages.

4. The certificate shall be carried on board the ship and a copy shall be deposited with the authorities who keep the record of the ship's registry or, if the ship is not registered in a Contracting State, with the authorities of the State issuing or certifying the certificate.

5. An insurance or other financial security shall not satisfy the requirements of this Article if it can cease, for reasons other than the expiry of the period of validity of the insurance or security specified in the certificate under paragraph 2 of this Article, before three months have elapsed from the date on which notice of its termination is given to the authorities referred to in paragraph 4 of this Article, unless the certificate has been surrendered to these authorities or a new certificate has been issued within the

said period. The foregoing provisions shall similarly apply to any modification which results in the insurance or security no longer satisfying the requirements of this Article.

6. The State of registry shall subject to the provisions of this Article, determine the conditions of issue and validit of the certificate.

7. Certificates issued or certified under the authority of a Contracting State in accordance with paragraph 2 shall be accepted by other Contracting States for the purposes of this Convention and shall be regarded by other Contracting States as having the same force as certificates issued or certified by them even if issued or certified in respect of a ship not registered in a Contracting State. A Contracting State may at any time request consultation with the issuing or certifying State should it believe that the insurer or guarantor named in the certificate is not financially capable of meeting the obligations imposed by this Convention.

8. Any claim for compensation for pollution damage may be brought directly against the insurer or other person providing financial security for the owner's liability for pollution damage. In such case the defendant may, even if the owner is not entitled to limit his liability according to Article V, paragraph 2, avail himself of the limits of liability prescribed in Article V, paragraph 1. He may further avail himself of the defences (other than the bankruptcy or winding up of the owner) which the owner himself would have been entitled to invoke. Furthermore, the defendant may avail himself of the defence that the pollution damage resulted from the wilful misconduct of the owner himself, but the defendant shall not avail himself of any other defence which he might have been entitled to invoke in proceedings brought by the owner against him. The defendant shall in any event have the right to require the owner to be joined in the proceedings.

9. Any sums provided by insurance or by other financial security maintained in accordance with paragraph 1 of this Article shall be available exclusively for the satisfaction of claims under this Convention.

10. A Contracting State shall not permit a ship under its flag to which this Article applies to trade unless a certificate has been issued under paragraph 2 or 12 of this Article.

11. Subject to the provisions of this Article, each Contracting State shall ensure, under its national legislation, that insurance or other security to the extent specified in paragraph 1 of this Article is in force in respect of any ship, wherever registered, entering or leaving a port in its territory, or arriving at or leaving an off-shore terminal in its territorial sea, if the ship actually carries more than 2,000 tons of oil in bulk as cargo.

12. If insurance or other financial security is not maintained in respect of a ship owned by a Contracting State, the provisions of this Article relating thereto shall not be applicable to such ship, but the ship shall carry a certificate issued by the appropriate authorities of the State of the ship's registry stating that the ship is owned by that State and that the ship's liability is covered within the limits prescribed by Article V, paragraph 1. Such a certificate shall follow as closely as practicable the model prescribed by paragraph 2 of this Article

Article VIII

Rights of compensation under this Convention shall be extinguished unless an action is brought thereunder within three years from the date when the damage occurred. However, in no case shall an action be brought after six years from the date of the incident which caused the damage. Where this incident consists of a series of occurrences, the six years' period shall run from the date of the first such occurrence.

Article IX

1. Where an incident has caused pollution damage in the territory, including the territorial sea or an area referred to in Article II, of one or more Contracting States or preventive measures have been taken to prevent or minimize pollution damage in such territory including the territorial sea or area, actions for compensation may only be brought in the Courts of any such Contracting State or States. Reasonable notice of any such action shall be given to the defendant.

2. Each Contracting State shall ensure that its Courts possess the necessary jurisdiction to entertain such actions for compensation.

3. After the fund has been constituted in accordance with Article V the Courts of the State in which the fund is constituted shall be exclusively competent to determine all matters relating to the apportionment and distribution of the fund.

Article X

1. Any judgment given by a Court with jurisdiction in accordance with Article IX which is enforceable in the State of origin where it is no longer subject to ordinary forms of review, shall be recognized in any Contracting State, except:
(a) where the judgment was obtained by fraud; or
(b) where the defendant was not given reasonable notice and a fair opportunity to present his case.

2. A judgment recognized under paragraph 1 of this Article shall be enforceable in each Contracting State as soon as the formalities required in that State have been complied with. The formalities shall not permit the merits of the case to be re-opened.

Article XI

1. The provisions of this Convention shall not apply to warships or other ships owned or operated by a State and used, for the time being, only on government non-commercial service.

2. With respect to ships owned by a Contracting State and used for commercial purposes, each State shall be subject to suit in the jurisdictions set forth in Article IX and shall waive all defences based in its status as a sovereign State.

Article XII

This Convention shall supersede any International Conventions in force or open for signature, ratification or accession at the date on which the Convention is opened for signature, but only to the extent that such Conventions would be in conflict with it; however, nothing in this Article shall affect the obligations of Contracting States to non-Contracting States arising under such International Conventions.

Article XII bis
Transitional provisions

The following transitional provisions shall apply in the case of a State which at the time of an incident is a Party both to this Convention and to the 1969 Liability Convention:
(a) where an incident has caused pollution damage within the scope of this Convention, liability under this Convention shall be deemed to be discharged if, and to the extent that, it also arises under the 1969 Liability Convention;

(b) where an incident has caused pollution damage within the scope of this Convention, and the State is a Party both to this Convention and to the International Convention on the Establishment of an International Fund for Compensation for Oil Pollution Damage, 1971, liability remaining to be discharged after the application of subparagraph (a) of this Article shall arise under this Convention only to the extent that pollution damage remains uncompensated after application of the said 1971 Convention;

(c) in the application of Article III, paragraph 4, of this Convention the expression 'this Convention' shall be interpreted as referring to this Convention or the 1969 Liability Convention, as appropriate;

(d) in the application of Article V, paragraph 3, of this Convention the total sum of the fund to be constituted shall be reduced by the amount by which liability has been deemed to be discharged in accordance with subparagraph (a) of this Article.

Article XII ter
Final clauses

The final clauses of this Convention shall be Articles 12 to 18 of the Protocol of 1992 to amend the 1969 Liability Convention. References in this Convention to Contracting States shall be taken to mean references to the Contracting States of that Protocol.

[The following Articles 10-18 are articles of CLC PROT 1992 which, according to Article 11(1), has to be read and interpreted together with CLC 1969 as one instrument.]

Article 10

The model of a certificate annexed to the 1969 Liability Convention is replaced by the model annexed to this Protocol.

Article 11

1. The 1969 Liability Convention and this Protocol shall, as between the Parties to this Protocol, be read and interpreted together as one single instrument.

2. Articles I to XII ter, including the model certificate, of the 1969 Liability Convention as amended by this Protocol shall be known as the International Convention on Civil Liability for Oil Pollution Damage, 1992 (1992 Liability Convention).

Final Clauses

Article 12
Signature, ratification, acceptance, approval and accession

1. This Protocol shall be open for signature at London from 15 January 1993 to 14 January 1994 by all States.

2. Subject to paragraph 4, any State may become a Party to this Protocol by:

(a) signature subject to ratification, acceptance or approval followed by ratification, acceptance or approval; or

(b) accession.

3. Ratification, acceptance, approval or accession shall be effected by the deposit of a formal instrument to that effect with the Secretary-General of the Organization.

4. Any Contracting State to the International Convention on the Establishment of an International Fund for Compensation for Oil Pollution Damage, 1971, hereinafter referred to as the 1971 Fund Convention, may ratify, accept, approve or accede to this Protocol only if it ratifies, accepts, approves or accedes to the Protocol of 1992 to amend that Convention at the same time, unless it denounces the 1971 Fund Convention to take effect on the date when this Protocol enters into force for that State.

5. A State which is a Party to this Protocol but not a Party to the 1969 Liability Convention shall be bound by the provisions of the 1969 Liability Convention as amended by this Protocol in relation to other States Parties hereto, but shall not be bound by the provisions of the 1969 Liability Convention in relation to States Parties thereto.

6. Any instrument of ratification, acceptance, approval or accession deposited after the entry into force of an amendment to the 1969 Liability Convention as amended by this Protocol shall be deemed to apply to the Convention so amended, as modified by such amendment.

Article 13
Entry into force

1. This Protocol shall enter into force twelve months following the date on which ten States including four States each with not less than one million units of gross tanker tonnage have deposited instruments of ratification, acceptance, approval or accession with the Secretary-General of the Organization.

2. However, any Contracting State to the 1971 Fund Convention may, at the time of the deposit of its instrument of ratification, acceptance, approval or accession in respect of this Protocol, declare that such instrument shall be deemed not to be effective for the purposes of this Article until the end of the six-month period in Article 31 of the Protocol of 1992 to amend the 1971 Fund Convention. A State which is not a Contracting State to the 1971 Fund Convention but which deposits an instrument of ratification, acceptance, approval or accession in respect of the Protocol of 1992 to amend the 1971 Fund Convention may also make a declaration in accordance with this paragraph at the same time.

3. Any State which has made a declaration in accordance with the preceding paragraph may withdraw it at any time by means of notification addressed to the Secretary-General of the Organization. Any such withdrawal shall take effect on the date the notification is received, provided that such State shall be deemed to have deposited its instrument of ratification, acceptance, approval or accession in respect of this Protocol on that date.

4. For any State which ratifies, accepts, approves or accedes to it after the conditions in paragraph 1 for entry into force have been met, this Protocol shall enter into force twelve months following the date of deposit by such State of the appropriate instrument.

Article 14
Revision and amendment

1. A Conference for the purpose of revising or amending the 1992 Liability Convention may be convened by the Organization.

2. The Organization shall convene a Conference of Contracting States for the purpose of revising or amending the 1992 Liability Convention at the request of not less than one third of the Contracting States.

Article 15
Amendments of limitation amounts

1. Upon the request of at least one quarter of the Contracting States any proposal to amend the limits of liability laid down in Article V, paragraph 1, of the 1969 Liability Convention as amended by this Protocol shall be circulated by the Secretary-General to all Members of the Organization and to all Contracting States.
2. Any amendment proposed and circulated as above shall be submitted to the Legal Committee of the Organization for consideration at a date at least six months after the date of its circulation.
3. All Contracting States to the 1969 Liability Convention as amended by this Protocol, whether or not Members of the Organization, shall be entitled to participate in the proceedings of the Legal Committee for the consideration and adoption of amendments.
4. Amendments shall be adopted by a two-thirds majority of the Contracting States present and voting in the Legal Committee, expanded as provided for in paragraph 3, on condition that at least one half of the Contracting States shall be present at the time of voting.
5. When acting on a proposal to amend the limits, the Legal Committee shall take into account the experience of incidents and in particular the amount of damage resulting therefrom, changes in the monetary values and the effect of the proposed amendment on the cost of insurance. It shall also take into account the relationship between the limits in Article V, paragraph 1, of the 1969 Liability Convention as amended by this Protocol and those in Article 4, paragraph 4, of the International Convention on the Establishment of an International Fund for Compensation for Oil Pollution Damage, 1992.
6(a) No amendment of the limits of liability under this Article may be considered before 15 January 1998 nor less than five years from the date of entry into force of a previous amendment under this Article. No amendment under this Article shall be considered before this Protocol has entered into force.
(b) No limit may be increased so as to exceed an amount which corresponds to the limit laid down in the 1969 Liability Convention as amended by this Protocol increased by 6 per cent per year calculated on a compound basis from 15 January 1993.
(c) No limit may be increased so as to exceed an amount which corresponds to the limit laid down in the 1969 Liability Convention as amended by this Protocol multiplied by 3.
7. Any amendment adopted in accordance with paragraph 4 shall be notified by the Organization to all Contracting States. The amendment shall be deemed to have been accepted at the end of a period of eighteen months after the date of notification, unless within that period not less than one quarter of the States that were Contracting States at the time of the adoption of the amendment by the Legal Committee have communicated to the Organization that they do not accept the amendment in which case the amendment is rejected and shall have no effect.
8. An amendment deemed to have been accepted in accordance with paragraph 7 shall enter into force eighteen months after its acceptance.
9. All Contracting States shall be bound by the amendment, unless they denounce this Protocol in accordance with Article 16, paragraphs 1 and 2, at least six months before

the amendment enters into force. Such denunciation shall take effect when the amendment enters into force.

10. When an amendment has been adopted by the Legal Committee but the eighteen-month period for its acceptance has not yet expired, a State which becomes a Contracting State during that period shall be bound by the amendment if it enters into force. A State which becomes a Contracting State after that period shall be bound by an amendment which has been accepted in accordance with paragraph 7. In the cases referred to in this paragraph, a State becomes bound by an amendment when that amendment enters into force, or when this Protocol enters into force for that State, if later.

Article 16
Denunciation

1. This Protocol may be denounced by any Party at any time after the date on which it enters into force for that Party.
2. Denunciation shall be effected by the deposit of an instrument with the Secretary-General of the Organization.
3. A denunciation shall take effect twelve months, or such longer period as may be specified in the instrument of denunciation, after its deposit with the Secretary-General of the Organization.
4. As between the Parties to this Protocol, denunciation by any of them of the 1969 Liability Convention in accordance with Article XVI thereof shall not be construed in any way as a denunciation of the 1969 Liability Convention as amended by this Protocol.
5. Denunciation of the Protocol of 1992 to amend the 1971 Fund Convention by a State which remains a Party to the 1971 Fund Convention shall be deemed to be a denunciation of this Protocol. Such denunciation shall take effect on the date on which denunciation of the Protcol of 1992 to amend the 1971 Fund Convention takes effect according to Article 34 of that Protocol.

Article 17
Depositary

1. This Protocol and any amendments accepted under Article 15 shall be deposited with the Secretary-General of the Organization.
2. The Secretary-General of the Organization shall:
   (a) inform all States which have signed or acceded to this Protocol of:
      (i) each new signature or deposit of an instrument together with the date thereof;
      (ii) each declaration and notification under Article 13 and each declaration and communication under Article V, paragraph 9, of the 1992 Liability Convention;
      (iii) the date of entry into force of this Protocol;
      (iv) any proposal to amend limits of liability which has been made in accordance with Article 15, paragraph 1;
      (v) any amendment which has been adopted in accordance with Article 15, paragraph 4;
      (vi) any amendment deemed to have been accepted under Article 15, paragraph 7, together with the date on which that amendment shall enter into force in accordance with paragraphs 8 and 9 of that Article;

(vii) the deposit of any instrument of denunciation of this Protocol together with the date of the deposit and the date on which it takes effect;

(viii) any denunciation deemed to have been made under Article 16, paragraph 5;

(ix) any communication called for by any Article of this Protocol.

(b) transmit certified true copies of this Protocol to all Signatory States and to all States which accede to this Protocol.

3. As soon as this Protocol enters into force, the text shall be transmitted by the Secretary-General of the Organization to the Secretariat of the United Nations for registration and publication in accordance with Article 102 of the Charter of the United Nations.

Article 18
Languages

This Protocol is established in a single original in the Arabic, Chinese, English, French, Russian and Spanish languages, each text being equally authentic.

DONE AT LONDON, this twenty-seventh day of November one thousand nine hundred and ninety-two.

IN WITNESS WHEREOF the undersigned, being duly authorized by their respective Governments for that purpose, have signed this Protocol.

[This 1992 version of the Annex is, under Articles 10 and 11(2) of CLC PROT 1992, part of the '1992 Liability Convention']

ANNEX

CERTIFICATE OF INSURANCE OR OTHER FINANCIAL SECURITY IN RESPECT OF CIVIL LIABILITY FOR OIL POLLUTION DAMAGE

Issued in accordance with the provisions of Article VII of the International Convention on Civil Liability for Oil Pollution Damage, 1992.

Name of Ship	Distinctive Number or Letters	Port of Registry	Name and Address of Owner

This is to certify that there is in force in respect of the above-named ship a policy of insurance or other financial security satisfying the requirements of Article VII of the International Convention on Civil Liability for Oil Pollution Damage, 1992.

Type of Security...

....

Duration of Security ....

....

Name and Address of the Insurer(s) and/or Guarantor(s)

Name ....

Address ....
    This certificate is valid until...
    Issued or certified by the Government of ....
....
    (Full designation of the State)
    At .... On ....
           (Place)   (Date)

....
Signature and Title of issuing or
certifying official

Explanatory Notes:

1. If desired, the designation of the State may include a reference to the competent public authority of the country where the certificate is issued.
2. If the total amount of security has been furnished by more than one source, the amount of each of them should be indicated.
3. If security is furnished in several forms, these should be enumerated.
4. The entry 'Duration of Security' must stipulate the date on which such security takes effect.

Notes

1. 11 ILM (1970), p.45; UK Treaty Series No.106 (1975), Cmnd. 6183; *Kiss*, p.235; IMO Doc. IMO-410E.
2. Protocol to CLC, 19 November 1976, IMO Doc. IMO-410E.
3. Protocol to amend CLC, 25 May 1984, 13 ILM (1984), p.177; IMO Doc. IMO-456E.
4. Protocol of 1992 to Amend the International Convention on Civil Liability for Oil Pollution Damage, 1969 (IMO Doc. LEG/CONF.9/15, 2 December 1992), Preamble, emphasis added.
5. Loc.cit. in note 4.
6. IMO Doc. LEG/CONF.9/DC/3, 26 November 1992, p.8.
7. Art.12.
8. Loc.cit. in note 6.

10.3 THE INTERNATIONAL CONVENTION ON THE ESTABLISHMENT OF AN INTERNATIONAL FUND FOR COMPENSATION FOR OIL POLLUTION DAMAGE, 1992

Introduction

The International Convention on the Establishment of an International Fund for Compensation for Oil Pollution Damage, 1971[1] (Fund Convention 1971) was amended by Protocol in 1976[2] (FUND PROT 1976) in order to change the unit of account prescribed in the Convention[3] from the gold franc to the Special Drawing Right (SDR) of the International Monetary Fund. Unfortunately, FUND PROT 1976 has not yet entered into force.[4]

Important substantive amendments to the Fund Convention 1971 were introduced by a second Protocol adopted in 1984[5] (FUND PROT 1984). Under Article 27, the Fund Convention 1971 and FUND PROT 1984 were, as between the parties to FUND PROT 1984, to be read and interpreted as one instrument and the Fund Convention 1971, as amended by FUND PROT 1984, was to be known as the 'International Convention on the Establishment of an International Fund for Compensation for Oil Pollution Damage, 1984'. Unfortunately, FUND PROT 1984 failed to attract sufficient support to satisfy the conditions for entry into force laid down in Article 30. To find a way out of the impasse, an IMO Conference met in 1992 and, 'Aware of the need to ensure the entry into force of *the content* of the 1984 Protocol as soon as possible',[6] drafted the Protocol of 1992 to Amend the Fund Convention 1971[7] (FUND PROT 1992). As is evident from Conference Resolution 4,[8] FUND PROT 1992 was intended to replace FUND PROT 1984 and, following the 1984 model, provides in Article 27 that the Fund Convention 1971 and FUND PROT 1992 shall, as between the parties to the Protocol, be read and interpreted together as a single instrument and Articles 1 to 36 quinquies of the Fund Convention 1971, as amended by FUND PROT 1992, are to be known as the 'International Convention on the Establishment of an International Fund for Compensation for Oil Pollution Damage, 1992' (Fund Convention 1992).

Since no authentic composite text has so far been produced, the writer has prepared such a text below.

FUND PROT 1992 was open for signature from 15 January 1993 to 14 January 1994.[9] According to Conference Resolution 4, '... it is unlikely that the conditions for ... entry into force [of FUND PROT 1984] will be met following the adoption of the 1992 Protocol ...'[10]

COMPOSITE TEXT OF 1992 FUND CONVENTION AND ADDITIONAL PROVISIONS OF FUND PROT 1992

[Preamble and Article 1 of FUND PROT 1992]

THE PARTIES TO THE PRESENT PROTOCOL,

HAVING CONSIDERED the International Convention on the Establishment of an International Fund for Compensation for Oil Pollution Damage, 1971, and the 1984 Protocol thereto,

HAVING NOTED that the 1984 Protocol to that Convention, which provides for improved scope and enhanced compensation, has not entered into force,

AFFIRMING the importance of maintaining the viability of the international oil pollution liability and compensation system,

AWARE of the need to ensure the entry into force of the content of the 1984 Protocol as soon as possible,

RECOGNIZING the advantage for the States Parties of arranging for the amended Convention to coexist with and be supplementary to the original Convention for a transitional period,

CONVINCED that the economic consequences of pollution damage resulting from the carriage of oil in bulk at sea by ships should continue to be shared by the shipping industry and by the oil cargo interests,

BEARING IN MIND the adoption of the Protocol of 1992 to amend the International Convention on Civil Liability for Oil Pollution Damage, 1969,
HAVE AGREED as follows:

Article 1

The Convention which the provisions of this Protocol amend is the International Convention on the Establishment of an International Fund for Compensation for Oil Pollution Damage, 1971, hereinafter referred to as the '1971 Fund Convention'. For States Parties to the Protocol of 1976 to the 1971 Fund Convention, such reference shall be deemed to include the 1971 Fund Convention as amended by that Protocol.

[Preamble of original Fund Convention 1971]

The States Parties to the present Convention,
BEING PARTIES to the International Convention on Civil Liability for Oil Pollution Damage, adopted at Brussels on 29 November 1969,
CONSCIOUS of the dangers of pollution posed by the world-wide maritime carriage of oil in bulk,
CONVINCED of the need to ensure that adequate compensation is available to persons who suffer damage caused by pollution resulting from the escape or discharge of oil from ships,
CONSIDERING that the International Convention of 29 November 1969, on Civil Liability for Oil Pollution Damage, by providing a régime for compensation for pollution damage in Contracting States and for the costs of measures, wherever taken, to prevent or minimize such damage, represents a considerable progress towards the achievement of this aim,
CONSIDERING HOWEVER that this régime does not afford full compensation for victims of oil pollution damage in all cases while it imposes an additional financial burden on shipowners,
CONSIDERING FURTHER that the economic consequences of oil pollution damage resulting from the escape or discharge of oil carried in bulk at sea by ships should not exclusively be borne by the shipping industry but should in part be borne by the oil cargo interests,
CONVINCED of the need to elaborate a compensation and indemnification system supplementary to the International Convention on Civil Liability for Oil Pollution Damage with a view to ensuring that full compensation will be available to victims of oil pollution incidents and that the shipowners are at the same time given relief in respect of the additional financial burdens imposed on them by the said Convention,
TAKING NOTE of the Resolution on the Establishment of an International Compensation Fund for Oil Pollution Damage which was adopted on 29 November 1969 by the International Legal Conference on Marine Pollution Damage,
HAVE AGREED as follows:

General Provisions

Article 1

1. '1992 Liability Convention' means the International Convention on Civil Liability for Oil Pollution Damage, 1992.

1 *bis*. '1971 Fund Convention' means the International Convention on the Establishment of an International Fund for Compensation for Oil Pollution Damage, 1971. For States Parties to the Protocol of 1976 to that Convention, the term shall be deemed to include the 1971 Fund Convention as amended by that Protocol.

2. 'Ship', 'Person', 'Owner', 'Pollution Damage', 'Preventive Measures', 'Incident' and 'Organization' have the same meaning as in Article I of the 1992 Liability Convention.

3. 'Contributing Oil' means crude oil and fuel oil as defined in sub-paragraphs (a) and (b) below:

    (a) 'Crude Oil' means any liquid hydrocarbon mixture occurring naturally in the earth whether or not treated to render it suitable for transportation. It also includes crude oils from which certain distillate fractions have been removed (sometimes referred to as 'topped crudes') or to which certain distillate fractions have been added (sometimes referred to as 'spiked' or 'reconstituted' crudes).

    (b) 'Fuel Oil' means heavy distillates or residues from crude oil or blends of such materials intended for use as a fuel for the production of heat or power of a quality equivalent to the 'American Society for Testing and Materials' Specification for Number Four Fuel Oil (Designation D 396-69)', or heavier.

4. 'Unit of account' has the same meaning as in Article V, paragraph 9, of the 1992 Liability Convention.

5. 'Ship's tonnage' has the same meaning as in Article V, paragraph 10, of the 1992 Liability Convention.

6. 'Ton', in relation to oil, means a metric ton.

7. 'Guarantor' means any person providing insurance or other financial security to cover an owner's liability in pursuance of Article VII, paragraph 1, of the 1992 Liability Convention.

8. 'Terminal Installation' means any site for the storage of oil in bulk which is capable of receiving oil from waterborne transportation, including any facility situated off-shore and linked to such site.

9. Where an incident consists of a series of occurrences, it shall be treated as having occurred on the date of the first such occurrence.

Article 2

1. An International Fund for compensation for pollution damage, to be named 'The International Oil Pollution Compensation Fund 1992' and hereinafter referred to as 'the Fund', is hereby established with the following aims:

(a) to provide compensation for pollution damage to the extent that the protection afforded by the 1992 Liability Convention is inadequate;

(b) to give effect to the related purposes set out in this Convention.

2. The Fund shall in each Contracting State be recognized as a legal person capable under the laws of that State of assuming rights and obligations and of being a party in legal proceedings before the courts of that State. Each Contracting State shall recognize the Director of the Fund (hereinafter referred to as 'The Director') as the legal representative of the Fund.

Article 3

This Convention shall apply exclusively:

(a) to pollution damage caused:

(i) in the territory, including the territorial sea, of a Contracting State, and

(ii) in the exclusive economic zone of a Contracting State, established in accordance with international law, or, if a Contracting State has not established such a zone, in an area beyond and adjacent to the territorial sea of that State determined by that State in accordance with international law and extending not more than 200 nautical miles from the baselines from which the breadth of its territorial sea is measured;

(b) to preventive measures, wherever taken, to prevent or minimize such damage.

Compensation

Article 4

1. For the purpose of fulfilling its function under Article 2, paragraph 1(a), the Fund shall pay compensation to any person suffering pollution damage if such person has been unable to obtain full and adequate compensation for the damage under the terms of the 1992 Liability Convention,

(a) because no liability for the damage arises under the 1992 Liability Convention;

(b) because the owner liable for the damage under the 1992 Liability Convention is financially incapable of meeting his obligations in full and any financial security that may be provided under Article VII of that Convention does not cover or is insufficient to satisfy the claims for compensation for the damage; an owner being treated as financially incapable of meeting his obligations and a financial security being treated as insufficient if the person suffering the damage has been unable to obtain full satisfaction of the amount of compensation due under the 1992 Liability Convention after having taken all reasonable steps to pursue the legal remedies available to him;

(c) because the damage exceeds the owner's liability under the 1992 Liability Convention as limited pursuant to Article V, paragraph 1, of that Convention or under the terms of any other international Convention in force or open for signature, ratification or accession at the date of this Convention.

Expenses reasonably incurred or sacrifices reasonably made by the owner voluntarily to prevent or minimize pollution damage shall be treated as pollution damage for the purposes of this Article.

2. The Fund shall incur no obligation under the preceding paragraph if:

(a) it proves that the pollution damage resulted from an act of war, hostilities, civil war or insurrection or was caused by oil which has escaped or been discharged from a warship or other ship owned or operated by a State and used, at the time of the incident, only on Government non-commercial service; or

(b) the claimant cannot prove that the damage resulted from an incident involving one or more ships.

3. If the Fund proves that the pollution damage resulted wholly or partially either from an act or omission done with the intent to cause damage by the person who suffered the damage or from the negligence of that person, the Fund may be exonerated wholly or partially from its obligation to pay compensation to such person. The Fund shall in any event be exonerated to the extent that the shipowner may have been exonerated under Article III, paragraph 3, of the 1992 Liability Convention. However, there shall be no such exoneration of the Fund with regard to preventive measures.

4. (a) Except as otherwise provided in subparagraphs (b) and (c) of this paragraph, the aggregate amount of compensation payable by the Fund under this Article shall in respect of any one incident be limited, so that the total sum of that

amount and the amount of compensation actually paid under the 1992 Liability Convention for pollution damage within the scope of application of this Convention as defined in Article 3 shall not exceed 135 million units of account.

(b) Except as otherwise provided in subparagraph (c), the aggregate amount of compensation payable by the Fund under this Article for pollution damage resulting from a natural phenomenon of an exceptional, inevitable and irresistible character shall not exceed 135 million units of account.

(c) The maximum amount of compensation referred to in subparagraphs (a) and (b) shall be 200 million units of account with respect to any incident occurring during any period when there are three Parties to this Convention in respect of which the combined relevant quantity of contributing oil received by persons in the territories of such Parties, during the preceding calendar year, equalled or exceeded 600 million tons.

(d) Interest accrued on a fund constituted in accordance with Article V, paragraph 3, of the 1992 Liability Convention, if any, shall not be taken into account for the computation of the maximum compensation payable by the Fund under this Article.

(e) The amounts mentioned in this Article shall be converted into national currency on the basis of the value of that currency by reference to the Special Drawing Right on the date of the decision of the Assembly of the Fund as to the first date of payment of compensation.

5. Where the amount of established claims against the Fund exceeds the aggregate amount of compensation payable under paragraph 4, the amount available shall be distributed in such a manner that the proportion between any established claim and the amount of compensation actually recovered by the claimant under this Convention shall be the same for all claimants.

6. The Assembly of the Fund may decide that, in exceptional cases, compensation in accordance with this Convention can be paid even if the owner of the ship has not constituted a fund in accordance with Article V, paragraph 3, of the 1992 Liability Convention. In such case paragraph 4(e) of this Article applies accordingly.

7. The Fund shall, at the request of a Contracting State, use its good offices as necessary to assist that State to secure promptly such personnel, material and services as are necessary to enable the State to take measures to prevent or mitigate pollution damage arising from an incident in respect of which the Fund may be called upon to pay compensation under this Convention.

8. The Fund may on conditions to be laid down in the Internal Regulations provide credit facilities with a view to the taking of preventive measures against pollution damage arising from a particular incident in respect of which the Fund may be called upon to pay compensation under this Convention.

Article 5

[Article 5 of the Fund Convention 1971 is deleted]

Article 6

Rights to compensation under Article 4 shall be extinguished unless an action is brought thereunder or a notification has been made pursuant to Article 7, paragraph 6, within three years from the date when the damage occurred. However, in no case shall an action be brought after six years from the date of the incident which caused the damage.

Article 7

1.   Subject to the subsequent provisions of this Article, any action against the Fund for compensation under Article 4 of this Convention shall be brought only before a court competent under Article IX of the 1992 Liability Convention in respect of actions against the owner who is or who would, but for the provisions of Article III, paragraph 2, of that Convention, have been liable for pollution damage caused by the relevant incident.

2.   Each Contracting State shall ensure that its courts possess the necessary jurisdiction to entertain such actions against the Fund as are referred to in paragraph 1.

3.   Where an action for compensation for pollution damage has been brought before a court competent under Article IX of the 1992 Liability Convention against the owner of a ship or his guarantor, such court shall have exclusive jurisdictional competence over any action against the Fund for compensation under the provisions of Article 4 of this Convention in respect of the same damage. However, where an action for compensation for pollution damage under the 1992 Liability Convention has been brought before a court in a State Party to the 1992 Liability Convention but not to this Convention, any action against the Fund under Article 4 of this Convention shall at the option of the claimant be brought either before a court of the State where the Fund has its headquarters or before any court of a State Party to this Convention competent under Article IX of the 1992 Liability Convention.

4.   Each Contracting State shall ensure that the Fund shall have the right to intervene as a party to any legal proceedings instituted in accordance with Article IX of the 1992 Liability Convention before a competent court of that State against the owner of a ship or his guarantor.

5.   Except as otherwise provided in paragraph 6, the Fund shall not be bound by any judgment or decision in proceedings to which it has not been a party or by any settlement to which it is not a party.

6.   Without prejudice to the provisions of paragraph 4, where an action under the 1992 Liability Convention for compensation for pollution damage has been brought against an owner or his guarantor before a competent court in a Contracting State, each party to the proceedings shall be entitled under the national law of that State to notify the Fund of the proceedings. Where such notification has been made in accordance with the formalities required by the law of the court seized and in such time and in such a manner that the Fund has in fact been in a position effectively to intervene as a party to the proceedings, any judgment rendered by the court in such proceedings shall, after it has become final and enforceable in the State where the judgment was given, become binding upon the Fund in the sense that the facts and findings in that judgment may not be disputed by the Fund even if the Fund has not actually intervened in the proceedings.

Article 8

Subject to any decision concerning the distribution referred to in Article 4, paragraph 5, any judgment given against the Fund by a court having jurisdiction in accordance with Article 7, paragraphs 1 and 3, shall, when it has become enforceable in the State of origin and is in that State no longer subject to ordinary forms of review, be recognized and enforceable in each Contracting State on the same conditions as are prescribed in Article X of the 1992 Liability Convention.

Article 9

1. The Fund shall, in respect of any amount of compensation for pollution damage paid by the Fund in accordance with Article 4, paragraph 1, of this Convention, acquire by subrogation the rights that the person so compensated may enjoy under the 1992 Liability Convention against the owner or his guarantor.

2. Nothing in this Convention shall prejudice any right of recourse or subrogation of the Fund against persons other than those referred to in the preceding paragraph. In any event the right of the Fund to subrogation against such person shall not be less favourable than that of an insurer of the person to whom compensation has been paid.

3. Without prejudice to any other rights of subrogation or recourse against the Fund which may exist, a Contracting State or agency thereof which has paid compensation for pollution damage in accordance with provisions of national law shall acquire by subrogation the rights which the person so compensated would have enjoyed under this Convention.

Article 10

Annual contributions to the Fund shall be made in respect of each Contracting State by any person who, in the calendar year referred to in Article 12, paragraphs 2(a) or (b), has received in total quantities exceeding 150,000 tons:

  (a) in the ports or terminal installations in the territory of that State contributing oil carried by sea to such ports or terminal installations; and

  (b) in any installations situated in the territory of that Contracting State contributing oil which has been carried by sea and discharged in a port or terminal installation of a non-Contracting State, provided that contributing oil shall only be taken into account by virtue of this sub-paragraph on first receipt in a Contracting State after its discharge in that non-Contracting State.

2. (a) For the purposes of paragraph 1, where the quantity of contributing oil received in the territory of a Contracting State by any person in a calendar year when aggregated with the quantity of contributing oil received in the same Contracting State in that year by any associated person or persons exceeds 150,000 tons, such person shall pay contributions in respect of the actual quantity received by him notwithstanding that that quantity did not exceed 150,000 tons.

  (b) 'Associated person' means any subsidiary or commonly controlled entity. The question whether a person comes within this definition shall be determined by the national law of the State concerned.

Article 11

[Article 11 of the Fund Convention 1971 is deleted]

Article 12

1. With a view to assessing the amount of annual contributions due, if any, and taking account of the necessity to maintain sufficient liquid funds, the Assembly shall for each calendar year make an estimate in the form of a budget of:

(i) Expenditure

(a) costs and expenses of the administration of the Fund in the relevant year and any deficit from operations in preceding years;

(b) payments to be made by the Fund in the relevant year for the satisfaction of claims against the Fund due under Article 4, including repayment on loans previously taken by the Fund for the satisfaction of such claims, to the extent that the aggregate amount of such claims in respect of any one incident does not exceed four million units of account;

(c) payments to be made by the Fund in the relevant year for the satisfaction of claims against the Fund due under Article 4, including repayments on loans previously taken by the Fund for the satisfaction of such claims, to the extent that the aggregate amount of such claims in respect of any one incident is in excess of four million units of account;

(ii) Income

(a) surplus funds from operations in preceding years, including any interest;

(b) annual contributions, if required to balance the budget;

(c) any other income.

2. The Assembly shall decide the total amount of contributions to be levied. On the basis of that decision, the Director shall, in respect of each Contracting State, calculate for each person referred to in Article 10 the amount of his annual contribution:

(a) in so far as the contribution is for the satisfaction of payments referred to in paragraph 1(i)(a) and (b) on the basis of a fixed sum for each ton of contributing oil received in the relevant State by such persons during the preceding calendar year; and

(b) in so far as the contribution is for the satisfaction of payments referred to in paragraph 1(i)(c) of this Article on the basis of a fixed sum for each ton of contributing oil received by such person during the calendar year preceding that in which the incident in question occurred, provided that State was a Party to this Convention at the date of the incident.

3. The sums referred to in paragraph 2 above shall be arrived at by dividing the relevant total amount of contributions required by the total amount of contributing oil received in all Contracting States in the relevant year.

4. The annual contribution shall be due on the date to be laid down in the Internal Regulations of the Fund. The Assembly may decide on a different date of payment.

5. The Assembly may decide, under conditions to be laid down in the Financial Regulations of the Fund, to make transfers between funds received in accordance with Article 12.2(a) and funds received in accordance with Article 12.2(b).

Article 13

1. The amount of any contribution due under Article 12 and which is in arrears shall bear interest at a rate which shall be determined in accordance with the Internal Regulations of the Fund, provided that different rates may be fixed for different circumstances.

2. Each Contracting State shall ensure that any obligation to contribute to the Fund arising under this Convention in respect of oil received within the territory of that State is fulfilled and shall take any appropriate measures under its law, including the imposing of such sanctions as it may deem necessary, with a view to the effective execution of any such obligation; provided, however, that such measures shall only be directed against those persons who are under an obligation to contribute to the Fund.

3. Where a person who is liable in accordance with the provisions of Articles 10 and 12 to make contributions to the Fund does not fulfil his obligations in respect of any

such contribution or any part thereof and is in arrear, the Director shall take all appropriate action against such person on behalf of the Fund with a view to the recovery of the amount due. However, where the defaulting contributor is manifestly insolvent or the circumstances otherwise so warrant, the Assembly may, upon recommendation of the Director, decide that no action shall be taken or continued against the contributor.

Article 14

1. Each Contracting State may at the time when it deposits its instrument of ratification or accession or at any time thereafter declare that it assumes itself obligations that are incumbent under this Convention on any person who is liable to contribute to the Fund in accordance with Article 10, paragraph 1, in respect of oil received within the territory of that State. Such declaration shall be made in writing and shall specify which obligations are assumed.
2. Where a declaration under paragraph 1 is made prior to the entry into force of this Convention in accordance with Article 40, it shall be deposited with the Secretary-General of the Organization who shall after the entry into force of the Convention communicate the declaration to the Director.
3. A declaration under paragraph 1 which is made after the entry into force of this Convention shall be deposited with the Director.
4. A declaration made in accordance with this Article may be withdrawn by the relevant State giving notice thereof in writing to the Director. Such notification shall take effect three months after the Director's receipt thereof.
5. Any State which is bound by a declaration made under this Article shall, in any proceedings brought against it before a competent court in respect of any obligation specified in the declaration, waive any immunity that it would otherwise be entitled to invoke.

Article 15

1. Each Contracting State shall ensure that any person who receives contributing oil within its territory in such quantities that he is liable to contribute to the Fund appears on a list to be established and kept up to date by the Director in accordance with the subsequent provisions of this Article.
2. For the purposes set out in paragraph 1, each Contracting State shall communicate, at a time and in the manner to be prescribed in the Internal Regulations, to the Director the name and address of any person who in respect of that State is liable to contribute to the Fund pursuant to Article 10, as well as data on the relevant quantities of contributing oil received by any such person during the preceding calendar year.
3. For the purposes of ascertaining who are, at any given time, the persons liable to contribute to the Fund in accordance with Article 10, paragraph 1, and of establishing, where applicable, the quantities of oil to be taken into account for any such person when determining the amount of his contribution, the list shall be *prima facie* evidence of the facts stated therein.
4. Where a Contracting State does not fulfil its obligations to submit to the Director the communication referred to in paragraph 2 and this results in a financial loss for the Fund, that Contracting State shall be liable to compensate the Fund for such loss. The Assembly shall, on the recommendation of the Director, decide whether such compensation shall be payable by that Contracting State.

Article 16

The Fund shall have an Assembly and a Secretariat headed by a Director.

Article 17

The Assembly shall consist of all Contracting States to this Convention.

Article 18

The functions of the Assembly shall be:
1. to elect at each regular session its Chairman and two Vice-Chairmen who shall hold office until the next regular session;
2. to determine its own rules of procedure, subject to the provisions of this Convention;
3. to adopt Internal Regulations necessary for the proper functioning of the Fund;
4. to appoint the Director and make provisions for the appointment of such other personnel as may be necessary and determine the terms and conditions of service of the Director and other personnel;
5. to adopt the annual budget and fix the annual contributions;
6. to appoint auditors and approve the accounts of the Fund;
7. to approve settlements of claims against the Fund, to take decisions in respect of the distribution among claimants of the available amount of compensation in accordance with Article 4, paragraph 5, and to determine the terms and conditions according to which provisional payments in respect of claims shall be made with a view to ensuring that victims of pollution damage are compensated as promptly as possible;
8. [Paragraph 8 is deleted];
9. to establish any temporary or permanent subsidiary body it may consider to be necessary, to define its terms of reference and to give it the authority needed to perform the functions entrusted to it; when appointing the members of such body, the Assembly shall endeavour to secure an equitable geographical distribution of members and to ensure that the Contracting States, in respect of which the largest quantities of contributing oil are being received, are appropriately represented; the Rules of Procedure of the Assembly may be applied, *mutatis mutandis*, for the work of such subsidiary body;
10. to determine which non-Contracting States and which inter-governmental and international non-governmental organizations shall be admitted to take part, without voting rights, in meetings of the Assembly, and subsidiary bodies;
11. to give instructions concerning the administration of the Fund to the Director and subsidiary bodies;
12. [Paragraph 12 is deleted];
13. to supervise the proper execution of the Convention and of its own decisions;
14. to perform such other functions as are allocated to it under the Convention or are otherwise necessary for the proper operation of the Fund.

Article 19

1. Regular sessions of the Assembly shall take place once every calendar year upon convocation by the Director.
2. Extraordinary sessions of the Assembly shall be convened by the Director at the request of at least one-third of the members of the Assembly and may be convened on

the Director's own initiative after consultation with the Chairman of the Assembly. The Director shall give members at least thirty days' notice of such sessions.

Articles 21-27

[Articles 21-27 of the Fund Convention 1971 are deleted]

Secretariat

Article 28

1. The Secretariat shall comprise the Director and such staff as the administration of the Fund may require.
2. The Director shall be the legal representative of the Fund.

Article 29

1. The Director shall be the chief administrative officer of the Fund. Subject to the instructions given to him by the Assembly, he shall perform those functions which are assigned to him by this Convention, the Internal Regulations of the Fund and the Assembly.
2. The Director shall in particular:
   (a) appoint the personnel required for the administration of the Fund;
   (b) take all appropriate measures with a view to the proper administration of the Fund's assets;
   (c) collect the contributions due under this Convention while observing in particular the provisions of Article 13, paragraph 3;
   (d) to the extent necessary to deal with claims against the Fund and carry out the other functions of the Fund, employ the services of legal, financial and other experts;
   (e) take all appropriate measures for dealing with claims against the Fund within the limits and on conditions to be laid down in the Internal Regulations, including the final settlement of claims without the prior approval of the Assembly where these regulations so provide;
   (f) prepare and submit to the Assembly the financial statements and budget estimates for each calendar year;
   (g) prepare, in consultation with the Chairman of the Assembly, and publish a report of the activities of the Fund during the previous calendar year;
   (h) prepare, collect and circulate the papers, documents, agenda, minutes and information that may be required for the work of the Assembly and subsidiary bodies.

Article 30

In the performance of their duties the Director and the staff and experts appointed by him shall not seek or receive instructions from any Government or from any authority external to the Fund. They shall refrain from any action which might reflect on their position as international officials. Each Contracting State on its part undertakes to respect the exclusively international character of the responsibilities of the Director and the staff and experts appointed by him, and not to seek to influence them in the discharge of their duties.

Finances

Article 31

1. Each Contracting State shall bear the salary, travel and other expenses of its own delegation to the Assembly and of its representatives on subsidiary bodies.
2. Any other expenses incurred in the operation of the Fund shall be borne by the Fund.

Voting

Article 32

The following provisions shall apply to voting in the Assembly:
(a) each member shall have one vote;
(b) except as otherwise provided in Article 33, decisions of the Assembly shall be by a majority vote of the members present and voting;
(c) decisions where a three-fourths or a two-thirds majority is required shall be by a three-fourths or two-thirds majority vote, as the case may be, of those present;
(d) for the purpose of this Article the phrase 'members present' means 'members present at the meeting at the time of the vote', and the phrase 'members present and voting' means 'members present and casting an affirmative or negative vote'. Members who abstain from voting shall be considered as not voting.

Article 33

[1. Paragraph 1 is deleted].
The following decisions of the Assembly shall require a two-thirds majority:
(a) a decision under Article 13, paragraph 3, not to take or continue action against a contributor;
(b) the appointment of the Director under Article 18, paragraph 4;
(c) the establishment of subsidiary bodies, under Article 18, paragraph 9, and matters relating to such establishment.

Article 34

1. The Fund, its assets, income, including contributions, and other property shall enjoy in all Contracting States exemption from all direct taxation.
2. When the Fund makes substantial purchases of movable or immovable property, or has important work carried out which is necessary for the exercise of its official activities and the cost of which includes indirect taxes or sales taxes, the Governments of Member States shall take, whenever possible, appropriate measures for the remission or refund of the amount of such duties and taxes.
3. No exemption shall be accorded in the case of duties, taxes or dues which merely constitute payment for public utility services.
4. The Fund shall enjoy exemption from all customs duties, taxes and other related taxes on articles imported or exported by it or on its behalf for its official use. Articles thus imported shall not be transferred either for consideration or gratis on the territory of the country into which they have been imported except on conditions agreed by the Government of that country.

5. Persons contributing to the fund and victims and owners of ships receiving compensation from the Fund shall be subject to the fiscal legislation of the State where they are taxable, no special exemption or other benefit being conferred on them in this respect.

6. Information relating to individual contributors supplied for the purpose of this Convention shall not be divulged outside the Fund except in so far as it may be strictly necessary to enable the Fund to carry out its functions including the bringing and defending of legal proceedings.

7. Independently of existing or future regulations concerning currency or transfers, Contracting States shall authorize the transfer and payment of any contribution to the Fund and of any compensation paid by the Fund without any restriction.

Transitional Provisions

Article 35

Claims for compensation under Article 4 arising from incidents occurring after the date of entry into force of this Convention may not be brought against the Fund earlier than the one hundred and twentieth day after that date.

Article 36

The Secretary-General of the Organization shall convene the first session of the Assembly. This session shall take place as soon as possible after entry into force of this Convention and, in any case, not more than thirty days after such entry into force.

[Article 26 of FUND PROT 1992]

After Article 36 of the 1971 Fund Convention four new articles are inserted as follows:

Article 36 bis

The following transitional provisions shall apply in the period, hereinafter referred to as the transitional period, commencing with the date of entry into force of this Convention and ending with the date on which the denunciations provided for in Article 31 of the 1992 Protocol to amend the 1971 Fund Convention take effect:

   (a) In the application of paragraph 1(a) of Article 2 of this Convention, the reference to the 1992 Liability Convention shall include reference to the International Convention on Civil Liability for Oil Pollution Damage, 1969, either in its original version or as amended by the Protocol thereto of 1976 (referred to in this Article as 'the 1969 Liability Convention'), and also the 1971 Fund Convention.

   (b) Where an incident has caused pollution damage within the scope of this Convention, the Fund shall pay compensation to any person suffering pollution damage only if, and to the extent that, such person has been unable to obtain full and adequate compensation for the damage under the terms of the 1969 Liability Convention, the 1971 Fund Convention and the 1992 Liability Convention, provided that, in respect of pollution damage within the scope of this Convention in respect of a Party to this Convention but not a Party to the 1971 Fund Convention, the Fund shall pay compensation to any person suffering pollution damage only if, and to the extent that, such person would have been unable to obtain full and adequate compensation had that State been party to each of the above-mentioned Conventions.

(c) In the application of Article 4 of this Convention, the amount to be taken into account in determining the aggregate amount of compensation payable by the Fund shall also include the amount of compensation actually paid under the 1969 Liability Convention, if any, and the amount of compensation actually paid or deemed to have been paid under the 1971 Fund Convention.

(d) Paragraph 1 of Article 9 of this Convention shall also apply to the rights enjoyed under the 1969 Liability Convention.

Article 36 ter

1. Subject to paragraph 4 of this Article, the aggregate amount of the annual contributions payable in respect of contributing oil received in a single Contracting State during a calendar year shall not exceed 27.5 per cent of the total amount of annual contributions pursuant to the 1992 Protocol to amend the 1971 Fund Convention, in respect of that calendar year.

2. If the application of the provisions in paragraphs 2 and 3 of Article 12 would result in the aggregate amount of the contributions payable by contributors in a single Contracting State in respect of a given calendar year exceeding 27.5 per cent of the total annual contributions, the contributions payable by all contributors in that State shall be reduced *pro rata* so that their aggregate contributions equal 27.5 per cent of the total annual contributions to the Fund in respect of that year.

3. If the contributions payable by persons in a given Contracting State shall be reduced pursuant to paragraph 2 of this Article, the contributions payable by persons in all other Contracting States shall be increased *pro rata* so as to ensure that the total amount of contributions payable by all persons liable to contribute to the Fund in respect of the calendar year in question will reach the total amount of contributions decided by the Assembly.

4. The provisions in paragraphs 1 to 3 of this Article shall operate until the total quantity of contributing oil received in all Contracting States in a calendar year has reached 750 million tonnes or until a period of 5 years after the date of entry into force of the said Protocol has elapsed, whichever occurs earlier.

Article 36 quater

Notwithstanding the provisions of this Convention, the following provisions shall apply to the administration of the Fund during the period in which both the 1971 Fund Convention and this Convention are in force:

(a) The Secretariat of the Fund, established by the 1971 Fund Convention (hereinafter referred to as 'the 1971 Fund'), headed by the Director, may also function as the Secretariat and the Director of the Fund.

(b) If, in accordance with subparagraph (a), the Secretariat and the Director of the 1971 Fund also perform the function of Secretariat and Director of the Fund, the Fund shall be represented, in cases of conflict of interests between the 1971 Fund and the Fund, by the Chairman of the Assembly of the Fund.

(c) The Director and the staff and experts appointed by him, performing their duties under this Convention and the 1971 Fund Convention, shall not be regarded as contravening the provisions of Article 30 of this Convention in so far as they discharge their duties in accordance with this Article.

(d) The Assembly of the Fund shall endeavour not to take decisions which are incompatible with decisions taken by the Assembly of the 1971 Fund. If differences of opinion with respect to common administrative issues arise, the Assembly of the Fund shall try to reach a consensus with the Assembly of the 1971 Fund, in a spirit of mutual co-operation and with the common aims of both organizations in mind.

(e) The Fund may succeed to the rights, obligations and assets of the 1971 Fund if the Assembly of the 1971 Fund so decides, in accordance with Article 44, paragraph 2, of the 1971 Fund Convention.

(f) The Fund shall reimburse to the 1971 Fund all costs and expenses arising from administrative services performed by the 1971 Fund on behalf of the Fund.

Article 36 quinquies
Final clauses

The final clauses of this Convention shall be Articles 28 to 39 of the Protocol of 1992 to amend the 1971 Fund Convention. References in this Convention to Contracting States shall be taken to mean references to the Contracting States of that Protocol.

[Article 27 of FUND PROT 1992]

Article 27

1. The 1971 Fund Convention and this Protocol shall, as between the Parties to this Protocol, be read and interpreted together as one single instrument.
2. Articles 1 to 36 quinquies of the 1971 Fund Convention as amended by this Protocol shall be known as the International Convention on the Establishment of an International Fund for Compensation for Oil Pollution Damage, 1992 (1992 Fund Convention).

[The following Articles 28 to 39 of FUND PROT 1992 constitute the final clauses of the Fund Convention 1992 under Article 36 quinquies]

Final Clauses

Article 28
Signature, ratification, acceptance, approval and accession

1. This Protocol shall be open for signature at London from 15 January 1993 to 14 January 1994 by any State which has signed the 1992 Liability Convention.
2. Subject to paragraph 4, this Protocol shall be ratified, accepted or approved by States which have signed it.
3. Subject to paragraph 4, this Protocol is open for accession by States which did not sign it.
4. This Protocol may be ratified, accepted, approved or acceded to, only by States which have ratified, accepted, approved or acceded to the 1992 Liability Convention.
5. Ratification, acceptance, approval or accession shall be effected by the deposit of a formal instrument to that effect with the Secretary-General of the Organization.
6. A State which is a Party to this Protocol but is not a Party to the 1971 Fund Convention shall be bound by the provisions of the 1971 Fund Convention as amended by this Protocol in relation to other Parties hereto, but shall not be bound by the provisions of the 1971 Fund Convention in relation to Parties thereto.

7. Any instrument of ratification, acceptance, approval or accession deposited after the entry into force of an amendment to the 1971 Fund Convention as amended by this Protocol shall be deemed to apply to the Convention so amended, as modified by such amendment.

Article 29
Information on contributing oil

1. Before this Protocol comes into force for a State, that State shall, when depositing an instrument referred to in Article 28, paragraph 5, and annually thereafter at a date to be determined by the Secretary-General of the Organization, communicate to him the name and address of any person who in respect of that State would be liable to contribute to the Fund pursuant to Article 10 of the 1971 Fund Convention as amended by this Protocol as well as data on the relevant quantities of contributing oil received by any such person in the territory of that State during the preceding calendar year.
2. During the transitional period, the Director shall, for Parties, communicate annually to the Secretary-General of the Organization data on quantities of contributing oil received by persons liable to contribute to the Fund pursuant to Article 10 of the 1971 Fund Convention as amended by this Protocol.

Article 30
Entry into Force

1. This Protocol shall enter into force twelve months following the date on which the following requirements are fulfilled:
   (a) at least eight States have deposited instruments of ratification, acceptance, approval or accession with the Secretary-General of the Organization; and
   (b) the Secretary-General of the Organization has received information in accordance with Article 29 that those persons who would be liable to contribute pursuant to Article 10 of the 1971 Fund Convention as amended by this Protocol have received during the preceding calendar year a total quantity of at least 450 million tons of contributing oil.
2. However, this Protocol shall not enter into force before the 1992 Liability Convention has entered into force.
3. For each State which ratifies, accepts, approves or accedes to this Protocol after the conditions in paragraph 1 for entry into force have been met, the Protocol shall enter into force twelve months following the date of the deposit by such State of the appropriate instrument.
4. Any State may, at the time of the deposit of its instrument of ratification, acceptance, approval or accession in respect of this Protocol declare that such instrument shall not take effect for the purpose of this Article until the end of the six-month period in Article 31.
5. Any State which has made a declaration in accordance with the preceding paragraph may withdraw it at any time by means of a notification addressed to the Secretary-General of the Organization. Any such withdrawal shall take effect on the date the notification is received, and any State making such a withdrawal shall be deemed to have deposited its instrument of ratification, acceptance, approval or accession in respect of this Protocol on that date.
6. Any State which has made a declaration under Article 13, paragraph 2, of the Protocol of 1992 to amend the 1969 Liability Convention shall be deemed to have also made a declaration under paragraph 4 of this Article. Withdrawal of a declaration under

the said Article 13, paragraph 2, shall be deemed to constitute withdrawal also under paragraph 5 of this Article.

Article 31
Denunciation of 1969 and 1971 Conventions

Subject to Article 30, within six months following the date on which the following requirements are fulfilled:

(a) at least eight States have become Parties to this Protocol or have deposited instruments of ratification, acceptance, approval or accession with the Secretary-General of the Organization, whether or not subject to Article 30, paragraph 4, and

(b) the Secretary-General of the Organization has received information in accordance with Article 29 that those persons who are or would be liable to contribute pursuant to Article 10 of the 1971 Fund Convention as amended by this Protocol have received during the preceding calendar year a total quantity of at least 750 million tons of contributing oil;

each Party to this Protocol and each State which has deposited an instrument of ratification, acceptance, approval or accession, whether or not subject to Article 30, paragraph 4, shall, if party thereto, denounce the 1971 Fund Convention and the 1969 Liability Convention with effect twelve months after the expiry of the above-mentioned six-month period.

Article 32
Revision and amendment

1. A conference for the purpose of revising or amending the 1992 Fund Convention may be convened by the Organization.

2. The Organization shall convene a Conference of Contracting States for the purpose of revising or amending the 1992 Fund Convention at the request of not less than one third of all Contracting States.

Article 33
Amendment of compensation limits

1. Upon the request of at least one quarter of the Contracting States, any proposal to amend the limits of amounts of compensation laid down in Article 4, paragraph 4, of the 1971 Fund Convention as amended by this Protocol shall be circulated by the Secretary-General to all Members of the Organization and to all Contracting States.

2. Any amendment proposed and circulated as above shall be submitted to the Legal Committee of the Organization for consideration at a date at least six months after the date of its circulation.

3. All Contracting States to the 1971 Fund Convention as amended by this Protocol, whether or not Members of the Organization, shall be entitled to participate in the proceedings of the Legal Committee for the consideration and adoption of amendments.

4. Amendments shall be adopted by a two-thirds majority of the Contracting States present and voting in the Legal Committee, expanded as provided for in paragraph 3, on condition that at least one half of the Contracting States shall be present at the time of voting.

5. When acting on a proposal to amend the limits, the Legal Committee shall take into account the experience of incidents and in particular the amount of damage resulting therefrom and changes in the monetary values. It shall also take into account the

relationship between the limits in Article 4, paragraph 4, of the 1971 Fund Convention as amended by this Protocol and those in Article V, paragraph 1, of the International Convention on Civil Liability for Oil Pollution Damage, 1992.

6. (a) No amendment of the limits under this Article may be considered before 15 January 1998 nor less than five years from the date of entry into force of a previous amendment under this Article. No amendment under this Article shall be considered before this Protocol has entered into force.

(b) No limit may be increased so as to exceed an amount which corresponds to the limit laid down in the 1971 Fund Convention as amended by this Protocol increased by six per cent per year calculated on a compound basis from 15 January 1993.

(c) No limit may be increased so as to exceed an amount which corresponds to the limit laid down in the 1971 Fund Convention as amended by this Protocol multiplied by three.

7. Any amendment adopted in accordance with paragraph 4 shall be notified by the Organization to all Contracting States. The amendment shall be deemed to have been accepted at the end of a period of eighteen months after the date of notification unless within that period not less than one quarter of the States that were Contracting States at the time of the adoption of the amendment by the Legal Committee have communicated to the Organization that they do not accept the amendment in which case the amendment is rejected and shall have no effect.

8. An amendment deemed to have been accepted in accordance with paragraph 7 shall enter into force eighteen months after its acceptance.

9. All Contracting States shall be bound by the amendment, unless they denounce this Protocol in accordance with Article 34, paragraphs 1 and 2, at least six months before the amendment enters into force. Such denunciation shall take effect when the amendment enters into force.

10. When an amendment has been adopted by the Legal Committee but the eighteen-month period for its acceptance has not yet expired, a State which becomes a Contracting State during that period shall be bound by the amendment if it enters into force. A State which becomes a Contracting State after that period shall be bound by an amendment which has been accepted in accordance with paragraph 7. In the cases referred to in this paragraph, a State becomes bound by an amendment when that amendment enters into force, or when this Protocol enters into force for that State, if later.

Article 34
Denunciation

1. This Protocol may be denounced by any Party at any time after the date on which it enters into force for that Party.

2. Denunciation shall be effected by the deposit of an instrument with the Secretary-General of the Organization.

3. A denunciation shall take effect twelve months, or such longer period as may be specified in the instrument of denunciation, after its deposit with the Secretary-General of the Organization.

4. Denunciation of the 1992 Liability Convention shall be deemed to be a denunciation of this Protocol. Such denunciation shall take effect on the date on which denunciation of the Protocol of 1992 to amend the 1969 Liability Convention takes effect according to Article 16 of that Protocol.

5. Any Contracting State to this Protocol which has not denounced the 1971 Fund Convention and the 1969 Liability Convention as required by Article 31 shall be

deemed to have denounced this Protocol with effect twelve months after the expiry of the six-month period mentioned in that Article. As from the date on which the denunciations provided for in Article 31 take effect, any Party to this Protocol which deposits an instrument of ratification, acceptance, approval or accession to the 1969 Liability Convention shall be deemed to have denounced this Protocol with effect from the date on which such instrument takes effect.

6.   As between the Parties to this Protocol, denunciation by any of them of the 1971 Fund Convention in accordance with Article 41 thereof shall not be construed in any way as a denunciation of the 1971 Fund Convention as amended by this Protocol.

7.   Notwithstanding a denunciation of this Protocol by a Party pursuant to this Article, any provisions of this Protocol relating to the obligations to make contributions under Article 10 of the 1971 Fund Convention as amended by this Protocol with respect to an incident referred to in Article 12, paragraph 2(b), of that amended Convention and occurring before the denunciation takes effect shall continue to apply.

Article 35
Extraordinary sessions of the Assembly

1.   Any Contracting State may, within ninety days after the deposit of an instrument of denunciation the result of which it considers will significantly increase the level of contributions for the remaining Contracting States, request the Director to convene an extraordinary session of the Assembly. The Director shall convene the Assembly to meet not later than sixty days after receipt of the request.

2.   The Director may convene, on his own initiative, an extraordinary session of the Assembly to meet within sixty days after the deposit of any instrument of denunciation, if he considers that such denunciation will result in a significant increase in the level of contributions of the remaining Contracting States.

3.   If the Assembly at an extraordinary session convened in accordance with paragraph 1 or 2 decides that the denunciation will result in a significant increase in the level of contributions for the remaining Contacting State, any such State may, not later than one hundred and twenty days before the date on which the denunciation takes effect, denounce this Protocol with effect from the same date.

Article 36
Termination

1.   This Protocol shall cease to be in force on the date when the number of Contracting States falls below three.

2.   States which are bound by this Protocol on the day before the date it ceases to be in force shall enable the Fund to exercise its functions as described under Article 37 of this Protocol and shall, for that purpose only, remain bound by this Protocol.

Article 37
Winding up of the Fund

1.   If this Protocol ceases to be in force, the Fund shall nevertheless:
   (a) meet its obligations in respect of any incident occurring before the Protocol ceased to be in force;
   (b) be entitled to exercise its rights to contributions to the extent that these contributions are necessary to meet the obligations under subparagraph (a), including expenses for the administration of the Fund necessary for this purpose.

2. The Assembly shall take all appropriate measures to complete the winding up of the Fund including the distribution in an equitable manner of any remaining assets among those persons who have contributed to the Fund.

3. For the purposes of this Article the Fund shall remain a legal person.

Article 38
Depositary

1. This Protocol and any amendments accepted under Article 33 shall be deposited with the Secretary-General of the Organization.

2. The Secretary-General of the Organization shall:
   (a) inform all States which have signed or acceded to this Protocol of:
      (i) each new signature or deposit of an instrument together with the date thereof;
      (ii) each declaration and notification under Article 30 including declarations and withdrawals deemed to have been made in accordance with that Article;
      (iii) the date of entry into force of this Protocol;
      (iv) the date by which denunciations provided for in Article 31 are required to be made;
      (v) any proposal to amend limits of amounts of compensation which has been made in accordance with Article 33, paragraph 1;
      (vi) any amendment which has been adopted in accordance with Article 33, paragraph 4;
      (vii) any amendment deemed to have been accepted under Article 3, paragraph 7, together with the date on which that amendment shall enter into force in accordance with paragraphs 8 and 9 of that Article;
      (viii) the deposit of an instrument of denunciation of this Protocol together with the date of the deposit and the date on which it takes effect;
      (ix) any denunciation deemed to have been made under Article 34, paragraph 5;
      (x) any communication called for by any Article in this Protocol;
   (b) transmit certified true copies of this Protocol to all Signatory States and to all States which accede to the Protocol.

3. As soon as this Protocol enters into force, the text shall be transmitted by the Secretary-General of the Organization to the Secretariat of the United Nations for registration and publication in accordance with Article 102 of the Charter of the United Nations.

Article 39
Languages

This Protocol is established in a single original in the Arabic, Chinese, English, French, Russian and Spanish languages, each text being equally authentic.

DONE AT LONDON this twenty-seventh day of November one thousand nine hundred and ninety-two.

IN WITNESS WHEREOF the undersigned being duly authorized for that purpose have signed this Protocol.

Notes

1. 11 ILM (1972), p.284; UK Treaty Series No.95 (1978), Cmnd. 7383; *Kiss*, p.255; IMO Doc. IMO-420B.
2. Protocol to Fund Convention 1971, 19 November 1976, *Singh*, Vol.3, p.2517; IMO Doc. IMO-420B, Supplement.
3. Amounts are expressed in francs and the franc is defined in Art.1(4) by reference to CLC 1969, Art.V(9), *i.e.*, the Poincaré gold franc.
4. See further Vol.1, Chap.15, text, following note 466.
5. 23 ILM (1984), p.195; IMO Doc. IMO-456E.
6. Protocol of 1992 to Amend the International Convention on the Establishment of an International Fund for Compensation for Oil Pollution Damage, 1971 (IMO Doc. LEG/CONF.9/16, 2 December 1992), Preamble, emphasis added.
7. Loc.cit. in note 6.
8. IMO Doc. LEG/CONF.9/DC/3, 26 November 1992, p.8.
9. Art.28.
10. Loc.cit. in note 8.

10.4 BASEL CONVENTION ON THE CONTROL OF TRANSBOUNDARY MOVEMENTS OF HAZARDOUS WASTES AND THEIR DISPOSAL, 1989

Preamble

The Parties to this Convention,

Aware of the risk of damage to human health and the environment caused by hazardous wastes and other wastes and the transboundary movement thereof,

Mindful of the growing threat to human health and the environment posed by the increased generation and complexity, and transboundary movement of hazardous wastes and other wastes,

Mindful also that the most effective way of protecting human health and the environment from the dangers posed by such wastes is the reduction of their generation to a minimum in terms of quantity and/or hazard potential,

Convinced that States should take necessary measures to ensure that the management of hazardous wastes and other wastes including their transboundary movement and disposal is consistent with the protection of human health and the environment whatever the place of their disposal,

Noting that States should ensure that the generator should carry out duties with regard to the transport and disposal of hazardous wastes and other wastes in a manner that is consistent with the protection of the environment, whatever the place of disposal,

Fully recognizing that any State has the sovereign right to ban the entry or disposal of foreign hazardous wastes and other wastes in its territory,

Recognizing also the increasing desire for the prohibition of transboundary movements of hazardous wastes and their disposal in other States, especially developing countries,

Convinced that hazardous wastes and other wastes should, as far as is compatible with environmentally sound and efficient management, be disposed of in the State where they were generated.

Aware also that transboundary movements of such wastes from the State of their generation to any other State should be permitted only when conducted under conditions which do not endanger human health and the environment, and under conditions in conformity with the provisions of this Convention,

Considering that enhanced control of transboundary movement of hazardous wastes and other wastes will act as an incentive for their environmentally sound management and for the reduction of the volume of such transboundary movement,

Convinced that States should take measures for the proper exchange of information on and control of the transboundary movement of hazardous wastes and other wastes from and to those States,

Noting that a number of international and regional agreements have addressed the issue of protection and preservation of the environment with regard to the transit of dangerous goods,

Taking into account the Declaration of the United Nations Conference on the Human Environment (Stockholm, 1972), the Cairo Guidelines and Principles for the Environmentally Sound Management of Hazardous Wastes adopted by the Governing Council of the United Nations Environment Programme (UNEP) by decision 14/30 of 17 June 1987, the Recommendations of the United Nations Committee of Experts on the Transport of Dangerous Goods (formulated in 1957 and updated biennially), relevant recommendations, declarations, instruments and regulations adopted within the United Nations system and the work and studies done within other international and regional organizations,

Mindful of the spirit, principles, aims and functions of the World Charter for Nature adopted by the General Assembly of the United Nations at its thirty-seventh session (1982) as the rule of ethics in respect of the protection of the human environment and the conservation of natural resources,

Affirming that States are responsible for the fulfilment of their international obligations concerning the protection of human health and protection and preservation of the environment, and are liable in accordance with international law,

Recognizing that in the case of a material breach of the provisions of this Convention or any protocol thereto the relevant international law of treaties shall apply,

Aware of the need to continue the development and implementation of environmentally sound low-waste technologies, recycling options, good house-keeping and management systems with a view to reducing to a minimum the generation of hazardous wastes and other wastes,

Aware also of the growing international concern about the need for stringent control of transboundary movement of hazardous wastes and other wastes, and of the need as far as possible to reduce such movement to a minimum,

Concerned also about the problem of illegal transboundary traffic in hazardous wastes and other wastes,

Taking into account also the limited capabilities of the developing countries to manage hazardous wastes and other wastes,

Recognizing the need to promote the transfer of technology for the sound management of hazardous wastes and other wastes produced locally, particularly to the developing countries in accordance with the spirit of the Cairo Guidelines and decision 14/16 of the Governing Council of UNEP on Promotion of the transfer of environmental protection technology,

Recognizing also that hazardous wastes and other wastes should be transported in accordance with relevant international conventions and recommendations,

Convinced also that the transboundary movement of hazardous wastes and other wastes should be permitted only when the transport and the ultimate disposal of such wastes is environmentally sound, and

Determined to protect, by strict control, human health and the environment against the adverse effects which may result from the generation and management of hazardous wastes and other wastes,

HAVE AGREED AS FOLLOWS:

Article 1
Scope of the Convention

1. The following wastes that are subject to transboundary movement shall be "hazardous wastes" for the purposes of this Convention:

   (a) Wastes that belong to any category contained in Annex I, unless they do not possess any of the characteristics contained in Annex III; and

   (b) Wastes that are not covered under paragraph (a) but are defined as, or are considered to be, hazardous wastes by the domestic legislation of the Party of export, import or transit.

2. Wastes that belong to any category contained in Annex II that are subject to transboundary movement shall be "other wastes" for the purposes of this Convention.

3. Wastes which, as a result of being radioactive, are subject to other international control systems, including international instruments, applying specifically to radioactive materials, are excluded from the scope of this Convention.

4. Wastes which derive from the normal operations of a ship, the discharge of which is covered by another international instrument, are excluded from the scope of this Convention.

Article 2
Definitions

For the purposes of this Convention:

1. "Wastes" are substances or objects which are disposed of or are intended to be disposed of or are required to be disposed of by the provisions of national law;

2. "Management" means the collection, transport and disposal of hazardous wastes or other wastes, including after-care of disposal sites;

3. "Transboundary movement" means any movement of hazardous wastes or other wastes from an area under the national jurisdiction of one State to or through an area under the national jurisdiction of another State or to or through an area not under the national jurisdiction of any State, provided at least two States are involved in the movement;

4. "Disposal" means any operation specified in Annex IV to this Convention;

5. "Approved site or facility" means a site or facility for the disposal of hazardous wastes or other wastes which is authorized or permitted to operate for this purpose by a relevant authority of the State where the site or facility is located;

6. "Competent authority" means one governmental authority designated by a Party to be responsible, within such geographical areas as the Party may think fit, for receiving the notification of a transboundary movement of hazardous wastes or other wastes, and any information related to it, and for responding to such a notification, as provided in article 6;

7. "Focal point" means the entity of a Party referred to in article 5 responsible for receiving and submitting information as provided for in articles 13 and 16;

8. "Environmentally sound manage of hazardous wastes or other wastes" means taking all practicable steps to ensure that hazardous wastes or other wastes are managed in a manner which will protect human health and the environment against the adverse effects which may result from such wastes;

9. "Area under the national jurisdiction of a State" means any land, marine area or airspace within which a State exercises administrative and regulatory responsibility in accordance with international law in regard to the protection of human health or the environment;

10. "State of export" means a Party from which a transboundary movement of hazardous wastes or other wastes is planned to be initiated or is initiated;

11. "State of import" means a Party to which a transboundary movement of hazardous wastes or other wastes is planned or takes place for the purpose of disposal therein or for the purpose of loading prior to disposal in an area not under the national jurisdiction of any State;

12. "State of transit" means any State, other than the State of export or import, through which a movement of hazardous wastes or other wastes is planned or takes place;

13. "States concerned" means Parties which are States of export or import, or transit States, whether or not Parties;

14. "Person" means any natural or legal person;

15. "Exporter" means any person under the jurisdiction of the State of export who arranges for hazardous wastes or other wastes to be exported;

16. "Importer" means any person under the jurisdiction of the State of import who arranges for hazardous wastes or other wastes to be imported;

17. "Carrier" means any person who carries out the transport of hazardous wastes or other wastes;

18. "Generator" means any person whose activity produced hazardous wastes or other wastes or, if that person is not known, the person who is in possession and/or control of those wastes;

19. "Disposer" means any person to whom hazardous wastes or other wastes are shipped and who carries out the disposal of such wastes;

20. "Political and/or economic integration organization" means an organization constituted by sovereign States to which its member States have transferred competence in respect of matters governed by this Convention and which has been duly authorized, in accordance with its internal procedures, to sign, ratify, accept, approve, formally confirm or accede to it;

21. "Illegal traffic" means any transboundary movement of hazardous wastes or other wastes as specified in article 9.

Article 3
National definitions of hazardous wastes

1. Each Party shall, within six months of becoming a Party to this Convention, inform the secretariat of the Convention of the wastes, other than those listed in Annexes I and II, considered or defined as hazardous under its national legislation and of any requirements concerning transboundary movement procedures applicable to such wastes.

2. Each Party shall subsequently inform the secretariat of any significant changes to the information it has provided pursuant to paragraph 1.

3. The secretariat shall forthwith inform all Parties of the information it has received pursuant to paragraphs 1 and 2.

4. Parties shall be responsible for making the information transmitted to them by the secretariat under paragraph 3 available to their exporters.

Article 4
General obligations

1. (a) Parties exercising their right to prohibit the import of hazardous wastes or other wastes for disposal shall inform the other Parties of their decision pursuant to article 13;

(b) Parties shall prohibit or shall not permit the export of hazardous wastes and other wastes to the Parties which have prohibited the import of such wastes, when notified pursuant to subparagraph (a) above;

(c) Parties shall prohibit or shall not permit the export of hazardous wastes and other wastes if the State of import does not consent in writing to the specific import, in the case where that State of import has not prohibited the import of such wastes.

2. Each Party shall take the appropriate measures to:

(a) Ensure that the generation of hazardous wastes and other wastes within it is reduced to a minimum, taking into account social, technological and economic aspects;

(b) Ensure the availability of adequate disposal facilities, for the environmentally sound management of hazardous wastes and other wastes, that shall be located, to the extent possible, within it, whatever the place of their disposal;

(c) Ensure that persons involved in the management of hazardous wastes or other wastes within it take such steps as are necessary to prevent pollution due to hazardous wastes and other wastes arising from such management and, if such pollution occurs, to minimize the consequences thereof for human health and the environment;

(d) Ensure that the transboundary movement of hazardous wastes and other wastes is reduced to the minimum consistent with the environmentally sound and efficient management of such wastes, and is conducted in a manner which will protect human health and the environment against the adverse effects which may result from such movement;

(e) Not allow the export of hazardous wastes or other wastes of a State or group of States belonging to an economic and/or political integration organization that are Parties, particular developing countries, which have prohibited by their legislation all imports, or if it has reason to believe that the wastes in question will not be managed in an environmentally sound manner, according to criteria to be decided on by the Parties at their first meeting;

(f) Require that information about a proposed transboundary movement of hazardous wastes and other wastes be provided to the States concerned, according to annex V A, to state clearly the effects of the proposed movement on human health and the environment;

(g) Prevent the import of hazardous wastes and other wastes if it has reason to believe that the wastes in question will not be managed in an environmentally sound manner;

(h) Co-operate in activities with other Parties and interested organizations, directly and through the secretariat, including the dissemination of information on the transboundary movement of hazardous wastes and other wastes, in order to improve the environmentally sound management of such wastes and to achieve the prevention of illegal traffic.

3. The Parties consider that illegal traffic in hazardous wastes or other wastes is criminal.

4. Each Party shall take appropriate legal, administrative and other measures to implement and enforce the provisions of this Convention, including measures to prevent and punish conduct in contravention of the Convention.

5. A Party shall not permit hazardous wastes or other wastes to be exported to a non-Party or to be imported from a non-Party.

6. The Parties agree not to allow the export of hazardous wastes or other wastes for disposal within the area south of 60° South latitude, whether or not such wastes are subject to transboundary movement.

7. Furthermore, each party shall:

(a) Prohibit all persons under its national jurisdiction from transporting or disposing of hazardous wastes unless such persons are authorized or allowed to perform such types of operations;

(b) Require that hazardous wastes and other wastes that are to be the subject of a transboundary movement be packaged, labelled, and transported in conformity with generally accepted and recognized international rules and standards in the field of packaging, labelling, and transport, and that due account is taken of relevant internationally recognized practices;

(c) Require that hazardous wastes and other wastes be accompanied by a movement document from the point at which a transboundary movement commences to the point of disposal.

8. Each Party shall require that hazardous wastes or other wastes, to be exported, are managed in an environmentally sound manner in the State of import or elsewhere. Technical guidelines for the environmentally sound management of wastes subject to this Convention shall be decided by the Parties at their first meeting.

9. Parties shall take the appropriate measures to ensure that the transboundary movement of hazardous wastes and other wastes only be allowed if:

(a) The State of export does not have the technical capacity and the necessary facilities, capacity or suitable disposal sites in order to dispose of the wastes in question in an environmentally sound and efficient manner; or

(b) The wastes in question are required as a raw material for recycling or recovery industries in the State of import; or

(c) The transboundary movement in question is in accordance with other criteria to be decided by the Parties, provided those criteria do not differ from the objectives of this Convention.

10. The obligation under this Convention of States in which hazardous wastes and other wastes are generated to require that those wastes are managed in an environmentally sound manner may not under any circumstances be transferred to the States of import or transit.

11. Nothing in this Convention shall prevent a Party from imposing additional requirements that are consistent with the provisions of this Convention, and are in accordance with the rules of international law, in order better to protect human health and the environment.

12. Nothing in this Convention shall affect in any way the sovereignty of States over their territorial sea established in accordance with international law, and the sovereign rights and the jurisdiction which States have in their exclusive economic zones and their continental shelves in accordance with international law, and the exercise by ships and aircraft of all States of navigational rights and freedoms as provided for in international law and as reflected in relevant international instruments.

13. Parties shall undertake to review periodically the possibilities for the reduction of the amount and/or the pollution potential of hazardous wastes and other wastes which are exported to other States, in particular to developing countries.

Article 5
Designation of competent authorities and focal point

To facilitate the implementation of this Convention, the Parties shall:

1. Designate or establish one or more competent authorities and one focal point. One competent authority shall be designated to receive the notification in case of a State of transit.

2. Inform the secretariat, within three months of the date of the entry into force of this Convention for them, which agencies they have designated as their focal point and their competent authorities.

3. Inform the secretariat, within one month of the date of decision, of any changes regarding the designation made by them under paragraph 2 above.

Article 6
Transboundary movement between Parties

1. The State of export shall notify, or shall require the generator or exporter to notify, in writing, through the channel of the competent authority of the State of export, the competent authority of the States concerned of any proposed transboundary movement of hazardous wastes or other wastes. Such notification shall contain the declarations and information specified in annex V A, written in a language acceptable to the State of import. Only one notification needs to be sent to each State concerned.

2. The State of import shall respond to the notifier in writing, consenting to the movement with or without conditions, denying permission for the movement, or requesting additional information. A copy of the final response of the State of import shall be sent to the competent authorities of the States concerned which are Parties.

3. The State of export shall not allow the generator or exporter to commence the transboundary movement until it has received written confirmation that:

(a) The notifier has received the written consent of the State of import; and

(b) The notifier has received from the State of import confirmation of the existence of a contract between the exporter and the disposer specifying environmentally sound management of the wastes in question.

4. Each State of transit which is a Party shall promptly acknowledge to the notifier receipt of the notification. It may subsequently respond to the notifier in writing, within 60 days, consenting to the movement with or without conditions, denying permission for the movement, or requesting additional information. The State of export shall not allow the transboundary movement to commence until it has received the written consent of the State of transit. However, if at any time a party decided not to require prior written consent, either generally or under specific conditions, for transit transboundary movements of hazardous wastes or other wastes, or modifies its requirements in this respect, it shall forthwith inform the other Parties of its decision pursuant to article 13. In this latter case, if no response is received by the State of export within 60 days of the receipt of a given notification by the State of transit, the State of export may allow the export to proceed through the State of transit.

5. In the case of a transboundary movement of wastes where the wastes are legally defined as or considered to be hazardous wastes only:

(a) By the State of export, the requirements of paragraph 9 of this article that apply to the importer or disposer and the State of import shall apply *mutatis mutandis* to the exporter and State of export, respectively;

(b) By the State of import, or by the States of import and transit which are Parties, the requirements of paragraphs 1, 3, 4 and 6 of this article that apply to the exporter and State of export shall apply *mutatis mutandis* to the importer or disposer and State of import, respectively; or

(c) By any State of transit which is a Party, the provisions of paragraph 4 shall apply to such State.

6. The State of export may, subject to the written consent of the States concerned, allow the generator or the exporter to use a general notification where hazardous wastes or other wastes having the same physical and chemical characteristics are shipped regularly to the same disposer via the same customs office of exit of the State of export via the same customs office of entry of the State of import, and, in the case of transit, via the same customs office of entry and exit of the State or States of transit.

7. The States concerned may make their written consent to the use of the general notification referred to in paragraph 6 subject to the supply of certain information, such as the exact quantities or periodical lists of hazardous wastes or other wastes to be shipped.

8. The general notification and written consent referred to in paragraphs 6 and 7 may cover multiple shipments of hazardous wastes or other wastes during a maximum period of 12 months.

9. The Parties shall require that each person who takes charge of a transboundary movement of hazardous wastes or other wastes sign the movement document either upon delivery or receipt of the wastes in question. They shall also require that the disposer inform both the exporter and the competent authority of the State of export of receipt by the disposer of the wastes in question and, in due course, of the completion of disposal as specified in the notification. If no such information is received within the State of export, the competent authority of the State of export or the exporter shall so notify the State of import.

10. The notification and response required by this article shall be transmitted to the competent authority of the Parties concerned or to such governmental authority as may be appropriate in the case of non-Parties.

11. Any transboundary movement of hazardous wastes or other wastes shall be covered by insurance, bond or other guarantee as may be required by the State of import or any State of transit which is a Party.

Article 7
Transboundary movement from a Party through States which are not Parties

Paragraph 2 of article 6 of the Convention shall apply *mutatis mutandis* to transboundary movement of hazardous wastes or other wastes from a Party through a State or States which are not Parties.

Article 8
Duty to re-import

When a transboundary movement of hazardous wastes or other wastes to which the consent of the States concerned has been given, subject to the provisions of this Convention, cannot be completed in accordance with the terms of the contract, the State of export shall ensure that the wastes in question are taken back into the State of export, by the exporter, if alternative arrangements cannot be made for their disposal in an environmentally sound manner, within 90 days from the time that the importing State informed the State of export and the secretariat, or such other period of time as the States concerned agree. To this end, the State of export and any party of transit shall not oppose, hinder or prevent the return of those wastes to the State of export.

Article 9
Illegal traffic

1. For the purpose of this Convention, any transboundary movement of hazardous wastes or other wastes:

(a) without notification pursuant to the provisions of this Convention to all States concerned; or

(b) without the consent pursuant to the provisions of this Convention of a State concerned; or

(c) with consent obtained from States concerned through falsification, misrepresentation or fraud; or

(d) that does not conform in a material way with the documents; or

(e) that results in deliberate disposal (e.g. dumping) of hazardous wastes or other wastes in contravention of this Convention and of general principles of international law,

shall be deemed to be illegal traffic.

2. In case of a transboundary movement of hazardous wastes or other wastes deemed to be illegal traffic as the result of conduct on the part of the exporter or generator, the State of export shall ensure that the wastes in question are:

(a) taken back by the exporter or the generator or, if necessary, by itself into the State of export, or, if impracticable,

(b) are otherwise disposed of in accordance with the provisions of this Convention,

within 30 days from the time the State of export has been informed about the illegal traffic or such other period of time as States concerned may agree. To this end the Parties concerned shall not oppose, hinder or prevent the return of those wastes to the State of export.

3. In the case of a transboundary movement of hazardous wastes or other wastes deemed to be illegal traffic as the result of conduct on the part of the importer or disposer, the State of import shall ensure that the wastes in question are disposed of in an environmentally sound manner by the importer or disposer or, if necessary, by itself within 30 days from the time the illegal traffic has come to the attention of the State of import or such other period of time as the States concerned may agree. To this end, the Parties concerned shall co-operate, as necessary, in the disposal of the wastes in an environmentally sound manner.

4. In cases where the responsibility for the illegal traffic cannot be assigned either to the importer or generator or to the importer or disposer, the Parties concerned or other Parties, as appropriate, shall ensure, through co-operation, that the wastes in question are disposed of as soon as possible in an environmentally sound manner either in the State of export or the State of import or elsewhere as appropriate.

5. Each Party shall introduce appropriate national/domestic legislation to prevent and punish illegal traffic. The Parties shall co-operate with a view to achieving the objects of this article.

Article 10
International co-operation

1. The Parties shall co-operate with each other in order to improve and achieve environmentally sound management of hazardous wastes and other wastes.
2. To this end, the Parties shall:
    (a) Upon request, make available information, whether on a bilateral or multilateral basis, with a view to promoting the environmentally sound management of hazardous wastes and other wastes, including harmonization of technical standards and practices for the adequate management of hazardous wastes and other wastes;
    (b) Co-operate in monitoring the effects of the management of hazardous wastes on human health and the environment;
    (c) Co-operate, subject to their national laws, regulations and policies, in the development and implementation of new environmentally sound low-waste technologies and the improvement of existing technologies with a view to eliminating, as far as practicable, the generation of hazardous wastes and other wastes and achieving more effective and efficient methods of ensuring their management in an environmentally sound manner, including the study of the economic, social and environmental effects of the adoption of such new or improved technologies;
    (d) Co-operate actively, subject to their national laws, regulations and policies, in the transfer of technology and management systems related to the environmentally sound management of hazardous wastes and other wastes.   They shall also co-operate in developing the technical capacity among Parties, especially those which may need and request technical assistance in this field;
    (e) Co-operate in developing appropriate technical guidelines and/or codes of practice;
3. The Parties shall employ appropriate means to co-operate in order to assist developing countries in the implementation of subparagraphs (a), (b), (c) and (d) of paragraph 2 of article 4.
4. Taking into account the needs of developing countries, co-operation between Parties and the competent international organizations is encouraged to promote, *inter alia*, public awareness, the development of sound management of hazardous wastes and other wastes and the adoption of new low-waste technologies.

Article 11
Bilateral, multilateral and regional agreements

1. Notwithstanding the provisions of article 4, paragraph 5, Parties may enter into bilateral, multilateral, or regional agreements or arrangements regarding transboundary movement of hazardous wastes or other wastes with Parties or non-Parties provided that such agreements or arrangements do not derogate from the environmentally sound management of hazardous wastes and other wastes as required by this Convention. These agreements or arrangements shall stipulate provisions which are not less environmentally sound than those provided for by this Convention, in particular taking into account the interests of developing countries.
2. Parties shall notify the secretariat of any bilateral, multilateral or regional agreements or arrangements referred to in paragraph 1 and those which they have entered into prior to the entry into force of this Convention for them, for the purpose of controlling transboundary movements of hazardous wastes and other wastes which take place entirely among the Parties to such agreements.   The provisions of this Convention shall not affect transboundary movements which take place pursuant to such

agreements provided that such agreements are compatible with the environmentally sound management of hazardous wastes and other wastes as required by this Convention.

Article 12
Consultations on liability

The Parties shall co-operate with a view to adopting, as soon as practicable, a protocol setting out appropriate rules and procedures in the field of liability and compensation for damage resulting from the transboundary movement and disposal of hazardous wastes and other wastes.

Article 13
Transmission of information

1. The Parties shall, whenever it comes to their knowledge, ensure that, in the case of an accident occurring during the transboundary movement of hazardous wastes or other wastes or their disposal, which are likely to present risks to human health and the environment in other States, those States are immediately informed.
2. The Parties shall inform each other, through the secretariat, of:
    (a) Changes regarding the designation of competent authorities and/or focal points, pursuant to article 5;
    (b) Changes in their national definition of hazardous wastes, pursuant to article 3; and, as soon as possible,
    (c) Decisions made by them not to consent totally or partially to the import of hazardous wastes or other wastes for disposal within the area under their national jurisdiction;
    (d) Decisions taken by them to limit or ban the export of hazardous wastes or other wastes;
    (e) Any other information required pursuant to paragraph 4 of this article.
3. The Parties, consistent with national laws and regulations, shall transmit, through the secretariat, to the Conference of the Parties established under article 15, before the end of each calendar year, a report on the previous calendar year, containing the following information:
    (a) Competent authorities and focal points that have been designated by them pursuant to article 5;
    (b) Information regarding transboundary movements of hazardous wastes or other wastes in which they have been involved, including:
    (i) The amount of hazardous wastes and other wastes exported, their category, characteristics, destination, any transit country and disposal method as stated on the response to notification;
    (ii) The amount of hazardous wastes and other wastes imported, their category, characteristics, origin, and disposal methods;
    (iii) Disposals which did not proceed as intended;
    (iv) Efforts to achieve a reduction of the amount of hazardous wastes or other wastes subject to transboundary movement.
    (c) Information on the measures adopted by them in implementation of this Convention;
    (d) Information on available qualified statistics which have been compiled by them on the effects on human health and the environment of the generation, transportation and disposal of hazardous wastes or other wastes;

(e) Information concerning bilateral, multilateral and regional agreements and arrangements entered into pursuant to article 11 of this Convention;

(f) Information on accidents occurring during the transboundary movement and disposal of hazardous wastes and other wastes and on the measures undertaken to deal with them;

(g) Information on disposal options operated within the area of their national jurisdiction;

(h) Information on measures undertaken for development of technologies for the reduction and/or elimination of production of hazardous wastes and other wastes; and

(i) Such other matters as the Conference of the Parties shall deem relevant.

4. The Parties, consistent with national laws and regulations, shall ensure that copies of each notification concerning any given transboundary movement of hazardous wastes or other wastes, and the response to it, are sent to the secretariat when a Party [which?] considers that its environment may be affected by that transboundary movement has requested that this should be done.

Article 14
Financial aspects

1. The Parties agree that, according to the specific needs of different regions and subregions, regional or subregional centres for training and technology transfers regarding the management of hazardous wastes and other wastes and the minimization of their generation should be established.   The Parties shall decide on the establishment of appropriate funding mechanisms of a voluntary nature.

2. The Parties shall consider the establishment of a revolving fund to assist on an interim basis in case of emergency situations to minimize damage from accidents arising from transboundary movements of hazardous wastes and other wastes or during the disposal of those wastes.

Article 15
Conference of the Parties

1. A Conference of the Parties is hereby established.   The first meeting of the Conference of the Parties shall be convened by the Executive Director of UNEP not later than one year after the entry into force of this Convention.   Thereafter, ordinary meetings of the Conference of the Parties shall be held at regular intervals to be determined by the Conference at its first meeting.

2. Extraordinary meetings of the Conference of the Parties shall be held at such other times as may be deemed necessary by the Conference at its first meeting.

3. The Conference of the Parties shall by consensus agree upon and adopt rules of procedure for itself and for any subsidiary body it may establish, as well as financial rules to determine in particular the financial participation of the Parties under this Convention.

4. The Parties at their first meeting shall consider any additional measures needed to assist them in fulfilling their responsibilities with respect to the protection and the preservation of the marine environment in the context of this Convention.

5. The Conference of the Parties shall keep under continuous review and evaluation the effective implementation of this Convention, and, in addition, shall:

(a) Promote the harmonization of appropriate policies, strategies and measures for minimizing harm to human health and the environment by hazardous wastes and other wastes;

(b) Consider and adopt, as required, amendments to this Convention and its annexes, taking into consideration, *inter alia*, available scientific, technical, economic and environmental information;

(c) Consider and undertake any additional action that may be required for the achievement of the purposes of this Convention in the light of experience gained in its operation and in the operation of the agreements and arrangements envisaged in article 11;

(d) Consider and adopt protocols as required; and

(e) Establish such subsidiary bodies as are deemed necessary for the implementation of this Convention.

6. The United nations, its specialised agencies, as well as any State not party to this Convention, may be represented as observers at meetings of the Conference of the Parties. Any other body or agency, whether national or international, governmental or non-governmental, qualified in fields relating to hazardous wastes or other wastes which has informed the secretariat of its wish to be represented as an observer at a meeting of the Conference of the Parties, may be admitted unless at least one-third of the Parties present object. The admission and participation of observers shall be subject to the rules of procedure adopted by the Conference of the Parties.

7. The Conference of the Parties shall undertake three years after the entry into force of this Convention, and at least every six years thereafter, an evaluation of its effectiveness and, if deemed necessary, to consider the adoption of a complete or partial ban on transboundary movements of hazardous wastes and other wastes in the light of the latest scientific, environmental, technical and economic information.

Article 16
Secretariat

1. The functions of the secretariat shall be:

(a) To arrange for and service meetings provided for in articles 15 and 17;

(b) To prepare and transmit reports based upon information received in accordance with articles 3, 4, 6, 11 and 13 as well as upon information derived from meetings of subsidiary bodies established under article 15 as well as upon, as appropriate, information provided by relevant inter-governmental and non-governmental entities;

(c) To prepare reports on its activities carried out in implementation of its functions under this Convention and present them to the Conference of the Parties;

(d) To ensure the necessary co-ordination with relevant international bodies, and in particular to enter into such administrative and contractual arrangements as may be required for the effective discharge of its functions;

(e) To communicate with focal points and competent authorities established by the Parties in accordance with article 5 of this Convention;

(f) To compile information concerning authorized national sites and facilities of Parties available for the disposal of their hazardous wastes and other wastes and to circulate this information among Parties;

(g) To receive and convey information from and to Parties on:
- sources of technical assistance and training;
- available technical and scientific know-how;
- sources of advice and expertise; and
- availability of resources

with a view to assisting them, upon request, in such areas as:
- the handling of the notification system of this Convention;
- the management of hazardous wastes and other wastes;

- environmentally sound technologies relating to hazardous wastes and other wastes, such as low- and non-waste technology;
- the assessment of disposal capabilities and sites;
- the monitoring of hazardous wastes and other wastes; and
- emergency responses.

(h) To provide Parties, upon request, with information on consultants or consulting firms having the necessary technical competence in the field, which can assist them to examine a notification for a transboundary movement, the concurrence of a shipment of hazardous wastes or other wastes with the relevant notification, and/or the fact that the proposed disposal facilities for hazardous wastes or other wastes are environmentally sound, when they have reason to believe that the wastes in question will not be managed in an environmentally sound manner. Any such examination would not be at the expense of the secretariat;

(i) To assist Parties upon request in their identification of cases of illegal traffic and to circulate immediately to the Parties concerned any information it has received regarding illegal traffic;

(j) To co-operate with Parties and with relevant and competent international organizations and agencies in the provision of experts and equipment for the purpose of rapid assistance to States in the event of an emergency situation; and

(k) To perform such other functions relevant to the purposes of this Convention as may be determined by the Conference of the Parties.

2. The secretariat functions will be carried out on an interim basis by UNEP until the completion of the first meeting of the Conference of the Parties held pursuant to article 15.

3. At its first meeting, the Conference of the Parties shall designate the secretariat from among those existing competent intergovernmental organizations which have signified their willingness to carry out the secretariat functions under this Convention. At this meeting, the Conference of the Parties shall also evaluate the implementation by the interim secretariat of the functions assigned to it, in particular under paragraph 1 above, and decide upon the structures appropriate for those functions.

Article 17
Amendment of the Convention

1. Any Party may propose amendments to this Convention and any party to a protocol may propose amendments to that protocol. Such amendments shall take due account, *inter alia*, of relevant scientific and technical considerations.

2. Amendments to this Convention shall be adopted at a meeting of the Conference of the Parties. Amendments to any protocol shall be adopted at a meeting of the Parties to the protocol in question. The text of any proposed amendment to this Convention or to any protocol, except as may otherwise be provided in such protocol, shall be communicated to the Parties by the secretariat at least six months before the meeting at which it is proposed for adoption. The secretariat shall also communicate proposed amendments to the Signatories to this Convention for information.

3. The Parties shall make every effort to reach agreement on any proposed amendment to this Convention by consensus. If all efforts at consensus have been exhausted, and no agreement reached, the amendment shall as a last resort be adopted by a three-fourths majority vote of the Parties present and voting at the meeting, and shall be submitted by the Depositary to all Parties for ratification, approval, formal confirmation or acceptance.

4. The procedure mentioned in paragraph 3 above shall apply to amendments to any protocol, except that a two-thirds majority of the Parties to that protocol present and voting at the meeting shall suffice for their adoption.

5. Instruments of ratification, approval, formal confirmation or acceptance of amendments shall be deposited with the Depositary.   Amendments adopted in accordance with paragraphs 3 or 4 above shall enter into force between Parties having accepted them on the ninetieth day after the receipt by the Depositary of their instrument of ratification, approval, formal confirmation or acceptance by at least three-fourths of the Parties who accepted the amendments to the protocol concerned, except as may otherwise be provided in such protocol.   The amendments shall enter into force for any other Party on the ninetieth day after that party deposits its instrument of ratification, approval, formal confirmation or acceptance of the amendments.

6. For the purpose of this article, "Parties present and voting" means Parties present and casting an affirmative or negative vote.

Article 18
Adoption and amendment of annexes

1. The annexes to this Convention or to any protocol shall form an integral part of this Convention or of such a protocol, as the case may be and, unless expressly provided otherwise, a reference to this Convention or its protocols constitutes at the same time a reference to any annexes thereto.   Such annexes shall be restricted to scientific, technical and administrative matters.

2. Except as may be otherwise provided in any protocol with respect to its annexes, the following procedure shall apply to the proposal, adoption and entry into force of additional annexes to this Convention or of annexes to a protocol:

(a) Annexes to this Convention and its protocols shall be proposed and adopted according to the procedure laid down in article 17, paragraphs 2, 3 and 4;

(b) Any Party that is unable to accept an additional annex to this Convention or an annex to any protocol to which it is party shall so notify the Depositary, in writing, within six months from the date of the communication of the adoption by the Depositary.   The Depositary shall without delay notify all Parties of any such notification received.   A Party may at any time substitute an acceptance for a previous declaration of objection and the annexes shall thereupon enter into force for that Party;

(c) On the expiry of six months from the date of the circulation of the communication by the Depositary, the annex shall become effective for all Parties to this Convention or to any protocol concerned, which have not submitted a notification in accordance with the provision of subparagraph (b) above.

3. The proposal, adoption and entry into force of amendments to annexes to this Convention or to any protocol shall be subject to the same procedure as for the proposal, adoption and entry into force of annexes to the Convention or annexes to a protocol.   Annexes and amendments thereto shall take due account, *inter alia*, of relevant scientific and technical considerations.

4. If an additional annex or an amendment to an annex involves an amendment to this Convention or to any protocol, the additional annex or amended annex shall not enter into force until such time as the amendment to this Convention or to the protocol enters into force.

Article 19
Verification

Any Party which has reason to believe that another Party is acting or has acted in breach of its obligations under this Convention may inform the secretariat thereof, and in such an event, shall simultaneously and immediately inform, directly or through the secretariat, the Party against whom the allegations are made. All relevant information should be submitted by the secretariat to the Parties.

Article 20
Settlement of disputes

1. In case of a dispute between Parties as to the interpretation or application of, or compliance with, this Convention or any protocol thereto, they shall seek a settlement of the dispute through negotiation or any other peaceful means of their own choice.
2. If the Parties concerned cannot settle their dispute through the means mentioned in the preceding paragraph, the dispute, if the parties to the dispute agree, shall be submitted to the International Court of Justice or to arbitration under the conditions set out in annex VI on arbitration. However, failure to reach common agreement on submission of the dispute to the International Court of Justice or to arbitration shall not absolve the Parties from the responsibility of continuing to seek to resolve it by the means referred to in paragraph 1.
3. When ratifying, accepting, approving, formally confirming or acceding to this Convention, or at any time thereafter, a State or political and/or economic integration organization may declare that it recognizes as compulsory *ipso facto* and without special agreement, in relation to any Party accepting the same obligation:
   (a) submission of the dispute to the International Court of Justice; and/or
   (b) arbitration in accordance with the procedures set out in annex VI.
Such declaration shall be notified in writing to the secretariat which shall communicate it to the Parties.

Article 21
Signature

This Convention shall be open for signature by States, by Namibia, represented by the United Nations Council for Namibia, and by political and/or economic integration organizations, in Basel on 22 March 1989, at the Federal Department of Foreign Affairs of Switzerland in Berne from 23 March 1989 to 30 June 1989, and at United Nations Headquarters in New York from 1 July 1989 to 22 March 1990.

Article 22
Ratification, acceptance, formal confirmation or approval

1. This Convention shall be subject to ratification, acceptance or approval by States and by Namibia, represented by the United Nations Council for Namibia, and to formal confirmation or approval by political and/or economic integration organizations. Instruments of ratification, acceptance, formal confirmation, or approval shall be deposited with the Depositary.
2. Any organization referred to in paragraph 1 above which becomes a Party to this Convention without any of its member States being a Party shall be bound by all the obligations under the Convention. In the case of such organizations, one or more of whose member States is a Party to the Convention, the organization and its member

States shall decide on their respective responsibilities for the performance of their obligations under the Convention. In such cases, the organization and the member States shall not be entitled to exercise rights under the Convention concurrently.

3. In their instruments of formal confirmation or approval, the organizations referred to in paragraph 1 above shall declare the extent of their competence with respect to the matters governed by the Convention. These organizations shall also inform the Depositary, who will inform the Parties of any substantial modification in the extent of their competence.

Article 23
Accession

1. This Convention shall be open for accession by States, by Namibia, represented by the United Nations Council for Namibia, and by political and/or economic integration organizations from the day after the date on which the Convention is closed for signature. The instruments of accession shall be deposited with the Depositary.

2. In their instruments of accession, the organizations referred to in paragraph 1 above shall declare the extent of their competence with respect to the matters governed by the Convention. These organizations shall also inform the Depositary of any substantial modification in the extent of their competence.

3. The provisions of article 22, paragraph 2, shall apply to political and/or economic integration organizations which accede to this Convention.

Article 24
Right to vote

1. Except as provided for in paragraph 2 below, each Contracting Party to this Convention shall have one vote.

2. Political and/or economic integration organizations, in matters within their competence, in accordance with article 22, paragraph 3, and article 23, paragraph 2, shall exercise their right to vote with a number of votes equal to the number of their member States which are Parties to the Convention or the relevant protocol. Such organizations shall not exercise their right to vote if their member States exercise theirs, and vice versa.

Article 25
Entry into force

1. This Convention shall enter into force on the ninetieth day after the date of deposit of the twentieth instrument of ratification, acceptance, formal confirmation, approval or accession.

2. For each State or political and/or economic integration organization which ratifies, accepts, approves or formally confirms this Convention or acceded thereto after the date of the deposit of the twentieth instrument of ratification, acceptance, approval, formal confirmation or accession, it shall enter into force on the ninetieth day after the date of deposit by such State or political and/or economic integration organization of its instrument of ratification, acceptance, approval, formal confirmation or accession.

3. For the purposes of paragraphs 1 and 2 above, any instrument deposited by a political and/or economic integration organization shall not be counted as additional to those deposited by member States of such organizations.

Article 26
Reservations and declarations

1. No reservation or exception may be made to this Convention.
2. Paragraph 1 of this article does not preclude a State or political and/or economic integration organization, when signing, ratifying, accepting, approving, formally confirming or acceding to this Convention, from making declarations or statements, however phrased or named, with a view, *inter alia*, to the harmonization of its laws and regulations with the provisions of this Convention, provided that such declarations or statements do not purport to exclude or to modify the legal effects of the provisions of the Convention in their application to that State.

Article 27
Withdrawal

1. At any time after three years from the date on which this Convention has entered into force for a Party, that Party may withdraw from the Convention by giving written notification to the Depositary.
2. Withdrawal shall be effective one year from receipt of notification by the Depositary, or on such later date as may be specified in the notification.

Article 28
Depositary

The Secretary-General of the United Nations shall be the Depositary of this Convention and of any protocol thereto.

Article 29
Authentic texts

The original Arabic, Chinese, English, French, Russian and Spanish texts of this Convention are equally authentic.

IN WITNESS WHEREOF the undersigned, being duly authorized to that effect, have signed this Convention.

[Annexes I-VI, Final Act of Basel Conference and Conference Resolutions 1-8 omitted]

10.5 INTERNATIONAL CONVENTION ON SALVAGE, 1989

THE STATES PARTIES TO THE PRESENT CONVENTION,

RECOGNIZING the desirability of determining by agreement uniform international rules regarding salvage operations,

NOTING that substantial developments, in particular the increased concern for the protection of the environment, have demonstrated the need to review the international rules presently contained in the Convention for the Unification of Certain Rules of Law relating to Assistance and Salvage at Sea, done at Brussels, 23 September 1910,

CONSCIOUS of the major contribution which efficient and timely salvage operations can make to the safety of vessels and other property in danger and to the protection of the environment,

CONVINCED of the need to ensure that adequate incentives are available to persons who undertake salvage operations in respect of vessels and other property in danger,

HAVE AGREED as follows:

Chapter I – General provisions

Article 1
Definitions

For the purpose of this Convention:

(a) *Salvage operation* means any act or activity undertaken to assist a vessel or any other property in danger in navigable waters or in any other waters whatsoever;

(b) *Vessel* means any ship or craft, or any structure capable of navigation;

(c) *Property* means any property not permanently and intentionally attached to the shoreline and includes freight at risk;

(d) *Damage to the environment* means substantial physical damage to human health or to marine life or resources in coastal or inland waters or areas adjacent thereto, caused by pollution, contamination, fire, explosion or similar major incidents;

(e) *Payment* means any reward, remuneration or compensation due under this Convention;

(f) *Organization* means the International Maritime Organization;

(g) *Secretary-General* means the Secretary-General of the Organization.

Article 2
Application of the Convention

This Convention shall apply whenever judicial or arbitral proceedings relating to matters dealt with in this Convention are brought in a State Party.

Article 3
Platforms and drilling units

This Convention shall not apply to fixed or floating platforms or to mobile offshore drilling units when such platforms or units are on location engaged in the exploration, exploitation or production of sea-bed mineral resources.

Article 4
State-owned vessels

1. Without prejudice to article 5, this Convention shall not apply to warships or other non-commercial vessels owned or operated by a State and entitled, at the time of salvage operations, to sovereign immunity under generally recognized principles of international law unless that State decides otherwise.

2. Where a State Party decides to apply the Convention to its warships or other vessels described in paragraph 1, it shall notify the Secretary-General thereof specifying the terms and conditions of such application.

Article 5
Salvage operations controlled by public authorities

1. This Convention shall not affect any provisions of national law or any international convention relating to salvage operations by or under the control of public authorities.

2. Nevertheless, salvors carrying out such salvage operations shall be entitled to avail themselves of the rights and remedies provided for in this Convention in respect of salvage operations.

3. The extent to which a public authority under a duty to perform salvage operations may avail itself of the rights and remedies provided for in this Convention shall be determined by the law of the State where such authority is situated.

Article 6
Salvage contracts

1. This Convention shall apply to any salvage operations save to the extent that a contract otherwise provides expressly or by implication.

2. The master shall have the authority to conclude such contracts for salvage operations on behalf of the owner of the vessel. The master or the owner of the vessel shall have the authority to conclude such contracts on behalf of the owner of the property on board the vessel.

3. Nothing in this article shall affect the application of article 7 or duties to prevent or minimize damage to the environment.

Article 7
Annulment and modification of contracts

A contract or any terms thereof may be annulled or modified if:

(a) the contract has been entered into under undue influence or the influence of danger and its terms are inequitable; or

(b) the payment under the contract is in an excessive degree too large or too small for the services actually rendered.

Chapter II – Performance of salvage operations

Article 8
Duties of the salvor and of the owner and master

1. The salvor shall owe a duty to the owner of the vessel or other property in danger:

(a) to carry out the salvage operations with due care;

(b) in performing the duty specified in subparagraph (a), to exercise due care to prevent or miminize damage to the environment;

(c) whenever circumstances reasonably require, to seek assistance from other salvors; and

(d) to accept the intervention of other salvors when reasonably requested to do so by the owner or master of the vessel or other property in danger; provided however that the amount of his reward shall not be prejudiced should it be found that such a request was unreasonable.

2. The owner and master of the vessel or the owner of other property in danger shall owe a duty to the salvor:

(a) to co-operate fully with him during the course of the salvage operations;

(b) in so doing, to exercise due care to prevent or minimize damage to the environment; and

(c) when the vessel or other property has been brought to a place of safety, to accept redelivery when reasonably requested by the salvor to do so.

Article 9
Rights of coastal States

Nothing in this Convention shall affect the right of the coastal State concerned to take measures in accordance with generally recognized principles of international law to protect its coastline or related interests from pollution or the threat of pollution following upon a maritime casualty or acts relating to such a casualty which may reasonably be expected to result in major harmful consequences, including the right of a coastal State to give directions in relation to salvage operations.

Article 10
Duty to render assistance

1. Every master is bound, so far as he can do so without serious danger to his vessel and persons thereon, to render assistance to any person in danger of being lost at sea.
2. The States Parties shall adopt the measures necessary to enforce the duty set out in paragraph 1.
3. The owner of the vessel shall incur no liability for a breach of the duty of the master under paragraph 1.

Article 11
Co-operation

A State Party shall, whenever regulating or deciding upon matters relating to salvage operations such as admittance to ports of vessels in distress or the provision of facilities to salvors, take into account the need for co-operation between salvors, other interested parties and public authorities in order to ensure the efficient and successful performance of salvage operations for the purpose of saving life or property in danger as well as preventing damage to the environment in general.

Chapter III – Rights of salvors

Article 12
Conditions for reward

1. Salvage operations which have had useful result give right to a reward.
2. Except as otherwise provided, no payment is due under this Convention if the salvage operations have had no useful result.
3. This chapter shall apply, notwithstanding that the salved vessel and the vessel undertaking the salvage operations belong to the same owner.

Article 13
Criteria for fixing the reward

1. The reward shall be fixed with a view to encouraging salvage operations, taking into account the following criteria without regard to the order in which they are presented below:
    (a) the salved value of the vessel and other property;
    (b) the skill and efforts of the salvors in preventing or minimizing damage to the environment;
    (c) the measure of success obtained by the salvor;
    (d) the nature and degree of the danger;
    (e) the skill and efforts of the salvors in salving the vessel, other property and life;

(f) the time used and expenses and losses incurred by the salvors;

(g) the risk of liability and other risks run by the salvors or their equipment;

(h) the promptness of the services rendered;

(i) the availability and use of vessels or other equipment intended for salvage operations;

(j) the state of readiness and efficiency of the salvor's equipment and the value thereof.

2. Payment of a reward fixed according to paragraph 1 shall be made by all of the vessel and other property interests in proportion to their respective salved values. However, a State Party may in its national law provide that the payment of a reward has to be made by one of these interests, subject to a right of recourse of this interest against the other interests for their respective shares.   Nothing in this article shall prevent any right of defence.

3. The rewards, exclusive of any interest and recoverable legal costs that may be payable thereon, shall not exceed the salved value of the vessel and other property.

Article 14
Special compensation

1. If the salvor has carried out salvage operations in respect of a vessel which by itself or its cargo threatened damage to the environment and has failed to earn a reward under article 13 at least equivalent to the special compensation assessable in accordance with this article, he shall be entitled to special compensation from the owner of that vessel equivalent to his expenses as herein defined.

2. If, in the circumstances set out in paragraph 1, the salvor by his salvage operations has prevented or minimised damage to the environment, the special compensation payable by the owner to the salvor under paragraph 1 may be increased up to a maximum of 30 per cent of the expenses incurred by the salvor.   However, the tribunal, if it deems it fair and just to do so and bearing in mind the relevant criteria set out in article 13, paragraph 1, may increase such special compensation further, but in no event shall the total increase be more than 100 per cent of the expenses incurred by the salvor.

3. Salvor's expenses for the purpose of paragraphs 1 and 2 means the out-of-pocket expenses reasonably incurred by the salvor in the salvage operation and a fair rate for equipment and personnel actually and reasonably used in the salvage operation, taking into consideration the criteria set out in article 13, paragraph 1(h), (i) and (j).

4. The total special compensation under this article shall be paid only if and to the extent that such compensation is greater than any reward recoverable by the salvor under article 13.

5. If the salvor has been negligent and has thereby failed to prevent or minimize damage to the environment, he may be deprived of the whole or part of any special compensation due under this article.

6. Nothing in this article shall affect any right of recourse on the part of the owner of the vessel.

Article 15
Apportionment between salvors

1. The apportionment of a reward under article 13 between salvors shall be made on the basis of the criteria contained in that article.

2. The apportionment between the owner, master and other persons in the service of each salving vessel shall be determined by the law of the flag of that vessel. If the salvage has not been carried out from a vessel, the apportionment shall be determined by the law governing the contract between the salvor and his servants.

Article 16
Salvage of persons

1. No remuneration is due from persons whose lives are saved, but nothing in this article shall affect the provisions of national law on this subject.
2. A salvor of human life, who has taken part in the services rendered on the occasion of the accident giving rise to salvage, is entitled to a fair share of the payment awarded to the salvor for salving the vessel or other property or preventing or minimizing damage to the environment.

Article 17
Services rendered under existing contracts

No payment is due under the provisions of this Convention unless the services rendered exceed what can be reasonably considered as due performance of a contract entered into before the danger arose.

Article 18
The effect of salvor's misconduct

A salvor may be deprived of the whole or part of the payment due under this Convention to the extent that the salvage operations have become necessary or more difficult because of fault or neglect on his part or if the salvor has been guilty of fraud or other dishonest conduct.

Article 19
Prohibition of salvage operations

Services rendered notwithstanding the express and reasonable prohibition of the owner or master of the vessel or the owner of any other property in danger which is not and has not been on board the vessel shall not give rise to payment under this Convention.

Chapter IV – Claims and actions

Article 20
Maritime lien

1. Nothing in this Convention shall affect the salvor's maritime lien under any international convention or national law.
2. The salvor may not enforce his maritime lien when satisfactory security for his claim, including interest and costs, has been duly tendered or provided.

Article 21
Duty to provide security

1. Upon the request of the salvor a person liable for a payment due under this Convention shall provide satisfactory security for the claim, including interest and costs of the salvor.

2. Without prejudice to paragraph 1, the owner of the salved vessel shall use his best endeavours to ensure that the owners of the cargo provide satisfactory security for the claims against them including interest and costs before the cargo is released.

3 The salved vessel and other property shall not, without the consent of the salvor, be removed from the port or place at which they first arrive after the completion of the salvage operations until satisfactory security has been put up for the salvor's claim against the relevant vessel or property.

Article 22
Interim payment

1. The tribunal having jurisdiction over the claim of the salvor may, by interim decision, order that the salvor shall be paid on account such amount as seems fair and just, and on such terms including terms as to security where appropriate, as may be fair and just according to the circumstances of the case.

2. In the event of an interim payment under this article the security provided under article 21 shall be reduced accordingly.

Article 23
Limitation of actions

1. Any action relating to payment under this Convention shall be time-barred if judicial or arbitral proceedings have not been instituted within a period of two years. The limitation period commences on the day on which the salvage operations are terminated.

2. The person against whom a claim is made may at any time during the running of the limitation period extend that period by a declaration to the claimant. This period may in the like manner be further extended.

3. An action for indemnity by a person liable may be instituted even after the expiration of the limitation period provided for in the preceding paragraphs, if brought within the time allowed by the law of the State where proceedings are instituted.

Article 24
Interest

The right of the salvor to interest on any payment due under this Convention shall be determined according to the law of the State in which the tribunal seized of the case is situated.

Article 25
State-owned cargoes

Unless the State owner consents, no provision of this Convention shall be used as a basis for the seizure, arrest or detention by any legal process of, nor for any proceedings *in rem* against, non-commercial cargoes owned by a State and entitled, at the time of the salvage operations, to sovereign immunity under generally recognized principles of international law.

Article 26
Humanitarian cargoes

No provision of this Convention shall be used as a basis for the seizure, arrest or detention of humanitarian cargoes donated by a State, if such State has agreed to pay for salvage services rendered in respect of such humanitarian cargoes.

Article 27
Publication of arbitral awards

States Parties shall encourage, as far as possible and with the consent of the parties, the publication of arbitral awards made in salvage cases.

Chapter V – Final clauses

Article 28
Signature, ratification, acceptance, approval and accession

1. This Convention shall be open for signature at the headquarters of the Organization from 1 July 1989 to 30 June 1990 and shall thereafter remain open for accession.
2. States may express their consent to be bound by this Convention by:
    (a) signature without reservation as to ratification, acceptance or approval; or
    (b) signature subject to ratification, acceptance or approval, followed by ratification, acceptance or approval; or
    (c) accession.
3. Ratification, acceptance, approval or accession shall be effected by the deposit of an instrument to that effect with the Secretary-General.

Article 29
Entry into Force

1. This Convention shall enter into force one year after the date on which 15 States have expressed their consent to be bound by it.
2. For a State which expresses its consent to be bound by this Convention after the conditions for entry into force thereof have been met, such consent shall take effect one year after the date of expression of such consent.

Article 30
Reservations

1. Any State may, at the time of signature, ratification, acceptance, approval or accession, reserve the right not to apply the provisions of this Convention:
    (a) when the salvage operation takes place in inland waters and all vessels involved are of inland navigation;
    (b) when the salvage operations take place in inland waters and no vessel is involved.
    (c) when all interested parties are nationals of that State;
    (d) when the property involved is maritime cultural property of prehistoric, archaeological or historical interest and is situated on the sea-bed.
2. Reservations made at the time of signature are subject to confirmation upon ratification, acceptance or approval.
3. Any State which has made a reservation to this Convention may withdraw it at any time by means of a notification addressed to the Secretary-General. Such withdrawal

shall take effect on the date the notification is received. If the notification states that the withdrawal of a reservation is to take effect on a date specified therein, and such date is later than the date the notification is received by the Secretary-General, the withdrawal shall take effect on such later date.

Article 31
Denunciation

1. This Convention may be denounced by any State Party at any time after the expiry of one year from the date on which this Convention enters into force for that State.
2. Denunciation shall be effected by the deposit of an instrument of denunciation with the Secretary-General.
3. A denunciation shall take effect one year, or such longer period as may be specified in the instrument of denunciation, after the receipt of the instrument of denunciation by the Secretary-General.

Article 32
Revision and amendment

1. A conference for the purpose of revising or amending this Convention may be convened by the Organization.
2. The Secretary-General shall convene a conference of the States Parties to this Convention for revising or amending the Convention, at the request of eight States Parties, or one-fourth of the States Parties, whichever is the higher figure.
3. Any consent to be bound by this Convention expressed after the date of entry into force of an amendment to this Convention shall be deemed to apply to the Convention as amended.

Article 33
Depositary

1. This Convention shall be deposited with the Secretary-General.
2. The Secretary-General shall:
   (a) inform all States which have signed this Convention or acceded thereto, and all members of the Organization, of:
   (i)   each new signature or deposit of an instrument of ratification, acceptance, approval or accession together with the date thereof;
   (ii)   the date of the entry into force of this Convention;
   (iii)   the deposit of any instrument of denunciation of this Convention together with the date on which it is received and the date on which the denunciation takes effect;
   (iv)   any amendment adopted in conformity with article 32;
   (v)   the receipt of any reservation, declaration or notification made under this Convention.
   (b) transmit certified true copies of this Convention to all States which have signed this Convention or acceded thereto.
3. As soon as this Convention enters into force, a certified true copy thereof shall be transmitted by the Depositary to the Secretary-General of the United Nations for registration and publication in accordance with Article 102 of the Charter of the United Nations.

Article 34
Languages

This Convention is established in a single original in the Arabic, Chinese, English, French, Russian and Spanish languages, each text being equally authentic.

IN WITNESS WHEREOF the undersigned, being duly authorized by their respective Governments for that purpose, have signed this Convention.

DONE AT LONDON this twenty-eighth day of April one thousand nine hundred and eighty-nine.

11 The Regime of Marine Scientific Research

11.1 UNITED NATIONS CONVENTION ON THE LAW OF THE SEA, 1982: PART XIII: MARINE SCIENTIFIC RESEARCH; AND PART XIV: DEVELOPMENT AND TRANSFER OF MARINE TECHNOLOGY

PART XIII
MARINE SCIENTIFIC RESEARCH
SECTION 1. GENERAL PROVISIONS

Article 238
Right to conduct marine scientific research

All States, irrespective of their geographical location, and competent international organizations have the right to conduct marine scientific research subject to the rights and duties of other States as provided for in this Convention.

Article 239
Promotion of marine scientific research

States and competent international organizations shall promote and facilitate the development and conduct of marine scientific research in accordance with this Convention.

Article 240
General principles for the conduct of marine scientific research

In the conduct of marine scientific research the following principles shall apply:

(a) marine scientific research shall be conducted exclusively for peaceful purposes;
(b) marine scientific research shall be conducted with appropriate scientific methods and means compatible with this Convention;
(c) marine scientific research shall not unjustifiably interfere with other legitimate uses of the sea compatible with this Convention and shall be duly respected in the course of such uses;
(d) marine scientific research shall be conducted in compliance with all relevant regulations adopted in conformity with this Convention including those for the protection and preservation of the marine environment.

Article 241
Non-recognition of marine scientific research activities as the legal basis for claims

Marine scientific research activities shall not constitute the legal basis for any claim to any part of the marine environment or its resources.

SECTION 2. INTERNATIONAL CO-OPERATION

Article 242
Promotion of international co-operation

1. States and competent international organizations shall, in accordance with the principle of respect for sovereignty and jurisdiction and on the basis of mutual benefit, promote international co-operation in marine scientific research for peaceful purposes.
2. In this context, without prejudice to the rights and duties of States under this Convention, a State, in the application of this Part, shall provide, as appropriate, other States with a reasonable opportunity to obtain from it, or with its co-operation, information necessary to prevent and control damage to the health and safety of persons and to the marine environment.

Article 243
Creation of favourable conditions

States and competent international organizations shall co-operate, through the conclusion of bilateral and multilateral agreements, to create favourable conditions for the conduct of marine scientific research in the marine environment and to integrate the efforts of scientists in studying the essence of phenomena and processes occurring in the marine environment and the inter-relations between them.

Article 244
Publication and dissemination of information and knowledge

1. States and competent international organizations shall, in accordance with this Convention, make available by publication and dissemination through appropriate channels information on proposed major programmes and their objectives as well as knowledge resulting from marine scientific research.
2. For this purpose, States, both individually and in co-operation with other States and with competent international organizations, shall actively promote the flow of scientific data and information and the transfer of knowledge resulting from marine scientific

research, especially to developing States, as well as the strengthening of the autonomous marine scientific research capabilities of developing States through, *inter alia*, programmes to provide adequate education and training of their technical and scientific personnel.

SECTION 3. CONDUCT AND PROMOTION OF MARINE SCIENTIFIC RESEARCH

Article 245
Marine scientific research in the territorial sea

Coastal States, in the exercise of their sovereignty, have the exclusive right to regulate, authorize and conduct marine scientific research in their territorial sea. Marine scientific research therein shall be conducted only with the express consent of and under the conditions set forth by the coastal State.

Article 246
Marine Scientific research in the exclusive economic zone and on the continental shelf

1. Coastal States, in the exercise of their jurisdiction, have the right to regulate, authorize and conduct marine scientific research in their exclusive economic zone and on their continental shelf in accordance with the relevant provisions of this Convention.
2. Marine scientific research in the exclusive economic zone and on the continental shelf shall be conducted with the consent of the coastal State.
3. Coastal States shall, in normal circumstances, grant their consent for marine scientific research projects by other States or competent international organizations in their exclusive economic zone or on their continental shelf to be carried out in accordance with this Convention exclusively for peaceful purposes and in order to increase scientific knowledge of the marine environment for the benefit of all mankind. To this end, coastal States shall establish rules and procedures ensuring that such consent will not be delayed or denied unreasonably.
4. For the purposes of applying paragraph 3, normal circumstances may exist in spite of the absence of diplomatic relations between the coastal State and the researching State.
5. Coastal States may however in their discretion withhold their consent to the conduct of a marine scientific research project of another State or competent international organization in the exclusive economic zone or on the continental shelf of the coastal State if that project:
(a) is of direct significance for the exploration and exploitation of natural resources, whether living or non-living;
(b) involves drilling into the continental shelf, the use of explosives or the introduction of harmful substances into the marine environment;
(c) involves the construction, operation or use of artificial islands, installations and structures referred to in articles 60 and 80;
(d) contains information communicated pursuant to article 248 regarding the nature and objectives of the project which is inaccurate or if the researching State or competent international organization has outstanding obligations to the coastal State from a prior research project.
6. Notwithstanding the provisions of paragraph 5, coastal States may not exercise their discretion to withhold consent under subparagraph (a) of that paragraph in respect of marine scientific research projects to be undertaken in accordance with the provisions

of this Part on the continental shelf, beyond 200 nautical miles from the baselines from which the breadth of the territorial sea is measured, outside those specific areas which coastal States may at any time publicly designate as areas in which exploitation or detailed exploratory operations focused on those areas are occurring or will occur within a reasonable period of time. Coastal States shall give reasonable notice of the designation of such areas, as well as any modifications thereto, but shall not be obliged to give details of the operations therein.

7. The provisions of paragraph 6 are without prejudice to the rights of coastal States over the continental shelf as established in article 77.

8. Marine scientific research activities referred to in this article shall not unjustifiably interfere with activities undertaken by coastal States in the exercise of their sovereign rights and jurisdiction provided for in this Convention.

Article 247
Marine scientific research projects undertaken by or under the auspices of international organizations

A coastal State which is a member of or has a bilateral agreement with an international organization, and in whose exclusive economic zone or on whose continental shelf that organization wants to carry out a marine scientific research project, directly or under its auspices, shall be deemed to have authorized the project to be carried out in conformity with the agreed specifications if that State approved the detailed project when the decision was made by the organization for the undertaking of the project, or is willing to participate in it, and has not expressed any objection within four months of notification of the project by the organization to the coastal State.

Article 248
Duty to provide information to the coastal State

States and competent international organizations which intend to undertake marine scientific research in the exclusive economic zone or on the continental shelf of a coastal State shall, not less than six months in advance of the expected starting date of the marine scientific research project, provide that State with a full description of:

(a) the nature and objectives of the project;

(b) the method and means to be used, including name, tonnage, type and class of vessels and a description of scientific equipment;

(c) the precise geographical areas in which the project is to be conducted;

(d) the expected date of first appearance and final departure of the research vessels, or deployment of the equipment and its removal, as appropriate;

(e) the name of the sponsoring institution, its director, and the person in charge of the project; and

(f) the extent to which it is considered that the coastal State should be able to participate or to be represented in the project.

Article 249
Duty to comply with certain conditions

1. States and competent international organizations when undertaking marine scientific research in the exclusive economic zone or on the continental shelf of a coastal State shall comply with the following conditions:

(a) ensure the right of the coastal State, if it so desires, to participate or be represented in the marine scientific research project, especially on board research vessels and

other craft or scientific research installations, when practicable, without payment of any remuneration to the scientists of the coastal State and without obligation to contribute towards the coasts of the project;
(b) provide the coastal State, at its request, with preliminary reports, as soon as practicable, and with the final results and conclusions after the completion of the research;
(c) undertake to provide access for the coastal State, at its request, to all data and samples derived from the marine scientific research project and likewise to furnish it with data which may be copied and samples which may be divided without detriment to their scientific value;
(d) if requested, provide the coastal State with an assessment of such data, samples and research results or provide assistance in their assessment or interpretation;
(e) ensure, subject to paragraph 2, that the research results are made internationally available through appropriate national or international channels, as soon as practicable;
(f) inform the coastal State immediately of any major change in the research programme;
(g) unless otherwise agreed, remove the scientific research installations or equipment once the research is completed.
2. This article is without prejudice to the conditions established by the laws and regulations of the coastal State for the exercise of its discretion to grant or withhold consent pursuant to article 246, paragraph 5, including requiring prior agreement for making internationally available the research results of a project of direct significance for the exploration and exploitation of natural resources.

Article 250
Communications concerning marine scientific research projects

Communications concerning the marine scientific research projects shall be made through appropriate official channels, unless otherwise agreed.

Article 251
General criteria and guidelines

States shall seek to promote through competent international organizations the establishment of general criteria and guidelines to assist States in ascertaining the nature and implications of marine scientific research.

Article 252
Implied consent

States or competent international organizations may proceed with a marine scientific research project six months after the date upon which the information required pursuant to article 248 was provided to the coastal State unless within four months of the receipt of the communication concerning such information the coastal State has informed the State or organization conducting the research that:
(a) it has withheld its consent under the provisions of article 246; or
(b) the information given by that State or competent international organization regarding the nature or objectives of the project does not conform to the manifestly evident facts; or
(c) it requires supplementary information relevant to conditions and the information provided for under articles 248 and 249; or

(d) outstanding obligations exist with respect to a previous marine scientific research project carried out by that State or organization, with regard to conditions established in article 249.

Article 253
Suspension or cessation of marine scientific research activities

1. A coastal State shall have the right to require the suspension of any marine scientific research activities in progress within its exclusive economic zone or on its continental shelf if:
(a) the research activities are not being conducted in accordance with the information communicated as provided under article 248 upon which the consent of the coastal State was based; or
(b) the State or competent international organization conducting the research activities fails to comply with the provisions of article 249 concerning the rights of the coastal State with respect to the marine scientific research project.
2. A coastal State shall have the right to require the cessation of any marine scientific research activities in case of any non-compliance with the provisions of article 248 which amounts to a major change in the research project or the research activities.
3. A coastal State may also require cessation of marine scientific research activities if any of the situations contemplated in paragraph 1 are not rectified within a reasonable period of time.
4. Following notification by the coastal State of its decision to order suspension or cessation, States or competent international organizations authorized to conduct marine scientific research activities shall terminate the research activities that are the subject of such a notification.
5. An order of suspension under paragraph 1 shall be lifted by the coastal State and the marine scientific research activities allowed to continue once the researching State or competent international organization has complied with the conditions required under articles 248 and 249.

Article 254
Rights of neighbouring land-locked and geographically disadvantaged States

1. States and competent international organizations which have submitted to a coastal State a project to undertake marine scientific research referred to in article 246, paragraph 3, shall give notice to the neighbouring land-locked and geographically disadvantaged States of the proposed research project, and shall notify the coastal State thereof.
2. After the consent has been given for the proposed marine scientific research project by the coastal State concerned, in accordance with article 246 and other relevant provisions of this Convention, States and competent international organizations undertaking such a project shall provide to the neighbouring land-locked and geographically disadvantaged States, at their request and when appropriate, relevant information as specified in article 248 and article 249, paragraph 1(f).
3. The neighbouring land-locked and geographically disadvantaged States referred to above shall, at their request, be given the opportunity to participate, whenever feasible, in the proposed marine scientific research project through qualified experts appointed by them and not objected to by the coastal State, in accordance with the conditions agreed for the project, in conformity with the provisions of this Convention, between

the coastal State concerned and the State or competent international organizations conducting the marine scientific research.

4. States and competent international organizations referred to in paragraph 1 shall provide to the above-mentioned land-locked and geographically disadvantaged States, at their request, the information and assistance specified in article 249, paragraph 1(d), subject to the provisions of article 249, paragraph 2.

Article 255
Measures to facilitate marine scientific research and assist research vessels

States shall endeavour to adopt reasonable rules, regulations and procedures to promote and facilitate marine scientific research conducted in accordance with this Convention beyond their territorial sea and, as appropriate, to facilitate, subject to the provisions of their laws and regulations, access to their harbours and promote assistance for marine scientific research vessels which comply with the relevant provisions of this Part.

Article 256
Marine scientific research in the Area

All States, irrespective of their geographical location, and competent international organizations have the right, in conformity with the provisions of Part XI, to conduct marine scientific research in the Area.

Article 257
Marine scientific research in the water column beyond the exclusive economic zone

All States, irrespective of their geographical location, and competent international organizations have the right, in conformity with this Convention, to conduct marine scientific research in the water column beyond the limits of the exclusive economic zone.

SECTION 4. SCIENTIFIC RESEARCH INSTALLATIONS OR EQUIPMENT IN THE MARINE ENVIRONMENT

Article 258
Deployment and use

The deployment and use of any type of scientific research installations or equipment in any area of the marine environment shall be subject to the same conditions as are prescribed in this Convention for the conduct of marine scientific research in any such area.

Article 259
Legal status

The installations or equipment referred to in this section do not possess the status of islands. They have no territorial sea of their own, and their presence does not affect the delimitation of the territorial sea, the exclusive economic zone or the continental shelf.

Article 260
Safety zones

Safety zones of a reasonable breadth not exceeding a distance of 500 metres may be created around scientific research installations in accordance with the relevant provisions of this Convention.   All States shall ensure that such safety zones are respected by their vessels.

Article 261
Non-interference with shipping routes

The deployment and use of any type of scientific research installations or equipment shall not constitute an obstacle to established international shipping routes.

Article 262
Identification markings and warning signals

Installations or equipment referred to in this section shall bear identification markings indicating the State of registry or the international organization to which they belong and shall have adequate internationally agreed warning signals to ensure safety at sea and the safety of air navigation, taking into account rules and standards established by competent international organizations.

SECTION 5. RESPONSIBILITY AND LIABILITY

Responsibility and liability

1.   States and competent international organizations shall be responsible for ensuring that marine scientific research, whether undertaken by them or on their behalf, is conducted in accordance with this Convention.
2.   States and competent international organizations shall be responsible and liable for the measures they take in contravention of this Convention in respect of marine scientific research conducted by other States, their natural or juridical persons or by competent international organizations, and shall provide compensation for damage resulting from such measures.
3.   States and competent international organizations shall be responsible and liable pursuant to article 235 for damage caused by pollution of the marine environment arising out of marine scientific research undertaken by them or on their behalf.

SECTION 6. SETTLEMENT OF DISPUTES AND INTERIM MEASURES

Article 264
Settlement of disputes

Disputes concerning the interpretation or application of the provisions of this Convention with regard to marine scientific research shall be settled in accordance with Part XV, sections 2 and 3.

Article 265
Interim measures

Pending settlement of a dispute in accordance with Part XV, sections 2 and 3, the State or competent international organization authorised to conduct a marine scientific research project shall not allow research activities to commence or continue without the express consent of the coastal State concerned.

PART XIV
DEVELOPMENT AND TRANSFER OF MARINE TECHNOLOGY

SECTION 1. GENERAL PROVISIONS

Article 266
Promotion of the development and transfer of marine technology

1. States, directly or through competent international organizations, shall co-operate in accordance with their capabilities to promote actively the development and transfer of marine science and marine technology on fair and reasonable terms and conditions.

2. States shall promote the development of the marine scientific and technological capacity of States which may need and request technical assistance in this field, particularly developing States, including land-locked and geographically disadvantaged States, with regard to the exploration, exploitation, conservation and management of marine resources, the protection and preservation of the marine environment, marine scientific research and other activities in the marine environment compatible with this Convention, with a view to accelerating the social and economic development of the developing States.

3. States shall endeavour to foster favourable economic and legal conditions for the transfer of marine technology for the benefit of all parties concerned on an equitable basis.

Article 267
Protection of legitimate interests

States, in promoting co-operation pursuant to article 266, shall have due regard for all legitimate interests including, *inter alia*, the rights and duties of holders, suppliers and recipients of marine technology.

Article 268
Basic objectives

States, directly or through competent international organizations, shall promote:
(a) the acquisition, evaluation and dissemination of marine technological knowledge and facilitate access to such information and data;
(b) the development of appropriate marine technology;
(c) the development of the necessary technological infrastructure to facilitate the transfer of marine technology;
(d) the development of human resources through training and education of nationals of developing States and countries and especially the nationals of the least developed among them;
(e) international co-operation at all levels, particularly at the regional, sub-regional and bilateral levels.

Article 269
Measures to achieve the basic objectives

In order to achieve the objectives referred to in article 268, States, directly or through competent international organizations, shall endeavour, *inter alia*, to:

(a) establish programmes of technical co-operation for the effective transfer of all kinds of marine technology to States which may need and request technical assistance in this field, particularly the developing land-locked and geographically disadvantaged States, as well as other developing States which have not been able either to establish or develop their own technological capacity in marine science and in the exploration and exploitation of marine resources or to develop the infrastructure of such technology;

(b) promote favourable conditions for the conclusion of agreements, contracts and other similar arrangements, under equitable and reasonable conditions;

(c) hold conferences, seminars and symposia on scientific and technological subjects, in particular on policies and methods for the transfer of marine technology;

(d) promote the exchange of scientists and of technological and other experts;

(e) undertake projects and promote joint ventures and other forms of bilateral and multilateral co-operation.

SECTION 2. INTERNATIONAL CO-OPERATION

Article 270
Ways and means of international co-operation

International co-operation for the development and transfer of marine technology shall be carried out, where feasible and appropriate, through existing bilateral, regional or multilateral programmes, and also through expanded and new programmes in order to facilitate marine scientific research, the transfer of marine technology, particularly in new fields, and appropriate international funding for ocean research and development.

Article 271
Guidelines, criteria and standards

States, directly or through competent international organizations, shall promote the establishment of generally accepted guidelines, criteria and standards for the transfer of marine technology on a bilateral basis or within the framework of international organizations and other fora, taking into account, in particular, the interests and needs of developing States.

Article 272
Co-ordination of international programmes

In the field of transfer of marine technology, States shall endeavour to ensure that competent international organizations co-ordinate their activities, including any regional or global programmes, taking into account the interests and needs of developing States, particularly land-locked and geographically disadvantaged States.

Article 273
Co-operation with international organizations and the Authority

States shall co-operate actively with competent international organizations and the Authority to encourage and facilitate the transfer to developing States, their nationals and the Enterprise of skills and marine technology with regard to activities in the Area.

Article 274
Objectives of the Authority

Subject to all legitimate interests including, *inter alia*, the rights and duties of holders, suppliers and recipients of technology, the Authority, with regard to activities in the Area, shall ensure that:

(a) on the basis of the principle of equitable geographical distribution, nationals of developing States, whether coastal, land-locked or geographically disadvantaged, shall be taken on for the purposes of training as members of the managerial, research and technical staff constituted for its undertakings;

(b) the technical documentation on the relevant equipment, machinery, devices and processes is made available to all States, in particular developing States, and the acquisition by their nationals of the necessary skills and know-how, including professional training;

(c) adequate provision is made by the Authority to facilitate the acquisition of technical assistance in the field of marine technology by States which may need and request it, in particular developing States, and the acquisition by their nationals of the necessary skills and know-how, including professional training;

(d) States which may need and request technical assistance in this field, in particular developing States, are assisted in the acquisition of necessary equipment, processes, plant and other technical know-how through any financial arrangements provided for in this Convention.

SECTION 3. NATIONAL AND REGIONAL MARINE SCIENTIFIC AND TECHNOLOGICAL CENTRES

Article 275
Establishment of national centres

1. States, directly or through competent international organizations and the Authority, shall promote the establishment, particularly in developing coastal States, of national marine scientific and technological research centres and the strengthening of existing national centres, in order to stimulate and advance the conduct of marine scientific research by developing coastal States and to enhance their national capabilities to utilize and preserve their marine resources for their economic benefit.

2. States, through competent international organizations and the Authority, shall give adequate support to facilitate the establishment and strengthening of such national centres so as to provide for advanced training facilities and necessary equipment, skills and know-how as well as technical experts to such States which may need and request such assistance.

Article 276
Establishment of regional centres

1. States, in co-ordination with the competent international organizations, the Authority and national marine scientific and technological research institutions, shall promote the establishment of regional marine scientific and technological research centres, particularly in developing States, in order to stimulate and advance the conduct of marine scientific research by developing States and foster the transfer of marine technology.
2. All States of a region shall co-operate with the regional centres therein to ensure the more effective achievement of their objectives.

Article 277
Functions of regional centres

The functions of such regional centres shall include, *inter alia*:
(a) training and educational programmes at all levels on various aspects of marine scientific and technological research, particularly marine biology, including conservation and management of living resources, oceanography, hydrography, engineering, geological exploration of the sea-bed, mining and desalination technologies;
(b) management studies;
(c) study programmes related to the protection and preservation of the marine environment and the prevention, reduction and control of pollution;
(d) organization of regional conferences, seminars and symposia;
(e) acquisition and processing of marine scientific and technological data and information;
(f) prompt dissemination of results of marine scientific and technological research in readily available publications;
(g) publicizing national policies with regard to the transfer of marine technology and systematic comparative study of those policies;
(h) compilation and systematization of information on the marketing of technology and on contracts and other arrangements concerning patents;
(i) technical co-operation with other States of the region.

SECTION 4. CO-OPERATION AMONG INTERNATIONAL ORGANIZATIONS

Article 278
Co-operation among international organizations

The competent international organizations referred to in this Part and in Part XIII shall take all appropriate measures to ensure, either directly or in close co-operation among themselves, the effective discharge of their functions and responsibilities under this Part.

12 The Regime of Seabed Mining

12.1 NOTE VERBALE OF 17 AUGUST 1967 FROM MALTA TO UN SECRETARY-GENERAL (A/6695, 18 AUGUST 1967)

REQUEST FOR THE INCLUSION OF A SUPPLEMENTARY ITEM IN THE AGENDA OF THE TWENTY-SECOND SESSION

DECLARATION AND TREATY CONCERNING THE RESERVATION EXCLUSIVELY FOR PEACEFUL PURPOSES OF THE SEABED AND OF THE OCEAN FLOOR, UNDERLYING THE SEAS BEYOND THE LIMITS OF PRESENT NATIONAL JURISDICTION, AND THE USE OF THEIR RESOURCES IN THE INTERESTS OF MANKIND

Note verbale dated 17 August 1967 from the Permanent Mission of Malta to the United Nations addressed to the Secretary-General

The Permanent Mission of Malta to the United Nations presents its compliments to the Secretary-General of the United Nations and has the honour to propose under rule 14 of the rules of procedure of the General Assembly the inclusion of the following item in the agenda of the twenty-second session of the General Assembly: "Declaration and treaty concerning the reservation exclusively for peaceful purposes of the seabed and of the ocean floor, underlying the seas beyond the limits of present national jurisdiction, and the use of their resources in the interests of mankind".

An explanatory memorandum is attached in accordance with rule 20 of the rules of procedure.

MEMORANDUM

1. The seabed and the ocean floor are estimated to constitute approximately five-sevenths of the world's area. The seabed and ocean floor, underlying the seas outside present territorial waters and/or the continental shelves, are the only areas of our planet which have not yet been appropriated for national use, because they have been relatively inaccessible and their use for defence purposes or the economic exploitation of their resources was not technologically feasible.

2. In view of rapid progress in the development of new techniques by technologically advanced countries, it is feared that the situation will change and that the seabed and the ocean floor, underlying the seas beyond present national jurisdiction, will become progressively and competitively subject to national appropriation and use. This is likely to result in the militarizarion of the accessible ocean floor through the establishment of fixed military installations and in the exploitation and depletion of resources of immense potential benefit to the world, for the national advantage of technologically developed countries.

3. It is, therefore, considered that the time has come to declare the seabed and the ocean floor a common heritage of mankind and that immediate steps should be taken to draft a treaty embodying, *inter alia*, the following principles:

(a) The seabed and the ocean floor, underlying the seas beyond the limits of present national jurisdiction, are not subject to national appropriation in any manner whatsoever;

(b) The exploration of the seabed and of the ocean floor, underlying the seas beyond the limits of present national jurisdiction, shall be undertaken in a manner consistent with the Principles and Purposes of the Charter of the United Nations;

(c) The use of the seabed and of the ocean floor, underlying the seas beyond the limits of present national jurisdiction, and their economic exploitation shall be undertaken with the aim of safeguarding the interests of mankind. The net financial benefits derived from the use and exploitation of the seabed and of the ocean floor shall be used primarily to promote the development of poor countries;

(d) The seabed and the ocean floor, underlying the seas beyond the limits of present national jurisdiction, shall be reserved exclusively for peaceful purposes in perpetuity.

4. It is believed that the proposed treaty should envisage the creation of an international agency (a) to assume jurisdiction, as a trustee for all countries, over the seabed and the ocean floor, underlying the seas beyond the limits of present national jurisdiction; (b) to regulate, supervise and control all activities thereon; and (c) to ensure that the activities undertaken conform to the principles and provisions of the proposed treaty.

12.2 DECLARATION OF PRINCIPLES GOVERNING THE SEABED AND THE OCEAN FLOOR AND THE SUBSOIL THEREOF BEYOND THE LIMITS OF NATIONAL JURISDICTION, ADOPTED BY UN GENERAL ASSEMBLY ON 17 DECEMBER 1970 (A/RES/2749 (XXV))

The General Assembly,
Recalling its resolutions 2340 (XXII) of 18 December 1967, 2467 (XXIII) of 21 December 1968, and 2574 (XXIV) of 15 December 1969, concerning the area to which the title of the item refers,

Affirming that there is an area of the seabed and the ocean floor, and the subsoil thereof, beyond the limits of national jurisdiction, the precise limits of which are yet to be determined,

Recognising that the existing legal regime of the high seas does not provide substantive rules for regulating the exploration of the aforesaid area and the exploitation of its resources,

Convinced that the area shall be reserved exclusively for peaceful purposes and that the exploration of the area and the exploitation of its resources shall be carried out for the benefit of mankind as a whole,

Believing it essential that an international regime applying to the area and its resources and including appropriate international machinery should be established as soon as possible,

Bearing in mind that the development and use of the area and its resources shall be undertaken in such a manner as to foster healthy development of the world economy and balanced growth of international trade, and to minimize any adverse economic effects caused by fluctuation of prices of raw materials resulting from such activities,

Solemnly declares that:

1. The seabed and ocean floor, and the subsoil thereof, beyond the limits of national jurisdiction (hereinafter referred to as the area), as well as the resources of the area, are the common heritage of mankind.

2. The area shall not be subject to appropriation by any means by States or persons, natural or juridical, and no State shall claim or exercise sovereignty or sovereign rights over any part thereof.

3. No State or person, natural or juridical, shall claim, exercise or acquire rights with respect to the area or its resources incompatible with the international regime to be established and the principles of this Declaration.

4. All activities regarding the exploration of the resources of the area and other related activities shall be governed by the international regime to be established.

5. The area shall be open to use exclusively for peaceful purposes by all States whether coastal or land-locked, without discrimination, in accordance with the international regime to be established.

6. States shall act in the area in accordance with applicable principles and rules of international law including the Charter of the United Nations and the Declaration on Principles of International Law concerning Friendly Relations and Co-operation among States in accordance with the Charter of the United Nations, adopted by the General Assembly on 24 October 1970, in the interests of maintaining international peace and security and promoting international co-operation and mutual understanding.

7. The exploration of the area and the exploitation of its resources shall be carried out for the benefit of mankind as a whole, irrespective of the geographical location of States, whether land-locked or coastal, and taking into particular consideration the interests and needs of the developing countries.

8. The area shall be reserved exclusively for peaceful purposes, without prejudice to any measures which have been or may be agreed upon in the context of international negotiations undertaken in the field of disarmament and which may be applicable to a broader area. One or more international agreements shall be concluded as soon as possible in order to implement effectively this principle and to constitute a step towards the exclusion of the seabed, the ocean floor and the subsoil thereof from the arms race.

9. On the basis of the principles of this Declaration, an international regime applying to the area and its resources and including appropriate international machinery to give effect to its provisions shall be established by an international treaty of a

universal character, generally agreed upon. The regime shall, *inter alia*, provide for the orderly and safe development and rational management of the area and its resources and for expanding opportunities in the use thereof and ensure the equitable sharing by States in the benefits therefrom, taking into particular consideration the interest and needs of the developing countries, whether land-locked or coastal.

10. States shall promote international co-operation in scientific research exclusively for peaceful purposes:

(a) By participation in international programmes and by encouraging co-operation in scientific research by personnel of different countries;

(b) Through effective publication of research programmes and dissemination of the results of research through international channels;

(c) By co-operation in measures to strengthen research capabilities of developing countries, including the participation of their nationals in research programmes.

No such activity shall form the legal basis for any claims with respect to any part of the area or its resources.

11. With respect to activities in the area and acting in conformity with the international regime to be established, States shall take appropriate measures for and shall co-operate in the adoption and implementation of international rules, standards and procedures for, *inter alia*:

(a) Prevention of pollution and contamination, and other hazards to the marine environment, including the coastline, and of interference with the ecological balance of the marine environment;

(b) Protection and conservation of the natural resources of the area and prevention of damage to the flora and fauna of the marine environment.

12. In their activities in the area, including those relating to its resources, States shall pay due regard to the rights and legitimate interests of coastal States in the region of such activities, as well as of all other States which may be affected by such activities. Consultations shall be maintained with the coastal States concerned with respect to activities relating to the exploration of the area and the exploitation of its resources with a view to avoiding infringement of such rights and interests.

13. Nothing herein shall affect:

(a) The legal status of the waters superjacent to the area or that of the air space above those waters;

(b) The rights of coastal States with respect to measures to prevent, mitigate or eliminate grave and imminent danger to their coastline or their related interests from pollution or threat thereof resulting from, or from other hazardous occurrences caused by, any activities in the area, subject to the international regime to be established.

14. Every State shall have the responsibility to ensure that activities in the area, including those relating to its resources, whether undertaken by governmental agencies, or non-governmental entities or persons under its jurisdiction, or acting on its behalf, shall be carried out in conformity with the international regime to be established. The same responsibility applies to international organisations and their members for activities undertaken by such organisations or on their behalf. Damage caused by such activities shall entail liability.

15. The parties to any dispute relating to activities in the area and its resources shall resolve such dispute by the measures mentioned in Article 33 of the Charter of the United Nations and such procedures for settling disputes as may be agreed upon in the international regime to be established.

12.3 UNITED NATIONS CONVENTION ON THE LAW OF THE SEA, 1982: ARTICLE I: EXCERPT; AND PART XI: THE AREA: EXCERPT

Article 1
Use of terms and scope

1. For the purposes of this Convention:
(1) "Area" means the seabed and ocean floor and subsoil thereof, beyond the limits of national jurisdiction;
(2) "Authority" means the International Seabed Authority;
(3) "activities in the Area" means all activities of exploration for, and exploitation of, the resources of the Area;
...

PART XI
THE AREA

SECTION 1. GENERAL PROVISIONS

Article 133
Use of terms

For the purposes of this part:
(a) "resources" means all solid, liquid or gaseous mineral resources *in situ* in the Area at or beneath the seabed, including polymetallic nodules;
(b) resources, when recovered from the Area, are referred to as "minerals".
...

Article 134
Scope of this Part

1. This Part applies to the Area.
2. Activities in the Area shall be governed by the provisions of this Part.
3. The requirements concerning deposit of, and publicity to be given to, the charts or lists of geographical co-ordinates showing the limits referred to in article 2, paragraph 1(1), are set forth in Part VI.
4. Nothing in this article affects the establishment of the outer limits of the continental shelf in accordance with Part VI or the validity of agreements relating to delimitation between States with opposite or adjacent coasts.

Article 135
Legal status of the superjacent waters and air space

Neither this Part nor any rights granted or exercised pursuant thereto shall affect the legal status of the waters superjacent to the Area or that of the air space above those waters.

SECTION 2. PRINCIPLES GOVERNING THE AREA

Article 136
Common heritage of mankind

The Area and its resources are the common heritage of mankind.

Article 137
Legal status of the Area and its resources

1. No State shall claim or exercise sovereignty or sovereign rights over any part of the Area or its resources, nor shall any State or natural or juridical person appropriate any part thereof. No such claim or exercise of sovereignty or sovereign rights nor such appropriation shall be recognized.
2. All rights in the resources of the Area are vested in mankind as a whole, on whose behalf the Authority shall act. These resources are not subject to alienation. The minerals recovered from the Area, however, may only be alienated in accordance with this Part and the rules, regulations and procedures of the Authority.
3. No State or natural or juridical person shall claim, acquire or exercise rights with respect to the minerals recovered from the Area except in accordance with this Part. Otherwise, no such claim, acquisition or exercise of such rights shall be recognized.

Article 138
General conduct of States in relation to the Area

The general conduct of States in relation to the Area shall be in accordance with the provisions of this Part, the principles embodied in the Charter of the United Nations and other rules of international law in the interests of maintaining peace and security and promoting international co-operation and mutual understanding.

Article 139
Responsibility to ensure compliance and liability for damage

1. States Parties shall have the responsibility to ensure that activities in the Area, whether carried out by States Parties, or state enterprises or natural or juridical persons which possess the nationality of States Parties or are effectively controlled by them or their nationals, shall be carried out in conformity with this Part. The same responsibility applies to international organizations for activities in the Area carried out by such organizations.
2. Without prejudice to the rules of international law and Annex III, article 22, damage caused by the failure of a State Party or international organization to carry out its responsibilities under this Part shall entail liability; States parties or international organizations acting together shall bear joint and several liability. A State Party shall not however be liable for damage caused by any failure to comply with this Part by a person whom it has sponsored under article 153, paragraph 2(b), if the State Party has taken all necessary and appropriate measures to secure effective compliance under article 153, paragraph 4, and Annex III, article 4, paragraph 4.
3. States Parties that are members of international organizations shall take appropriate measures to ensure the implementation of this article with respect to such organizations.

Article 140
Benefit of mankind

1. Activities in the Area shall, as specifically provided for in this Part, be carried out for the benefit of mankind as a whole, irrespective of the geographical location of States, whether coastal or land-locked, and taking into particular consideration the interests and needs of developing States and of peoples who have not attained full independence or other self-governing status recognized by the United Nations in accordance with General Assembly resolution 1514 (XV) and other relevant General Assembly resolutions.
2. The Authority shall provide for the equitable sharing of financial and other economic benefits derived from activities in the Area through any appropriate mechanism, on a non-discriminatory basis, in accordance with article 160, paragraph 2(f)(i).

Article 141
Use of the Area exclusively for peaceful purposes

The Area shall be open to use exclusively for peaceful purposes by all States, whether coastal or land-locked, without discrimination and without prejudice to the other provisions of this Part.

Article 142
Rights and legitimate interests of coastal States

1. Activities in the Area, with respect to resource deposits in the Area which lie across limits of national jurisdiction, shall be conducted with due regard to the rights and legitimate interests of any coastal State across whose jurisdiction such deposits lie.
2. Consultations, including a system of prior notification, shall be maintained with the State concerned, with a view to avoiding infringement of such rights and interests. In cases where activities in the Area may result in the exploitation of resources lying within national jurisdiction, the prior consent of the coastal State concerned shall be required.
3. Neither this Part nor any rights granted or exercised pursuant thereto shall affect the rights of coastal States to take such measures consistent with the relevant provisions of Part XII as may be necessary to prevent, mitigate or eliminate grave and imminent danger to their coastline, or related interests from pollution or threat thereof or from other hazardous occurrences resulting from or caused by any activities in the Area.

Article 143
Marine scientific research

1. Marine scientific research in the Area shall be carried out exclusively for peaceful purposes and for the benefit of mankind as a whole, in accordance with Part XIII.
2. The Authority may carry out marine scientific research concerning the Area and its resources, and may enter into contracts for that purpose. The Authority shall promote and encourage the conduct of marine scientific research in the Area, and shall co-ordinate and disseminate the results of such research in the Area when available.
3. States Parties may carry out marine scientific research in the Area. States Parties shall promote international co-operation in marine scientific research in the Area by:
(a) participating in international programmes and encouraging co-operation in marine scientific research by personnel of different countries and of the Authority;

(b) ensuring that programmes are developed through the Authority or other international organizations as appropriate for the benefit of developing States and technologically less developed States with a view to:

    (i)   strengthening their research capabilities;

    (ii)   training their personnel and the personnel of the Authority in the techniques and applications of research;

    (iii) fostering the employment of their qualified personnel in research in the Area;

(c) effectively disseminating the results of research and analysis when available, through the Authority or other international channels when appropriate.

Article 144
Transfer of technology

1. The Authority shall take measures in accordance with this Convention;

(a) to acquire technology and scientific knowledge relating to activities in the Area; and

(b) to promote and encourage the transfer to developing States of such technology and scientific knowledge so that all States Parties benefit therefrom.

2. To this end the Authority and States Parties shall co-operate in promoting the transfer of technology and scientific knowledge relating to activities in the Area so that the Enterprise and all States Parties may benefit therefrom. In particular they shall initiate and promote:

(a) programmes for the transfer of technology to the Enterprise and to developing States with regard to activities in the Area, including, *inter alia*, facilitating the access of the Enterprise and of developing States to the relevant technology, under fair and reasonable terms and conditions;

(b) measures directed towards the advancement of the technology of the Enterprise and the domestic technology of developing States, particularly by providing opportunities to personnel from the Enterprise and from developing States for training in marine science and technology and for their full participation in activities in the Area.

Article 145
Protection of the marine environment

Necessary measures shall be taken in accordance with this Convention with respect to activities in the Area to ensure effective protection for the marine environment from harmful effects which may arise from such activities. To this end the Authority shall adopt appropriate rules, regulations and procedures for *inter alia*:

(a) the prevention, reduction and control of pollution and other hazards to the marine environment, including the coastline, and of interference with the ecological balance of the marine environment, particular attention being paid to the need for protection from harmful effects of such activities as drilling, dredging, excavation, disposal of waste, construction and operation or maintenance of installations, pipelines and other devices related to such activities;

(b) the protection and conservation of the natural resources of the Area and the prevention of damage to the flora and fauna of the marine environment.

Article 146
Protection of human life

With respect to activities in the Area, necessary measures shall be taken to ensure effective protection of human life. To this end the Authority shall adopt appropriate rules, regulations and procedures to supplement existing international law as embodied in relevant treaties.

Article 147
Accommodation of activities in the Area and in the marine environment

1. Activities in the Area shall be carried out with reasonable regard for other activities in the marine environment.
2. Installations used for carrying out activities in the Area shall be subject to the following conditions:
(a) such installations shall be erected, emplaced and removed solely in accordance with this Part and subject to the rules, regulations and procedures of the Authority. Due notice must be given of the erection, emplacement and removal of such installations, and permanent means for giving warning of their presence must be maintained.
(b) such installations may not be established where interference may be caused to the use of recognized sea lanes essential to international navigation or in areas of intense fishing activity;
(c) safety zones shall be established around such installations with appropriate markings to ensure the safety of both navigation and the installations. The configuration and location of such safety zones shall not be such as to form a belt impeding the lawful access of shipping to particular maritime zones or navigation along international sea lanes;
(d) such installations shall be used exclusively for peaceful purposes;
(e) such installations do not possess the status of islands. They have no territorial sea of their own, and their presence does not affect the delimitation of the territorial sea, the exclusive economic zone or the continental shelf.
3. Other activities in the marine environment shall be conducted with reasonable regard for activities in the Area.

Article 148
Participation of developing States in activities in the Area

The effective participation of developing States in activities in the Area shall be promoted as specifically provided for in this Part, having due regard to their special interests and needs, and in particular to the special need of the land-locked and geographically disadvantaged among them to overcome obstacles arising from their disadvantaged location, including remoteness from the Area and difficulty of access to and from it.

Article 149
Archaeological and historical objects

All objects of an archaeological and historical nature found in the area shall be preserved or disposed of for the benefit of mankind as a whole, particular regard being paid to the preferential rights of the State or country of origin, or the State of cultural origin, or the State of historical and archaeological origin.

12.4 RESOLUTION I OF UNCLOS III: ESTABLISHMENT OF THE PREPARATORY COMMISSION FOR THE INTERNATIONAL SEABED AUTHORITY AND FOR THE INTERNATIONAL TRIBUNAL FOR THE LAW OF THE SEA

The Third United Nations Conference on the Law of the Sea,

Having adopted the Convention on the Law of the Sea which provides for the establishment of the International Seabed Authority and the International Tribunal for the Law of the Sea,

Having decided to take all possible measures to ensure the entry into effective operation without undue delay of the Authority and the Tribunal and to make the necessary arrangements for the commencement of their functions,

Having decided that a Preparatory Commission should be established for the fulfilment of these purposes,

Decides as follows:

1. There is hereby established the Preparatory Commission for the International Seabed Authority and for the International Tribunal for the Law of the Sea. Upon signature of or accession to the Convention by 50 States, the Secretary-General of the United Nations shall convene the Commission, and it shall meet no sooner than 60 days and no later than 90 days thereafter.

2. The Commission shall consist of the representatives of States and of Namibia, represented by the United Nations Council for Namibia, which have signed the Convention or acceded to it. The representatives of signatories of the Final Act may participate fully in the deliberations of the Commission as observers but shall not be entitled to participate in the taking of decisions.

3. The Commission shall elect its Chairman and other officers.

4. The Rules of Procedure of the Third United Nations Conference on the Law of the Sea shall apply *mutatis mutandis* to the adoption of the rules of procedure of the Commission.

5. The Commission shall:

(a) prepare the provisional agenda for the first session of the Assembly and of the Council and, as appropriate, make recommendations relating to items thereon;

(b) prepare draft rules of procedure of the Assembly and of the Council;

(c) make recommendations concerning the budget for the first financial period of the Authority;

(d) make recommendations concerning the relationship between the Authority and the United Nations and other international organizations;

(e) make recommendations concerning the Secretariat of the Authority in accordance with the relevant provisions of the Convention;

(f) undertake studies, as necessary, concerning the establishment of the headquarters of the Authority, and make recommendations relating thereto;

(g) prepare draft rules, regulations and procedures, as necessary, to enable the Authority to commence its functions, including draft regulations concerning the financial management and the internal administration of the Authority;

(h) exercise the powers and functions assigned to it by resolution II of the Third United Nations Conference on the Law of the Sea relating to preparatory investment;

(i) undertake studies on the problems which would be encountered by developing land-based producer States likely to be most seriously affected by the production of minerals derived from the Area with a view to minimizing their difficulties and helping them to make the necessary economic adjustment, including studies on the establishment of a compensation fund, and submit recommendations to the Authority thereon.

6. The Commission shall have such legal capacity as may be necessary for the exercise of its functions and the fulfilment of its purposes as set forth in this resolution.

7. The Commission may establish such subsidiary bodies as are necessary for the exercise of its functions and shall determine their functions and rules of procedure. It may also make use, as appropriate, of outside sources of expertise in accordance with United Nations practice to facilitate the work of bodies so established.

8. The Commission shall establish a special commission for the Enterprise and entrust to it the functions referred to in paragraph 12 of resolution II of the Third United Nations Conference on the Law of the Sea relating to preparatory investment. The special commission shall take all measures necessary for the early entry into effective operation of the Enterprise.

9. The Commission shall establish a special commission on the problems which would be encountered by developing land-based producer States likely to be most seriously affected by the production of minerals derived from the Area and entrust to it the functions referred to in paragraph 5(i).

10. The Commission shall prepare a report containing recommendations for submission to the meeting of the States Parties to be convened in accordance with Annex VI, article 4, of the Convention regarding practical arrangements for the establishment of the International Tribunal for the Law of the Sea.

11. The Commission shall prepare a final report on all matters within its mandate, except as provided in paragraph 10, for the presentation to the Assembly at its first session. Any action which may be taken on the basis of the report must be in conformity with the provisions of the Convention concerning the powers and functions entrusted to the respective organs of the Authority.

12. The Commission shall meet at the seat of the Authority if facilities are available; it shall meet as often as necessary for the expeditious exercise of its functions.

13. The Commission shall remain in existence until the conclusion of the first session of the Assembly, at which time its property and records shall be transferred to the Authority.

14. The expenses of the Commission shall be met from the regular budget of the United Nations, subject to the approval of the General Assembly of the United Nations.

15. The Secretary-General of the United Nations shall make available to the Commission such secretariat services as may be required.

16. The Secretary-General of the United Nations shall bring this resolution, in particular paragraphs 14 and 15, to the attention of the General Assembly for necessary action.

12.5 RESOLUTION II OF UNCLOS III GOVERNING PREPARATORY INVESTMENT IN PIONEER ACTIVITIES RELATING TO POLYMETALLIC NODULES

The Third United Nations Conference on the Law of the Sea,
  Having adopted the Convention on the Law of the Sea (the "Convention"),
  Having established by resolution I the Preparatory Commission for the International Seabed Authority and for the International Tribunal for the Law of the

Sea (the "Commission") and directed it to prepare draft rules, regulations and procedures, as necessary to enable the Authority to commence its functions, as well as to make recommendations for the early entry into effective operation of the Enterprise,

Desirous of making provision for investments by States and other entities made in a manner compatible with the international regime set forth in Part XI of the Convention and the Annexes relating thereto, before the entry into force of the Convention,

Recognizing the need to ensure that the Enterprise will be provided with the funds, technology and expertise necessary to enable it to keep pace with the States and other entities referred to in the preceding paragraph with respect to activities in the Area,

Decides as follows:

1. For the purposes of this resolution:
   (a) "pioneer investor" refers to:
      (i) France, India, Japan and the Union of Soviet Socialist Republics, or a state enterprise of each of those States or one natural or juridical person which possesses the nationality of or is effectively controlled by each of those States, or their nationals, provided that the State concerned signs the Convention and the State or state enterprise or natural or juridical person has expended , before 1 January 1983, an amount equivalent to at least $US 30 million (United States dollars calculated in constant dollars relative to 1982) in pioneer activities and has expended no less than 10 per cent of that amount in the location, survey and evaluation of the area referred to in paragraph 3(a);
      (ii) four entities, whose components being natural or juridical persons[1] possess the nationality of one or more of the following States, or are effectively controlled by one or more of them or their nationals: Belgium, Canada, the Federal Republic of Germany, Italy, Japan, the Netherlands, the United Kingdom of Great Britain and Northern Ireland, and the United States of America, provided that the certifying State or States sign the Convention and the entity concerned has expended, before 1 January 1983, the levels of expenditure for the purpose stated in subparagraph (i);
      (iii) any developing State which signs the Convention or any state enterprise or natural or juridical person which possesses the nationality of such State or is effectively controlled by it or its nationals, or any group of the foregoing, which, before 1 January 1985, has expended the levels of expenditure for the purpose stated in subparagraph (i);

   The rights of the pioneer investor may devolve upon its successor in interest.
   (b) "pioneer activities" means undertakings, commitments of financial and other assets, investigations, findings, research, engineering development and other activities relevant to the identification, discovery, and systematic analysis and evaluation of polymetallic nodules and to the determination of the technical and economic feasibility of exploitation. Pioneer activities include:
      (i) any at-sea observation and evaluation activity which has as its objective the establishment and documentation of the nature, shape, concentration, location and grade of polymetallic nodules and of the environmental, technical and other appropriate factors which must be taken into account before exploitation;

---

1. For their identity and composition see "Sea-bed mineral resource development: recent activities of the international Consortia" and addendum, published by the Department of International Economic and Social Affairs of the United Nations (ST/ESA/107 and Add.1).

    (ii) the recovery from the Area of polymetallic nodules with a view to the designing, fabricating and testing of equipment which is intended to be used in the exploitation of polymetallic nodules;

(c) "certifying State" means a State which signs the Convention, standing in the same relation to a pioneer investor as would a sponsoring State pursuant to Annex III, article 4, of the Convention and which certifies the levels of expenditure specified in subparagraph (a);

(d) "polymetallic nodules" means one of the resources of the Area consisting of any deposit or accretion of nodules, on or just below the surface of the deep sea-bed, which contain manganese, nickel, cobalt and copper;

(e) "pioneer area" means an area allocated by the Commission to a pioneer investor for pioneer activities pursuant to this resolution. A pioneer area shall not exceed 150,000 square kilometres. The pioneer investor shall relinquish portions of the pioneer area to revert to the Area, in accordance with the following schedule:

    (i) 20 per cent of the area allocated by the end of the third year from the date of the allocation;

    (ii) an additional 10 per cent of the area allocated by the end of the fifth year from the date of the allocation;

    (iii) an additional 20 per cent of the area allocated or such larger amount as would exceed the exploitation area decided upon by the Authority in its rules, regulations and procedures, after eight years from the date of the allocation of the area or the date of the award of a production authorization, whichever is earlier;

(f) "Area", "Authority", "activities in the Area" and "resources" have the meanings assigned to those terms in the Convention.

2. As soon as the Commission begins to function, any State which has signed the Convention may apply to the Commission on its behalf or on behalf of any state enterprise or entity or natural or juridical person specified in paragraph 1(a) for registration as a pioneer investor. The Commission shall register the applicant as a pioneer investor if the application:

(a) is accompanied, in the case of a State which has signed the Convention, by a statement certifying the level of expenditure made in accordance with paragraph 1(a), and, in all other cases, a certificate concerning such level of expenditure issued by a certifying State or States; and

(b) is in conformity with the other provisions of this resolution, including paragraph 5.

3. (a) Every application shall cover a total area which need not be a single continuous area, sufficiently large and of sufficient estimated commercial value to allow two mining operations. The application shall indicate the co-ordinates of the area defining the total area and dividing it into two parts of equal estimated commercial value and shall contain all the data available to the applicant with respect to both parts of the area. Such data shall include, *inter alia*, information relating to mapping, testing, the density of polymetallic nodules and their metal content. In dealing with such data, the Commission and its staff shall act in accordance with the relevant provisions of the Convention and its Annexes concerning the confidentiality of data.

(b) Within 45 days of receiving the data required by subparagraph (a), the Commission shall designate the part of the area which is to be reserved in accordance with the Convention for the conduct of activities in the Area by the Authority through the

Enterprise or in association with developing States. The other part of the area shall be allocated to the pioneer investor as a pioneer area.

4. No pioneer investor may be registered in respect of more than one pioneer area. In the case of a pioneer investor which is made up of two or more components, none of such components may apply to be registered as a pioneer investor in its own right or under paragraph 1(a)(iii).

5. (a) Any State which has signed the Convention and which is a prospective certifying State shall ensure, before making applications to the Commission under paragraph 2, that areas in respect of which applications are made do not overlap one another or areas previously allocated as pioneer areas. The States concerned shall keep the Commission currently and fully informed of any efforts to resolve conflicts with respect to overlapping claims and of the results thereof.

   (b) Certifying States shall ensure, before the entry into force of the Convention, that pioneer activities are conducted in a manner compatible with it.

   (c) The prospective certifying States, including all potential claimants, shall resolve their conflicts as required under subparagraph (a) by negotiations within a reasonable period. If such conflicts have not been resolved by 1 March 1983, the prospective certifying States shall arrange for the submission of all such claims to binding arbitration in accordance with UNCITRAL Arbitration Rules to commence not later than 1 May 1983 and to be completed by 1 December 1984. If one of the States concerned does not wish to participate in the arbitration, it shall arrange for a juridical person of its nationality to represent it in the arbitration. The arbitral tribunal may, for good cause, extend the deadline for the making of the award for one or more 30-day periods.

   (d) In determining the issue as to which applicant involved in a conflict shall be awarded all or part of each area in conflict, the arbitral tribunal shall find a solution which is fair and equitable, having regard, with respect to each applicant involved in the conflict, to the following factors:

      (i) the deposit of the list of relevant co-ordinates with the prospective certifying State or States not later than the date of adoption of the Final Act or 1 January 1983, whichever is earlier;

      (ii) the continuity and extent of past activities relevant to each area in conflict and to the application area of which it is a part;

      (iii) the date on which each pioneer investor concerned or predecessor in interest or component organization thereof commenced activities at sea in the application area;

      (iv) the financial cost of activities measured in constant United States dollars relevant to each area in conflict and to the application area of which it is a part; and

      (v) the time when those activities were carried out and the quality of activities.

6. A pioneer investor registered pursuant to this resolution shall, from the date of registration, have the exclusive right to carry out pioneer activities in the pioneer area allocated to it.

7. (a) Every applicant for registration as a pioneer investor shall pay to the Commission a fee of $US 250,000. When the pioneer investor applies to the Authority for a plan of work for exploration and exploitation the fee referred to in Annex III, article 13, paragraph 2, of the Convention shall be $US 250,000.

(b) Every registered pioneer investor shall pay an annual fixed fee of $US 1 million commencing from the date of the allocation of the pioneer area. The payments shall be made by the pioneer investor to the Authority upon the approval of its plan of work for exploration and exploitation. The financial arrangements undertaken pursuant to such plan of work shall be adjusted to take account of the payments made pursuant to this paragraph.

(c) Every registered pioneer investor shall agree to incur periodic expenditures, with respect to the pioneer area allocated to it, until approval of its plan of work pursuant to paragraph 8, of an amount to be determined by the Commission. The amount should be reasonably related to the size of the pioneer area and the expenditures which would be expected of a *bona fide* operator who intends to bring that area into commercial production within a reasonable time.

8. (a) Within six months of the entry into force of the Convention and certification by the Commission in accordance with paragraph 11, of compliance with this resolution, the pioneer investor so registered shall apply to the Authority for approval of a plan of work for exploration and exploitation, in accordance with the Convention. The plan of work in respect of such application shall comply with and be governed by the relevant provisions of the Convention and the rules, regulations and procedures of the Authority, including those on the operational requirements, the financial requirements and the undertakings concerning the transfer of technology. Accordingly, the Authority shall approve such application.

(b) When an application for approval of a plan of work is submitted by an entity other than a State, pursuant to subparagraph (a), the certifying State or States shall be deemed to be the sponsoring State for the purposes of Annex III, article 4, of the Convention, and shall thereupon assume such obligations.

(c) No plan of work for exploration and exploitation shall be approved unless the certifying State is a Party to the Convention. In the case of the entities referred to in paragraph 1(a)(ii), the plan of work for exploration and exploitation shall not be approved unless all the States whose natural or juridical persons comprise those entities are Parties to the Convention. If any such State fails to ratify the Convention within six months after it has received a notification from the Authority that an application by it, or sponsored by it, is pending, its status as a pioneer investor or certifying State, as the case may be, shall terminate, unless the Council, by a majority of three-fourths of its members present and voting, decides to postpone the terminal date for a period not exceeding six months.

9. (a) In the allocation of production authorizations, in accordance with article 151 and Annex III, article 7, of the Convention, the pioneer investors who have obtained approval of plans of work for exploration and exploitation shall have priority over all applicants other than the Enterprise which shall be entitled to production authorizations for two mine sites including that referred to in article 151, paragraph 5, of the Convention. After each of the pioneer investors has obtained production authorization for its first mine site, the priority for the Enterprise contained in Annex III, article 7, paragraph 6, of the Convention shall apply.

(b) Production authorizations shall be issued to each pioneer investor within 30 days of the date on which that pioneer investor notifies the Authority that it will commence commercial production within five years. If a pioneer investor is unable to begin production within the period of five years for reasons beyond its control, it shall apply to the Legal and Technical Commission for an extension of time.   That Commission shall grant the extension of time, for a period not exceeding five years and not subject to further extension, if it is satisfied that the pioneer investor cannot begin on an economically viable basis at the time originally planned.   Nothing in this subparagraph shall prevent the Enterprise or any other pioneer applicant, who has notified the Authority that it will commence commercial production within five years, from being given a priority over any applicant who has obtained an extension of time under this subparagraph.

(c) If the Authority, upon being given notice, pursuant to subparagraph (b), determines that the commencement of commercial production within five years would exceed the production ceiling in article 151, paragraphs 2 to 7, of the Convention, the applicant shall hold a priority over any other applicant for the award of the next production authorization allowed by the production ceiling.

(d) If two or more pioneer investors apply for production authorizations to begin commercial production at the same time and article 151, paragraphs 2 to 7, of the Convention, would not permit all such production to commence simultaneously, the Authority shall notify the pioneer investors concerned. Within three months of such notification, they shall decide whether and, if so, to what extent they wish to apportion the allowable tonnage among themselves.

(e) If, pursuant to subparagraph (d), the pioneer investors concerned decide not to apportion the available production among themselves they shall agree on an order of priority for production authorizations and all subsequent applications for production authorizations will be granted after those referred to in this subparagraph have been approved.

(f) If, pursuant to subparagraph (d), the pioneer investors concerned decide to apportion the available production among themselves, the Authority shall award each of them a production authorization for such lesser quantity as they have agreed.   In each case the stated production requirements of the applicant will be approved and their full production will be allowed as soon as the production ceiling admits of additional capacity sufficient for the applicants involved in the competition.   All subsequent applications for production authorizations will only be granted after the requirements of this subparagraph have been met and the applicant is no longer subject to the reduction of production provided for in this subparagraph.

(g) If the parties fail to reach agreement within the stated time period, the matter shall be decided immediately by the means provided for in paragraph 5(c) in accordance with the criteria set forth in Annex III, article 7, paragraphs 3 and 5, of the Convention.

10. (a) Any rights acquired by entities or natural or juridical persons which possess the nationality of or are effectively controlled by a State or States whose status as certifying State has been terminated, shall lapse unless the pioneer investor changes its nationality and sponsorship within six months of the date of such termination, as provided for in subparagraph (c).

(b) A pioneer investor may change its nationality and sponsorship from that existing at the time of its registration as a pioneer investor to that of any State Party to the Convention which has effective control over the pioneer investor in terms of paragraph 1(a).

(c) Changes of nationality and sponsorship pursuant to this paragraph shall not affect any right or priority conferred on a pioneer investor pursuant to paragraphs 6 and 8.

11. The Commission shall:
    (a) provide each pioneer investor with the certificate of compliance with the provisions of this resolution referred to in paragraph 8; and
    (b) include in its final report required by paragraph 11 of resolution 1 of the Conference details of all registrations of pioneer investors and allocations of pioneer areas pursuant to this resolution.

12. In order to ensure that the Enterprise is able to carry out activities in the Area in such a manner as to keep pace with States and other entities:
    (a) every registered pioneer investor shall:
        (i) carry out exploration, at the request of the Commission, in the area reserved, pursuant to paragraph 3 in connection with its application, for activities in the Area by the Authority through the Enterprise or in association with developing States, on the basis that the costs so incurred plus interest thereon at the rate of 10 per cent per annum shall be reimbursed;
        (ii) provide training at all levels for personnel designated by the Commission;
        (iii) undertake before the entry into force of the Convention, to perform the obligations prescribed in the Convention relating to transfer of technology;
    (b) every certifying State shall:
        (i) ensure that the necessary funds are made available to the Enterprise in a timely manner in accordance with the Convention, upon its entry into force; and
        (ii) report periodically to the Commission on the activities carried out by it, by its entities or natural or juridical persons.

13. The Authority and its organs shall recognize and honour the rights and obligations arising from this resolution and the decisions of the Commission taken pursuant to it.

14. Without prejudice to paragraph 13, this resolution shall have effect until the entry into force of the Convention.

15. Nothing in this resolution shall derogate from Annex III, article 6, paragraph 3(c), of the Convention.

12.6 UNITED KINGDOM: DEEP SEA MINING (TEMPORARY PROVISIONS) ACT 1981: EXCERPTS

An Act to make provision with respect to deep sea mining operations; and for purposes connected therewith.   [28th July 1981]
...

Prohibition of unlicensed deep sea mining
1. – (1) Subject to the following provisions of this Act, a person to whom this section applies shall not explore for the hard mineral resources of any part of the deep seabed unless he holds an exploration licence granted under section 2 below in respect of that part of the deep seabed or is the agent or employee of the holder of that licence (acting in his capacity as such).

(2) Subject to the following provisions of this Act, a person to whom this section applies shall not exploit the hard mineral resources of any part of the deep seabed

unless he holds an exploitation licence granted under section 2 below in respect of that part of the deep seabed or is the agent or employee of the holder of that licence (acting in his capacity as such).

...

(6) In this Act –
"deep seabed" means that part of the bed of the high seas in respect of which sovereign rights in relation to the natural resources of the seabed are neither exercisable by the United Kingdom nor recognised by Her Majesty's Government in the United Kingdom as being exercisable by another Sovereign Power or, in a case where disputed claims are made by more than one Sovereign Power, by one or other of these Sovereign Powers;
"hard mineral resources" means deposits of nodules containing (in quantities greater than trace) at least one of the following elements, that is to say, manganese, nickel, cobalt, copper, phosphorus and molybdenum;

...

(7) In any proceedings, a certificate issued by the Secretary of State certifying that sovereign rights are not exercisable in relation to any part of the seabed by the United Kingdom or by any other Sovereign Power shall be conclusive as to that fact; and any document purporting to be such a certificate shall be received in evidence and shall, unless the contrary is proved, be deemed to be such a certificate.

Exploration and exploitation licences
2. – (1) In this Act –
"exploration licence" means a licence authorising the licensee to explore for the hard mineral resources of such part of the deep seabed as may be specified in the licence; and
"exploitation licence" means a licence authorising the licensee to exploit the hard mineral resources of such part of the deep seabed as may be specified in the licence.

(2) Subject to subsection (4) and section 3 below, the Secretary of State may on payment of such fee as may with the consent of the Treasury be prescribed grant to such persons as he thinks fit exploration or exploitation licences; and in determining whether to grant a licence in any case he shall have regard to any relevant factors including in particular the desirability of keeping an area or areas of the deep seabed free from deep seabed mining operations so as to provide an area or areas for comparison with licensed areas in assessing the effects of such operations.

(3) An exploration or an exploitation licence shall be granted for such period as the Secretary of State thinks fit and shall contain such terms and conditions as he thinks fit and, in particular but without prejudice to the generality of the foregoing, a licence may include terms and conditions –

...

(b) relating to the processing or other treatment of any hard mineral resources won in pursuance of the licence which is carried out by or on behalf of the licensee on any ship;
(c) relating to the disposal of any waste material resulting from such processing or other treatment;

...

(f) requiring any exploration or exploitation of the hard mineral resources of the licensed area to be diligently carried out;

(g) requiring the payment to the Secretary of State of such sums as may with the consent of the Treasury be prescribed at such times as may be prescribed; and

(h) permitting the transfer of the licence in prescribed cases or with the written consent of the Secretary of State.

(4) An exploration licence shall not be granted in respect of any period before 1st July 1981 and an exploitation licence shall not be granted in respect of any period before 1st January 1988.

(5) Where the Secretary of State has granted an exploration licence he shall not grant an exploitation licence in respect of any part of the licensed area otherwise than to the licensee except with the licensee's written consent.

(6) Any fees or other sums received by the Secretary of State under this section shall be paid into the Consolidated Fund.

Licences granted by reciprocating countries

3. – (1) Where, in the opinion of Her Majesty, the law of any country contains provisions similar in their aims and effects to the provisions of this Act, Her Majesty may by Order in Council designate that country as a reciprocating country for the purposes of this Act.

(2) Where a person holds a licence or other authorisation issued and for the time being in force under the law of a reciprocating country for the exploration or exploitation of the hard mineral resources of any area of the deep seabed specified in that authorisation (the "authorised area") –

(a) the Secretary of State shall not grant an exploration or exploitation licence in respect of any part of the authorised area; and

(b) if section 1 above applies to that person, he shall not be prohibited by that section from engaging in the exploration or, as the case may be, exploitation of the hard mineral resources of the authorised area.

...

Prevention of interference with licensed operations

4. – (1) A person to whom section 1 above applies shall not intentionally interfere with any operations carried on in pursuance of an exploration or exploitation licence or a reciprocal authorisation.

...

Protection of the marine environment

5. – (1) In determining whether to grant an exploration or exploitation licence the Secretary of State shall have regard to the need to protect (so far as reasonably practicable) marine creatures, plants and other organisms and their habitat from any harmful effects which might result from any activities to be authorised by the licence; and the Secretary of State shall consider any representations made to him concerning such effects.

(2) Without prejudice to section 2(3) above, any exploration or exploitation licence granted by the Secretary of State shall contain such terms and conditions as he considers necessary or expedient to avoid or minimise any such harmful effects.

...

Freedom of the high seas

7. – It shall be the duty of the licensee to exercise his rights under the licence with reasonable regard to the interests of other persons in their exercise of the freedom of the high seas.

...

The Deep Sea Mining Levy

9. – (1) Subject to the following provisions of this section, the holder of an exploitation licence shall, at the prescribed times, pay to the Secretary of State –

(a) an amount equal to 3.75 per cent of the value of the hard mineral resources recovered in pursuance of the licence during any prescribed period; or

(b) if the value of the hard mineral resources so recovered cannot be ascertained under paragraph (a) above, 0.75 per cent of the value of any manganese, nickel, cobalt, copper, phosphorus or molybdenum ("the elements") or any compound containing any of the elements, found in those hard mineral resources.

(2) The value of any hard mineral resources, element or compound shall for the purposes of subsection (1) above be determined in accordance with such rules as may be prescribed.

(3) If any hard mineral resources recovered by the licensee during any prescribed period contain less than the amount prescribed in relation to that period (by weight or proportion or otherwise) of any of the elements or any compound containing any of the elements, the licensee shall not be liable to make any payment in respect of that element or compound.

(4) A licensee may elect, in writing and at the prescribed times, in respect of any element or compound specified in the election to defer payment under subsection (1) above until the element or compound is separated from any other matter with which it was recovered or, if earlier, until he disposes of the hard mineral resources containing that element or compound.

(5) Where a licensee fails at the prescribed time to pay to the Secretary of State any amount which he is required by subsection (1) above to pay at that time, the amount due shall as from that time carry interest at the relevant rate until payment.

For the purposes of this subsection, "relevant rate" means such rate as the Secretary of State may with the consent of the Treasury prescribe.

(6) Where any payment has been deferred under subsection (4) above and becomes due, the amount due shall be calculated in accordance with subsections (1) to (3) above, and, for the purposes of subsection (5) above, that amount shall be deemed to have become due on the date when it would have been due had the election not been made.

The Deep Sea Mining Fund

10. – (1) There shall be established under the control and management of the Treasury a fund to be called the Deep Sea Mining Fund ("the Fund") into which there shall be paid any sums paid to the Secretary of State under section 9 above.

(2) Subject to subsection (3) below, the Treasury shall prepare accounts of the Fund and shall send them to the Comptroller and Auditor General not later than the end of the month of November following the financial year to which the accounts relate; and the Comptroller and Auditor General shall examine and certify every such account and shall lay copies thereof, together with his report thereon, before Parliament.

(3) Subsection (2) above shall not have effect until the first payment into the Fund is made in pursuance of subsection (1) above.

(4) In subsection (2) above, "financial year" means a period of twelve months ending on 31st March except that the Secretary of State may direct that –

(a) the first financial year for the Fund shall be of such period not exceeding two years and ending on 31st March as he may specify in the direction; and

(b) where an order under subsection (7) below is made, the last financial year shall be of such period not exceeding twelve months as he may specify in the direction;

and, where a direction is given under paragraph (b) above, subsection (2) shall apply in relation to the accounts for that last financial year with the substitution for the reference to the end of the month of November of a reference to the end of the eighth month following the end of that year.

(5) If an international organisation for the deep sea bed is established in pursuance of an international agreement on the law of the sea which has been adopted by a United Nations Conference on the Law of the Sea and has entered into force for the United Kingdom, the Secretary of State may by order designate that organisation as the relevant international organisation for the purposes of this section.

(6) An order designating an international organisation as the relevant international organisation for the purposes of this section may also make provision for the payment to that organisation of any sums for the time being standing to the credit of the Fund.

(7) If within ten years of the coming into force of this section no organisation has been designated as the relevant international organisation the Secretary of State may by order made with the approval of the Treasury provide for the winding up of the Fund and the payment into the Consolidated Fund of any sums standing to its credit and for the repeal of section 9 above.

(8) An order under subsection (7) above shall not be made unless a draft thereof has been approved by resolution of the Commons House of Parliament.

(9) Until such time as an international organisation is so designated, any money in the Fund may from time to time be paid over to the National Debt Commissioners and invested by them, in accordance with such directions as may be given by the Treasury, in any such manner as may be specified by an order of the Treasury for the time being in force under section 22(1) of the National Savings Bank Act 1971.

...

Short title, etc.

18. – (1)   This Act may be cited as the Deep Sea Mining (Temporary Provisions) Act 1981.

...

(3) If it appears to the Secretary of State that an international agreement on the law of the sea which has been adopted by a United Nations Conference on the Law of the Sea is to be given effect within the United Kingdom the Secretary of State may by order provide for the repeal of this Act.

(4) An order under subsection (3) above shall not be made unless a draft thereof has been approved by resolution of each House of Parliament.

(5) Such an order may contain such incidental, supplementary and transitional provisions as the Secretary of State thinks fit.

...

12.7 UNITED STATES: DEEP SEABED HARD MINERAL RESOURCES ACT 1980: EXCERPTS

An Act

To establish an interim procedure for the orderly development of hard mineral resources in the deep seabed, pending adoption of an international regime relating thereto, and for other purposes.

...

SEC.2. FINDINGS AND PURPOSES

(a) Findings. – The Congress finds that –
(1) the United States' requirements for hard minerals to satisfy national industrial needs will continue to expand and the demand for such minerals will increasingly exceed the available domestic sources of supply;
(2) in the case of certain hard minerals, the United States is dependent upon foreign sources of supply and the acquisition of such minerals from foreign sources is a significant factor in the national balance-of-payments position;
(3) the present and future national interest of the United States requires the availability of hard mineral resources which is independent of the export policies of foreign nations;
(4) there is an alternate source of supply, which is significant in relation to national needs, of certain hard minerals, including nickel, copper, cobalt, and manganese, contained in the nodules existing in great abundance on the deep seabed;
(5) the nations of the world, including the United States, will benefit if the hard mineral resources of the deep seabed beyond limits of national jurisdiction can be developed and made available for their use;
(6) in particular, future access to the nickel, copper, cobalt, and manganese resources of the deep seabed will be important to the industrial needs of the nations of the world, both developed and developing;
(7) on December 17, 1970, the United States supported (by affirmative vote) the United Nations General Assembly Resolution 2749 (XXV) declaring *inter alia* the principle that the mineral resources of the deep seabed are the common heritage of mankind, with the expectation that this principle would be legally defined under the terms of a comprehensive international Law of the Sea Treaty yet to be agreed upon;
(8) it is in the national interest of the United States and other nations to encourage a widely acceptable Law of the Sea Treaty, which will provide a new legal order for the oceans covering a broad range of ocean interests, including exploration for and commercial recovery of hard mineral resources of the deep seabed;
(9) the negotiations to conclude such a Treaty and establish the international regime governing the exercise of rights over, and exploration of, the resources of the deep seabed, referred to in General Assembly Resolution 2749 (XXV) are in progress but may not be concluded in the near future;
(10) even if such negotiations are completed promptly, much time will elapse before such an international regime is established and in operation;
(11) development of technology required for the exploration and recovery of hard mineral resources of the deep seabed will require substantial investment for many years before commercial production can occur, and must proceed at this time if deep seabed minerals are to be available when needed;
(12) it is the legal opinion of the United States that exploration for and commercial recovery of hard mineral resources of the deep seabed are freedoms of the high seas subject to a duty of reasonable regard to the interests of other states in their exercise of those and other freedoms recognized by general principles of international law;
(13) pending a Law of the Sea Treaty, and in the absence of agreement among states on applicable principles of international law, the uncertainty among potential investors as to the future legal regime is likely to discourage or prevent the investments necessary to develop deep seabed mining technology;

(14) pending a Law of the Sea Treaty, the protection of the marine environment from damage caused by exploration or recovery of hard mineral resources of the deep seabed depends upon the enactment of suitable interim national legislation;

(15) a Law of the Sea Treaty is likely to establish financial arrangements which obligate the United States or United States citizens to make payments to an international organization with respect to exploration or recovery of the hard mineral resources of the deep seabed; and

(16) legislation is required to establish an interim legal regime under which technology can be developed and the exploration and recovery of the hard mineral resources of the deep seabed can take place until such time as a Law of the Sea Treaty enters into force with respect to the United States.

(b) Purposes. – The Congress declares that the purposes of this Act are –

(1) to encourage the successful conclusion of a comprehensive Law of the Sea Treaty, which will give legal definition to the principle that the hard mineral resources of the deep seabed are the common heritage of mankind and which will assure, among other things, non-discriminatory access to such resources for all nations;

(2) pending the ratification by, and entering into force with respect to, the United States of such a Treaty, to provide for the establishment of an international revenue-sharing fund the proceeds of which shall be used for sharing with the international community pursuant to such Treaty;

(3) to establish, pending the ratification by, and entering into force with respect to, the United States of such a Treaty, an interim program to regulate the exploration for and commercial recovery of hard mineral resources of the deep seabed by United States citizens;

(4) to accelerate the program of environmental assessment of exploration for and commercial recovery of hard mineral resources of the deep seabed and assure that such exploration and recovery activities are conducted in a manner which will encourage the conservation of such resources, protect the quality of the environment, and promote the safety of life and property at sea; and

(5) to encourage the continued development of technology necessary to recover the hard mineral resources of the deep seabed.

SEC.3. INTERNATIONAL OBJECTIVES OF THIS ACT

(a) Disclaimer of Extraterritorial Sovereignty. – By the enactment of this Act, the United States –

(1) exercises its jurisdiction over United States citizens and vessels, and foreign persons and vessels otherwise subject to its jurisdiction, in the exercise of the high seas freedom to engage in exploration for, and commercial recovery of, hard mineral resources of the deep seabed in accordance with generally accepted principles of international law recognized by the United States; but

(2) does not thereby assert sovereignty or sovereign or exclusive rights or jurisdiction over, or the ownership of, any areas or resources in the deep seabed.

(b) Secretary of State. – (1) The Secretary of State is encouraged to negotiate successfully a comprehensive Law of the Sea Treaty which, among other things, provides assured and nondiscriminatory access to the hard mineral resources of the deep seabed for all nations, gives legal definition to the principle that the resources of the deep seabed are the common heritage of mankind, and provides for the establishment of requirements for the protection of the quality of the environment as stringent as those promulgated pursuant to this Act.

(2) Until such a Treaty is concluded, the Secretary of State is encouraged to promote any international actions necessary to adequately protect the environment from adverse impacts which may result from any exploration for and commercial recovery of hard mineral resources of the deep seabed carried out by persons not subject to this Act.

...

TITLE 1 – REGULATION OF EXPLORATION AND COMMERCIAL RECOVERY BY UNITED STATES CITIZENS

SEC. 101. PROHIBITED ACTIVITIES BY UNITED STATES CITIZENS

(a) Prohibited Activities and Exceptions. – (1) No United States citizen may engage in any exploration or commercial recovery unless authorized to do so under -
(A) a license or a permit issued under this title;
(B) a license, permit, or equivalent authorization issued by a reciprocating state; or
(C) an international agreement which is in force with respect to the United States.

...

(c) Interference. – No United States citizen may interfere or participate in interference with any activity conducted by any licensee or permittee which is authorized to be undertaken under a license or permit issued by the United States to the licensee or permittee under this Act or with any activity conducted by the holder or permittee under this Act or with any activity conducted by the holder of, and authorized to be undertaken under, a license or permit or equivalent authorization issued by a reciprocating state for the exploration or commercial recovery of hard mineral resources. United States citizens shall exercise their rights on the high seas with reasonable regard for the interests of other states in their exercise of the freedoms of the high seas.

SEC. 102. LICENSES FOR EXPLORATION AND PERMITS FOR COMMERCIAL RECOVERY

(a) Authority to Issue. – Subject to the provisions of this Act, the Administrator shall issue to applicants who are eligible therefor licenses for exploration and permits for commercial recovery.

(b) Nature of Licenses and Permits. – (1) A license or permit issued under this title shall authorize the holder thereof to engage in exploration or commercial recovery, as the case may be, consistent with the provisions of this Act, the regulations issued by the Administrator to implement the provisions of this Act, and the specific terms, conditions, and restrictions applied to the license or permit by the Administrator.

(2) Any license or permit issued under this title shall be exclusive with respect to the holder thereof as against any other United States citizen or any citizen, national or governmental agency of, or any legal entity organized or existing under the laws of, any reciprocating state.

(3) A valid existing license shall entitle the holder, if otherwise eligible under the provisions of this Act and regulations issued under this Act, to a permit for commercial recovery. Such a permit recognizes the right of the holder to recover hard mineral resources, and to own, transport, use, and sell hard mineral resources recovered, under the permit and in accordance with the requirements of this Act.

(4) In the event of interference with the exploration or commercial recovery activities of a licensee or permittee by nationals of other states, the Secretary of State

shall use all peaceful means to resolve the controversy by negotiation, conciliation, arbitration, or resort to agreed tribunals.

...

SEC.118. RECIPROCATING STATES

(a) Designation. – The Administrator, in consultation with the Secretary of State and the heads of other appropriate departments and agencies, may designate any foreign nation as a reciprocating state if the Secretary of State finds that such foreign nation –

(1) regulates the conduct of its citizens and other persons subject to its jurisdiction engaged in exploration for, and commercial recovery of, hard mineral resources of the deep seabed in a manner compatible with that provided in this Act and the regulations issued under this Act, which includes adequate measures for the protection of the environment, the conservation of natural resources, and the safety of life and property at sea, and includes effective enforcement provisions;

(2) recognizes licenses and permits issued under this title to the extent that such nation, under its laws, (A) prohibits any person from engaging in exploration or commercial recovery which conflicts with that authorized under any such license or permit and (B) complies with the date for issuance of licenses and the effective date for permits provided in section 102(c)(1)(D) of this Act;

(3) recognizes, under its procedures, priorities of right, consistent with those provided in this Act and the regulations issued under this Act, for applications for licenses for exploration or permits for commercial recovery, which applications are made either under its procedures or under this Act; and

(4) provides an interim legal framework for exploration and commercial recovery which does not unreasonably interfere with the interests of other states in their exercise of the freedoms of the high seas, as recognized under general principles of international law.

(b) Effect of Designation. – No license or permit shall be issued under this title permitting any exploration or commercial recovery which will conflict with any license, permit, or equivalent authorization issued by any foreign nation which is designated as a reciprocating state under subsection (a).

(c) Notification. – Upon receipt of any application for a license or permit under this title, the Administrator shall immediately notify all reciprocating states of such application. The notification shall include those portions of the exploration plan or recovery plan submitted with respect to the application, or a summary thereof, and any other appropriate information not required to be withheld from public disclosure by section 113(c).

(d) Revocation of Reciprocating State Status. – The Administrator, in consultation with the Secretary of State and the heads of other appropriate departments and agencies, shall revoke the designation of a foreign nation as a reciprocating state if the Secretary of State finds that such foreign nation no longer complies with the requirements of subsection (a). At the request of any holder of a license, permit, or equivalent authorization of such foreign nation, who obtained the license, permit, or equivalent authorization while such foreign nation was a reciprocating state, the Administrator, in consultation with the Secretary of State, may decide to recognise the license, permit, or equivalent authorization for purposes of subsection (b).

(e) Authorization. – The President is authorized to negotiate agreements with foreign nations necessary to implement this section.

(f) International Consultations. – The Administrator, in consultation with the Secretary of State and the heads of other appropriate departments and agencies, shall consult with foreign nations which enact, or are preparing to enact, domestic legislation establishing an interim legal framework for exploration and commercial recovery of hard mineral resources. Such consultations shall be carried out with a view to facilitating the designation of such nations as reciprocating states and, as necessary, the negotiation of agreements with foreign nations authorized by subsection (e). In addition, the Administrator shall provide such foreign nations with information on environmental impacts of exploration and commercial recovery activities, and shall provide any technical assistance requested in designing regulatory measures to protect the environment.

TITLE II – TRANSITION TO INTERNATIONAL AGREEMENT

SEC.201. DECLARATION OF CONGRESSIONAL INTENT

It is the intent of Congress –

(1) that any international agreement to which the United States becomes a party should, in addition to promoting other national oceans objectives –

(A) provide assured and non-discriminatory access, under reasonable terms and conditions, to the hard mineral resources of the deep seabed for United States citizens, and

(B) provide security of tenure by recognizing the rights of United States citizens who have undertaken exploration or commercial recovery under title I before such agreement enters into force with respect to the United States to continue their operations under terms, conditions, and restrictions which do not impose significant new economic burdens upon such citizens with respect to such operations with the effect of preventing the continuation of such operations on a viable economic basis;

(2) that the extent to which any such international agreement conforms to the provisions of paragraph (1) should be determined by the totality of the provisions of such agreement, including, but not limited to, the practical implications for the security of investments of any discretionary powers granted to an international regulatory body, the structures and decision-making procedures of such body, the availability of impartial and effective procedures for the settlement of disputes, and any features that tend to discriminate against exploration and commercial recovery activities undertaken by United States citizens; and

(3) that this Act should be transitional pending –

(A) the adoption of an international agreement at the Third United Nations Conference on the Law of the Sea, and the entering into force of such agreement, or portions thereof, with respect to the United States, or

(B) if such adoption is not forthcoming, the negotiation of a multilateral or other treaty concerning the deep seabed, and the entering into force of such treaty with respect to the United States.

SEC.202. EFFECT OF INTERNATIONAL AGREEMENT

If an international agreement enters into force with respect to the United States, any provision of title I, this title, or title III, and any regulation issued under any such provision, which is not inconsistent with such international agreement shall continue in effect with respect to United States citizens. In the implementation of such international agreement the Administrator, in consultation with the Secretary of State, shall make every effort, to the maximum extent practicable consistent with the provisions of that agreement, to provide for the continued operation of exploration and commercial recovery activities undertaken by United States citizens prior to entry into force of the agreement. The Administrator shall submit to the Congress, within one year after the date of such entry into force, a report on the actions taken by the Administrator under this section, which report shall include, but not be limited to –

(1) a description of the status of deep seabed mining operations of United States citizens under the international agreement; and

(2) an assessment of whether United States citizens who were engaged in exploration or commercial recovery on the date such agreement entered into force have been permitted to continue their operations.

SEC.203. PROTECTION OF INTERIM INVESTMENTS

In order to further the objectives set forth in section 201, the Administrator, not more than one year after the date of enactment of this Act –

(1) shall submit to the Congress proposed legislation necessary for the United States to implement a system for the protection of interim investments that has been adopted as part of an international agreement and any resolution relating to such international agreement; or

(2) if a system for the protection of interim investments has not been so adopted, shall report to the Congress on the status of negotiations relating to the establishment of such a system.

SEC.204. DISCLAIMER OF OBLIGATION TO PAY COMPENSATION

Sections 201 and 202 of this Act do not create or express any legal or moral obligation on the part of the United States Government to compensate any person for any impairment of the value of that person's investment in any operation for exploration or commercial recovery under title I which might occur in connection with the entering into force of an international agreement with respect to the United States.

...

SEC.403. ESTABLISHMENT OF DEEP SEABED REVENUE SHARING TRUST FUND

(a) Creation of Trust Fund. – There is established in the Treasury of the United States a trust fund to be known as the "Deep Seabed Revenue Sharing Trust Fund" (hereinafter in this section referred to as the "Trust Fund"), consisting of such amounts as may be appropriated or credited to the Trust Fund as provided in this section.

(b) Transfer to Trust Fund of Amounts Equivalent to Certain Taxes. –

(1) In General. – There are hereby appropriated to the Trust Fund amounts determined by the Secretary of the Treasury to be equivalent to the amounts of the taxes received in the Treasury under section 4495 of the Internal Revenue Code of 1954.

...

(d) Expenditures from Trust Fund. – If an international deep seabed treaty is ratified by and in effect with respect to the United States on or before the date ten years after the date of the enactment of this Act, amounts in the Trust Fund shall be available, as provided by appropriations Acts, for making contributions required under such treaty for purposes of the sharing among nations of the revenues from deep seabed mining.　Nothing in this subsection shall be deemed to authorize any program or other activity not otherwise authorized by law.

(e)　Use of Funds. − If an international deep seabed treaty is not in effect with respect to the United States on or before the date ten years after the date of the enactment of this Act, amounts in the Trust Fund shall be available for such purposes as Congress may hereafter provide by law.

12.7.1　UNITED STATES:
DEEP SEABED MINING EXPLORATION LICENCE USA - 2
ISSUED TO OCEAN MANAGEMENT, INC.

By note dated 13 January 1986, the Government of the United States conveyed to the United Nations notices published in the *Federal Register* of the United States, which provided public notice of the issuance in 1984 by the National Oceanic and Atmospheric Administration (NOAA), United States Department of Commerce, of four licences authorizing deep seabed hard mineral resources exploration in specified areas of the east-central Pacific Ocean.　Included in the *Federal Register* notices were the geographical co-ordinates of the deep seabed areas within which deep seabed hard mineral exploration has been authorized.　That note and the related licence notices were printed in the United Nations *Law of the Sea Bulletin* [LOS Bull.], No.7, April 1986.

As a result of negotiations which in July 1987 produced the successful resolution of mine site overlaps, three of the above licences have been modified to incorporate changes in site co-ordinates.　These licence amendments are set forth in the attached *Federal Register* notices ... [source: LOS Bull. No.12, December 1988, p.29]

[Excerpts are given below from the public notices published in 1984 in respect of the licence issued to Ocean Management Inc. (source:　LOS Bull. No.7, April 1986, pp.81-3) and in 1988 in respect of amendments of the licence (source:　LOS Bull. No.12, December 1988, pp.29-31)]

DEEP SEABED MINING; ISSUANCE OF EXPLORATION LICENCE

Agency:　National Oceanic and Atmospheric Administration, Commerce.
Action:　Notice of issuance of exploration licence to Ocean Management Inc., subject to terms, conditions, and restrictions.
Summary:　Pursuant to the Deep Seabed Hard Mineral Resources Act and 15 CFR Part 970, the National Oceanic and Atmospheric Administration on 29 August 1984 issued to Ocean Management, Inc., One New York Plaza, New York, N.Y. 10004, a licence to engage in deep seabed mining exploration activities subject to terms, conditions and restrictions, for a site designated USA-2, which is located in the Clarion-Clipperton Fracture Zone of the Northeastern Equatorial Pacific Ocean ...

...

Dated:　7 September 1984 ...

DEEP SEABED MINING; NOTICE OF AVAILABILITY OF INFORMATION

Agency: National Oceanic and Atmospheric Administration, Commerce.

Action: Notice of location of Ocean Management, Inc. deep seabed mining licence area.

Summary: On 29 August 1984, the National Oceanic and Atmospheric Administration (NOAA) issued a licence (designated as USA-2) to Ocean Management, Inc. (OMI) to conduct deep seabed mining exploration activities in an area of 136,000 square kilometers in the Northeastern Equatorial Pacific Ocean within the sea-bed area generally known as the Clarion-Clipperton Fracture Zone. OMI has now formally withdrawn its request for confidential treatment of the precise location of its licence area and requested NOAA to apprise the public of this fact and to publish the co-ordinates as well.

In accordance with this request and pursuant to 15 CFR 970.902(d)(5), NOAA hereby is publishing the co-ordinates of the OMI licence area.

The OMI licence applies to an area bounded by a line with the following turning points:

Turning point	Latitude	Longitude
1	15°25'N	134°00'W
2	14°00'N	134°00'W
3	14°00'N	133°50'W
4	11°30'N	133°50'W
5	11°30'N	136°00'W
6	10°50'N	136°00'W
7	10°50'N	137°50'W
8	12°30'N	137°50'W
9	12°30'N	136°00'W
10	15°25'N	136°00'W
1	15°25'N	134°00'W

...

DEEP SEABED MINING: APPROVAL OF REVISIONS TO MINE SITE AREAS AND PUBLICATION OF REVISED CO-ORDINATES

Agency: National Oceanic and Atmospheric Administration, Commerce

Action: Notice of approval of amendments to Deep Seabed Mining Exploration Licence areas and publication of revised co-ordinates.

Summary: Pursuant to the Deep Seabed Hard Mineral Resources Act and 15 CFR Part 970, and at the request of the affected U.S. licensees, the National Oceanic and Atmospheric Administration (NOAA) on 22 February 1988 approved revisions to exploration licences USA-2 and USA-3, issued to Ocean Management, Inc. (OMI) and Ocean Mining Associates (OMA), respectively.

...

In accordance with the provisions of 15 CFR 970.512 through 970.514, NOAA has modified the licence terms, conditions and restrictions (TCR (5)) of licences USA-2 and

USA-3 to restrict exploration activities so as to reflect the resolution of site overlaps. All other licence TCRs will remain in effect.

USA-2, issued to Ocean Management, Inc.

NOAA published the co-ordinates for the Ocean Management, Inc. exploration licence at 49 FR 48205 on 11 December 1984. That licence area is now amended, resulting in a change in operating area from approximately 135,100 square kilometres to approximately 112,500 square kilometres; a reduction of approximately 22,600 square kilometres. This amendment is accomplished as follows:
1) The licence area is reduced by OMI relinquishment of the following area:

Turning Points	Latitude (North)	Longitude (West)
1	12°50'	133°50'
2	12°50'	134°00'
3	13°00'	134°00'
4	13°00'	134°15'
5	12°30'	134°15'
6	12°30'	134°04'
7	12°11.6'	134°04'
8	12°11.6'	133°50'
1	12°50'	133°50'

The above area has been applied for to be added to the licence area of Ocean Minerals Company.
2) The operating area within the original licence area is reduced by adding new paragraphs (b) and (c) to TCR(5) of the licence terms, conditions and restrictions. TCR(5) now provides as follows:

(5) Freedom of the High Seas Requirements

(a) The licensee shall conduct its exploration activities in a manner which will not unreasonably interfere with the interests of other nations in their exercise of the freedoms of the high seas, as recognized under general principles of international law, such as fishing, navigation, submarine pipeline and cable laying, and scientific research 915 CFR 970.520).
(b) In particular, pursuant to the resolution of the deep seabed mining site overlap between Ocean Management, Inc., and Yuzhmorgeologiya, which is to be implemented as set forth in the agreement of 14 August 1987 between the United States and the Union of Soviet Socialist Republics, Ocean Management, Inc., shall not engage in exploration, and shall not physically interfere with the exploration or commercial recovery activities of other operators, in the following area:

Turning Points	Latitude (North)	Longitude (West)
1	13°30'	134°45'
2	13°30'	133°50'
3	12°50'	133°50'
4	12°50'	134°50'
5	13°00'	134°00'

6	13°00'	134°15'
7	12°30'	134°15'
8	12°30'	134°04'
9	12°11.6'	134°04'
10	12°11.6'	133°50'
11	11°30'	133°50'
12	11°30'	134°45'
1	13°30'	134°45'

(c) In the event of actions which may constitute a breach of the above agreement of 14 August 1987, including the understandings related thereto, the State Department, on its own initiative or at the request of NOAA or any affected licensee, will determine within 60 days after such initiative or request, and in consultation with NOAA and any affected licensee, if such a breach has occurred. If this is determined to be the case, the Department of State and NOAA, in consultation with any affected licensee, will take appropriate action to seek to remedy the breach. If such breach cannot be remedied within 90 days after it is determined a breach has occurred, NOAA shall, in accordance with NOAA regulations, remove or modify the restrictions set forth in TCR(5)(b), or take promptly such other action as is appropriate and effective.
...
Dated: 26 February 1988

12.8 CERTIFICATE OF REGISTRATION AS A PIONEER INVESTOR OF INSTITUT FRANÇAIS DE RECHERCHE POUR L'EXPLOITATION DE LA MER

Certificate of Registration

This is to certify that
Pursuant to the United Nations Convention on the Law of the Sea,
Resolution II of the Third United Nations Conference on the Law of the Sea governing preparatory investment in pioneer activities relating to polymetallic nodules,
The statement on the implementation of resolution II of 5 September 1986 and
The statement of understanding on the implementation of resolution II of 10 April 1987 of the Preparatory Commission for the International Seabed Authority and for the International Tribunal for the Law of the Sea, and
Having noted that the Government of the Republic of France
Has signed the United Nations Convention on the Law of the Sea on 10 December 1982, and, as a certifying State,
Has submitted, on behalf of Institut français de recherche pour l'exploitation de la mer, a French public industrial and commercial corporation, acting on behalf of Association française d'études et de recherche des nodules, an application for registration as a pioneer investor on 22 August 1984 and a revised application on 15 November 1987,
Has undertaken to comply with its obligations under the said resolution II and the aforementioned statements, and
Has undertaken to ensure that the pioneer activities are conducted in a manner compatible with the United Nations Convention on the Law of the Sea, and Pursuant to

The decision of the Preparatory Commission for the International Sea-Bed Authority and for the International Tribunal for the Law of the Sea to register Institut français de recherche pour l'exploitation de la mer acting on behalf of Association française d'études et de recherche des nodules as a pioneer investor adopted by its General Committee on 17 December 1987 in accordance with the Rules of Procedure of the Preparatory Commission,

Institut français de recherche pour l'exploitation de la mer acting on behalf of Association française d'études et de recherche des nodules,

Having undertaken to comply with its obligations under the said the resolution II and the aforementioned statements, and

Having made payment to the Preparatory Commission of the fee for registration as a pioneer investor, is registered as a Pioneer Investor and has been allocated the pioneer area, defined in the Schedule hereto, in accordance with the said the resolution II and with the aforementioned statements; and By virtue of the aforementioned decision and registration Institut français de recherche pour l'exploitation de la mer acting on behalf of Association française d'études et de recherche des nodules as a pioneer investor shall have the exclusive right to carry out pioneer activities in the pioneer area in accordance with the said resolution II.

GIVEN UNDER MY HAND and the official seal of the United Nations for and on behalf of the Preparatory Commission for the International Sea-Bed Authority and for the International Tribunal for the Law of the Sea at United Nations Headquarters, This 16th day of May 1988.

Javier Pérez de Cuéllar
Secretary-General of the United Nations

Schedule

The pioneer area shall be defined as that bounded by the lines joining the following turning points, the co-ordinates of which are:

[List of co-ordinates omitted.]

[source: *Law of the Sea Bulletin*, No, 12, December 1988, pp.39-40.]

12.9 GENERAL ASSEMBLY RESOLUTION A/48/263 OF 28 JULY 1994 ON AGREEMENT IMPLEMENTING PART XI OF THE UNITED NATIONS CONVENTION ON THE LAW OF THE SEA

The General Assembly,

Prompted by the desire to achieve universal participation in the United Nations Convention on the Law of the Sea of 10 December 1982 (hereinafter referred to as "the Convention")[1] and to promote appropriate representation in the institutions established by it,

Reaffirming that the seabed and ocean floor and subsoil thereof, beyond the limits of national jurisdiction (hereinafter referred to as the "Area"), as well as the resources of the Area, are the common heritage of mankind,[2]

Recalling that the Convention in its Part XI and related provisions (hereinafter referred to as "Part XI") established a regime for the Area and its resources,

Taking note of the consolidated provisional final report of the Preparatory Commission for the International Seabed Authority and for the International Tribunal for the Law of the Sea,[3]

Recalling its resolution 48/28 of 9 December 1993 on the law of the sea,

Recognizing that political and economic changes, including in particular a growing reliance on market principles, have necessitated the re-evaluation of some aspects of the regime for the Area and its resources,

Noting the initiative of the Secretary-General which began in 1990 to promote dialogue aimed at achieving universal participation in the Convention,

Welcoming the report of the Secretary-General on the outcome of his informal consultations, including the draft of an agreement relating to the implementation of Part XI,

Considering that the objective of universal participation in the Convention may best be achieved by the adoption of an agreement relating to the implementation of Part XI,

Recognizing the need to provide for the provisional application of such an agreement from the date of entry into force of the Convention on 16 November 1994,

1. *Expresses its appreciation* to the Secretary-General for his report on the informal consultations;

2. *Reaffirms* the unified character of the United Nations Convention on the Law of the Sea of 10 December 1982;

3. *Adopts* the Agreement relating to the Implementation of Part XI of the United Nations Convention on the Law of the Sea of 10 December 1982 (hereinafter referred to as "the Agreement"), the text of which is annexed to the present resolution;

4. *Affirms* that the Agreement shall be interpreted and applied together with Part XI as a single instrument;

5. *Considers* that future ratifications or formal confirmations of or accessions to the Convention shall represent also consent to be bound by the Agreement and that no State or entity may establish its consent to be bound by the Agreement unless it has previously established or establishes at the same time its consent to be bound by the Convention;

6. *Calls upon* States which consent to the adoption of the Agreement to refrain from any act which would defeat its object and purpose;

7. *Expresses its satisfaction* at the entry into force of the Convention on 16 November 1994;

8. *Decides* to fund the administrative expenses of the International Seabed Authority in accordance with section 1, paragraph 14, of the annex to the Agreement;

9. *Requests* the Secretary-General to transmit immediately certified copies of the Agreement to the States and entities referred to in article 3 thereof, with a view to facilitating universal participation in the Convention and the Agreement, and to draw attention to articles 4 and 5 of the Agreement;

10. *Also requests* the Secretary-General to open the Agreement for signature in accordance with article 3 thereof immediately after its adoption;

11. *Urges* all States and entities referred to in article 3 of the Agreement to consent to its provisional application as from 16 November 1994 and to establish their consent to be bound by the Agreement at the earliest possible date;

12. *Also urges* all such States and entities that have not already done so to take all appropriate steps to ratify, formally confirm or accede to the Convention at the earliest possible date in order to ensure universal participation in the Convention;

13. *Calls upon* the Preparatory Commission for the International Seabed Authority and for the International Tribunal for the Law of the Sea to take into account the terms of the Agreement when drawing up its final report.

Notes

1. *Official Records of the Third United Nations Conference on the Law of the Sea*, vol. XVII (United Nations publication, Sales No. E.84.V.3), document A/CONF.62/122.
2. General Assembly resolution 2749 (XXV); article 136 of the United Nations Convention on the Law of the Sea.
3. LOS/PCN/130 and Add. 1.

12.10 NEW YORK AGREEMENT OF 28 JULY 1994 RELATING TO THE IMPLEMENTATION OF PART XI OF THE UNITED NATIONS CONVENTION ON THE LAW OF THE SEA OF 10 DECEMBER 1982

The States Parties to this Agreement,

Recognizing the important contribution of the United Nations Convention on the Law of the Sea of 10 December 1982 (hereinafter referred to as "the Convention") to the maintenance of peace, justice and progress for all peoples of the world,

Reaffirming that the seabed and ocean floor and subsoil thereof, beyond the limits of national jurisdiction (hereinafter referred to as "the Area"), as well as the resources of the Area, are the common heritage of mankind,

Mindful of the importance of the Convention for the protection and preservation of the marine environment and of the growing concern for the global environment,

Having considered the report of the Secretary-General of the United Nations on the results of the informal consultations among States held from 1990 to 1994 on outstanding issues relating to Part XI and related provisions of the Convention (hereinafter referred to as "Part XI"),

Noting the political and economic changes, including market-orientated approaches, affecting the implementation of Part XI,

Wishing to facilitate universal participation in the Convention,

Considering that an agreement relating to the implementation of Part XI would best meet that objective,

Have agreed as follows:

Article 1
Implementation of Part XI

1. The States Parties to this Agreement undertake to implement Part XI in accordance with this Agreement.
2. The Annex forms an integral part of this Agreement.

Article 2
Relationship between this Agreement and Part XI

1. The provisions of this Agreement and Part XI shall be interpreted and applied together as a single instrument. In the event of any inconsistency between this Agreement and Part XI, the provisions of this Agreement shall prevail.
2. Articles 309 to 319 of the Convention shall apply to this Agreement as they apply to the Convention.

Article 3
Signature

This Agreement shall remain open for signature at United Nations Headquarters by the States and entities referred to in article 305, paragraph 1 (a), (c), (d), (e) and (f), of the Convention for 12 months from the date of its adoption.

Article 4
Consent to be bound

1. After the adoption of this Agreement, any instrument of ratification or formal confirmation of or accession to the Convention shall also represent consent to be bound by this Agreement.
2. No State or entity may establish its consent to be bound by this Agreement unless it has previously established or establishes at the same time its consent to be bound by the Convention.
3. A State or entity referred to in article 3 may express its consent to be bound by this Agreement by:
   (a) Signature not subject to ratification, formal confirmation or the procedure set out in article 5;
   (b) Signature subject to ratification or formal confirmation, followed by ratification or formal confirmation;
   (c) Signature subject to the procedure set out in article 5; or
   (d) Accession.
4. Formal confirmation by the entities referred to in article 305, paragraph 1 (f), of the Convention shall be in accordance with Annex IX of the Convention.
5. The instruments of ratification, formal confirmation or accession shall be deposited with the Secretary-General of the United Nations.

Article 5
Simplified procedure

1. A State or entity which has deposited before the date of the adoption of this Agreement an instrument of ratification or formal confirmation of or accession to the Convention and which has signed this Agreement in accordance with article 4, paragraph 3 (c), shall be considered to have established its consent to be bound by this Agreement 12 months after the date of its adoption, unless that State or entity notifies the depositary in writing before that date that it is not availing itself of the simplified procedure set out in this article.
2. In the event of such notification, consent to be bound by this Agreement shall be established in accordance with article 4, paragraph 3 (b).

Article 6
Entry into force

1. This Agreement shall enter into force 30 days after the date on which 40 States have established their consent to be bound in accordance with articles 4 and 5, provided that such States include at least seven of the States referred to in paragraph 1 (a) of resolution II of the Third United Nations Conference on the Law of the Sea (hereinafter referred to as "resolution II") and that at least five of those States are developed States.

If these conditions for entry into force are fulfilled before 16 November 1994, this Agreement shall enter into force on 16 November 1994.

2. For each State or entity establishing its consent to be bound by this Agreement after the requirements set out in paragraph 1 have been fulfilled, this Agreement shall enter into force on the thirtieth day following the date of establishment of its consent to be bound.

Article 7
Provisional application

1. If on 16 November 1994 this Agreement has not entered into force, it shall be applied provisionally pending its entry into force by:

(a) States which have consented to its adoption in the General Assembly of the United Nations, except any such State which before 16 November 1994 notifies the depositary in writing either that it will not so apply this Agreement or that it will consent to such application only upon subsequent signature or notification in writing;

(b) States and entities which sign this Agreement, except any such State or entity which notifies the depositary in writing at the time of signature that it will not so apply this Agreement;

(c) States and entities which consent to its provisional application by so notifying the depositary in writing;

(d) States which accede to this Agreement.

2. All such States and entities shall apply this Agreement provisionally in accordance with their national or internal laws and regulations, with effect from 16 November 1994 or the date of signature, notification of consent or accession, if later.

3. Provisional application shall terminate upon the date of entry into force of this Agreement. In any event, provisional application shall terminate on 16 November 1998 if at that date the requirement in article 6, paragraph 1, of consent to be bound by this Agreement by at least seven of the States (of which at least five must be developed States) referred to in paragraph 1 (a) of resolution II has not been fulfilled.

Article 8
States Parties

1. For the purposes of this Agreement, "States Parties" means States which have consented to be bound by this Agreement and for which this Agreement is in force.

2. This Agreement applies *mutatis mutandis* to the entities referred to in article 305, paragraph 1 (c), (d), (e) and (f), of the Convention which become Parties to this Agreement in accordance with the conditions relevant to each, and to that extent "States Parties" refers to those entities.

Article 9
Depositary

The Secretary-General of the United Nations shall be the depositary of this Agreement.

Article 10
Authentic texts

The original of this Agreement, of which the Arabic, Chinese, English, French, Russian and Spanish texts are equally authentic, shall be deposited with the Secretary-General of the United Nations.

IN WITNESS WHEREOF, the undersigned Plenipotentiaries, being duly authorized thereto, have signed this Agreement.

DONE AT NEW YORK, this twenty eighth day of July, one thousand nine hundred and ninety-four.

ANNEX

SECTION 1. COSTS TO STATES PARTIES AND INSTITUTIONAL ARRANGEMENTS

1. The International Seabed Authority (hereinafter referred to as "the Authority") is the organization through which States Parties to the Convention shall, in accordance with the regime for the Area established in Part XI and this Agreement, organize and control activities in the Area, particularly with a view to administering the resources of the Area. The powers and functions of the Authority shall be those expressly conferred upon it by the Convention. The Authority shall have such incidental powers, consistent with the Convention, as are implicit in, and necessary for, the exercise of those powers and functions with respect to activities in the Area.

2. In order to minimise costs to States Parties, all organs and subsidiary bodies to be established under the Convention and this Agreement shall be cost-effective. This principle shall also apply to the frequency, duration and scheduling of meetings.

3. The setting up and the functioning of the organs and subsidiary bodies of the Authority shall be based on an evolutionary approach, taking into account the functional needs of the organs and subsidiary bodies concerned in order that they may discharge effectively their respective responsibilities at various stages of the development of activities in the Area.

4. The early functions of the Authority upon entry into force of the Convention shall be carried out by the Assembly, the Council, the Secretariat, the Legal and Technical Commission and the Finance Committee. The functions of the Economic Planning Commission shall be performed by the Legal and Technical Commission until such time as the Council decides otherwise or until the approval of the first plan of work for exploitation.

5. Between the entry into force of the Convention and the approval of the first plan of work for exploitation, the Authority shall concentrate on:

(a) Processing of applications for approval of plans of work for exploration in accordance with Part XI and this Agreement;

(b) Implementation of decisions of the Preparatory Commission for the International Seabed Authority and for the International Tribunal for the Law of the Sea (hereinafter referred to as "the Preparatory Commission") relating to the registered pioneer investors and their certifying States, including their rights and obligations, in accordance with article 308, paragraph 5, of the Convention and resolution II, paragraph 13;

(c) Monitoring of compliance with plans of work for exploration approved in the form of contracts;

(d) Monitoring and review of trends and developments relating to deep seabed mining activities, including regular analysis of world metal market conditions and metal prices, trends and prospects;

(e) Study of the potential impact of mineral production from the Area on the economies of developing land-based producers of those minerals which are likely to be most seriously affected, with a view to minimizing their difficulties and assisting them in their economic adjustment, taking into account the work done in this regard by the Preparatory Commission;

(f) Adoption of rules, regulations and procedures necessary for the conduct of activities in the Area as they progress. Notwithstanding the provisions of Annex III, article 17, paragraph 2 (b) and (c), of the Convention, such rules, regulations and procedures shall take into account the terms of this Agreement, the prolonged delay in commercial deep seabed mining and the likely pace of activities in the Area;

(g) Adoption of rules, regulations and procedures incorporating applicable standards for the protection and preservation of the marine environment;

(h) Promotion and encouragement of the conduct of marine scientific research with respect to activities in the Area and the collection and dissemination of the results of such research and analysis, when available, with particular emphasis on research related to the environmental impact of activities in the Area;

(i) Acquisition of scientific knowledge and monitoring of the development of marine technology relevant to activities in the Area, in particular technology relating to the protection and preservation of the marine environment;

(j) Assessment of available data relating to prospecting and exploration;

(k) Timely elaboration of rules, regulations and procedures for exploitation, including those relating to the protection and preservation of the marine environment.

6. (a) An application for approval of a plan of work for exploration shall be considered by the Council following the receipt of a recommendation on the application from the Legal and Technical Commission. The processing of an application for approval of a plan of work for exploration shall be in accordance with the provisions of the Convention, including Annex II thereof, and this Agreement, and subject to the following:

(i) A plan of work for exploration submitted on behalf of a State or entity, or any component of such entity, referred to in resolution II, paragraph 1 (a) (ii) or (iii), other than a registered pioneer investor, which had already undertaken substantial activities in the Area prior to the entry into force of the Convention, or its successor in interest, shall be considered to have met the financial and technical qualifications necessary for approval of a plan of work if the sponsoring State or States certify that the applicant has expended an amount equivalent to at least US\$ 30 million in research and exploration activities and has expended no less than 10 per cent of that amount in the location, survey and evaluation of the area referred to in the plan of work. If the plan of work otherwise satisfies the requirements of the Convention and any rules, regulations and procedures adopted pursuant thereto, it shall be approved by the Council in the form of a contract. The provisions of section 3, paragraph 11, of this Annex shall be interpreted and applied accordingly;

(ii) Notwithstanding the provisions of resolution II, paragraph 8 (a), a registered pioneer investor may request approval of a plan of work for exploration within 36 months of the entry into force of the Convention. The plan of work for exploration shall consist of documents, reports and other data submitted to the Preparatory Commission both before and after registration and shall be accompanied by a certificate of compliance, consisting of a factual report describing the status of fulfilment of obligations under the pioneer investor regime, issued by the Preparatory Commission in accordance with resolution II, paragraph 11 (a). Such a plan of work shall be considered to be approved. Such an approved plan of work shall be in the form of a contract concluded between the Authority and the registered pioneer investor in accordance with Part XI and this Agreement. The fee of US$ 250,000 paid pursuant to resolution II, paragraph 7 (a), shall be deemed to be the fee relating to the exploration phase pursuant to section 8, paragraph 3, of this Annex. Section 3, paragraph 11, of this Annex shall be interpreted and applied accordingly;

(iii) In accordance with the principle of non-discrimination, a contract with a State or entity or any component of such entity referred to in subparagraph (a) (i) shall include arrangements which shall be similar to and no less favourable than those agreed with any registered pioneer investor referred to in subparagraph (a) (ii). If any of the States or entities or any components of such entities referred to in subparagraph (a) (i) are granted more favourable arrangements, the Council shall make similar and no less favourable arrangements with investors referred to in subparagraph (a) (ii), provided that such arrangements do not affect or prejudice the interests of the Authority;

(iv) A State sponsoring an application for a plan of work pursuant to the provisions of subparagraph (a) (i) or (ii) may be a State Party or a State which is applying this Agreement provisionally in accordance with article 7, or a State which is a member of the Authority on a provisional basis in accordance with paragraph 12;

(v) Resolution II, paragraph 8 (c), shall be interpreted and applied in accordance with subparagraph (a) (iv).

(b) The approval of a plan of work for exploration shall be in accordance with article 153, paragraph 3, of the Convention.

7. An application for approval of a plan of work shall be accompanied by an assessment of the potential environmental impacts of the proposed activities and by a description of a programme for oceanographic and baseline environmental studies in accordance with the rules, regulations and procedures adopted by the Authority.

8. An application for approval of a plan of work for exploration, subject to paragraph 6 (a) (i) or (ii), shall be processed in accordance with the procedures set out in section 3, paragraph 11, of this Annex.

9. A plan of work for exploration shall be approved for a period of 15 years. Upon the expiration of a plan of work for exploration, the contractor shall apply for a plan of work for exploitation unless the contractor has already done so or has obtained an extension for the plan of work for exploration. Contractors may apply for such extensions for periods of not more than five years each. Such extensions shall be approved if the contractor has made efforts in good faith to comply with the requirements of the plan of work but for reasons beyond the contractor's control has been unable to complete the necessary preparatory work for proceeding to the exploitation stage or if the prevailing economic circumstances do not justify proceeding to the exploitation stage.

10. Designation of a reserved area for the Authority in accordance with Annex III, article 8, of the Convention shall take place in connection with approval of an application for a plan of work for exploration or approval of an application for a plan of work for exploration and exploitation.

11. Notwithstanding the provisions of paragraph 9, an approved plan of work for exploration which is sponsored by at least one State provisionally applying this

Agreement shall terminate if such a State ceases to apply this Agreement provisionally and has not become a member on a provisional basis in accordance with paragraph 12 or has not become a State Party.

12. Upon the entry into force of this Agreement, States and entities referred to in article 3 of this Agreement which have been applying it provisionally in accordance with article 7 and for which it is not in force may continue to be members of the Authority on a provisional basis pending its entry into force for such States and entities, in accordance with the following subparagraphs:

(a) If this Agreement enters into force before 16 November 1996, such States and entities shall be entitled to continue to participate as members of the Authority on a provisional basis upon notification to the depositary of the Agreement by such a State or entity of its intention to participate as a member on a provisional basis. Such membership shall terminate either on 16 November 1996 or upon the entry into force of this Agreement and the Convention for such member, whichever is earlier. The Council may, upon the request of the State or entity concerned, extend such membership beyond 16 November 1996 for a further period or periods not exceeding a total of two years provided that the Council is satisfied that the State or entity concerned has been making efforts in good faith to become a party to the Agreement and the Convention;

(b) If this Agreement enters into force after 15 November 1996, such States and entities may request the Council to grant continued membership in the Authority on a provisional basis for a period or periods not extending beyond 16 November 1998. The Council shall grant such membership with effect from the date of the request if it is satisfied that the State or entity has been making efforts in good faith to become a party to the Agreement and the Convention;

(c) States and entities which are members of the Authority on a provisional basis in accordance with subparagraph (a) or (b) shall apply the terms of Part XI and this Agreement in accordance with their national or internal laws, regulations and annual budgetary appropriations and shall have the same rights and obligations as other members, including:

(i) The obligation to contribute to the administrative budget of the Authority in accordance with the scale of assessed contributions;

(ii) The right to sponsor an application for approval of a plan of work for exploration. In the case of entities whose components are natural or juridical persons possessing the nationality of more than one State, a plan of work for exploration shall not be approved unless all the States whose natural or juridical persons comprise those entities are States Parties or members on a provisional basis;

(d) Notwithstanding the provisions of paragraph 9, an approved plan of work in the form of a contract for exploration which was sponsored pursuant to subparagraph (c) (ii) by a State which was a member on a provisional basis shall terminate if such membership ceases and the State or entity has not become a State Party;

(e) If such a member has failed to make its assessed contributions or otherwise failed to comply with its obligations in accordance with this paragraph, its membership on a provisional basis shall be terminated.

13. The reference in Annex III, article 10, of the Convention to performance which has not been satisfactory shall be interpreted to mean that the contractor has failed to comply with the requirements of an approved plan of work in spite of a written warning or warnings from the Authority to the contractor to comply therewith.

14. The Authority shall have its own budget. Until the end of the year following the year during which this Agreement enters into force, the administrative expenses of the Authority shall be met through the budget of the United Nations. Thereafter, the administrative expenses of the Authority shall be met by assessed contributions of its members, including any members on a provisional basis, in accordance with articles 171, subparagraph (a), and 173 of the Convention and this Agreement, until the Authority has sufficient funds from other sources to meet those expenses. The Authority shall not exercise the power referred to in article 174, paragraph 1, of the Convention to borrow funds to finance its administrative budget.

15. The Authority shall elaborate and adopt, in accordance with article 162, paragraph 2 (o) (ii), of the Convention, rules, regulations and procedures based on the principles contained in sections 2, 5, 6, 7 and 8 of this Annex, as well as any additional rules, regulations and procedures necessary to facilitate the approval of plans of work for exploration or exploitation, in accordance with the following subparagraphs:

(a) The Council may undertake such elaboration any time it deems that all or any of such rules, regulations or procedures are required for the conduct of activities in the Area, or when it determines that commercial exploitation is imminent, or at the request of a State whose national intends to apply for approval of a plan of work for exploitation;

(b) If a request is made by a State referred to in subparagraph (a) the Council shall, in accordance with article 162, paragraph 2 (o), of the Convention, complete the adoption of such rules, regulations and procedures within two years of the request;

(c) If the Council has not completed the elaboration of the rules, regulations and procedures relating to exploitation within the prescribed time and an application for approval of a plan of work for exploitation is pending, it shall none the less consider and provisionally approve such plan of work based on the provisions of the Convention and any rules, regulations and procedures that the Council may have adopted provisionally, or on the basis of the norms contained in the Convention and the terms and principles contained in this Annex as well as the principle of non-discrimination among contractors.

16. The draft rules, regulations and procedures and any recommendations relating to the provisions of Part XI, as contained in the reports and recommendations of the Preparatory Commission, shall be taken into account by the Authority in the adoption of rules, regulations and procedures in accordance with Part XI and this Agreement.

17. The relevant provisions of Part XI, section 4, of the Convention shall be interpreted and applied in accordance with this Agreement.

SECTION 2. THE ENTERPRISE

1. The Secretariat of the Authority shall perform the functions of the Enterprise until it begins to operate independently of the Secretariat. The Secretary-General of the Authority shall appoint from within the staff of the Authority an interim Director-General to oversee the performance of these functions by the Secretariat. These functions shall be:

(a) Monitoring and review of trends and developments relating to deep seabed mining activities, including regular analysis of world metal market conditions and metal prices, trends and prospects;

(b) Assessment of the results of the conduct of marine scientific research with respect to activities in the Area, with particular emphasis on research related to the environmental impact of activities in the Area;

(c) Assessment of available data relating to prospecting and exploration, including the criteria for such activities;

(d) Assessment of technological developments relevant to activities in the Area, in particular technology relating to the protection and preservation of the marine environment;

(e) Evaluation of information and data relating to areas reserved for the Authority;

(f) Assessment of approaches to joint-venture operations;

(g) Collection of information on the availability of trained manpower;

(h) Study of managerial policy options for the administration of the Enterprise at different stages of its operations.

2. The Enterprise shall conduct its initial deep seabed mining operations through joint ventures. Upon the approval of a plan of work for exploitation for an entity other than the Enterprise, or upon receipt by the Council of an application for a joint-venture operation with the Enterprise, the Council shall take up the issue of the functioning of the Enterprise independently of the Secretariat of the Authority. If joint-venture operations with the Enterprise accord with sound commercial principles, the Council shall issue a directive pursuant to article 170, paragraph 2, of the Convention providing for such independent functioning.

3. The obligation of States Parties to fund one mine site of the Enterprise as provided for in Annex IV, article 11, paragraph 3, of the Convention shall not apply and States Parties shall be under no obligation to finance any of the operations in any mine site of the Enterprise or under its joint-venture arrangements.

4. The obligations applicable to contractors shall apply to the Enterprise. Notwithstanding the provisions of article 153, paragraph 3, and Annex III, article 3, paragraph 5, of the Convention, a plan of work for the Enterprise upon its approval shall be in the form of a contract concluded between the Authority and the Enterprise.

5. A contractor which has contributed a particular area to the Authority as a reserved area has the right of first refusal to enter into a joint-venture arrangement with the Enterprise for exploration and exploitation of that area. If the Enterprise does not submit an application for a plan of work for activities in respect of such a reserved area within 15 years of the commencement of its functions independent of the Secretariat of the Authority or within 15 years of the date on which that area is reserved for the Authority, whichever is the later, the contractor which contributed the area shall be entitled to apply for a plan of work for that area provided it offers in good faith to include the Enterprise as a joint-venture partner.

6. Article 170, paragraph 4, Annex IV and other provisions of the Convention relating to the Enterprise shall be interpreted and applied in accordance with this section.

SECTION 3. DECISION-MAKING

1. The general policies of the Authority shall be established by the Assembly in collaboration with the Council.

2. As a general rule, decision-making in the organs of the Authority should be by consensus.

3. If all efforts to reach a decision by consensus have been exhausted, decisions by voting in the Assembly on questions of procedure shall be taken by a majority of members present and voting, and decisions on questions of substance shall be taken by

a two-thirds majority of members present and voting, as provided for in article 159, paragraph 8, of the Convention.

4. Decisions of the Assembly on any matter for which the Council also has competence or on any administrative, budgetary or financial matter shall be based on the recommendations of the Council. If the Assembly does not accept the recommendation of the Council on any matter, it shall return the matter to the Council for further consideration. The Council shall reconsider the matter in the light of the views expressed by the Assembly.

5. If all efforts to reach a decision by consensus have been exhausted, decisions by voting in the Council on questions of procedure shall be taken by a majority of members present and voting, and decisions on questions of substance, except where the Convention provides for decisions by consensus in the Council, shall be taken by a two-thirds majority of members present and voting, provided that such decisions are not opposed by a majority in any one of the chambers referred to in paragraph 9. In taking decisions the Council shall seek to promote the interests of all the members of the Authority.

6. The Council may defer the taking of a decision in order to facilitate further negotiation whenever it appears that all efforts at achieving consensus on a question have not been exhausted.

7. Decisions by the Assembly or the Council having financial or budgetary implications shall be based on the recommendations of the Finance Committee.

8. The provisions of article 161, paragraph 8 (b) and (c), of the Convention shall not apply.

9. (a) Each group of States elected under paragraph 15 (a) to (c) shall be treated as a chamber for the purposes of voting in the Council. The developing States elected under paragraph 15 (d) and (e) shall be treated as a single chamber for the purposes of voting in the Council.

(b) Before electing the members of the Council, the Assembly shall establish lists of countries fulfilling the criteria for membership in the groups of States in paragraph 15 (a) to (d). If a State fulfils the criteria for membership in more than one group, it may only be proposed by one group for election to the Council and it shall represent only that group in voting in the Council.

10. Each group of States in paragraph 15 (a) to (d) shall be represented in the Council by those members nominated by that group. Each group shall nominate only as many candidates as the number of seats required to be filled by that group. When the number of potential candidates in each of the groups referred to in paragraph 15 (a) to (e) exceeds the number of seats available in each of those respective groups, as a general rule, the principle of rotation shall apply. States members of each of those groups shall determine how this principle shall apply in those groups.

11. (a) The Council shall approve a recommendation by the Legal and Technical Commission for approval of a plan of work unless by a two-thirds majority of its members present and voting, including a majority of members present and voting in each of the chambers of the Council, the Council decides to disapprove a plan of work. If the Council does not take a decision on a recommendation for approval of a plan of work within a prescribed period, the recommendation shall be deemed to have been approved by the Council at the end of that period. The prescribed period shall normally be 60 days unless the Council decides to provide for a longer period. If the Commission recommends the disapproval of a plan of work or does not make a recommendation, the Council may nevertheless approve the plan of work in accordance with its rules of procedure for decision-making on questions of substance.

(b) The provisions of article 162, paragraph 2 (j), of the Convention shall not apply.

12. Where a dispute arises relating to the disapproval of a plan of work, such dispute shall be submitted to the dispute settlement procedures set out in the Convention.

13. Decisions by voting in the Legal and Technical Commission shall be by a majority of members present and voting.

14. Part XI, section 4, subsections B and C, of the Convention shall be interpreted and applied in accordance with this section.

15. The Council shall consist of 36 members of the Authority elected by the Assembly in the following order:

(a) Four members from among those States Parties which, during the last five years for which statistics are available, have either consumed more than 2 per cent in value terms of total world consumption or have had net imports of more than 2 per cent in value terms of total world imports of the commodities produced from the categories of minerals to be derived from the Area, provided that the four members shall include one State from the Eastern European region having the largest economy in that region in terms of gross domestic product and the State, on the date of entry into force of the Convention, having the largest economy in terms of gross domestic product, if such States wish to be represented in this group;

(b) Four members from among the eight States Parties which have made the largest investments in preparation for and in the conduct of activities in the Area, either directly or through their nationals;

(c) Four members from among States Parties which, on the basis of production in areas under their jurisdiction, are major net exporters of the categories of minerals to be derived from the Area, including at least two developing States whose exports of such minerals have a substantial bearing upon their economies;

(d) Six members from among developing States Parties, representing special interests. The special interests to be represented shall include those of States with large populations, States which are land-locked or geographically disadvantaged, island States, States which are major importers of the categories of minerals to be derived from the Area, States which are potential producers of such minerals and least developed States;

(e) Eighteen members elected according to the principle of ensuring an equitable geographical distribution of seats in the Council as a whole, provided that each geographical region shall have at least one member elected under this subparagraph. For this purpose, the geographical regions shall be Africa, Asia, Eastern Europe, Latin America and the Caribbean and Western Europe and Others.[*]

16. The provisions of article 161, paragraph 1, of the Convention shall not apply.

SECTION 4. REVIEW CONFERENCE

The provisions relating to the Review Conference in article 155, paragraphs 1, 3 and 4, of the Convention shall not apply. Notwithstanding the provisions of article 314, paragraph 2, of the Convention, the Assembly, on the recommendation of the Council, may undertake at any time a review of the matters referred to in article 155, paragraph 1, of the Convention. Amendments relating to this Agreement and Part XI shall be subject to the procedures contained in articles 314, 315 and 316 of the Convention, provided that the principles, regime and other terms referred to in article 155, paragraph 2, of the Convention shall be maintained and the rights referred to in paragraph 5 of that article shall not be affected.

SECTION 5. TRANSFER OF TECHNOLOGY

1. In addition to the provisions of article 144 of the Convention, transfer of technology for the purposes of Part XI shall be governed by the following principles:

(a) The Enterprise, and developing States wishing to obtain deep seabed mining technology, shall seek to obtain such technology on fair and reasonable commercial terms and conditions on the open market, or through joint-venture arrangements;

(b) If the Enterprise or developing States are unable to obtain deep seabed mining technology, the Authority may request all or any of the contractors and their respective sponsoring State or States to cooperate with it in facilitating the acquisition of deep seabed mining technology by the Enterprise or its joint venture, or by a developing State or States seeking to acquire such technology on fair and reasonable commercial terms and conditions, consistent with the effective protection of intellectual property rights. States Parties undertake to cooperate fully and effectively with the Authority for this purpose and to ensure that contractors sponsored by them also cooperate fully with the Authority;

(c) As a general rule, States Parties shall promote international technical and scientific cooperation with regard to activities in the Area either between the parties concerned or by developing training, technical assistance and scientific cooperation programmes in marine science and technology and the protection and preservation of the marine environment.

2. The provisions of Annex III, article 5, of the Convention shall not apply.

SECTION 6. PRODUCTION POLICY

1. The production policy of the Authority shall be based on the following principles:

(a) Development of the resources of the Area shall take place in accordance with sound commercial principles;

(b) The provisions of the General Agreement on Tariffs and Trade, its relevant codes and successor or superseding agreements shall apply with respect to activities in the Area;

(c) In particular, there shall be no subsidization of activities in the Area except as may be permitted under the agreements referred to in subparagraph (b). Subsidization for the purpose of these principles shall be defined in terms of the agreements referred to in subparagraph (b);

(d) There shall be no discrimination between minerals derived from the Area and from other sources. There shall be no preferential access to markets for such minerals or for imports of commodities produced from such minerals, in particular:

(i) By the use of tariff or non-tariff barriers; and

(ii) Given by States Parties to such minerals or commodities produced by their state enterprises or by natural or juridical persons which possess their nationality or are controlled by them or their nationals;

(e) The plan of work for exploitation approved by the Authority in respect of each mining area shall indicate an anticipated production schedule which shall include the estimated maximum amounts of minerals that would be produced per year under the plan of work;

(f) The following shall apply to the settlement of disputes concerning the provisions of the agreements referred to in subparagraph (b):

(i) Where the States Parties concerned are parties to such agreements, they shall have recourse to the dispute settlement procedures of those agreements;

(ii) Where one or more of the States Parties concerned are not parties to such agreements, they shall have recourse to the dispute settlement procedures set out in the Convention;

(g) In circumstances where a determination is made under the agreements referred to in subparagraph (b) that a State Party has engaged in subsidization which is prohibited or has resulted in adverse effects on the interests of another State Party and appropriate steps have not been taken by the relevant State Party or States Parties, a State Party may request the Council to take appropriate measures.

2. The principles contained in paragraph 1 shall not affect the rights and obligations under any provision of the agreements referred to in paragraph 1 (b), as well as the relevant free trade and customs union agreements, in relations between States Parties which are parties to such agreements.

3. The acceptance by a contractor of subsidies other than those which may be permitted under the agreements referred to in paragraph 1 (b) shall constitute a violation of the fundamental terms of the contract forming a plan of work for the carrying out of activities in the Area.

4. Any State Party which has reason to believe that there has been a breach of the requirements of paragraphs 1 (b) to (d) or 3 may initiate dispute settlement procedures in conformity with paragraph 1 (f) or (g).

5. A State Party may at any time bring to the attention of the Council activities which in its view are inconsistent with the requirements of paragraph 1 (b) to (d).

6. The Authority shall develop rules, regulations and procedures which ensure the implementation of the provisions of this section, including relevant rules, regulations and procedures governing the approval of plans of work.

7. The provisions of article 151, paragraphs 1 to 7 and 9, article 162, paragraph 2 (q), article 165, paragraph 2 (n), and Annex III, article 6, paragraph 5, and article 7, of the Convention shall not apply.

SECTION 7. ECONOMIC ASSISTANCE

1. The policy of the Authority of assisting developing countries which suffer serious adverse effects on their export earnings or economies resulting from a reduction in the price of an affected mineral or in the volume of exports of that mineral, to the extent that such reduction is caused by activities in the Area, shall be based on the following principles:

(a) The Authority shall establish an economic assistance fund from a portion of the funds of the Authority which exceeds those necessary to cover the administrative expenses of the Authority. The amount set aside for this purpose shall be determined by the Council from time to time, upon the recommendation of the Finance Committee. Only funds from payments received from contractors, including the Enterprise, and voluntary contributions shall be used for the establishment of the economic assistance fund;

(b) Developing land-based producer States whose economies have been determined to be seriously affected by the production of minerals from the deep seabed shall be assisted from the economic assistance fund of the Authority;

(c) The Authority shall provide assistance from the fund to affected developing land-based producer States, where appropriate, in cooperation with existing global or regional development institutions which have the infrastructure and expertise to carry out such assistance programmes;

(d) The extent and period of such assistance shall be determined on a case-by-case basis. In doing so, due consideration shall be given to the nature and magnitude of the problems encountered by affected developing land-based producer States.

2. Article 151, paragraph 10, of the Convention shall be implemented by means of measures of economic assistance referred to in paragraph 1. Article 160, paragraph 2 (1), article 162, paragraph 2 (n), article 164, paragraph 2 (d), article 171, subparagraph (f), and article 173, paragraph 2 (c), of the Convention shall be interpreted accordingly.

SECTION 8. FINANCIAL TERMS OF CONTRACTS

1. The following principles shall provide the basis for establishing rules, regulations and procedures for financial terms of contracts:

(a) The system of payments to the Authority shall be fair both to the contractor and to the Authority and shall provide adequate means of determining compliance by the contractor with such system;

(b) The rates of payments under the system shall be within the range of those prevailing in respect of land-based mining of the same or similar minerals in order to avoid giving deep seabed miners an artificial competitive advantage or imposing on them a competitive disadvantage;

(c) The system should not be complicated and should not impose major administrative costs on the Authority or on a contractor. Consideration should be given to the adoption of a royalty system or a combination of a royalty and profit-sharing system. If alternative systems are decided upon, the contractor has the right to choose the system applicable to its contract. Any subsequent change in choice between alternative systems, however, shall be made by agreement between the Authority and the contractor;

(d) An annual fixed fee shall be payable from the date of commencement of commercial production. This fee may be credited against other payments due under the system adopted in accordance with subparagraph (c). The amount of the fee shall be established by the Council;

(e) The system of payments may be revised periodically in the light of changing circumstances. Any changes shall be applied in a non-discriminatory manner. Such changes may apply to existing contracts only at the election of the contractor. Any subsequent change in choice between alternative systems shall be made by agreement between the Authority and the contractor;

(f) Disputes concerning the interpretation or application of the rules and regulations based on these principles shall be subject to the dispute settlement procedures set out in the Convention.

2. The provisions of Annex III, article 13, paragraphs 3 to 10, of the Convention shall not apply.

3. With regard to the implementation of Annex III, article 13, paragraph 2, of the Convention, the fee for processing applications for approval of a plan of work limited

to one phase, either the exploration phase or the exploitation phase, shall be US$ 250,000.

SECTION 9.   THE FINANCE COMMITTEE

1.   There is hereby established a Finance Committee.   The Committee shall be composed of 15 members with appropriate qualifications relevant to financial matters. States Parties shall nominate candidates of the highest standards of competence and integrity.

2.   No two members of the Finance Committee shall be nationals of the same State Party.

3.   Members of the Finance Committee shall be elected by the Assembly and due account shall be taken of the need for equitable geographical distribution and the representation of special interests.   Each group of States referred to in section 3, paragraph 15 (a), (b), (c) and (d), of this Annex shall be represented on the Committee by at least one member.   Until the Authority has sufficient funds other than assessed contributions to meet its administrative expenses, the membership of the Committee shall include representatives of the five largest financial contributors to the administrative budget of the Authority.   Thereafter, the election of one member from each group shall be on the basis of nomination by the members of the respective group, without prejudice to the possibility of further members being elected from each group.

4.   Members of the Finance Committee shall hold office for a term of five years. They shall be eligible for re-election for a further term.

5.   In the event of the death, incapacity or resignation of a member of the Finance Committee prior to the expiration of the term of office, the Assembly shall elect for the remainder of the term a member from the same geographical region or group of States.

6.   Members of the Finance Committee shall have no financial interest in any activity relating to matters upon which the Committee has the responsibility to make recommendations.   They shall not disclose, even after the termination of their functions, any confidential information coming to their knowledge by reason of their duties for the Authority.

7.   Decisions by the Assembly and the Council on the following issues shall take into account recommendations of the Finance Committee:

(a)   Draft financial rules, regulations and procedures of the organs of the Authority and the financial management and internal financial administration of the Authority;

(b)   Assessment of contributions of members to the administrative budget of the Authority in accordance with article 160, paragraph 2 (e) of the Convention;

(c)   All relevant financial matters, including the proposed annual budget prepared by the Secretary-General of the Authority in accordance with article 172 of the Convention and the financial aspects of the implementation of the programmes of work of the Secretariat;

(d)   The administrative budget;

(e)   Financial obligations of States Parties arising from the implementation of this Agreement and Part XI as well as the administrative and budgetary implications of proposals and recommendations involving expenditure from the funds of the Authority;

(f)   Rules, regulations and procedures on the equitable sharing of financial and other economic benefits derived from activities in the Area and the decisions to be made thereon.

8.   Decisions in the Finance Committee on questions of procedure shall be taken by a majority of members present and voting. Decisions on questions of substance shall be taken by consensus.

9.   The requirement of article 162, paragraph 2 (y), of the Convention to establish a subsidiary organ to deal with financial matters shall be deemed to have been fulfilled by the establishment of the Finance Committee in accordance with this section.

[* Section 3, paragraph 15(e) of the Annex to the New York Agreement, concerning the representation of regional groups in the Council, should be read with the following 'Informal Understanding' read by the President of the UN General Assembly at the time of the adoption of Resolution A/48/263 on 28 July 1994 and annexed to it as Annex II:]

Informal Understanding to be read by the President of the General Assembly at the time of the adoption of the resolution

Once there is a widespread participation in the International Seabed Authority and the number of members of each regional group participating in the Authority is substantially similar to its membership in the United Nations, it is understood that each regional group would be represented in the Council of the Authority as a whole by at least three members.

13 Status of conventions

Table 13.1

**Status of the United Nations Convention on the Law of the Sea, 1982
as at 30 June 1994**

Date of entry into force: 16 November 1994

State	Final Act Signature	Convention Signature[a]	Convention Ratification or Accession
Afghanistan		18.3.83	
Albania			
Algeria[b]	x	x	
Angola[b]	x	x	5.12.90
Antigua and Barbuda		7.2.83	2.2.89
Argentina[b]		5.10.84	
Australia	x	x	
Austria	x	x	
Bahamas	x	x	29.7.83
Bahrain	x	x	30.5.85
Bangladesh	x	x	
Barbados	x	x	12.10.93
Belarus[b]	x	x	
Belgium[b]	x	5.12.84	
Belize	x	x	13.8.83
Benin	x	30.8.83	

State	Final Act Signature	Convention Signature	Convention Ratification or Accession
Bhutan	x	x	
Bolivia[b]		27.11.84	
Botswana	x	5.12.84	2.5.90
Bosnia-Herzegovina			18.2.94
Brazil [bc]	x	x	22.12.88
Brunei Darussalam		5.12.84	
Bulgaria	x	x	
Burkino Faso	x	x	
Burundi	x	x	
Cambodia		1.7.83	
Cameroon	x	x	19.11.85
Canada	x	x	
Cape Verde[bc]	x	x	10.8.87
Central African Republic		4.12.84	
Chad	x	x	
Chile[b]	x	x	
China	x	x	
Colombia	x	x	
Comoros		6.12.84	21.6.94
Congo	x	x	
Costa Rica[b]	x	x	21.9.92
Côte d'Ivoire	x	x	26.3.84
Cuba[bc]	x	x	15.8.84
Cyprus	x	x	12.12.88
Czechoslovakia	x	x	
Dem. People's Republic of Korea	x	x	
Denmark	x	x	
Djibouti	x	x	8.10.91
Dominica		28.3.83	24.10.91
Dominican Republic	x	x	
Ecuador	x		
Egypt[c]	x	x	26.8.83
El Salvador		5.12.84	
Equatorial Guinea	x	30.1.84	
Estonia			
Ethiopia	x	x	
Fiji	x	x	10.12.82
Finland[b]	x	x	
France[b]	x	x	
Gabon	x	x	
Gambia	x	x	22.5.84
Germany[(b-GDR)]	x		
Ghana	x	x	7.6.83
Greece[b]	x	x	

State	Final Act Signature	Convention Signature	Convention Ratification or Accession
Grenada	x	x	25.4.91
Guatemala		8.7.83	
Guinea[b]		4.10.84	6.9.85
Guinea-Bissau[c]	x	x	25.8.86
Guyana	x	x	16.11.93
Haiti	x	x	
Holy See	x		
Honduras	x	x	5.10.93
Hungary	x	x	
Iceland[c]	x	x[c]	21.6.85
India	x	x	
Indonesia	x	x	3.2.86
Iran (Islamic Republic of)[b]	x	x	
Iraq[b]	x	x	30.7.85
Ireland	x	x	
Israel	x		
Italy[b]	x	7.12.84	
Jamaica	x	x	21.3.83
Japan	x	7.2.83	
Jordan	x		
Kenya	x	x	2.3.89
Kiribati			
Kuwait[c]	x	x	2.5.86
Lao People's Democratic Republic	x	x	
Latvia			
Lebanon		7.12.84	
Lesotho	x	x	
Liberia	x	x	
Libyan Arab Jamahiriya	x	3.12.84	
Liechtenstein		30.11.84	
Lithuania			
Luxembourg[b]	x	5.12.84	
Madagascar		25.2.83	
Malawi		7.12.84	
Malaysia	x	x	
Maldives	x	x	
Mali[b]		19.10.83	16.7.85
Malta[c]	x	x	20.5.93
Marshall Islands	x		9.8.91
Mauritania	x	x	
Mauritius	x	x	
Mexico	x	x	18.3.83
Micronesia (Federated States of)	x		29.4.91
Monaco	x	x	

State	Final Act Signature	Convention Signature	Convention Ratification or Accession
Mongolia	x	x	
Morocco	x	x	
Mozambique	x	x	
Myanmar	x	x	
Namibia	x	x	18.4.83
Nauru	x	x	
Nepal	x	x	
Netherlands	x	x	
New Zealand	x	x	
Nicaragua[b]		9.12.84	
Niger	x	x	
Nigeria	x	x	14.8.86
Northern Mariana Islands	x		
Norway	x	x	
Oman[bc]	x	1.7.83	17.8.89
Pakistan	x	x	
Panama	x	x	
Papua New Guinea	x	x	
Paraguay	x	x	26.9.86
Peru	x		
Philippines[bc]	x	x	8.5.84
Poland	x	x	
Portugal	x	x	
Qatar[b]		27.11.84	
Republic of Korea	x	14.3.83	
Romania[b]	x	x	
Russian Federation[b]	x	x	
Rwanda	x	x	
Saint Kitts and Nevis		7.12.84	7.1.93
Saint Lucia	x	x	27.3.85
Saint Vincent and the Grenadines	x	x	1.10.93
Samoa	x	28.9.84	
San Marino			
Sao Tome and Principe[b]		13.7.83	3.11.87
Saudi Arabia		7.12.84	
Senegal	x	x	25.10.84
Seychelles	x	x	16.9.91
Sierra Leone	x	x	
Singapore	x	x	
Solomon Islands	x	x	
Somalia	x	x	24.7.89
South Africa[b]		5.12.84	
Spain[b]	x	4.12.84	
Sri Lanka	x	x	

State	Final Act Signature	Convention Signature	Convention Ratification or Accession
Sudanᵇ	x	x	23.1.85
Suriname	x	x	
Swaziland		18.1.84	
Swedenᵇ	x	x	
Switzerland	x	17.10.84	
Syrian Arab Republic			
Thailand	x	x	
Togo	x	x	16.4.85
Tonga			
Trinidad and Tobago	x	x	25.4.86
Tunisiaᶜ	x	x	24.4.85
Turkey			
Tuvalu	x	x	
Uganda	x	x	9.11.90
Ukraineᵇ	x	x	
United Arab Emirates	x	x	
United Kingdom	x		
United Rep. of Tanzaniaᶜ	x	x	30.9.85
United States of America	x		
Uruguayᵇ	x	x	10.12.92
Vanuatu	x	x	
Venezuela	x		
Viet Nam	x	x	
Yemenᵇ	x	x	21.7.87
Yugoslaviaᶜ	x	x	5.5.86
Zaire	x	22.8.83	17.2.89
Zambia	x	x	7.3.83
Zimbabwe	x	x	24.2.93
Total for States	142	154	62

Others (Under Art. 305(1)(b),(c), (d), (e) and (f))	Final Act Signature	Convention Signature	Convention Ratification or Accession
Cook Islands	x	x	
European Economic Communityᵇ	x	7.12.84	
Niue		5.12.84	
Trust Territory of the Pacific Islands (Palau)	x		
West Indies Associated States			
Total for States and Others	145	157	62

Other Entities which signed the Final Act of the Conference

African National Congress of South Africa
Netherlands Antilles
Palestine Liberation Organization
Pan Africanist Congress of Azania
South West Africa People's Organization

a   Those states which signed the Convention on 10 December 1982 are indicated
    by an 'x'. Those which signed at a later date are indicated by that date.
b   States so marked made declarations or statements on signature. See further
    Volume I, Chapter 3, section II.4.
c   States so marked made declarations or statements on ratification. See further
    Volume I, Chapter 3, section II.4.

Table 13.2

Status of the Geneva Conventions on the Law of the Sea, 1958
as at 31 December 1993

The following Conventions are included in Table 13.2:
1. The Geneva Convention on the Territorial Sea and the Contiguous Zone, 1958
2. The Geneva Convention on the High Seas, 1958
3. The Geneva Convention on Fishing and Conservation of the Living Resources of
   the High Seas, 1958
4. The Geneva Convention on the Continental Shelf, 1958
5. Optional Protocol of Signature concerning the Compulsory Settlement of Disputes,
   1958

The status of the Conventions is stated as at 31 December 1993.   The dates tabulated
refer to the date of ratification, accession or succession by the State concerned.   In
some cases parties are bound by the Convention concerned subject to declarations or
reservations.   No indication of such declarations or reservations has been included in
the Table.   For texts of declarations, reservations and objections thereto, see
*Multilateral Treaties Deposited with the Secretary-General.   Status as at 31 December
1992*, ST/LEG/SER.E/11, 1993, pp.744-60.

Convention	Territorial Sea Convention	High Seas Convention	Fishing Convention	Continental Shelf Convention	Optional Disputes Protocol
Date of Signature	29.4.58	29.4.58	29.4.58	29.4.58	29.4.58
Date of Entry into Force	10.9.64	30.9.62	20.3.66	10.6.64	30.9.62
Afghanistan		28.4.59			
Albania		7.12.64		7.12.64	
Australia	14.5.63	14.5.63	14.5.63	14.5.63	14.5.63
Austria		10.1.74			
Belarus	27.2.61	27.2.61		27.2.61	

Convention	Territorial Sea Convention	High Seas Convention	Fishing Convention	Continental Shelf Convention	Optional Disputes Protocol
Belgium	6.1.72	6.1.72	6.1.72		6.1.72
Bolivia					17.10.58
Bosnia/Herzegovina	1.9.93	1.9.9.3			
Bulgaria	31.8.62	31.8.62		31.8.62	
Burkina Faso		4.10.65	4.10.65		
Cambodia	18.3.60	18.3.60	18.3.60	18.3.60	
Canada				6.2.70	
Central African Rep.		15.10.62			
Colombia			3.1.63	8.1.62	29.4.58
Costa Rica		16.2.72		16.2.72	29.4.58
Croatia	3.8.92	3.8.92		3.8.92	
Cuba					29.4.58
Cyprus		23.5.88		11.4.74	
Czech Republic	22.2.93	22.2.93		22.2.93	
Denmark	26.9.68	26.9.68	26.9.68	12.6.63	26.9.68
Dominican Republic	11.8.64	11.8.64	11.8.64	11.8.64	29.4.58
Fiji	25.3.71	25.3.71	25.3.71	25.3.71	
Finland	16.2.65	16.2.65	16.2.65	16.2.65	27.10.58/ 16.2.65
France			18.9.70	14.6.65	30.10.58
Germany		26.7.73			30.10.58/ 26.7.73
Ghana					29.4.58
Greece				6.11.72	
Guatemala		27.11.61		27.11.61	
Haiti	29.3.60	29.3.60	29.3.60	29.3.60	29.4.58/ 29.3.60
Holy See					30.4.58
Hungary	6.12.61	6.12.61			8.12.89
Indonesia		10.8.61			
Israel	6.9.61	6.9.61		6.9.61	
Italy	17.12.64	17.12.64			
Jamaica	8.10.65	8.10.65	16.4.64	8.10.65	
Japan	10.6.68	10.6.68			
Kenya	20.6.69	20.6.69	20.6.69	20.6.69	
Latvia	17.11.92	17.11.92		2.12.92	
Lesotho	23.10.73	23.10.73	23.10.73	23.10.73	
Liberia					27.5.58
Madagascar	31.7.62	31.7.62	31.7.62	31.7.62	10.8.62
Malawi	3.11.65	3.11.65	3.11.65	3.11.65	17.2.65
Malaysia	21.12.60	21.12.60	21.12.60	21.12.60	1.5.61
Malta	19.5.66			19.5.66	19.5.66
Mauritius	5.10.70	5.10.70	5.10.70	5.10.70	5.10.70
Mexico	2.8.66	2.8.66	2.8.66	2.8.66	
Mongolia		15.10.76			
Nepal		28.12.62			29.4.58
Netherlands	18.2.66	18.2.66	18.2.66	18.2.66	18.2.66

Convention	Territorial Sea Convention	High Seas Convention	Fishing Convention	Continental Shelf Convention	Optional Disputes Protocol
New Zealand				18.1.65	29.10.58
Nigeria	26.6.61	26.6.61	26.6.61	28.4.71	
Norway				9.9.71	
Pakistan					6.11.58
Panama					2.5.58
Poland		29.6.62		29.6.62	
Portugal	8.1.63	8.1.63	8.1.63	8.1.63	8.1.63
Romania	12.12.61	12.12.61		12.12.61	
Russian Federation	22.11.60	22.11.60		22.11.60	
Senegal	25.4.61	25.4.61	25.4.61	25.4.61	
Sierra Leone	13.3.62	13.3.62	13.3.62	25.11.66	14.2.63
Slovak Republic	28.5.93	28.5.93		28.5.93	
Slovenia	6.7.92	6.7.92			
Solomon Islands	3.9.81	3.9.81	3.9.81	3.9.81	3.9.81
South Africa	9.4.63	9.4.63	9.4.63	9.4.63	
Spain	25.2.71	25.2.71	25.2.71	25.2.71	
Sri Lanka					30.10.58
Swaziland	16.10.70	16.10.70		16.10.70	
Sweden				1.6.66	28.6.66
Switzerland	18.5.66	18.5.66	18.5.66	18.5.66	18.5.66
Thailand	2.7.68	2.7.68	2.7.68	2.7.68	
Tonga	29.6.71	29.6.71	29.6.71	29.6.71	
Trinidad and Tobago	11.4.66	11.4.66	11.4.66	11.7.68	
Uganda	14.9.64	14.9.64	14.9.64	14.9.64	15.9.64
Ukraine	12.1.61	12.1.61		12.1.61	
United Kingdom	14.3.60	14.3.60	14.3.60	11.5.64	9.9.58
United States	12.4.61	12.4.61	12.4.61	12.4.61	
Uruguay					29.4.58
Venezuela	15.8.61	15.8.61	10.7.63	15.8.61	
Yugoslavia	28.1.66	28.1.66	28.1.66	28.1.66	28.1.66

Table 13.3

Status of Conventions on Civil Liability for Oil Pollution Damage as at 31 December 1993

Table 13.3 includes the following instruments:
1. International Convention on Civil Liability for Oil Pollution Damage, 1969 (CLC 1969)
2. Protocol to CLC 1969, 1976 (CLC PROT 1976)
3. Protocol of 1992 to Amend CLC 1969 (CLC PROT 1992)
4. International Convention on the Establishment of an International Fund for Compensation for Oil Pollution Damage, 1971 (Fund 1971)
5. Protocol to FUND 1971, 1976 (FUND PROT 1976)
6. Protocol of 1992 to Amend FUND 1971, 1992 (FUND PROT 1992)

The dates tabulated refer to the dates of ratification, accession or other form of acceptance by the States concerned.   No indication is given of any reservations or declarations made by the Contracting States.   See also the introductory notes to Documents 10.2 and 10.3.

Convention	1 CLC 1969	2 CLC PROT 1976	3 CLC PROT 1992	4 FUND 1971	5 FUND PROT 1976	6 FUND PROT 1992
Date of Entry into Force	19.6.75	8.4.81		16.10.78		
Algeria	14.6.74			2.6.75		
Australia	7.11.83	7.11.83				
Bahamas	22.7.76	3.3.80		22.7.76	3.3.80	
Belgium	12.1.77	15.6.89				
Belize	2.4.91	2.4.91				
Benin	1.11.85			1.11.85		
Brazil	17.12.76					
Brunei Darussalam	29.9.92	29.9.92		29.9.92		
Cameroon	14.5.84	14.5.84		14.5.84		
Canada	24.1.89	24.1.89		24.1.89		
Chile	2.8.77					
China	30.1.80	29.9.86				
Colombia	26.3.90	26.3.90				
Côte d'Ivoire	21.6.73			5.10.87		
Croatia	8.10.91			8.10.91		
Cyprus	19.6.89	19.6.89		26.7.89	26.7.89	
Denmark	2.4.75	3.6.81		2.4.75	3.6.81	
Djibouti	1.3.90			1.3.90		
Dominican Republic	2.4.75					
Ecuador	23.12.76					
Egypt	3.2.89	3.2.89				
Estonia	1.12.92			1.12.92		
Fiji	15.8.72			4.3.83		
Finland	10.10.80	8.1.81		10.10.80	8.1.81	
France	17.3.75	7.11.80		11.5.78	7.11.80	
Gabon	21.1.82			21.1.82		
Gambia	1.11.91			1.11.91		
Germany	20.5.75	28.8.80		30.12.76	28.8.80	
Ghana	20.4.78			20.4.78		
Greece	29.6.76	10.5.89		16.12.86		
Guatemala	20.10.82					
Iceland	17.7.80			17.7.80		
India	1.5.87	1.5.87		10.7.90	10.7.90	
Indonesia	1.9.78			1.9.78		
Ireland	19.11.92	19.11.92		19.11.92	19.11.92	
Italy	27.2.79	3.6.83		27.2.79	21.9.83	
Japan	3.6.76			7.7.76		
Kenya	15.12.92			15.12.92		
Kuwait	2.4.81	1.7.81		2.4.81		
Latvia	10.7.92					

Convention	1 CLC 1969	2 CLC PROT 1976	3 CLC PROT 1992	4 FUND 1971	5 FUND PROT 1976	6 FUND PROT 1992
Lebanon	9.4.74					
Liberia	25.9.72	17.2.81		25.9.72	17.2.81	
Luxembourg	14.2.91	14.2.91				
Maldives	16.3.81	14.6.81		16.3.81		
Malta	27.9.91	27.9.91		27.9.91	27.9.91	
Monaco	21.8.75			23.8.79		
Morocco	11.4.74			31.12.92	31.12.92	
Netherlands	9.9.75	3.8.82		3.8.82	1.11.82	
New Zealand	27.4.76					
Nigeria	7.5.81			11.9.87		
Norway	21.3.75	17.7.78		21.3.75	17.7.78	
Oman	24.1.85	24.1.85		10.5.85		
Panama	7.1.76					
Papua New Guinea	12.3.80			12.3.80		
Peru	24.2.87	24.2.87				
Poland	18.3.76	30.10.85		16.9.85	30.10.85	
Portugal	26.11.76	2.1.86		11.9.85	11.9.85	
Qatar	2.6.88	2.6.88		2.6.88		
Republic of Korea	18.12.78	8.12.92		8.12.92		
Russian Federation	25.6.75	2.12.88		17.6.87	30.1.89	
St. Vincent and the Grenadines	19.4.89					
Saudi Arabia	15.4.93	15.4.93				
Senegal	27.3.72					
Seychelles	12.4.88			12.4.88		
Sierra Leone	13.8.93			13.8.93		
Singapore	16.9.81	15.12.81				
Slovenia	25.6.91			25.6.91		
South Africa	17.3.76					
Spain	8.12.75	22.10.81		8.10.81	5.4.82	
Sri Lanka	12.4.83			12.4.83		
Sweden	17.3.75	7.7.78		17.3.75	7.7.78	
Switzerland	15.12.87	15.12.87				
Syrian Arab Republic	6.2.75			6.2.75		
Tunisia	4.5.76			4.5.76		
Tuvalu	1.10.78			16.10.78		
United Arab Emirates	15.12.83	14.3.84		15.12.83		
United Kingdom	17.3.75	31.1.80		2.4.76	31.1.80	
Vanuatu	2.2.83	13.1.89		13.1.89	13.1.89	
Venezuela	21.1.92	21.1.92		21.1.92	21.1.92	
Yemen	6.3.79	4.6.79				
Yugoslavia	18.6.76			16.3.78		

14 Bibliographies

The most comprehensive bibliography on the law of the sea, though limited to publications in English or French, is:

The Law of the Sea. A Bibliography on the Law of the Sea 1968-1988 (Office for Ocean Affairs and the Law of the Sea, UN Publication, Sales No. E/F.91.V.7, New York, 1991; multilingual version (Arabic/Chinese/German/Russian/Spanish) published in 1993, Sales No. Mult.93.V.15).   This 472-page volume draws upon and expands the coverage of the following earlier bibliographies and lists other bibliographies at pp.404-8.

Published by the Dag Hammarskjöld Library, United Nations

The Sea: Legal and Political Aspects: A Select Bibliography (ST/LIB/SER.B/14, UN Publication, Sales No. E/F.74.I.9).

The Sea: Economic and Technological Aspects: A Select Bibliography (ST/LIB/SER.B/15, UN Publication, Sales No. E/F.74.I.16).

The Sea: A Select Bibliography on the Legal, Political, Economic and Technological Aspects, 1974-1975 (ST/LIB/SER.B/16, UN Publication, Sales No. E/F.75.I.7).

The Sea: A Select Bibliography on the Legal, Political and Technological Aspects, 1975-1976 (ST/LIB/SER.B/21, UN Publication, Sales No. E/F.76.I.6).

The Sea: A Select Bibliography on the Legal, Political, Economic and Technical Aspects, 1976-1978 (ST/LIB/SER.B/25, UN Publication, Sales No. E/F.78.I.3).

The Sea: A Select Bibliography on the Legal, Political, Economic and Technical Aspects, 1978-1979 (ST/LIB/SER.B/29, UN Publication, Sales No. E/F.80.I.6).

Published by Division for Ocean Affairs and the Law of the Sea, Office of Legal Affairs, United Nations and its predecessors

The Law of the Sea: A Select Bibliography (LOS/LIB 1, UN Publication, Sales No. E.85.V.2).
The Law of the Sea: A Select Bibliography (LOS/LIB 2, UN Publication, Sales No. E.87.V.2).
The Law of the Sea: A Select Bibliography (LOS/LIB 3, UN Publication, Sales No. E.88.V.2).
The Law of the Sea: A Select Bibliography – 1988 (LOS/LIB 4, UN Publication, Sales No. E.89.V.3).
Further issues were published in 1992 and 1993:
The Law of the Sea: A Select Bibliography – 1991 (LOS/LIB/7, UN Publication, Sales No. E.92.V.6).
The Law of the Sea: A Select Bibliography – 1992 (LOS/LIB/8, UN Publication, Sales No. E.93.V.12).

Learning Resources
Centre